Core Competency-Based Strategy

Core Competency-Based Strategy

Edited by
Andrew Campbell and
Kathleen Sommers Luchs

INTERNATIONAL THOMSON BUSINESS PRESS
I(T)P® An International Thomson Publishing Company

London • Bonn • Boston • Johannesburg • Madrid • Melbourne • Mexico City • New York • Paris
Singapore • Tokyo • Toronto • Albany, NY • Belmont, CA • Cincinnati, OH • Detroit, MI

Core Competency-Based Strategy

Copyright selection ©1997 Andrew Campbell and Kathleen Sommers Luchs

First published by International Thomson Business Press

 A division of International Thomson Business Press
The ITP logo is a trademark under licence

British Library Cataloguing-in-Publication Data
A catalogue record for this book is available from the British Library

First edition 1997
Reprinted 1997

Typeset by J & L Composition, Filey, North Yorkshire
Printed in the UK by T.J. International Ltd, Padstow, Cornwall

ISBN 1861522738

International Thomson Business Press
Berkshire House
168–173 High Holborn
London WC1V 7AA
UK

International Thomson Business Press
20 Park Plaza
13th Floor
Boston MA 02116
USA

http://www.itbp.com

Contents

Introduction   1

Part I Understanding Competencies

1 Looking Inside for Competitive Advantage   13
  Jay B. Barney

2 Understanding Organizations as Learning Systems   30
  Edwin C. Nevis, Anthony J. DiBella and Janet M. Gould

3 Managing Core Competency for Corporate Renewal:
  Towards a Managerial Theory of Core Competencies   53
  Yves Doz

Part II Competencies and Corporate Strategy

4 Unexplored Assets for Diversification   83
  Gordon R. Conrad

5 Related Diversification, Core Competences and Corporate
  Performance   96
  Constantinos C. Markides and Peter J. Williamson

6 Targeting a Company's Real Core Competencies   123
  Amy Snyder and H. William Ebeling, Jr.

7 Corporate Strategy: The Quest for Parenting Advantage   134
  Andrew Campbell, Michael Goold and Marcus Alexander

Part III Managing Core Competencies across Business Units

8 Building Core Skills   163
  Andrew Campbell and Michael Goold

9 Knowledge Creator vs. Knowledge Broker: Corporate Roles
in Technology Development in Diversified Firms 188
Anil K. Gupta and Ilkka Eerola

10 Intra-Firm Transfer of Best Practices 208
Gabriel Szulanski

11 The Factory as a Learning Laboratory 236
Dorothy Leonard-Barton

12 Creating Knowledge in Practice 266
Ikujiro Nonaka and Hiro Takeuchi

13 Leveraging Competencies Across Businesses 295
Michael Goold, Andrew Campbell and Marcus Alexander

Appendix 1: Sources of Readings by Chapter 321

Introduction

Competence or skill is at the heart of any successful activity. It is particularly important to competitive activities such as sport or business. As a result, much of the thinking about business strategy over the last thirty years has been about what competencies a business needs to have to compete in a specific market, and what markets a business should plan on competing in given its current and potential competencies. Business strategy is like career strategy. What competencies does the individual need to succeed in a chosen career? What career should an individual choose given his or her current and potential competencies?

This book, though, is not intended to be a reader on competence and business strategy. It has a narrower objective. It is aimed at providing guidance to managers, academics and students who are thinking about the management of competence across business units within the same organization. In other words, this book is looking specifically at competence approaches to corporate level strategy, and competence management in multibusiness companies.

The reason for this focus stems from a research project launched by the Ashridge Strategic Management Centre on sharing skills across business units. We began by surveying the literature on skills and skill management in the business organization. We discovered that over the last fifty years, many business academics and management theorists have contributed to the thinking on this topic. For example, it was the American academic Philip Selznick who in 1957 first coined the phrase 'distinctive competence' to describe a company's relative skill in executing its chosen strategy. Writers of classic management texts, such as Igor Ansoff in the 1960s and Kenneth Andrews and his co-authors at the Harvard Business School, advocated an audit of internal strengths and weaknesses as an essential prelude to strategy formulation.[1] The quantity of writing in the area began to gather pace during the 1980s and early 1990s, with academics of the resource-based school[2] reviving the debate started by Selznick on the relationship between internal resources and business strategy. Not only is there a substantial theoretical literature on the subject of skills, but there are many different areas of the management literature that touch on the subject of competencies. We found relevant topics included change management and corporate renewal, organizational learning, resource management, technology and know-how, competitive advantage, strategy formulation techniques, and diversification theory.

Much of the work that we found in our survey examined the question of skills and competencies at the level of the business unit, and how a business's unique competencies can be the source of its competitive advantage. But we also found work relevant to corporate-level strategy. The work on skills and competencies suggested new ways to understand corporations – as bundles of competencies or resources rather than as portfolios of business units. This thinking provides a new perspective on the multibusiness company and can help in making decisions on allocating resources, portfolio building and diversification. A competence approach can be a powerful tool in thinking about strategic issues at the corporate level, and we hope that this selection of readings contributes to managers' understanding of both the strengths and limitations of a skills-based approach to corporate strategy. The main purpose of this book, however, is practical. We hope it will help managers trying to build skills and competencies across a number of business units.

Part I, 'Understanding Competencies', explores the subject of competence and strategy fairly broadly. Most writers do not distinguish between single business and multibusiness companies and the broad concepts are equally relevant to both sectors. The readings in this section cover resource-based thinking, organizational learning, and managerial theory of core competencies. We do not pretend that these readings provide a complete survey of the academic literature on these topics, but they do introduce the reader to the critical issues and fundamental concepts.

In Part II, 'Competencies and Corporate Strategy', we have selected readings that provide guidance on key issues in corporate strategy. The readings in this section demonstrate how a competence approach can be used in assessing the corporate portfolio of businesses, in making decisions about resource allocation, and in diversification. The authors included in this section help to bridge the gap between theory and practice by exploring the applications of the concepts and theories covered in the first section.

Part III, 'Managing Competencies across Business Units', is the heart of the book. It provides examples and insights on how multibusiness companies manage skill sharing and learning. The readings in this section examine how capabilities are developed and diffused among multiple business units and the role of headquarters in these processes. The experiences and practices of the companies discussed in these readings demonstrate both the complexity and rewards of skill-sharing in multi-business companies. They should provide managers with insights and advice about how to improve competency management in their own companies.

In short, the book is organized into three parts – theory, applications and practice. There are introductions to the readings in each part, to help you understand the major issues and identify the readings most relevant to your own interests and questions. We hope that this selection of readings and the organization of the book help you make sense of the substantial literature on skills and competencies and provides insights into both the theory and practice of skills-based management in multi-business companies.

NOTES

1 Ansoff, Igor, *Corporate Strategy*, McGraw-Hill, 1965; Learned, Christensen, Andrews and Guth, *Business Policy: Text and Cases*, Richard D. Irwin, Inc., Homewood, Illinois, 1965 (revised edition 1969); Andrews, Kenneth R., *The Concept of Corporate Strategy*, revised edition, Richard D. Irwin, Inc., Homewood, Illinois, 1980 (first published 1965).
2 Wernerfelt, B. 'A Resource Based Perspective', *Strategic Management Journal*, vol. 5, no. 2, April–June 1984, pp. 171–180; Barney, J. B. 'Firm Resources and Sustained Competitive Advantage', *Journal of Management*, vol. 17, no. 1, 1991, pp. 99–120; Conner, Kathleen R., 'A Historical Comparison of Resource-Based Theory and Five Schools of Thought Within Industrial Organization Economics: Do We Have a New Theory of the Firm?' *Journal of Management* vol. 17, no. 1, 1991, pp. 121–154; Peteraf, M. A. 'The Cornerstones of Competitive Advantage: A Resource Based View', *Strategic Management Journal*, 1993 (14), pp. 179–191.

Part I

Understanding competencies

One of the difficulties of the literature on skills-based management is the range of terms writers in this field use to describe their ideas. Similar terms – strengths, skills, competencies, capabilities, organizational knowledge, intangible assets – are used interchangeably by different authors. Kenneth Andrews uses the term 'distinctive competence' to define not just what an organization does, but what it does particularly well.[1] C. K. Prahalad and Gary Hamel introduced the phrase 'core competence' in their landmark article in the *Harvard Business Review* in 1990. They define core competence as an integrated bundle of skills and technologies; 'a messy accumulation of learning' which contributes to a business's competitive success.[2] Some authors, wishing to place particular emphasis on 'collective learning in the corporation' have chosen to use the phrase 'capability' or 'core capability' as better expressing the dynamic learning processes involved. What these terms have in common is that they define those unique capabilities, knowledge and behavioural routines which are a potential source of an organization's advantage.

The idea that complex internal capabilities are critical to a firms's success is not new. Phillip Selznick, in his book *Leadership in Adminis-tration*,[3] was one of the first writers to acknowledge that factors internal to an organization, such as its personnel and its previous experiences, are crucial to its chances of success in executing a chosen policy. In essence, Selznick argued that in the field of business activity, the past determines the present. He said that an organization's developmental history results in its having 'special limitations and capabilities' – a character, or 'emer-gent institutional pattern that decisively affects the competence of an organization to frame and execute desired policies'. Selznick called the peculiar character of an organization its 'distinctive competence'. He defined the art of good management as the ability to make a practical assessment of an organization's suitability to its task or strategy. To illustrate this, he gave an example of a master boat-building firm, specializing in high quality craftsmanship whose management decided to expand into mass production of low cost speed boats. It proved impossible to adapt worker attitudes away from their historical commitment to quality and craftsmanship, and the management were obliged to relocate the speed boat production and recruit a separate workforce. The new venture failed because the history and culture of the organization did not fit it to the new task. Thus Selznick observed that a 'distinctive competence' in one area – quality craftsmanship – may amount to a 'distinctive incompetence' in another – low cost mass production. Selznick concluded that internal social forces affect an organization's chances of success as much, if not more, than do the vagaries of the external market place.

This conclusion influenced many business policy writers, who saw that strategy formulation and opportunity surveillance were useless exercises unless the company had the internal abilities to execute its decisions, or at least a good chance of developing the required capabilities. With this in mind, Igor Ansoff in his book *Corporate Strategy*[4] advocated that managers compile a comprehensive checklist of their firm's skills and resources, a 'grid of competencies'. Similar grids were to be compiled on competitors, and a cross-comparison made of all the results. The profile emerging from this exercise would be a ready guide to the relative strengths of competitors already operating in a given market. Ansoff proposed that this document, regularly updated, would form a permanent reference guide for future strategy decisions and could be used in assessing the likely success of diversification. Also writing in the 1960s, joint authors Learned, Christensen, Andrews and Guth,[5] influential academics of the Harvard Business School, suggested that a company's competitive strength derived from its 'distinctive competence', or what the company could do especially well. The goal of corporate strategy was to match a firm's distinctive competence with available opportunities and thereby gain competitive advantage. The familiar SWOT framework – the analysis of a business's strengths, weaknesses, opportunities and threats – emerged from the work of these writers on business policy.

After the early 1970s, though, the thinking on distinctive competencies or corporate strengths stalled. One reason was that managers had a hard time deciding just what were corporate strengths or weaknesses. Howard Stevenson,[6] in an empirical study on assessing corporate capabilities, found that there was often little consensus on a company's strengths among its managers and that higher level managers tended to be more optimistic about their firm's capabilities than lower level managers. Charles Hofer and Dan Schendel, in their 1978 text *Strategy Formulation: Analytical Concepts*[7] advocated the process of assessing corporate resources, strengths and weakness but noted that many strategy formulation models skipped this step. The reason, they explained, was because such an analysis can be fruitless in isolation: 'Thus, one cannot tell whether it is a strength or a weakness to be seven feet tall until one specifies what that tall individual is supposed to do.'

Another reason that the thinking on competencies remained relatively dormant during the 1970s and early 1980s, was that influential academics and consultants turned their attention to other approaches to strategy. At the level of the business strategy, the environmental school exemplified by Michael Porter[8] developed frameworks such as the five-forces analysis, which helped managers understand external opportunities and competitive threats. In this approach, the strategist analyses industry attractiveness and market opportunities and formulates a strategy based on these analyses. The next step is to determine if the business has the requisite skills to implement the chosen strategy, or if it can acquire those skills at reasonable cost. At the corporate level, techniques of portfolio planning, developed by the Boston Consulting Group and others, helped corporate managers analyse the often disparate businesses in corporate portfolios in terms of competitive position and industry attractiveness. Portfolio management offered guidance to corporate managers on building portfolios of businesses with complementary growth and cash generating characteristics.[9]

These approaches to business level and corporate level strategy dominated management thinking through the 1980s, but the thinking on a firm's internal competencies was not entirely forgotten. Robert Hayes,[10] for example, writing in the *Harvard Business Review* in 1985, criticized what he called the ends–ways–means approach to strategic planning. He questioned whether managers should decide on a strategy before deciding on the means of implementing that strategy. He advised managers 'Do not develop plans and then seek capabilities; instead, build capabilities and then encourage the development of plans for exploiting them'. The Japanese academic Hiroyuko Itami,[11] in his influential book *Mobilizing Invisible Assets*, also stressed the importance of building on a firm's strengths, or what he called its invisible assets. He defined invisible assets as properties of a company with the potential for producing profit that do not show up on a printed balance sheet: reputation, brand-name, technical expertise and customer loyalty as compared to physical assets such as plant, real estate or manufactured stock. Itami argued that although invisible assets are often overlooked, they are the most enduring source of a company's competitive advantage. In his view, a successful strategy rests on finding ways of fully exploiting such invisible assets in the marketplace. For these authors, the starting point of strategy was the analysis of the firm's internal resources and capabilities. This thinking gathered momentum with the emergence of the resource based school during the 1980s.

The resource based school focuses on the firm's internal characteristics to explain why firms pursue different strategies with different outcomes.

The central proposition of this group of writers is that the organization is an accretion of specialized resources which can be used to gain a privileged market position – in other words, a sustainable competitive advantage. Firms acquire, develop and expand their resource bundles over time, and because organizations follow different developmental paths, firms have different resources. Thus, firms pursue different strategies in order to exploit their specific resources. The resource based school accepts that an organization's history and experiences, its character and culture, and its strengths and capabilities all contribute to its strategy and, indeed, are crucial in determining the success of that strategy.

These concepts are relevant to both business unit strategy and to corporate level strategy. At the business level, a key idea is that competitive advantage stems from a firm's unique resources and capabilities which are hard for competitors to imitate or acquire. At the corporate level, resource based theorists perceive the firm as bundles of resources which can have different applications; that is, the firm's resources can be deployed in different businesses with different end products. A successful corporate strategy depends on accumulating specialized resources and exploiting them by matching these resources to market opportunities through the creation of business units. Resource based thinkers regard internal attributes and capabilities as a more stable anchor for both business level and corporate level strategy than the varying demands of a volatile marketplace, and this is similar to earlier thinking on a firm's strengths and current work on competencies and capabilities. The work of the resource based school can help managers to appreciate why competencies are often the firm's most valuable resources, and to understand how these valuable resources can be exploited.

The first reading in this section is by the American academic Jay Barney, one of the best-known exponents of the resource based school. The article 'Looking Inside for Competitive Advantage', is written for a managerial audience, and in it Barney explores how the theoretical concepts of the resource based school can help managers understand strategic issues at both the business and corporate levels. Barney defines resources as a firm's assets, knowledge, information, capabilities, characteristics and organizational procedures. These can be conveniently categorized as financial, physical, human and organizational resources. An understanding of these internal attributes, Barney argues, is as essential as analysis of external opportunities and threats in assessing a firm's strategic position and options.

Using the language of the resource based school, Barney argues that a firm's resources and capabilities are competitively important if they are (1) valuable, (2) rare and (3) difficult to imitate. The value of a resource depends on the opportunities available for exploiting it, and these opportunities can change. For example, IBM's capabilities in mainframe computers became less valuable as personal computers became more sophisticated and cheaper. Competitively important resources are also rare. If many competitors have the same or similar capabilities, none of them will have a competitive advantage.

The third criteria for competitively important resources is that they are difficult to imitate. As Barney points out, many physical resources are easily imitated; rivals can build similar plants or copy a process technology. It is far more difficult to imitate capabilities which depend on teamwork, culture and organizational routines. These resources are usually complex, the result of a firm's own history and of numerous small decisions over time which contribute to the development of unique capabilities. Barney cites the example of Hewlett Packard's corporate culture, which encourages teamwork and co-operation across divisions. This has enabled HP to use its technologies in varied products – printers, plotters, computers and electronic instruments – and to make these products compatible. Rival firms may be able to duplicate the technology of HP's products, but it is not easy for competitors to imitate the culture and organization which underpins HP's success.

Capabilities are often a firm's most important resources because they are valuable, rare and difficult to imitate. At the same time, the complexity and opaqueness of a firm's capabilities creates a management problem of its own. To capitalize on an organization's resources, managers need to be able to identify them, make decisions about how to exploit them, and know how to expand them. Without this knowledge, successful strategies would only be the lucky result of historical decisions or accidents. To understand how firms acquire and expand their capabilities, we have to turn to learning theory, and the second reading in this section explores the ongoing process of organizational learning and managerial responsibility for this process.

The authors are Edwin Nevis and Janet Gould of the Organizational Learning Center at MIT Sloan School of Management and Anthony DiBella. In their article, 'Understanding Organizations as Learning Systems', the authors define organizational learning as 'the capacity or processes within an organisation to maintain or improve performance based on experience'. The authors argue that improving a firm's learning processes can enhance its performance.

Nevis, Gould and DiBella identify three stages in the learning process: knowledge acquisition, knowldege sharing and knowledge utilization, but they caution that learning is not necessarily linear through these stages. Their research, at companies such as Motorola, Electricité de France and Fiat, revealed that firms learn in different ways. For example, some firms develop knowledge internally while others more readily accept knowledge developed externally. Knowledge dissemination is highly formal in some companies, but in other companies it occurs informally, through networking or casual interactions. Companies also differ in the areas in which they invest in learning; an engineering company is likely to focus on production or process improvements while a consumer goods company may devote more time and effort to better delivery or service systems. The authors suggest that there is no single type of a successful 'learning organization'; instead, there are many different learning systems, each of which can be effective. The authors also identify facilitating factors, or approaches which can enhance learning in all organizations. A concern with measurement, a climate of openness, champions and involved leadership are among the factors which contribute to an organization's learning system.

Nevis and his co-authors also suggest strategies for improving learning in an organization. One option is to make the existing learning system more effective by strengthening or modifying the firm's learning orientations. For example, a firm that traditionally invests heavily in production improvements may improve service by putting more resources into the education and training of sales personnel. Another option is to improve facilitating factors, such as developing measurement systems or encouraging more communication across units. A third option is to try and change both learning orientations and facilitating factors. This is the most difficult option, amounting to transformational change. Nevis, Gould and DiBella urge managers to evaluate their firm's current learning system, and its facilitating factors, to understand its strengths and weaknesses. This will help managers select appropriate strategies for improving or changing the ways in which the firm acquires, shares and utilizes knowledge.

The third reading in this section, by Yves Doz, draws on many of the concepts developed by the resource based school and in the literature on learning organizations to discuss the management of core competencies. Doz, a professor of international management at INSEAD, writes that his work is 'a modest attempt to move in the direction of a managerial theory of core competencies'. His aim is to identify the major dilemmas managers confront in trying to manage core competencies, and to suggest some approaches which can help address these dilemmas.

Doz begins by discussing how difficult it is to manage competencies. In the first place, competencies are complex organizational routines and therefore difficult to define or to understand fully. They develop in different ways, even in a single organization, and the developmental path is often unclear. The learning which underpins competencies is often tacit and therefore difficult to communicate and share. Doz aims to make sense of the 'messiness' of competencies by identifying five key processes in competence management: the development, diffusion, integration, leverage and renewal of competencies. Each process may follow a natural track, but managers can also intervene to manage it more actively. For example, every firm must have some competencies if it is to survive. These usually develop through 'learning by doing', which demands no specific intervention from managers. At times, though, managers may need to accelerate the development of competencies. The firm may face competitive threats from new rivals, or it may be in a position where its existing competencies are becoming less valuable. Doz examines the managerial tools available to accelerate the development of competencies. These include business process reengineering, quality management, professional training. Yet, the use of such tools also involves risks. Organizational focus on improving or gaining a specific competence may challenge existing power structures, or undermine naturally emerging competencies. Managers may mis-identify the competencies which should be encouraged. Similar dilemmas arise with each of the key processes of competence management. Should managers leave the diffusion of competencies to the informal network of the organization, or should they try to improve diffusion through best practice exchange or by managing the internal labour market? Is it likely that the organization will fully exploit its competencies, or should managers deliberately explore new ways of leveraging its competencies? Doz's article provides a framework for addressing these major issues in managing core competencies.

The three readings in this section provide a brief introduction to the resource based view of the firm and to learning theory, with the final reading by Doz demonstrating how these different concepts are relevant to core competencies. Parts II and III of this reader explore some of the ways these concepts can be used in thinking about corporate strategy, and how multibusiness companies manage competencies in practice.

NOTES

1 Andrews, Kenneth R., *The Concept of Corporate Strategy*, revised edition, Richard D. Irvin, Inc., Homewood, Illinois, 1980 (first published 1965).
2 Prahalad, C. K. and Hamel, Gary, 'The Core Competence of the Corporation,' *Harvard Business Review*, May–June 1990, pp. 79–91. Hamel, Gary, 'The Concept of Core Competence,' in Hamel, Gary and Aimé Heene, eds., *Competence-Based Competition*, John Wiley & Sons, New York, 1994, pp. 11–16.
3 Selznick, Phillip, *Leadership in Administration*, Harper, New York, 1957.
4 Ansoff, Igor, *Corporate Strategy*, McGraw-Hill, 1965.
5 Learned, Edmund P., Christensen, Roland C., Andrews, Kenneth R., and Guth, William D., *Business Policy: Text and Cases*, Richard D. Irwin, Inc., Homewood, Illinois 1965 (revised edition 1969); Andrews Kenneth R., *The Concept of Corporate Strategy*.
6 Stevenson, Howard K. 'Analyzing Corporate Strengths and Weaknesses', *Sloan Management Review*, vol. 17, no. 3 (Spring 1976), pp. 51–68.
7 Hofer, Charles W. and Schendel, Dan, *Strategy Formulation: Analytical Concepts*, West Publishing Company, St. Paul, Minn., 1978.

8 Porter, Michael, *Competitive Strategy*, The Free Press, New York, 1980; Porter, Michael E., *Competitive Advantage*, The Free Press, New York, 1985.

9 Hamermesh, Richard G., *Making Strategy Work*, John Wiley & Sons, New York, 1986.

10 Hayes, Robert H. 'Strategic planning-forward in reverse?' *Harvard Business Review*, November–December 1985, pp. 111–119.

11 Itami, Hiroyuki and Roehl, Thomas, *Mobilizing Invisible Assets*, Harvard University Press, 1987.

Chapter 1

Looking inside for competitive advantage

Jay B. Barney

ABSTRACT

Strategic managers and researchers have long been interested in understanding sources of competitive advantage for firms. Traditionally, this effort has focused on the relationship between a firm's environmental opportunities and threats on the one hand, and its internal strengths and weaknesses on the other. Summarized in what has come to be known as SWOT (Strengths, Weaknesses, Opportunities, and Threats) analysis, this traditional logic suggests that firms that use their internal strengths in exploiting environmental opportunities and neutralizing environmental threats, while avoiding internal weaknesses, are more likely to gain competitive advantages than other kinds of firms.[1]

This simple SWOT framework points to the importance of both external and internal phenomena in understanding the sources of competitive advantage. To date, the development of tools for analyzing environmental opportunities and threats has proceeded much more rapidly than the development of tools for analyzing a firm's internal strengths and weaknesses. To address this deficiency, this article offers a simple, easy-to-apply approach to analyzing the competitive implications of a firm's internal strengths and weaknesses.

The history of strategic management research can be understood as an attempt to 'fill in the blanks' created by the SWOT framework; i.e., to move beyond suggesting that strengths, weaknesses, opportunities, and threats are important for understanding competitive advantage to suggest models and frameworks that can be used to analyze and evaluate these phenomena. Michael Porter and his associates have developed a number of these models and frameworks for analyzing environmental opportunities and threats.[2] Porter's work on the 'five forces model,' the relationship between industry structure and strategic opportunities, and strategic groups can all be understood as an effort to unpack the concepts of environmental opportunities and threats in a theoretically rigorous, yet highly applicable way.

However, the SWOT framework tells us that environmental analysis – no matter how rigorous – is only half the story. A complete understanding of sources of competitive advantage requires the analysis of a firm's internal strengths and weaknesses as well.[3] The importance of integrating internal with environmental analyses can be seen when evaluating the sources of competitive advantage of many firms. Consider, for example,

- WalMart, a firm that has, for the last twenty years, consistently earned a return on sales twice the average of its industry;
- Southwest Airlines, a firm whose profits continued to increase, despite losses at other U.S. airlines that totalled almost $10 billion from 1990 to 1993; and
- Nucor Steel, a firm whose stock price continued to soar through the 1980s and '90s, despite the fact that the market value of most steel companies has remained flat or fallen during the same time period.[4]

These firms, and many others, have all gained competitive advantages – despite the unattractive, high threat, low opportunity environments within which they operate. Even the most careful and complete analysis of these firms' competitive environments cannot, by itself, explain their success. Such explanations must also include these firms' internal attributes – their strengths and weaknesses – as sources of competitive advantage. Following more recent practice, internal attributes will be referred to as *resources* and *capabilities* throughout the following discussion.[5]

A firm's resources and capabilities include all of the financial, physical, human, and organizational assets used by a firm to develop, manufacture, and deliver products or services to its customers. Financial resources include debt, equity, retained earnings, and so forth. Physical resources include the machines, manufacturing facilities, and buildings firms use in their operations. Human resources include all the experience, knowledge, judgment, risk taking propensity, and wisdom of individuals associated with a firm. Organizational resources include the history, relationships, trust, and organizational culture that are attributes of groups of individuals associated with a firm, along with a firm's formal reporting structure, explicit management control systems, and compensation policies.

In the process of filling in the 'internal blanks' created by SWOT analysis, managers must address four important questions about their resources and capabilities: (1) the question of value, (2) the question of rareness, (3) the question of imitability, and (4) the question of organization.

THE QUESTION OF VALUE

To begin evaluating the competitive implications of a firm's resources and capabilities, managers must first answer the question of value: Do a firm's resources and capabilities add value by enabling it to exploit opportunities and/or neutralize threats?

The answer to this question, for some firms, has been yes. Sony, for example, has a great deal of experience in designing, manufacturing, and selling miniaturized electronic technology. Sony has used these resources to exploit numerous market opportunities, including portable tape players, portable disc players, portable televisions, and easy-to-hold 8mm video cameras. 3M has used its skills and experience in substrates, coatings, and adhesives, along with an organizational culture that rewards risk taking and creativity, to exploit numerous market opportunities in office products, including invisible tape and Post-It™ Notes. Sony's and 3M's resources – including their specific technological skills and their creative organizational cultures – made it possible for these firms to respond to, and even create, new environmental opportunities.

Unfortunately, for other firms, the answer to the question of value has been no. For example, USX's long experience in traditional steel-making technology and the traditional steel market made it almost impossible for USX to recognize and respond to fundamental changes in the structure of the steel industry. Because they could not recognize new opportunities and threats, USX delayed its investment in, among other opportunities, thin slab continuous casting steel manufacturing technology. Nucor Steel, on the other hand, was not shackled by its experience, made these investments early, and has become a major player in the international steel industry. In a similar way, Sears was unable to recognize or respond to changes in the retail market that had been created by WalMart and specialty retail stores. In a sense, Sears' historical success, along with a commitment to stick with a traditional way of doing things, led it to miss some significant market opportunities.[6]

Although a firm's resources and capabilities may have added value in the past, changes in customer tastes, industry structure, or technology can render them less valuable in the future. General Electric's capabilities in transistor manufacturing became much less valuable when semiconductors were invented. American Airlines' skills in managing their relationship with the Civil Aeronautics Board (CAB) became much less valuable after airline deregulation. IBM's numerous capabilities in the mainframe computing business became less valuable with the increase in power, and reduction in price, of personal and mini computers. One of the most important responsibilities of strategic managers is to constantly evaluate whether or not their firm's resources and capabilities continue to add value, despite changes in the competitive environment.

Some environmental changes are so significant that few, if any, of a firm's resources remain valuable in any enviromental context.[7] However, this kind of radical environmental change is unusual. More commonly, changes in a firm's environment may reduce the value of a firm's resources in their current use, while leaving the value of those resources in other uses unchanged. Such changes might even *increase* the value of those resources in those other uses. In this situation, the critical issue facing managers is: how can we use our traditional strengths in new ways to exploit opportunities and/or neutralize threats?

Numerous firms have weathered these environmental shifts by finding new ways to apply their traditional strengths. AT&T had developed a reputation for providing high-quality long distance telephone service. It moved rapidly to exploit this reputation in the newly competitive long distance market by aggressively marketing its services against MCI, Sprint, and other carriers. Also, AT&T had traditional strengths in research and development with its Bell Labs subsidiary. To exploit these strengths in its new competitive context, AT&T shifted Bell Labs' mission from basic research to applied research, and then leveraged those skills by forming numerous joint ventures, acquiring NCR, and other actions. Through this process, AT&T has been able to use some of its historically important capabilities to try to position itself as a major actor in the global telecommunications and computing industry.

Another firm that has gone through a similar transformation is the Hunter Fan Company. Formed in 1886, Hunter Fan developed the technology it needed to be the market share leader in ceiling fans used to cool large manufacturing facilities. Unfortunately, the invention of air conditioning significantly reduced demand for industrial fans, and Hunter Fan's performance deteriorated rapidly. However, in the 1970s, rising energy prices made energy conservation more important to home owners. Since ceiling fans can significantly reduce home energy consumption, Hunter Fan was able to move quickly to exploit this new opportunity. Of course, Hunter Fan had to develop some new skills as well, including brass-plating capabilities and new distribution networks. However, by building on its traditional strengths in new ways, Hunter Fan has become a leader in the home ceiling fan market.[8]

By answering the question of value, managers link the analysis of internal resources and capabilities with the analysis of environmental opportunities and threats. Firm resources are not valuable in a vacuum, but rather are valuable only when they exploit opportunities and/or neutralize threats. The models developed by Porter and his associates can be used to isolate potential opportunities and threats that the resources a firm controls can exploit or neutralize.

Of course, the resources and capabilities of different firms can be valuable in different ways. This can be true, even if firms are competing in the same industry. For example, while both Rolex and Timex manufacture watches, they exploit very different valuable resources. Rolex emphasizes its quality manufacturing, commitment to excellence, and high-status reputation in marketing its watches. Timex emphasizes its high-volume, low-cost manufacturing skills and abilities. Rolex exploits its capabilities in responding to demand for very expensive watches; Timex exploits its resources in responding to demand for practical, reliable, low-cost timekeeping.

THE QUESTION OF RARENESS

That a firm's resources and capabilities are valuable is an important first consideration in understanding internal sources of competitive advantage. However, if a particular resource and capability is controlled by numerous competing firms, then that resource is unlikely to be a source of competitive advantage for any one of them. Instead, valuable but common (i.e. not rare) resources and capabilities are sources of competitive parity. For managers evaluating the competitive implications of their resources and capabilities, these observations lead to the second critical issue: how many competing firms already possess these valuable resources and capabilities?

Consider, for example, two firms competing in the global communications and computing industries: NEC and AT&T. Both these firms are developing many of the same capabilities that are likely to be needed in these industries over the next decade. These capabilities are clearly valuable, although – since at least these two firms, and maybe others, are developing them – they may not be rare. If they are not rare, they cannot – by themselves – be sources of competitive advantage for either NEC or AT&T. If either of these firms is to gain competitive advantages, they must exploit resources and capabilities that are different from the communication and computing skills they are *both* cited as developing. This may be part of the reason why AT&T recently restructured its telecommunications and computer businesses into separate firms.[9]

While resources and capabilities must be rare among competing firms in order to be a source of competitive advantage, this does not mean that common, but valuable, resources are not important. Indeed, such resources and capabilities may be essential for a firm's survival. On the other hand, if a firm's resources are valuable and rare, those resources may enable a firm to gain at least a temporary competitive advantage. WalMart's skills in developing and using point-of-purchase data collection to control inventory have given it a competitive advantage over K-Mart, a firm that until recently has not had access to this timely information. Thus, for many years, WalMart's valuable point-of-purchase inventory control systems were rare, at least relative to its major U.S. competitor, K-Mart.[10]

THE QUESTION OF IMITABILITY

A firm that possesses valuable and rare resources and capabilities can gain, at least, a temporary competitive advantage. If, in addition, competing firms face a cost disadvantage in imitating these resources and capabilities, firms with these special abilities can obtain a sustained competitive advantage. These observations lead to the question of imitability: do firms without a resource or capability face a cost disadvantage in obtaining it compared to firms that already possess it?

Obviously, imitation is critical to understanding the ability of resources and capabilities to generate sustained competitive advantages. Imitation can occur in at least two ways: duplication and substitution. Duplication occurs when an imitating firm builds the same kinds of resources as the firm it is imitating. If one firm has a competitive advantage because of its research and development skills, then a duplicating firm will try to imitate that resource by developing its own research and development skills. In addition, firms may be able to substitute some resources for other resources. If these substitute resources have the same strategic implications and are no more costly to develop, then imitation through substitution will lead to competitive parity in the long run.

So, when will firms be at a cost disadvantage in imitating another's resources and capabilities, either through duplication of substitution? While there are numerous reasons why some of these internal attributes of firms may be costly to imitate, most of these reasons can be grouped into three categories: the importance of history in creating firm resources; the importance of numerous 'small decisions' in developing, nurturing, and exploiting resources; and the importance of socially complex resources.

The importance of history

As firms evolve, they pick up skills, abilities, and resources that are unique to them, reflecting their particular path through history. These resources and capabilities reflect the unique personalities, experiences, and relationship that exist in only a single firm. Before the Second World War, Caterpillar was one of several medium-sized firms in the heavy construction equipment industry struggling to survive intense competition. Just before the outbreak of war, the Department of War (now the Department of Defense) concluded that, in order to pursue a global war, they would need one worldwide supplier of heavy construction equipment to build roads, air strips, army bases, and so forth. After a brief competition, Caterpillar was awarded this contract and, with the support of the Allies, was able to develop a worldwide service and supply network for heavy construction equipment at very low cost.

After the war, Caterpillar continued to own and operate this worldwide service and supply network. Indeed, Caterpillar management still advertises their ability to deliver any part, for any piece of Caterpillar equipment, to any place in the world, in under two days. By using this valuable capability, Caterpillar was able to become the dominant firm in the heavy construction equipment industry. Even today, despite recessions and labor strife, Caterpillar remains the market share leader in most categories of heavy construction equipment.[11]

Consider the position of a firm trying to duplicate Caterpillar's worldwide service and supply network, at the same cost as Caterpillar. This competing firm would have to receive the same kind of government support that Caterpillar received during the Second World War. This kind of government support is very unlikely.

It is interesting to note that at least one firm in the heavy construction equipment industry has begun to effectively compete against Caterpillar: Komatsu. However, rather than attempting to duplicate Caterpillar's service and supply network, Komatsu has attempted to exploit its own unique design and manufacturing resources by building machines that do not break down as frequently. Since Komatsu's machines break down less frequently, Komatsu does not require as extensive a worldwide service and supply network as Caterpillar. In this sense, Komatsu's special design and manufacturing skills in building machines that break down less frequently may be a strategic substitute for Caterpillar's worldwide service and supply network.[12]

In general, whenever the acquisition or development of valuable and rare resources depends upon unique historical circumstances, those imitating these resources will be at a cost disadvantage building them. Such resources can be sources of sustained competitive advantage.

The importance of numerous small decisions

Strategic managers and researchers are often enamored with the importance of 'Big Decisions' as determinants of competitive advantage. IBM's decision to bring out the 360 series of computers in the 1960s was a 'Big Decision' that had enormous competitive implications until the rise of personal computers. General Electric's decision to invest in the medical imaging business was a 'Big Decision' whose competitive ramifications are still unfolding. Sometimes such 'Big Decisions' are critical in understanding a firm's competitive position. However, more and more frequently, a firm's competitive advantage seems to depend on numerous 'small decisions' through which a firm's resources and capabilities are developed and exploited. Thus, for example, a firm's competitive advantage in quality does not depend just upon its announcing that it is seeking the Malcolm Baldridge Quality Award. It depends upon literally hundreds of thousands of decisions made each day by employees in the firm – small decisions about whether or not to tighten a screw a little more, whether or not to share a small idea for improvement, or whether or not to call attention to a quality problem.[13] From the point of view of sustaining a competitive advantage, 'small decisions' have some advantages over 'Big Decisions'. In particular, small decisions are essentially invisible to firms seeking to imitate a successful firm's resources and capabilities. 'Big Decisions', on the other hand, are more obvious, easier to describe, and, perhaps, easier to imitate. While competitors may be able to observe the consequences of numerous little decisions, they often have a difficult time understanding the sources of the advantages.[14] A case in point is The Mailbox, Inc., a very successful firm in the bulk mailing business in the Dallas–Ft. Worth market. If there was ever a business where it seems unlikely that a firm would have a sustained competitive advantage, it is bulk mailing. Firms in this industry gather mail from customers, sort it by postal code, and then take it to the post office to be mailed. Where is the competitive advantage here? And yet, The Mailbox has enjoyed an enormous market share advantage in the Dallas–Ft. Worth area for several years. Why?

   When asked, managers at The Mailbox have a difficult time describing the sources of their sustained advantages. Indeed, they can point to *no* 'Big Decisions' they have made to generate this advantage. However, as these managers begin to discuss their firm, what becomes clear is that their success does not depend on doing a few big things right, but on doing lots of little things right. The way they manage accounting, finance, human resources, production, or other business functions, separately, is not exceptional. However, to manage all these functions so well, and so consistently over time is truly exceptional. Firms seeking to compete against The Mailbox will not have to imitate just a few internal attributes; they will have to imitate thousands or even hundreds of thousands of such attributes – a daunting task indeed.[15]

The importance of socially complex resources

A final reason that firms may be at a cost disadvantage in imitating resources and capabilities is that these resources may be socially complex. Some physical resources (e.g. computers, robots, and other machines) controlled by firms are very complex. However, firms seeking to imitate these physical resources need only purchase them, take them apart, and duplicate the technology in question. With just a couple of exceptions (including the pharmaceutical and specialty chemicals industries), patents provide little protection from the imitation of a firm's physical resources.[16] On the other hand, socially complex resources and capabilities – organizational phenomena like reputation, trust, friendship, teamwork and culture – while not patentable, are much more difficult to imitate. Imagine the difficulty of imitating Hewlett Packard's (HP) powerful and enabling culture. One of the most important components of HP's culture is that it supports and encourages teamwork and cooperation, even across divisional boundaries. HP has used this socially complex capability to enhance the compatibility of its numerous products, including printers, plotters, personal computers, mini-computers, and electronic instruments. By cooperating across these product categories, HP has been able to almost double its market value, all without introducing any radical new products or technologies.[17]

In general, when a firm's resources and capabilities are valuable, rare, and socially complex, those resources are likely to be sources of sustained competitive advantage. One firm that apparently violates this assertion is Sony. Most observers agree that Sony possesses some special management and coordination skills that enables it to conceive, design, and manufacture high quality, miniaturized consumer electronics. However, it appears that every time Sony brings out a new miniaturized product, several of its competitors quickly duplicate that product, through reverse engineering, thereby reducing Sony's technological advantage. In what way can Sony's socially complex miniaturization skills be a source of sustained competitive advantage, when most of Sony's products are quickly imitated?

The solution to this paradox depends on shifting the unit of analysis from the performance of Sony's products over time to the performance of Sony over time. After it introduces each new product, Sony experiences a rapid increase in sales and profits associated with that product. However, this leads other firms to reverse engineer the Sony product and introduce their own version. Increased competition leads the sales and profits associated with the new product to be reduced. Thus, at the level of individual products introduced by Sony, Sony apparently enjoys only very short-lived competitive advantages.

However, by looking at the total returns earned by Sony across all of its new products over time, the source of Sony's sustained competitive advantage becomes clear. By exploiting its capabilities in miniaturization, Sony is able to constantly introduce new and exciting personal electronics products. No one of these products generate a sustained competitive advantage. However, over time, across several such product introductions, Sony's capability advantages do lead to a sustained competitive advantage.[18]

THE QUESTION OF ORGANIZATION

A firm's competitive advantage potential depends on the value, rareness, and imitability of its resources and capabilities. However, to fully realize this potential, a firm must also be organized to exploit its resources and capabilities. These observations lead to the question of organization: is a firm organized to exploit the full competitive potential of its resources and capabilities?

Numerous components of a firm's organization are relevant when answering the question of organization, including its formal reporting structure, its explicit management control systems, and its compensation policies. These components are referred to as *complementary resources* because they have limited ability to generate competitive advantage in isolation. However, in combination with other resources and capabilities, they can enable a firm to realize its full competitive advantage.[19]

Much of Caterpillar's sustained competitive advantage in the heavy construction industry can be traced to its becoming the sole supplier of this equipment to Allied forces in the Second World War. However, if Caterpillar's management had not taken advantage of this opportunity by implementing a global formal reporting structure, global inventory and other control systems, and compensation policies that created incentives for its employees to work around the world, then Caterpillar's potential for competitive advantage would not have been fully realized. These attributes of Caterpillar's organization, by themselves, could not be a source of competitive advantage; i.e. adopting a global organizational form was only relevant for Caterpillar because it was pursuing a global opportunity, However, this organization was essential for Caterpillar to realize its full competitive advantage potential.

In a similar way, much of WalMart's continuing competitive advantage in the discount retailing industry can be attributed to its early entry into rural markets in the southern United States. However, to fully exploit this geographic advantage, WalMart needed to implement appropriate reporting structures, control systems, and compensation policies. We have already seen that one of these components of Wal-Mart's organization – its point-of-purchase inventory control system – is being imitated by K-Mart, and thus, by itself, is not likely to be a source of sustained competitive advantage. However, this inventory control system has enabled WalMart to take full advantage of its rural locations by decreasing the probability of stock outs and by reducing inventory costs.

While a complementary organization enabled Caterpillar and WalMart to realize their full competitive advantage, Xerox was prevented from taking full advantage of some of its most critical valuable, rare, and costly-to-imitate resources and capabilities because it lacked such organizational skills. Through the 1960s and early 1970s, Xerox invested in a series of very innovative technology development research efforts. Xerox managed this research effort by creating a stand alone research laboratory (Xerox PARC, in Palo Alto, California), and by assembling a large group of highly creative and innovative scientists and engineers to work there. Left to their own devices, these scientists and engineers developed an amazing array of technological innovations, including the personal computer, the 'mouse', windows-type software, the laser printer, the 'paperless office', ethernet, and so forth. In retrospect, the market potential of these technologies was enormous. Moreover, since these technologies were developed at Xerox PARC, they were rare. Finally, Xerox may have been able to gain some important first mover advantages if they had been able to translate these technologies into products, thereby increasing the cost to other firms of imitating these technologies.

Unfortunately, Xerox did not have an organization in place to take advantage of these resources. For example, no structure existed whereby Xerox PARC's innovations could become known to managers at Xerox. Indeed, most Xerox managers – even many senior managers – were unaware of these technological developments through the mid-1970s. Once they finally became aware of them, very few of the innovations survived Xerox's highly bureaucratic product development process – a process where product development projects were divided into hundreds of minute tasks, and progress in each task was reviewed by dozens of large committees. Even those innovations that survived the product development process were not exploited by Xerox managers. Management compensation at Xerox depended almost exclusively on maximizing current revenue. Short-term profitability was relatively less important in compensation calculations, and the development of markets for future sales and profitability was essentially irrelevant. Xerox's formal reporting structure, its explicit management control systems, and its compensation policies were all inconsistent with exploiting the valuable, rare, and costly-to-imitate resources developed at Xerox PARC. Not surprisingly, Xerox failed to exploit any of these potential sources of sustained competitive advantage.[20]

This set of questions can be applied in understanding the competitive implications of phenomena as diverse as the 'cola wars' in the soft drink industry and competition among different types of personal computers.

THE COMPETITIVE IMPLICATIONS OF THE 'COLA WARS'

Almost since they were founded, Coca-Cola, Inc. and PepsiCo, Inc. have battled each other for market share in the soft drink industry. In many ways, the intensity of these 'cola wars' increased in the mid-1970s with the introduction of PepsiCo's 'Pepsi Challenge' advertising campaign. While significant advertising and other marketing expenditures have been made by both these firms, and while market share has shifted back and forth between them over time, it is not at all clear that these efforts have generated competitive advantages for either Coke or Pepsi.

Obviously, market share is a very valuable commodity in the soft drink industry. Market share translates directly into revenues, which, in turn, has a large impact on profits and profitability. Strategies pursued by either Coke or Pepsi designed to acquire market share will usually be valuable.

But are these market share acquisition strategies rare or does either Coca-Cola or Pepsi have a cost advantage in implementing them? Both Coca-Cola and PepsiCo are marketing powerhouses; both have enormous financial capabilities and strong management teams. Any effort by one to take share away can instantly be matched by the other to protect that share. In this sense, while Coke's and Pepsi's share acquisition strategies may be valuable, they are not rare, nor does either Coke or Pepsi have a cost advantage in implementing them. Assuming that these firms are appropriately organized (a reasonable assumption), then the cola wars should be a source of competitive parity for these firms.

This has, apparently, been the case. For example, Pepsi originally introduced its 'Pepsi Challenge' advertising campaign in the Dallas–Ft. Worth market. After six months of the Pepsi Challenge – including price discounts, coupon campaigns, numerous celebrity endorsements, and so on – Pepsi was able to double its share of the Dallas–Ft. Worth market from 7% to 14%. Unfortunately, the retail price of Pepsi's soft drinks, after six months of the Pepsi Challenge, was approximately one half the pre-challenge level. Thus Pepsi doubled its market share, but cut its prices in half – exactly the result one would expect in a world of competitive parity.[21]

It is interesting to note that both Coca-Cola and Pepsi are beginning to recognize the futility of going head-to-head against an equally skilled competitor in a battle for market share to gain competitive advantages. Instead, these firms seem to be altering both their market share and other strategies. Coke, through its Diet Coke brand name, is targeting older consumers with advertisements that use personalities for the 1950s, '60s, and '70s (e.g. Elton John and Gene Kelly). Pepsi continues its focus on attracting younger drinkers with its 'choice of a new generation' advertising campaigns. Coke continues its traditional focus on the soft drink industry, while Pepsi has begun diversifying into fast food restaurants and other related businesses. Coke has extended its marketing efforts internationally, whereas Pepsi focuses mostly on the market in the United States (although it is beginning to alter this strategy). In all these ways, Coke and Pepsi seem to be moving away from head-to-head competition for market share, and moving towards exploiting *different* resources.

THE COMPETITIVE POSITION OF THE MACINTOSH COMPUTER

Building on earlier research conducted by Xerox PARC, Apple Computer developed and marketed the first user-friendly alternative to DOS-based personal computers, the Macintosh. Most Macintosh users have a passion for their computers that is usually reserved for personal relationships. Macintosh users shake their heads and wonder why DOS-based computer users don't wake up and experience the 'joy of Macintosh'.

The first step in analyzing the competitive position of the Macintosh is to evaluate whether or not 'user friendliness' in a personal computer is valuable; i.e. does it exploit an environmental opportunity and/or neutralize an environmental threat? While user friendliness is not a requirement of all personal computer users, it is not unreasonable to conclude that many of these computer users, other things being equal, would prefer working on a user friendly machine compared with a user unfriendly machine. Thus, the Macintosh computer does seem to respond to a real market opportunity.

When the Macintosh was first introduced, was user friendliness rare? At that time, DOS-based machines were essentially the only alternative to the Macintosh, and DOS-based software, in those early days, was anything but user friendly. Thus, the Macintosh was apparently both valuable and rare, and thus a source of at least a temporary competitive advantage for Apple.

Was the user-friendliness of the Macintosh costly to imitate? At first, it seemed likely that user-friendly software would rapidly be developed for DOS-based machines, and thus that the user-friendly Macintosh would only enjoy a temporary competitive advantage. However, history has shown that user friendliness was not easy to imitate.

Imitation of the user-friendly Macintosh by DOS-based machines was slowed by a combination of at least two factors. First, the Macintosh hardware and software system had originally been developed by teams of software, hardware, and production engineers all working in Apple Computer. The teamwork, trust, commitment, and enthusiasm that these Apple employees enjoyed while working on Macintosh technology was difficult for other computer firms to duplicate, since most of those firms specialized either in hardware design and manufacturing (e.g. IBM) or software development (e.g. Microsoft, Lotus). In other words, the socially complex resources that Apple was able to bring to bear in the Macintosh project were difficult to duplicate in vertically non-integrated computer hardware and software firms.

Second, Apple managment had a different conception of the personal computer and its future than did managers at IBM and other computer firms. At IBM, for example, computers had traditionally meant mainframe computers, and mainframe computers were expected to be complicated and difficult to operate. User friendliness was never an issue in IBM mainframes (users of IBM's JCL know the truth of that assertion!), and thus was not an important concern when IBM entered into the personal computer market. However, at Apple, computers were Jobs' and Wozniak's toys – a hobby, to be used for fun. If management's mindset is that 'computers are supposed to be fun', then it suddenly becomes easier to develop and build user-friendly computers.

Obviously, these two mindsets – IBM's 'computers are complex tools run by technical specialists' versus Apples's 'computers are toys for everyone' – were deeply embedded in the cultures of these two firms, as well as those firms that worked closely with them. Such mindsets are socially complex, slow to change, and difficult to imitate. It took some time before the notion that a computer should be (or even could be) easy to use came to prominence in DOS-based systems.[22] Only recently, after almost ten years (an eternity in the rapidly changing personal computer business), has user-friendly software for DOS-based machines been developed. With the introduction of Windows by Microsoft, the rareness of Macintosh's user friendliness has been reduced, as has been the competitive advantage that Macintosh had generated.

Interestingly, just as Windows software was introduced, Apple began to radically change its pricing and product development strategies. First Apple cut the price of the Macintosh computer, reflecting the fact that user friendliness was not as rare after Windows as it was before Windows. Second, Apple seems to have recognized the need to develop new resources and capabilities to enhance their traditional user-friendly strengths. Rather than only competing with other hardware and software companies, Apple has begun developing strategic alliances with several other computer firms, including IBM and Microsoft. These alliances may help Apple develop the resources and capabilities they need to remain competitive in the personal computer industry over the next several years.

THE MANAGEMENT CHALLENGE

In the end, this discussion reminds us that sustained competitive advantage cannot be created simply by evaluating environmental opportunities and threats, and then conducting business only in high-opportunity, low-threat environments. Rather, creating sustained competitive advantage depends on the unique resources and capabilities that a firm brings to competition in its environment. To discover these resources and capabilities, managers must look inside their firm for valuable, rare and costly-to-imitate resources, and then exploit these resources through their organization.

NOTES

1. The original SWOT framework was proposed and developed by E. Learned, C. Christiansen, K. Andrews, and W. Guth in *Business Policy* (Homewood, IL: Irwin, 1969). Though the field of strategic management has evolved a great deal since then, this fundamental SWOT framework, as an organizing principle, has remained unchanged. See for example Michael Porter, 'The Contributions of Industrial Organization to Strategic Management,' *Academy of Management Review*, 6, 1981, 609–620; and Jay Barney, 'Firm Resources and Sustained Competitive Advantage,' *Journal of Management*, 17, 1991, 99–120.
2. Porter's work is described in detail in M. Porter, *Competitive Strategy* (New York, NY: Free Press, 1980), and M. Porter, *Competitive Advantage* (New York, NY: Free Press, 1985).
3. A variety of different authors have begun to explore the competitive implications of a firm's internal strengths and weaknesses. Building on some seminal insights by Edith Penrose [*The Theory of the Growth of the Firm* (New York, NY: Wiley, 1959)], this work has come to be known as the Resource-Based View of the Firm. Resource-based scholarly work includes: Birger Wernerfelt, 'A Resource-Based View of the Firm,' *Strategic Management Journal*, 5, 1984, 171–180; Richard Rumelt, 'Toward a Strategic Theory of the Firm,' in R. Lamb (ed.), *Competitive Strategic Management* (Englewood Cliffs, NJ: Prentice-Hall, 1984), 556–570; Jay Barney, 'Strategic Factor Markets,' *Management Science*, 41, 1980, 1231–1241; and Jay Barney, 'Organizational Culture: Can It Be A Source of Sustained Competitive Advantage?' *Academy of Management Review*, 11, 1986, 791–800. The framework developed in this article draws most closely from Jay Barney, 'Firm Resources and Sustained Competitive Advantage,' *op cit.*
4. For more detailed discussions of the internal resources and capabilities of these firms, see Pankaj Ghemewat, 'WalMart Stores' Discount Operations,' Case No. 9–387–018 (Harvard Business School, 1986); S. Chakravarty, 'Hit 'Em Hardest with the Mostest,' *Forbes*, 148, September 16, 1991, 48–54; and Pankaj Ghemewat, 'Nucor at a Crossroad,' Case No. 9–793–039 (Harvard Business School, 1992).
5. Different terms have been used to describe these internal phenomena, including core competencies (C. K. Prahalad and Gary Hamel, 'The Core Competence of the Organization,' *Harvard Business Review*, 90, 1990, 79–93), firm resources (Birger Wernerfelt, *op cit.*, and Jay B. Barney, 'Firm Resources and Sustained Competitive Advantage') and firm capabilities (George Stalk, Phillip Evans, and Lawrence Shulman, 'Competing on Capabilities: The New Rules of Corporate Strategy,' *Harvard Business Review*, March–April, 1992, 57–69). While distinctions among these terms can be drawn, for our purposes they can, and will, be used interchangeably.
6. For details, see B. Schlender, 'How Sony Keeps the Magic Going,' *Fortune*, 125, February 24, 1992, 76–84; L. Krogh, J. Praeger, D. Sorenson, and J. Tomlinson, 'How 3M Evaluates Its R&D Programs,' *Research Technology Management*, 31, November/December, 1988, 10–14; Richard Rosenbloom, 'Continuous Casting Investments at USX Corporation,' Case No. 9–392–232 (Harvard Business School, 1990); and Cynthia Montgomery, 'Sears, Roebuck and Co. in 1989,' Case No. 9–391–147 (Harvard Business School, 1989).

7. This kind of environmental or technological shift is called a Schumpeterian revolution, and firms in this setting have little systematic hope of gaining competitive advantages, unless the competitive environment shifts again, although they can be lucky. See Jay B. Barney, 'Types of Competitors and the Theory of Strategy: Toward an Integrative Framework,' *Academy of Management Review*, 1986, 791–800.

8. For a discussion of AT&T's attempt to develop new resources and capabilities, see D. Kirkpatrick, 'Could AT&T Rule the World?' *Fortune*, 127, May 17, 1993, 54–56. Hunter Fan's experience was described through personal communication with managers there, and in a publication celebrating Hunter Fan's 100th anniversary in 1986.

9. Prahalad and Hamel's 1990 discussion of NEC's attempt to develop the resources needed to compete in the global telecommunications and computer industry is insightful, especially in comparison to Kirkpatrick's discussion of AT&T's efforts in *Fortune*.

10. WalMart's point of purchase inventory control system and the impact of WalMart's rural stores on its performance, are described in Ghemewat, *op cit.*, 1986. K-Mart's inventory control response to WalMart is described in L. Steven's 'Front Line Systems,' *Computerworld*, 26, 1992, 61–63.

11. See M. G. Rukstad and J. Horn, 'Caterpillar and the Construction Equipment Industry in 1988,' Case No. 9–389–097 (Harvard Business School, 1989).

12. Komatsu's response to Caterpillar's competitive advantage is described in C. A. Bartlett and U. S. Rangan, 'Komatsu Ltd.,' Case No. 9–385–277 (Harvard Business School, 1985).

13. See Richard Blackburn and Benson Rosen, 'Total Quality and Human Resources Management: Lessons Learned from Baldridge Award-winning Companies,' *Academy of Management Executive*, 7, 1993, 49–66.

14. These invisible assets have been described by H. Itami, *Mobilizing Invisible Assets* (Cambridge, MA: Harvard University Press, 1987).

15. Personal communication.

16. See E. Mansfield, 'How Rapidly Does New Industrial Technology Leak Out?' *Journal of Industrial Economics*, 34, 1985, 217–223; and E. Mansfield, M. Schwartz, and S. Wagner, 'Imitation Costs and Patents: An Empirical Study,' *Economic Journal*, 91, 1981, 907–918.

17. See S. K. Yoder, 'A 1990 Reorganization at Hewlett Packard Already Is Paying Off,' *Wall Street Journal*, July 22, 1991, Section Ak, 1+. This is not to suggest that socially complex resources and capabilities do not change and evolve in an organization. They clearly do. Nor does this suggest that managers can never radically alter a firm's socially complex resources and capabilities. Such transformational leaders do seem to exist, and do have an enormous impact on these resources in a firm. Managers such as the late Mike Walsh at Tenneco, Lee Iacocca at Chrysler, and Jack Welch at General Electric apparently have been such leaders. However, this kind of leadership is a socially complex phenomenon, and thus very difficult to imitate. Even if a leader in one firm can transform its socially complex resources and capabilities, it does not necessarily mean that other firms will be able to imitate this feat at the same cost. The concept of transformational leaders is discussed in N. Tichy, *The Transformational Leader* (New York, NY: Wiley, 1986).

18. See Schlender, *op cit.*

19. See Raphael Amit and Paul Schoemaker, 'Strategic Assets and Organizational Rent,' *Strategic Management Journal*, 14, 1993, 33–46; David Teece, 'Profiting From Technological Innovation,' *Research Policy*, 15, 1986, 285–

305; and Ingemar Dierickx and Karel Cool, 'Asset Stock Accumulation and Sustainability of Competitive Advantage,' *Management Science*, 35, 1989, 1504–1511, for a discussion of complementary resources and capabilities. Of course, complementary organizational resources are part of a firm's over-all resource and capability base, and thus the competitive implications of these resources could be evaluated using the questions of value, rareness, and imitability. However, the question of organization is included in this discussion to emphasize the particular importance of complementary organizational resources in enabling a firm to fully exploit its competitive advantage potential.

20. Xerox's organizational problems with Xerox PARC are described, in detail, in David T. Kearns, and David A. Nadler, *Prophets in the Dark* (New York, NY: Harper Collins, 1992); Douglas K. Smith and Robert C. Alexander, *Fumbling the Future* (New York, NY: William Morrow, 1988); and L. Hooper, 'Xerox Tries to Shed Its Has Been Image with a Big New Machine,' *Wall Street Journal*, September 20, 1990, Section A, 1+.

21. See A. E. Pearson and C. L. Irwin, 'Coca-Cola vs. Pepsi-Cola (A),' Case No. 9–387–108 (Harvard Business School, 1988), for a discussion of the cola wars, and their competitive implications for Coke and Pepsi.

22. See D. B. Yoffie, 'Apple Computer – 1992,' Case No. 9–792–081 (Harvard Business School, 1992), for a complete discussion of Apple, IBM, and Apple's new strategies for the 1990s.

Chapter 2

Understanding organizations as learning systems

Edwin C. Nevis, Anthony J. DiBella and Janet M. Gould

How can you tell if your company is, indeed, a learning organization? What is a learning organization anyway? And how can you improve the learning systems in your company? The authors provide a framework for examining a company, based on its 'learning orientations', a set of critical dimensions to organizational learning, and 'facilitating factors', the processes that affect how easy or hard it is for learning to occur. They illustrate their model with examples from four firms they studied – Motorola, Mutual Investment Corporation, Electricité de France, and Fiat – and conclude that all organizations have systems that support learning.

With the decline of some well-established firms, the diminishing competitive power of many companies in a burgeoning world market, and the need for organizational renewal and transformation, interest in organizational learning has grown. Senior managers in many organizations are convinced of the importance of improving learning in their organizations. This growth in awareness has raised many unanswered questions: What is a learning organization? What determines the characteristics of a good learning organization (or are all learning organizations good by definition)? How can organizations improve their learning? In the literature in this area, authors have used different definitions or models of organizational learning or have not defined their terms.[1] Executives have frequently greeted us with comments like these:

- 'How would I know a learning organization if I stumbled over it?'
- 'You academics have some great ideas, but what do I do with a mature, large organization on Monday morning?'
- 'I'm not sure what a good learning organization is, but you should not study us because we are a bad learning organization.'

Our research is dedicated to helping organizations become better learning systems. We define organizational learning as the capacity or processes within an organization to maintain or improve performance based on experience. Learning is a systems-level phenomenon because it stays within the organization, even if individuals change. One of our assumptions is that organizations learn as they produce. Learning is as much a task as the production and delivery of goods and services. We do not imply that organizations should sacrifice the speed and quality of production in order to learn, but, rather, that production systems be viewed as learning systems. While companies do not usually regard learning as a function of production, our research on successful firms indicates that three learning-related factors are important for their success:

1 Well-developed core competencies that serve as launch points for new products and services. (Canon has made significant investments over time in developing knowledge in eight core competencies applied in the creation of more than thirty products.)
2 An attitude that supports continuous improvement in the business's value-added chain. (Wal-Mart conducts ongoing experiments in its stores.)
3 The ability to fundamentally renew or revitalize. (Motorola has a long history of renewing itself through its products by periodically exiting old lines and entering new ones.)

These factors identify some of the qualities of an effective learning organization that diligently pursues a constantly enhanced knowledge base. This knowledge allows for the development of competencies and incremental or transformational change. In these instances, there is assimilation and utilization of knowledge and some kind of integrated learning system to support such 'actionable learning'. Indeed, an organization's ability to survive and grow is based on advantages that stem from core competencies that represent collective learning.[2]

As a corollary to this assumption, we assume that all organizations engage in some form of collective learning as part of their development.[3] The creation of culture and the socialization of members in the culture rely on learning processes to ensure an institutionalized reality.[4] In this sense, it may be redundant to talk of 'learning organizations'. On the other hand, all learning is not the same; some learning is dysfunctional, and some insights or skills that might lead to useful new actions are often hard to attain. The current concern with the learning organization focuses on the gaps in organizational learning capacity and does not negate the usefulness of those learning processes that organizations may do well, even though they have a learning disability. Thus Argyris and Schön emphasize double-loop learning (generative) as an important, often missing, level of learning in contrast with single-loop learning (corrective), which they have found to be more common.[5] Similarly, Senge makes a highly persuasive case for generative learning, 'as contrasted with adaptive learning', which he sees as more prevalent.[6] The focus for these theorists is on the learning required to make transformational changes – changes in basic assumptions – that organizations need in today's fast-moving, often chaotic environment. Their approach does not negate the value of everyday incremental 'fixes'; it provides a more complete model for observing and developing organizational learning. After periods of significant discontinuous change, incremental, adaptive learning may be just the thing to help consolidate transformational or generative learning.

Another assumption we make is that the value chain of any organization is a domain of integrated learning. To think of the value chain as an integrated learning system is to think of the work in each major step, beginning with strategic decisions through to customer service, as a subsystem for learning experiments. Structures and processes to achieve outcomes can be seen simultaneously as operational tasks and learning exercises; this holds for discrete functions and for cross-functional activities, such as new product development. The organization encompasses each value-added stage as a step in doing business, not as a fixed classification scheme. Most organizations do not think this way, but it is useful for handling complexity. With this 'chunking', we are able to study learning better and to see how integration is achieved at the macro-organizational level. This viewpoint is consistent with a definition of organizations as *complex arrangements of people in which learning takes place*.

While we have not looked at organizations' full value-added chains, we selected our research sites so that we could examine learning in different organizational subsets. In addition, we gathered data indicating preferences or biases in investments in learning at different points of the chain and to understand how learning builds, maintains, improves, or shifts core competencies. Do organizations see certain stages of the chain where significant investment is more desirable than at others?

Our last assumption is that the learning process has identifiable stages. Following Huber, whose comprehensive review of the literature presented four steps in an organizational learning process, we arrived at a three-stage model:

1 Knowledge acquisition – The development or creation of skills, insights, relationships.
2 Knowledge sharing – The dissemination of what has been learned.
3 Knowledge utilization – The integration of learning so it is broadly available and can be generalized to new situations.[7]

Most studies of organizational learning have been concerned with the acquisition of knowledge and, to a lesser extent, with the sharing or dissemination of the acquired knowledge (knowledge transfer). Less is known about the assimilation process, the stage in which knowledge becomes institutionally available, as opposed to being the property of select individuals or groups. Huber refers to the assimilation and utilization process as 'organizational memory'. While this is an important aspect of knowledge utilization, it is limited and works better when discussing information, as distinct from knowledge. True knowledge is more than information; it includes the meaning or interpretation of the information, and a lot of intangibles such as the tacit knowledge of experienced people that is not well articulated but often determines collective organizational competence. Studies of organizational learning must be concerned with all three stages in the process.

Early in our research, it became clear that organizational learning does not always occur in the linear fashion implied by any stage model. Learning may take place in planned or informal, often unintended, ways. Moreover, knowledge and skill acquisition takes place in the sharing and utilization stages. It is not something that occurs simply by organizing an 'acquisition effort'. With this in mind, we shifted our emphasis to look for a more fluid and chaotic learning environment, seeking less-defined, more subtle embodiments.

The first phase of our research was based on intensive field observations in four companies, Motorola Corporation, Mutual Investment Corporation (MIC), Electricité de France (EDF), and Fiat Auto Company.[8] We wanted to have both service and manufacturing settings in US and European environments. We chose two sites where we had access to very senior management and two where we were able to study lower levels. We selected Motorola as an example of a good learning organization; we were able to observe organizational learning during its fourteen-year quality improvement effort.

We did not attempt to study entire firms or to concentrate on any single work units in these four organizations. For example, at Motorola, we began by studying two senior management teams of twenty to twenty-five executives each from all parts of the corporation. Each team focuses on a critical issue defined by the CEO and COO, to whom the groups report. The teams' structures were designed as executive education interventions and vehicles for 'real-time' problem solving. Our objective was to see how these teams reflected and utilized organizational learning at Motorola.

From our interview data, we identified what organizational members claimed they had learned and why. We wrote case descriptions of the learning processes in their organizations, which we shared with the organizations to ensure their accuracy. Using a grounded analysis, we identified categories that reflected learning orientations and then constructed a two-part model of the critical factors that describe organizations as learning systems.[9] We have since tested this model in data-gathering workshops with personnel from more than twenty *Fortune* '500' companies. Our testing led us to revise some of the model's components, while retaining its overall framework.

CORE THEMES

Next we discuss the core themes that emerged from our research and provided a basis for our model.

All organizations are learning systems

All the sites we studied function as learning systems. All have formal and informal processes and structures for the acquisition, sharing, and utilization of knowledge and skills. Members communicated broadly and assimilated values, norms, procedures, and outcome data, starting with early socialization and continuing through group communications, both formal and informal. We talked with staff people in some firms who claimed that their companies were not good learning organizations, but, in each, we were able to identify one or more core competencies that could exist only if there were learning investments in those areas. Some type of structure or process would have to support the informed experience and formal educational interventions required for knowledge acquisition, sharing, and utilization. We found this in both our field sites and other firms. For example, one firm that considers itself to be a poor learning organization because of its difficulty in changing some dysfunction has a reputation in its industry for superior field marketing. It is clear that this group has well-developed recruiting, socialization, training and development, and rotating assignment policies that support its cadre of respected marketing people. Obviously, some learning has been assimilated at a fairly deep level.

Learning conforms to culture

The nature of learning and the way in which it occurs are determined by the organization's culture or subcultures. For example, the entrepreneurial style of MIC's investment funds group results in a learning approach in which information is made available to fund managers and analysts, but its use is at the managers' discretion. In addition, there is a good deal of leeway in how fund managers make their investments; some are intuitive, some rely heavily on past performance, and a few use sophisticated computer programs. Thus the fund managers' use or application of learning is largely informal, not dictated by formal, firmwide programs. Meanwhile, the culture of MIC's marketing groups is more collaborative; learning is derived more from interaction within and between cross-functional work groups and from improved communication.

In contrast, there is no question that a great deal of organizational learning about quality has occurred at Motorola, but its emphasis on engineering and technical concerns resulted in an earlier, complete embrace of total quality by product manufacturing groups. In a culture that heavily rewards product group performance, total quality in products and processes that require integrated, intergroup action lags behind, particularly in the marketing of systems that cut across divisions.

Style varies between learning systems

There are a variety of ways in which organizations create and maximize their learning. Basic assumptions about the culture lead to learning values and investments that produce a different learning style from a culture with another pattern of values and investments. These style variations are based on a series of learning orientations (dimensions of learning) that members of the organization may not see. We have identified seven learning orientations, which we see as bipolar variables.

For example, each of two distinct groups at both Motorola and MIC had different approaches to the way it accrued and utilized knowledge and skills. One Motorola group had great concern for specifying the metrics to define and measure the targeted learning. The other group was less concerned with very specific measures but, instead, stressed broad objectives. In the two groups at MIC, the methods for sharing and utilizing knowledge were very different; one was informal, and the other more formal and collaborative. From these variations, we concluded that the pattern of the learning orientations largely makes up an organizational learning system. The pattern may not tell us how *well* learning is promoted but tells a lot about what is learned and where it occurs.

Generic processes facilitate learning

How well an organization maximizes learning within its chosen style does not occur haphazardly. Our data suggest that talking about 'the learning organization' is partially effective; some policies, structures, and processes do seem to make a difference. The difference is in how easy or hard it is for useful learning to happen, and in how effective the organization is in 'working its style'. By analyzing why learning took place in the companies we studied, we identified ten facilitating factors that induced or supported learning. While we did not observe all the factors at each site, we saw most of them and at other sites as well. Thus we view them as generic factors that any organization can benefit from,

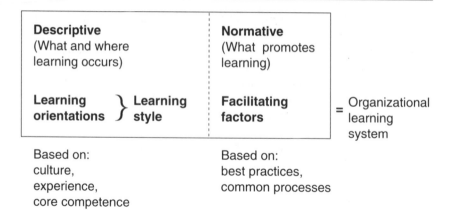

Figure 2.1 A model of organizations as learning systems

regardless of its learning style. For example, scanning, in which bench-marking plays an important role, was so central to learning at Motorola that it is now an integral, ongoing aspect of every important initiative in the company. Although MIC tends to create knowledge and skill intern-ally, it maintains an ongoing vigilance toward its external environment. On the negative side, the absence of solid, ongoing external scanning in other organizations is an important factor in their economic difficulties.

A MODEL OF ORGANIZATIONS AS LEARNING SYSTEMS

Our two-part model describes organizations as learning systems (see Figure 2.1). First, *learning orientations* are the values and practices that reflect where learning takes place and the nature of what is learned. These orientations form a pattern that defines a given organization's 'learning style'. In this sense, they are descriptive factors that help us to understand without making value judgments. Second, *facilitating factors* are the structures and processes that affect how easy or hard it is for learning to occur and the amount of effective learning that takes place. These are standards based on best practice in dealing with generic issues. (See Figure 2.2 for definitions of the learning orientations and facilitating factors we identified.)

Both parts of the model are required to understand an organization as a learning system; one without the other provides an incomplete picture. In addition, separating the parts enables organizations to see that they do indeed function as learning systems of some kind, and that their task is to understand better what they do well or poorly. (The idea of asses-sing what exists is more useful than the pejorative notion that there is only one good way to be a learning organization.) Finally, a refined,

Seven learning orientations

1. Knowledge source: internal–external. Preference for developing knowledge internally versus preference for acquiring knowledge developed externally.

2. Product–process focus: what?–how? Emphasis on accumulation of knowledge about what products/services are versus how organization develops, makes, and delivers its products/services.

3. Documentation mode: personal–public. Knowledge is something individuals possess versus publicly available know-how.

4. Dissemination mode: formal–informal. Formal, prescribed, organization-wide methods of sharing learning versus informal methods, such as role modeling and casual daily interaction.

5. Learning focus: incremental–transformative. Incremental or corrective learning versus transformative or radical learning.

6. Value-chain focus: design–deliver. Emphasis on learning investments in engineering/production activities ('design and make' functions) versus sales/service activities ('market and deliver' functions).

7. Skill development focus: individual–group. Development of individuals' skills versus team or group skills.

Ten facilitating factors

1. Scanning imperative. Information gathering about conditions and practices outside the unit; awareness of the environment; curiosity about the external environment in contrast to the internal environment.

2. Performance gap. Shared perception of a gap between actual and desired state of performance; performance shortfalls seen as opportunities for learning.

3. Concern for measurement. Considerable effort spent on defining and measuring key factors when venturing into new areas; striving for specific, quantifiable measures; discussion of metrics as a learning activity.

4. Experimental mind-set. Support for trying new things; curiosity about how things work; ability to 'play' with things; 'failures' are accepted, not punished; changes in work processes, policies, and structures are a continuous series of learning opportunities.

5. Climate of openness. Accessibility of information; open communications within the organization; problems/errors/lessons are shared, not hidden; debate and conflict are acceptable ways to solve problems.

6. Continuous education. Ongoing commitment to education at all levels of the organization; clear support for all members' growth and development.

7. Operational variety. Variety of methods, procedures, and systems; appreciation of diversity; pluralistic rather than singular definition of valued competencies.

8. Multiple advocates. New ideas and methods advanced by employees at all levels; more than one champion.

9. Involved leadership. Leaders articulate vision, are engaged in its implementation; frequently interact with members; become actively involved in educational programs.

10. System perspective. Interdependenence of organizational units; problems and solutions seen in terms of systemic relationships among processes; connection between the unit's needs and goals and the company's.

Figure 2.2 Definitions of the orientations and factors

detailed list of factors related to organizational learning may help companies select areas for learning improvement that do not demand drastic culture change but, rather, can lead to incremental change over time.

Learning orientations

In the next section, we expand on the definitions of the seven learning orientations and provide examples of each.

1. Knowledge source

To what extent does the organization develop new knowledge internally or seek inspiration in external ideas? This distinction is seen as the difference between innovation and adaptation – or imitation. In the United States, there is a tendency to value innovativeness more highly and look down on 'copiers'. American critiques of Japanese businesses often mention that the Japanese are good imitators but not good innovators. In our opinion, both of these approaches have great merit as opposing styles rather than as normative or negative behaviors.

Although our data show a tendency in organizations to prefer one mode over the other, the distinction is not clear-cut. While MIC does scan its environment, it prefers to innovate in responding to customer needs and problems and has been a leader in developing new financial products and services. EDF modeled its nuclear power plants on US technology. Motorola appears to be equally vigorous in innovation and in reflective imitation; it has been innovative in developing new products and adroit at adapting others' processes, such as benchmarking and TQM procedures. Among firms not in this study, American Airlines, Wal-Mart, Merck, and Rubbermaid appear to be innovative in producing knowledge. And American Home Products is a good example of a highly successful, reflective imitator, as are AT&T's Universal Credit Card, Tyco Toys (a Lego 'copier'), and Lexus and Infiniti automobiles.

2. Product–process focus

Does the organization prefer to accumulate knowledge about product and service outcomes or about the basic processes underlying various products? Many observers have stated that one reason Japanese companies are so competitive is that they make considerably more investments in process technologies in comparison to US companies. The difference is between interest in 'getting product out the door' and curiosity about the steps in the processes. All organizations give some attention to each side; the issue is to organize for learning in both domains.

Motorola makes learning investments on both sides. The executives we observed spent roughly equal amounts of time in collaborative learning about processes and outcomes. They paid less attention to 'people processes' than to 'hard' or technical processes, but many of them accepted the importance of process issues. MIC, EDF, and Fiat have traditionally focused almost exclusively on product issues but are now making greater learning investments in process issues.

3. Documentation mode

Do attitudes vary as to what constitutes knowledge and where knowledge resides? At one pole, knowledge is seen in personal terms, as something an individual possesses by virtue of education or experience. This kind of knowledge is lost when a long-time employee leaves an organization; processes and insights evaporate because they were not shared or made a part of collective memory. At the other pole, knowledge is defined in more objective, social terms, as being a consensually supported result of information processing. This attitude emphasizes organizational memory or a publicly documented body of knowledge.

MIC's investment funds group focuses on a personal documentation style, eschewing policy statements and procedure manuals. In keeping with its entrepreneurial orientation, MIC makes it possible for individuals to learn a great deal, but there is little pressure to codify this. Though engaged in a business that values 'hard data', the group supports subjective, tacit knowledge in decision-making processes. And at Fiat's Direzione Technica, where the individual has historically been the repository of knowledge, efforts are being made to establish a *memoria technica*, or engineering knowledge bank. Motorola shows evidence of both approaches but works hard to make knowledge explicit and broadly available.

4. Dissemination mode

Has the organization established an atmosphere in which learning evolves or in which a more structured, controlled approach induces learning? In the more structured approach, the company decides that valuable insights or methods should be shared and used by others across the organization. It uses written communication and formal educational methods or certifies learning through writing the procedures down. In the more informal approach, learning is spread through encounters between role models and gatekeepers who compellingly reinforce learning. In another approach, learning occurs when members of an occupational group or work team share their experiences in ongoing dialogue.[10]

MIC's investment funds group clearly prefers informal dissemination in which learning develops and is shared in loosely organized interactions. This method occurs in other MIC areas, although the marketing groups are becoming more structured in their dissemination. Motorola supports both approaches, though it invests heavily in structured, firmwide programs when senior management wants a basic value or method institutionalized. It considered quality so critical that it now includes vendors and customers in its dissemination. (Recently, some vendors were told that they had to compete for the Malcolm Baldrige Quality Award in order to be on the company's approved vendor list.) EDF prefers formal modes, emphasizing documented procedures that all share. Fiat's Direzione Technica formally spreads knowledge by accumulating it in specialist departments and then disseminating it to cross-functional design teams.

5. Learning focus

Is learning concentrated on methods and tools to improve what is already being done or on testing the assumptions underlying what is being done? Argyris and Schön call the former 'single-loop learning' and the latter 'double-loop learning'.[11] They have rightfully argued that organizational performance problems are more likely due to a lack of awareness and inability to articulate and check underlying assumptions than to a function of poor efficiency. In our opinion, these learning capabilities reinforce each other. Organizations may have a preference for one mode over the other, but a sound learning system can benefit from good work in both areas.

Our research sites displayed a range of behavior. EDF is primarily focused on incremental issues and does not question its basic assumptions. It prides itself on being the world's major nuclear power utility and devotes significant resources to being the most efficient, safe operator through small improvements rather than transformations. Though similar, Fiat's Direzione Technica is beginning to question assumptions about its new product development process. Since 1987, MIC has been in a transformational mode, particularly in the way that its marketing groups have focused on a questioning learning style. Motorola is fairly well balanced in its orientation; the founding family has historically accepted the concept of organizational renewal, which has led to far-reaching changes in the company's product lines through the years and to an inquisitive style. On the other hand, its strong dedication to efficiency learning often precludes questioning basic assumptions.

6. Value-chain focus

Which core competencies and learning investments does the organization value and support? By learning investments, we mean all allocations of personnel and money to develop knowledge and skill over time, including training and education, pilot projects, developmental assignments, available resources, and so on. If a particular organization is 'engineering focused' or 'marketing driven', it is biased in favor of substantial learning investments in those areas. We divided the value chain into two categories: internally directed activities of a 'design and make' nature, and those more externally focused of a 'sell and deliver' nature. The former include R&D, engineering, and manufacturing. The latter are sales, distribution, and service activities. Although this does some disservice to the value-chain concept, the breakdown easily accounts for our observations.

At MIC, the investment funds group focuses on the design and make side. While this is balanced by learning investments on the deliver side in the MIC marketing groups, there is a strong boundary between these groups, and the fund management side is regarded as the organization's core. Motorola's total quality effort clearly recognizes the importance of value-added at both sides, but 'design and make' is significantly ahead of 'deliver' in learning investments in quality. Fiat's Direzione Technica is clearly oriented toward design and make, although its new system of simultaneous engineering is balancing its approach with increased sensitivity to the deliver side. EDF nuclear operations focuses squarely on efficient production. While not in our study, Digital Equipment Corporation's learning investments traditionally were much more heavily focused on 'design and make' than on 'deliver'.

7. Skill development focus

Does the organization develop both individual and group skills? We believe it helps to view this as a stylistic choice, as opposed to seeing it in normative terms. In this way an organization can assess how it is doing and improve either one. It can also develop better ways of integrating individual learning programs with team needs by taking a harder look at the value of group development.

MIC designed the investment funds group to promote individual learning, which seems to fit with its culture and reward system. Heavy investment in team learning would probably improve its performance. On the other hand, MIC's marketing groups, more supportive of collective learning, are now investing in team development as one way to improve its total effectiveness. Fiat's Direzione Technica has been oriented toward more individual development, but, with its new reliance on cross-functional work teams, group development is increasingly more important. Recently, Motorola has become more team oriented and is making heavier investments in collaborative learning. It designed the two executive groups we observed to foster collective learning on two strategic issues affecting the entire company. EDF develops both individual and group skills, especially in control-room teams. All EDF employees follow individual training programs for certification or promotion. Control-room teams also learn, in groups, by using plant simulators. Some other firms that emphasize team learning are Federal Express, which invests heavily in teams for its quality effort, and Herman Miller, which stresses participative management and the Scanlon plan.

We view the seven learning orientations as a matrix. An organizational unit can be described by the pattern of its orientations in the matrix, which in turn provides a way to identify its learning style. Given the characteristics of the sites we studied and other sites we are familiar with, we believe it is possible to identify learning styles that represent a distinct pattern of orientations. Such styles may reflect the industry, size, or age of an organization, or the nature of its technology.

Facilitating factors

The second part of our model is the facilitating factors that expedite learning. The ten factors are defined in Figure 2.2.

1. Scanning imperative

Does the organization understand or comprehend the environment in which it functions? In recent years, researchers have emphasized the importance of environmental scanning and agreed that many organizations were in trouble because of limited or poor scanning efforts. Thus many firms have increased their scanning capacity. Five years into Motorola's quality program, a significant scanning effort showed it what others, particularly the Japanese, were doing. In reaction, Motorola substantially changed its approach and won the first Baldrige Award four years later. By contrast, the mainframe computer manufacturers (Cray, Unisys, IBM) and the US auto companies in the 1970s failed to respond to developing changes that sound investigative work would have made painfully visible. Recent changes at Fiat result from a concerted scanning effort in which fifty senior managers visited the manufacturing facilities of world-class auto and other durable goods companies.

2. Performance gap

First, how do managers, familiar with looking at the differences between targeted outcomes and actual performance, analyze variances? When feedback shows a gap, particularly if it implies failure, their analysis often leads to experimenting and developing new insights and skills.

One reason that well-established, long-successful organizations are often not good learning systems is that they experience lengthy periods in which feedback is almost entirely positive; the lack of disconfirming evidence is a barrier to learning.

Secondly, is there a potential new vision that is not simply a quantitative extension of the old or goes well beyond the performance level seen as achievable in the old vision? One or more firm members may visualize something not previously noted. Awareness of a performance gap is important because it often leads the organization to recognize that learning needs to occur or that something already known may not be working. Even if a group cannot articulate exactly what that need might be, its awareness of ignorance can motivate learning, as occurred at Motorola after its 1984 benchmarking. Currently, this 'humility' is driving Fiat's Direzione Technica to make a major study of what it needs to know.

In our findings, EDF provides perhaps the best instance of a performance gap leading to adaptive learning. Due to the nature of the nuclear power business, performance variations became the catalyst for learning effort to again achieve the prescribed standard. We also found that future-oriented CEOs encouraged performance-gap considerations related to generative learning at Motorola and MIC (parent company).

3. Concern for measurement

Does the organization develop and use metrics that support learning? Are measures internally or externally focused, specific, and custom-built or standard measures? The importance of metrics in total quality programs has been well documented and is used in target-setting programs such as management by objectives.[12] Our interest is in how the discourse about measurements, and the search for the most appropriate ones, is a critical aspect of learning, almost as much as learning that evolves from responding to the feedback that metrics provide.

Motorola executives believe that concern for measurement was one of the most critical reasons for their quality program's success. At three or four critical junctures, reexamination of measurement issues helped propel a move to a new level of learning. They are applying this factor to new initiatives, a major concern of the executive groups we observed. At EDF, the value of metrics is clearly associated with the performance gap. Its nuclear power plants are authorized to operate at certain specifications that, if not met, may suggest or predict an unplanned event leading to shutdown. Each occasion becomes an opportunity for learning to take place.

4. Experimental mind-set

Does the organization emphasize experimentation on an ongoing basis?
If learning comes through experience, it follows that the more one can
plan guided experiences, the more one will learn. Until managers see
organizing for production at any stage of the value chain as a learning
experiment as well as a production activity, learning will come slowly.
Managers need to learn to act like applied research scientists at the same
time they deliver goods and services.[13]

We did not see significant evidence of experimental mind-sets at our
research sites, with some notable exceptions at Motorola. At its paging
products operation, we observed the current production line for one
product, a blueprint and preparation for the new setup to replace the
line, and a 'white room' laboratory in which research is now underway
for the line that will replace the one currently being installed. Motorola
University constantly tries new learning approaches; the two executive
groups we observed at Motorola were also part of an experiment in
executive education.

We have seen evidence of experimental mind-sets in reports about
other firms. For example, on any given day, Wal-Mart conducts about
250 tests in its stores, concentrated on sales promotion, display, and
customer service. Although a traditional firm in many ways, 3M's
attitude toward new product development and operational unit size
suggests a strong experimental mind-set.

5. Climate of openness

Are the boundaries around information flow permeable so people can
make their own observations? Much informal learning is a function of
daily, often unplanned interactions among people. In addition, the
opportunity to meet with other groups and see higher levels of management in operation promotes learning.[14] People need freedom to express
their views through legitimate disagreement and debate. Another critical
aspect is the extent to which errors are shared and not hidden.[15]

Perhaps the most dramatic example of openness in our findings is
EDF, where abnormalities or deviations are publicly reported throughout the entire system of fifty-seven nuclear power plants. The company
treats such incidents as researchable events to see if the problem exists
anywhere else and follows up with a learning-driven investigation to
eliminate it. It then disseminates this knowledge throughout the company. While this openness may be explained by the critical nature of
problems in a nuclear power plant, we can only speculate as to what
would be gained if any organization functioned as though a mistake is
potentially disastrous and also an opportunity to learn.

6. Continuous education

Is there a commitment to lifelong education at all levels of the organization? This includes formal programs but goes well beyond that to more pervasive support of any kind of developmental experience. The mere presence of traditional training and development activities is not sufficient; it must be accompanied by a palpable sense that one is never finished learning and practising (something akin to the Samurai tradition). The extent to which this commitment permeates the entire organization, and not just the training and development groups, is another indicator. In many ways, this factor is another way of expressing what Senge calls 'personal mastery'.

MIC does an excellent job of exposing its young analysts to developmental experiences. Its chairman also seeks knowledge in many areas, not just direct financial matters. Motorola has a policy in which every employee has some educational experience every year; it has joint ventures with several community colleges around the country, joint programs with the state of Illinois for software competence development and training of school superintendents, and on-the-job and classroom experiences for managers up to the senior level. The company spends 3.6% of its revenues on education and plans to double this amount.[16] Among firms not in our study, General Electric, Unilever, and Digital Equipment Corporation have valued continuous education at all levels for many years.

7. Operational variety

Is there more than one way to accomplish work goals? An organization that supports variation in strategy, policy, process, structure, and personnel is more adaptable when unforeseen problems arise. It provides more options and, perhaps, even more important, allows for rich stimulation and interpretation for all its members. This factor helps enhance future learning in a way not possible with a singular approach.

We did not see a great deal of variety at our sites. EDF, perhaps due to the importance of total control over operations, shows little variation. Fiat's Direzione Technica follows similar response routines, although the change to a new structure should lead to greater variation because of its independent design teams. An exception is MIC investment funds group, where we identified at least three different methods that fund managers used in making investment decisions. Senior management, although a bit skeptical about one of the methods, seemed willing to support all three as legitimate approaches.

8. Multiple advocates

Along with involved leadership, is there more than one 'champion' who sets the stage for learning? This is particularly necessary in learning that is related to changing a basic value or a long-cherished method. The greater the number of advocates who promote a new idea, the more rapidly and extensively the learning will take place. Moreover, in an effective system, any member should be able to act as an awareness-enhancing agent or an advocate for new competence development. In this way, both top-down and bottom-up initiatives are possible.

One of the authors participated in two significant change efforts that failed, largely because there was only one champion in each case. One highly frustrated CEO said, 'It doesn't do me or the company any good if I'm the only champion of this new way of doing business.' At Motorola, we found that a major factor in the quality effort's success was the early identification, empowerment, and encouragement of a significant number of advocates. In a current initiative we observed, Motorola is enlisting a minimum of 300 champions in strategic parts of the company. Digital Equipment Corporation has had learning initiators throughout the company since its early days. Digital's problem has been in assimilating and integrating the lessons of its myriad educational and experimental efforts, rather than in creating an environment that enables broad-scale initiation. MIC's investment funds group encourages many individuals to initiate their own learning but not to proselytize.

9. Involved leadership

Is leadership at every organizational level engaged in hands-on implementaton of the vision? This includes eliminating management layers, being visible in the bowels of the organization, and being an active, early participant in any learning effort. Only through direct involvement that reflects coordination, vision, and integration can leaders obtain important data and provide powerful role models.

At Motorola, CEO Bob Galvin not only drove the quality vision, he was a student in the first seminars on quality and made it the first item on the agenda at monthly meetings with his division executives. Much-admired Wal-Mart CEO David Glass spends two or three days each week at stores and warehouses; employees can call him at home and are often transferred to his hotel when he is in the field. Mike Walsh of Tenneco (formerly of Union Pacific Railroad) meets with groups of employees at all levels in what Tom Peters calls 'conversation'.[17]

10. Systems perspective

Do the key actors think broadly about the interdependency of organizational variables? This involves the degree to which managers can look at their internal systems as a source of their difficulties, as opposed to blaming external factors. Research in the field of systems dynamics has demonstrated how managers elicit unintended consequences by taking action in one area without seeing its dynamic relationship to its effects.[18]

Despite its importance, this factor was relatively lacking at our research sites. MIC and Motorola are structured so that there are strong boundaries between groups and functions. Both have changed their perspectives recently, MIC as a consequence of unexpected internal problems related to the October 1987 stock market crash, and Motorola after experiencing difficulties in selling large-scale systems (as opposed to discrete products). In a 1992 survey of 3,000 Motorola employees that asked them to evaluate their unit based on Senge's five factors, they rated systems thinking the lowest and the one that required the most work to improve organizational learning. In contrast, Fiat's Direzione Technica took a systems approach to understanding the consequences of its structure on new product development. As a result, it changed the structure to establish mechanisms for simultaneous engineering. To reduce the new products' time to market, functions now work in parallel rather than sequentially.

GENERAL DIRECTIONS FOR ENHANCING LEARNING

We have divided the seven learning orientations and ten facilitating factors into three stages – knowledge acquisition, dissemination, and utilization. Figure 2.3 shows the orientations and factors within this framework. Within our two-part model, there are two general directions for enhancing learning in an organizational unit. One is to embrace the existing style and improve its effectiveness. This strategy develops a fundamental part of the culture to its fullest extent. For example, a firm that is a reflective imitator more than an innovator could adopt this strategy with heightened awareness of its value. A company that has benefited from heavy learning investments on the 'make' side of the value chain would see the value of those investments and decide to build further on them. This approach builds on the notion that full acceptance of what has been accomplished is validating and energizing for those involved. It is similar to the appreciative inquiry numerous organizational change consultants advocate.[19] The task is to select two or three facilitating factors to improve on.

The second direction is to change learning orientations. The organizational group would make more learning investments at a different part

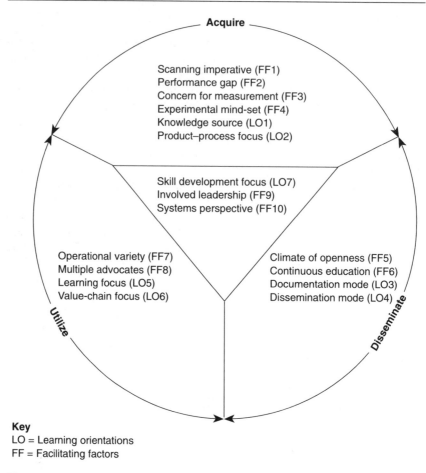

Key
LO = Learning orientations
FF = Facilitating factors

Figure 2.3 Elements of an organizational learning system

of the value chain, try to be an innovator if it is now more of an imitator, and so on. These are different changes from those involved in enhancing the facilitative factors, and the tactics will be different. Some changes will be seen as an attack on the organization's basic values, and it may be possible to avoid this by moving toward balance between the two poles, so members of the organization will support the existing style and advocate the 'new look' as a supplementary measure.

Supporting the learning orientations

In the second phase of our research, in which we worked closely with personnel from more than thirty *Fortune* '500' companies to identify their learning orientations, we validated our notion that organizations learn in varied ways. The singular 'learning organization' should be a pluralistic model.

Looking at 'what is' in a descriptive rather than normative way has another advantage in that you see better what you are *not* by examining better what you *are*. In the gestalt approach to dealing with resistance to organizational change, it has been well documented that change comes more readily if the targets of change first become more aware of and more accepting of their resistance.[20] In other works, it is important to gain full knowledge and appreciation of your organizational assumptions about learning whether you want to build on them or alter them.

This model may also be used to identify the complementarity of styles between coordinating organizations and to recognize that circumstances may dictate conditions and orientations in particular settings. For example, EDF's nuclear operations are constrained from transforming real-time operations due to the potentially dire consequences (e.g., the Chernobyl disaster) of operating under novel assumptions. However, at EDF, testing system assumptions is characteristic of its R&D division, which uses new technologies in the design of new plants. Thus changing one's style needs to be considered from a systems perspective; it may also be associated with the stage of organizational development.[21]

Strategies for improving organizational learning capability

When starting to improve its learning capabilities, an organization may decide to focus on any stage of the learning cycle – knowledge acquisition, dissemination, or utilization. While it may be possible or necessary to look at all three phases simultaneously, focusing on a single area is more manageable. The next task is to select an option for focus:

1 Improve on learning orientations. There are two reasons for selecting this option. First, the organization may decide to shift its position on one or more learning orientations. Second, the current pattern of learning orientations has resulted in identifiable strong competencies, so improving or expanding them may be the best way to enhance the unit's learning capabilities. This focus assumes that facilitating factors meet an acceptable standard and that more can be accomplished by adding to the strong base established by the learning orientations.

2 Improve on facilitating factors. In this option, the organization accepts its pattern of learning orientations as adequate or appropriate to its culture and decides that improving the systems and structures of the facilitating factors is the most useful course. This option assumes that maximizing the facilitating factors would add more to the organization's learning capabilities than enhancing or changing the current learning orientations.

3 Change both learning orientations and facilitating factors. An organization should select this option when it sees the other variable as inadequate. This option assumes that large-scale change is necessary and that changing one group of variables without changing the other will be only partially successful.

Each organizational unit or firm must make the decision to pursue one strategy or another for itself. While there are no rules for making this decision, the three options are incrementally more difficult to implement (i.e. one is the easiest to implement; three is the hardest). From the first to the third options, the resistance to change within the organization increases significantly. It is one thing to develop a plan for improving what is already done reasonably well; it is another to engage in nothing less than near-total transformation. It is one thing to stay within accepted, assimilated paradigms; it is another to replace institutionalized models.

Whatever the organization's choice, we offer three guidelines for developing and implementing a chosen strategy:

1 Before deciding to become something new, study and evaluate what you are now. Without full awareness and appreciation of current assumptions about management, organization, and learning, it is not possible to grasp what is being done well and what might be improved or changed.
2 Though the systemic issues and relationships in organizational life require that change be approached from multiple directions and at several points, organizations can change in major ways if people experience success with more modest, focused, and specific changes. As with many skills, there is a learning curve for the skill of managing and surviving transitions. Large-scale change requires that many initiatives be put into place in a carefully designed, integrated sequence.
3 Organizations must consider cultural factors in choosing and implementing any strategy, particularly when considering how it does specific things. For example, in a highly individualistic society like the United States or the United Kingdom, skill development focuses on individual skills; in comparison, more communitarian societies such as Japan or Korea have traditionally focused on group skill development. Moving from one pole to the other is a major cultural change; to simply improve on the existing orientation is much easier.

To help managers better understand the learning capabilities in their own organizations, we have developed and are testing an 'organizational learning inventory'. This diagnostic tool will enable an organization's members to produce a learning profile based on our model. The profile can guide managers to their choices for improving learning capability. Through further research, we intend to show how learning profiles vary within and across different companies and industries.

NOTES

1. C. Argyris, 'Double Loop Learning in Organizations,' *Harvard Business Review*, September–October 1977, pp. 115–124; K. Weick, *The Social Psychology of Organizing* (Reading, Massachusetts: Addison-Wesley, 1979); B. Leavitt and J. G. March, 'Organizational Learning,' *Annual Review of Sociology* 14 (1988): 319–340; P. M. Senge, *The Fifth Discipline* (New York: Doubleday, 1990); and E. H. Schein, 'How Can Organizations Learn Faster? The Challenge of Entering the Green Room,' *Sloan Management Review*, Winter 1993, pp. 85–92.
2. C. K. Prahalad and G. Hamel, 'The Core Competence of the Corporation,' *Harvard Business Review*, May–June 1990, pp. 79–91.
3. J. Child and A. Kieser, 'Development of Organizations over Time,' in N. C. Nystrom and W. H. Starbuck, eds., *Handbook of Organizational Design* (Oxford: Oxford University Press, 1981), pp. 28–64; and E. H. Schein, *Organizational Culture and Leadership* (San Francisco: Jossey-Bass, 1992).
4. J. Van Maanen and E. H. Schein, 'Toward a Theory of Organizational Socialization,' *Research in Organizational Behavior* 1 (1979): 1–37.
5. C. Argyris and D. A. Schön, *Organizational Learning: A Theory of Action Perspective* (Reading, Massachusetts: Addison-Wesley, 1978).
6. Senge (1990).
7. Huber identifies four constructs linked to organizational learning that he labels knowledge aquisition, information distribution, information interpretation, and organizational memory. Implicit in this formulation is that learning progresses through a series of stages. Our framework makes this sequence explicit and connects it to organizational action. Huber does not make this connection since to him learning alters the range of potential, rather than actual, behaviors. See: G. Huber, 'Organizational Learning: The Contributing Processes and Literature,' *Organization Science* 2 (1991): 88–115.
8. At Motorola, we observed and interviewed fifty senior managers, visited the paging products operations, and had access to about twenty-five internal documents. At Mutual Investment Corporation (a pseudonym for a large financial services company based in the United States), we observed and interviewed corporation employees in the investment funds group and the marketing groups. At Electricité de France, we observed and interviewed employees in the nuclear power operations. At Fiat, we observed and interviewed employees in the Direzione Technica (engineering division) in Torino, Italy.
9. A. Strauss, *Qualitative Analysis for Social Scientists* (Cambridge: Cambridge University Press, 1987).
10. For a discussion of 'communities of practice' see: J. S. Brown and P. Puguid, 'Organizational Learning and Communities of Practice,' *Organization Science* 2 (1991): 40–57.
11. Argyris and Schön (1978).
12. W. H. Schmidt and J. P. Finnegan, *The Race Without a Finish Line: America's Quest for Total Quality* (San Francisco: Jossey-Bass, 1992).
13. For the idea of the factory as a learning laboratory, see: D. Leonard-Barton

'The Factory as a Learning Laboratory,' *Sloan Management Review*, Fall 1992, pp. 39–52.

14. This skill has been referred to as 'legitimate peripheral participation.' See: J. Lave and E. Wenger, *Situated Learning: Legitimate Peripheral Participation* (Palo Alto, California: Institute for Research on Learning, IRL Report 90–0013, 1990).

15. C. Argyris, *Strategy, Change, and Defensive Routines* (Boston: Putman, 1985).

16. See 'Companies That Train Best,' *Fortune* 8 February 1993, pp. 44–48; and 'Motorola: Training for the Millenium,' *Business Week*, 28 March 1994, pp. 158–163.

17. T. Peters, *Liberation Management* (New York: Knopf, 1992).

18. Jay W. Forrester is considered to be the founder of the field of systems thinking.

19. S. Srivastra and D. L. Cooperrider and Associates, *Appreciative Management and Leadership* (San Francisco: Jossey-Bass, 1990).

20. E. Nevis, *Organizational Consulting: A Gestalt Approach* (Cleveland: Gestalt Institute of Cleveland Press, 1987).

21. W. R. Torbert, *Managing the Corporate Dream* (New York: Dow Jones-Irwin, 1987).

Chapter 3

Managing core competency for corporate renewal: towards a managerial theory of core competencies[1]

Yves Doz

ABSTRACT

Competence cultivation, competence diffusion, competence aggregation, competence leverage, and competence renewal, constitute the key processes in the management of core competencies. This paper seeks to define the key managerial issues and the tasks involved in the successful performance of these five processes. In that sense it constitutes a modest attempt to move in the direction of a managerial theory of core competencies.

INTRODUCTION

Partly as a reaction to the implicit bias in favour of the analysis of the external environment in much of the strategy literature of the 1970s, best exemplified by Porter's work (1980), many strands of research have recently converged to give more importance to the analysis of the firm's own resources and competencies. Building on seminal works by Penrose (1959) and Selznick (1957) considerable efforts have been deployed to build a theory of the firm's resources and competencies (Rumelt, 1984; Wernerfelt, 1984; Lippman and Rumelt, 1982; Itami, 1987; Barney, 1986; Dierickx and Cool, 1989; Teece, Pisano and Shuen, 1990), and to demonstrate to managers its value (Prahalad and Hamel, 1990). While this emerging theory does make a compelling case for the importance of resources and competencies to firm success, while it is intuitively appealing to managers, and while it presents business policy and organizational process researchers with a good opportunity not to let their fields of enquiry be reduced to a minor branch of economics, it lacks both a solid empirical base and a microtheoretical foundation. Competencies and resources are difficult to identify, isolate and measure (because they are often tacit, inimitable, collective, deeply embedded and interactive and integrative). Their performance effects are hard to isolate from others, thus making resource and competence based theories hard to test in the conventional I/O paradigm. This has led empirical researchers to be few, and to take radically different approaches. At one extreme one gets to competencies almost entirely by default, i.e. if nothing else explains performance differences between firms, firm- or business unit-specific factors must play a role (Rumelt, 1991). At the other extreme, painstakingly detailed small sample industry or corporate studies may shed light on the competencies of specific firms and on their use towards competitive advantage (Collis, 1991). Mid-range approaches, for example tracking the development of core technologies in specific industries (e.g. Miyazaki, 1991) or the development and exploitation of competencies by individual firms in industries (Cool and Dierickx, forthcoming 1994; Quinn, Doorley and Paquette, 1990) or focusing on the role of core competencies in new product development (Leonard Barton, 1992) start to be increasingly adopted by researchers. Another approach has been to rely on simulations of organizational learning and competence development processes (e.g. March, 1991; Marengo, 1992). At the same time a managerial theory of resourcres, capabilities and competencies is still not developed.[2]

Research on core competencies has so far been largely externally oriented and driven by theory building, and theory refutation. Theory has developed more in reaction to the economics-driven industry and environment analysis evolution of the business strategy field, and as a follow up on the seminal work of Nelson and Winter (1982). This has led more towards an economic theory rather than a managerial theory of core competencies. The difficulty, and resulting dearth, of empirical studies, whether large sample statistical or process-based, further contributed to an economic rather than managerial theory. Further, a managerial, or organizational process theory of core competencies quickly meets the relatively fragmented nature of the field of organizational learning, where proposed models and theories operate at very different levels and with very different priorities (e.g. intervention and action vs. conceptualization and modelization) (Huber, 1991). This did not help in the development of a managerial theory of core competencies either.

Without attempting to develop a managerial theory, this paper presents and analyses the major managerial challenges raised by core competence management. The paper starts with a broad discussion of the issues faced in managing core competencies, and draws a series of dilemmas from this discussion. Subsequent sections analyse each dilemma in turn, and provide a tentative set of observations on managerial approaches which can help address these dilemmas.

ISSUES AND DILEMMAS IN THE MANAGEMENT OF CORE COMPETENCIES

Competencies are not easy to manage. Competencies are not very tangible, nor measurable, and the more valuable competencies may well be the least manageable. Competencies are fragile. Unpractised, they wither away, stretched too thinly they lose their cut, explicited too fully they no longer improve, aggregated too widely they lose substance and reality, cultivated too long and too tightly they turn into rigidities, and breed incompetence in responding to new circumstances.

This section explores these issues, leading to the identification of a few managerial dilemmas that are at the heart of competence management.

Competencies develop in different ways in the context of an organization. Rather than at the level of a whole organization, or even at that of a small group, competence is most easily understood at the individual level, and most organizational competencies start with the individual. Individuals have skills and knowledge, benefit from intuition, and can develop expertise. Collective competencies start to develop with individual and small group learning by doing, rather than with top management-engineered grand designs. Competence develops partly as an individual action learning process, through reflective learning between practice and cognition (Schon, 1983). Learning also results from small group interaction involving know how development and exchange in communities of practice (Lave and Wenger, 1990). This allows the development and refining of procedural knowledge. Some such learning is shared informally in professional interactions (akin to the traditional apprenticeship processes), some may also be made easier to share through the reciprocal processes of knowledge articulation (making tacit knowledge and know how explicit) and knowledge internalization (bringing explicit knowledge to become in-action know how) in situation (Nonaka, 1991; Hedlund and Nonaka, 1993).

Beyond individual and small group learning, competencies in organizations are rooted in the interaction of distinctive skills, technical and management systems, dedicated processes and assets, and, finally, cultural attitudes and values which define competence and excellence in specific domains as valued goals (Leonard Barton, 1992). Organizational competencies are the underlying process routines that allow the combination of skills, systems, assets, and values, to result in predictable high-level performance of specific tasks, which yield an advantage over competitors, and provide valued functionalities for customers. Competencies are thus integrative task performance routines that combine resources (skills and knowledge, assets and processes, tangible and intangible) to result in superior competitive positions.

Competencies do not develop automatically. While individuals and small groups develop know how informally, more formal methodologies may be used to accelerate learning, or to trigger competence development. A number of management tools can be used to accelerate learning in organizations, some very structured and programmatic, such as total quality management, others more open-ended, such as the 'dialogue' methodologies which aim to improve content-free communication in the organization. Yet, competencies develop and evolve in partly unplanned creative ways, and structured methods can lead to an excessively deterministic approach.

One first issue for top management is thus to decide to what extent to leave competency development as an unstructured emergent process, or to what extent to structure and drive the process through a series of methods, programmes and tools.

Once developed, competencies are not communicated and shared easily. Deepening competencies requires ongoing cultivation, and most often growing specialization on the part of individuals and small groups. Competence deepening and competence sharing may conflict. Deepening competencies may require undivided focus and attention, and may also make communication and sharing more difficult. More tightly honed competencies may also be more difficult to share and communicate whatever the effort. Advanced tacit practices are not easily reproducible, and the learning process, for others, is slower and more difficult, except through a slow apprenticeship.

Moving know how from the individual to the collective level faster than through apprenticeship requires several processes, among which the articulation of the know how and its extension to other units (Hedlund and Nonaka, 1993). Yet, the articulation of competencies is unlikely to ever be fully feasible, because competencies cannot be entirely captured in explicit procedural knowledge. A tolerance for some tacitness and ambiguity is thus essential to the move from individual skills to collective competencies, unless one transfers procedures blindly with no room for learning. Indeed, less than fully specified rules foster learning, as they help learning, but one has to interpret and improve them, whereas fully explicit rules may block learning, or be ignored (Brown and Duguid, 1991). Either procedures are blindly adhered to, and learning stops, or procedures are increasingly ignored, and informal 'communities of practice' develop, often fostering significant collective 'learning by doing', within the local 'community', but making results from that learning increasingly difficult to share with other subunits which have developed other practices, following different learning paths.

One second key issue for management, therefore, is to create a 'tight–loose' process for competence diffusion, leaving enough variation and freedom to practices for learning to take place, and imposing enough commonality for sharing to remain possible. Large corporations, with multiple units performing comparable tasks, but each left with enough autonomy to experiment with new methods of task performance, and to develop different perspectives, may best take advantage of such 'tight–loose' processes. This may also involve a reliance on normative control, shared values, and common intents to provide organizational unity, rather than on detailed procedures and strict rules. Receptivity to practice sharing is fostered by shared attitudes, yet procedures and rules are flexible enough to encourage learning.

A third issue arises from the different levels of aggregation in competence management, from elemental skills, affecting a particular sub-task in what members of the organization do, to broad integration competencies that bring together these elemental competencies into an effective whole. Highly specialized elemental competencies are not easily integrated and combined. The firm may be good in parts, but ineffective in whole! Yet, poorly integrated disaggregated competencies are of little practical value. Conversely, though, integrating competencies that are not at the leading edge in their own right may also be of little practical value. Highly specialized elemental competencies are not easily integrated and combined.

One of the key tasks of management, therefore, is to facilitate competence aggregation. Again, a duality arises: honing leading edge competencies leads to increasing specialization, and makes the aggregation of competencies more difficult, just like their diffusion to the rest of the organization. Aggregation cannot be achieved at the cost of a substantial decay in the underlying competencies.

A fourth issue is rooted in the need to leverage competencies as widely and effectively as possible. Leveraging competencies across as wide a scope as is economically profitable may bring various types of benefits. First, leveraging maximizes the return on the competency. Second, leveraging accelerates the competence development process, by providing more opportunities to practise the competency. Third, by providing different but related application opportunities, leveraging allows not just the repetitive honing of the competence, but its enrichment and aggregation with other competencies in response to new needs or problems.

The major difficulty stems from the fact that the scope of competence leverage opportunities is difficult to establish precisely and leveraging faces three difficulties: the discovery of appropriate leveraging opportunities, the mobilization of competencies towards them, and the validation of the opportunity/competency match. Leveraging may run out of opportunities, or the identified opportunities may provide only a partial match for the firm's competencies. Conversely, opportunities may call for the development of additional competencies, which may be more or less feasible. The quality of the match between opportunities and competencies is thus important to competence enrichment and deepening, and to their widening, as well as to the achievement of competitive advantage in the new opportunities being sought. Striking a creative balance between focusing too much on existing opportunities, and

Table 3.1 Dilemmas in core competence management

Key processes	Natural path		Managed effort
1. Competence development	Emergent	vs.	Programmatic
2. Competence diffusion	Apprenticeship	vs.	Explicitation
3. Competence integration	Specificity	vs.	Aggregation
4. Competence leverage	Exploitation	vs.	Exploration
5. Competence renewal	Incrementalism	vs.	Discontinuity

mastered competencies, and discovering new opportunities, where the leverage potential may be uncertain, and for which new competencies will need to be developed, is a fourth, difficult trade-off in core competence management.

Finally, top management needs to be concerned with the renewal of core competencies. To talk of renewal competencies is almost an oxymoron. Competencies are the result of continuity, whereas renewal creates discontinuity. Competencies arise mainly from learning by doing and from reflection on action. Yet, competencies narrowly honed in the context of a procedurally defined process, or of a dominant paradigm (be it technological or about market or customer behaviour), may evolve into core rigidities (Leonard Barton, 1992) and turn into core liabilities or core incompetence if and when a new paradigm takes hold. Developing renewal competencies is likely to decrease the short to medium term efficiency of the organization (March, 1991), but may allow the organization to be less path dependent, and thus less vulnerable to changes in technology or market linkages (Henderson and Clark, 1990; Leonard Barton, 1992).

We have so far identified five facets to the management of competencies, each constituted by a process of organizational learning. Each of these processes gives rise to a managerial dilemma between letting the cultivation of competencies follow its 'natural' track (the left hand column in Table 3.1) and a more active management process (the right hand column in Table 3.1). We will discuss each of these processes and dilemmas in the next sections.

COMPETENCE DEVELOPMENT: EMERGENT VS. PROGRAMMATIC

In striving for survival, organizations will naturally develop some competencies, or die. In competitive environments, incompetent organizations are unlikely to survive for long. A competence is most often know how in action, i.e. it results from the 'learning by doing' that takes place in organizations. As such it is highly conservative: a competence does not arise without repetition, in particular for the more tacit collective types of know how. Competence grows with the repeated interactions between individual skills, systems and processes, and tangible and intangible resources of the organization. Honing skills and processes leads to better definition and increasing quality of the competence.

Yet, as the scope of competition widens, companies may face intense competitive challenges by firms with greater competencies. Concerned with the risks of such challenges, and in particular with the struggle of many Western industries fighting for survival against East Asian rivals, many firms have turned to programmatic managed approaches to accelerate the development of their competencies. Rather than allow the development of competencies to rely on an emergent repetitive tacit process, these companies have increasingly resorted to learning tools to foster faster core competence cultivation. Most such tools have their origin in the USA, where they were developed to manage effectively and efficiently the huge industrial build up during World War II, and have been diligently applied, and perfected in Japan after the war (Cole, 1989; Garvin, 1988; Imai, 1986), and 'rediscovered' in the West more recently.

Quality improvement and quality deployment methods in particular, have become key tools for the cultivation of a kernel of competencies. They offer a framework, a language, a systematic approach, and a set of procedures for the explicitation and the improvement of know how. Root cause analysis and other such tools provide a way to evolve from rough 'heuristics' in process design to much more accurate 'scripts' which reflect a deeper and more detailed understanding of cause and effect relationships. This allows the company to constantly refine, test, and validate its competence cultivation scripts and to confidently turn them into organizational routines (Chakravarthy and Kwun, 1990). Short of such a process, the competence kernel of the organization remains vulnerable and underdefined.

Competence development tools, such as the problem solving methodologies provided by TQM, have played a key role in the competitive responses of companies such as Ford, Motorola or Xerox to Japanese challenges. In some companies, Motorola and Xerox for example, these tools have become the backbone of a complete mobilization and transformation process. Similarly, Rover has learned a great deal from Honda in the use of these methods, and they played a key role in Rover's turnaround in the late 1980s, and are now applied to British Aerospace, Rover's parent company.

Yet, one should not underestimate the difficulties of accelerating competence development, in particular when the relative importance, and/or pace of improvement of various types of competencies is shifting. Competencies display great inertia. Competence development is intrinsically conservative, not just because of its cumulative and repetitive nature. Beyond task performance, a growing competence in some specific field usually leads to strong emotional and organizational commitment. First, successful learning by doing requires continuity of tasks and of performance criteria. This is typically achieved through a dominant process logic being applied to a dominant product design. As cumulative learning is achieved, and cumulative excellence develops, a growing commitment to the existing skill set and vested interest in its continued value develop. More rewards accrue from the successful use of the competence. Second, competence results from, and reinforces specific mindsets. Successful procedures, and what they deliver, are sources of satisfaction, which cannot be questioned without questioning the worth of the individuals and communities which breed them. How people think and how they perceive their environment is shaped by their skills and tools (cf. the famous hammer holder looking for nails metaphor). This shaping leads to strong value judgements and orthodoxies. Third, organizational routines are the result of a satisfactory compromise between stakeholders in an organization (of an 'organisational truce' as March puts it) and they implicitly reflect the relative credibility and relative power of various categories of stakeholders (Leonard Barton, 1992). A shift in the relative criticality of competencies may threaten the balance of power in the organization, and question the continued validity of existing arrangements between different groups of stakeholders. Fourth, existing competencies provide the basis for deciding on future commitments and bias them. Commitments, both to investments and to product and markets, are made as a function of existing competencies by the dominant groups in the organization, in a way most likely to perpetuate their relative dominance.

Efforts to increase quality at Xerox faced difficulties largely because they challenged the power base of strong groups. For example, more reliable copiers challenged the position, and the skills, of the large maintenance and service field force that Xerox had built over the years. Yet, inputs from that field force on the specifics of machine breakdowns and on maintenance issues were essential to improve machine quality. Similarly, engineering groups may be more concerned with engineering processes than with designing products for manufacturability.

Thus the use of various integration tools, such as the 'dialogue' processes and the business process reengineering approaches currently much in vogue, also have a key role to play to foster the development of transversal competencies, in particular where the efforts and the benefits of competency development may not be shared equally across functions, specialists, or subunits of the organization.

Beyond the tools, processes that favour the identification of individuals to the success of the organization may also contribute considerably to the development of collective competencies, in particular when the balance of costs and benefits to individuals is uneven across individuals and their subunits. One approach is to even costs and benefits. While this has long been seen as a cornerstone of Japanese management, it has also been practised by professional service firms confronted with the impossibility of forecasting accurately the future value of the skills of their members (Gilson and Mnookin, 1985) and, more generally, has been seen as an important contributor to the successful functioning of complex organizations (Prahalad and Doz, 1987, ch. 12). This approach collectivizes costs and benefits, and risks and returns, to the development of organizational competencies.

Stretching the collective ambition of the members of the organization, and imposing a sense of competitive urgency to accelerating and deepening of competence development are some of the key merits of setting an ambitious strategic intent (Hamel and Prahalad, 1989). This is largely what external benchmarking, and the very hard pressure of Japanese competition did to Motorola and Xerox, two of the more successful 'systematisers' of competence development. Articulating a sequence of competence development milestones, some measurable (e.g. Motorola's six standard deviations ['66'] approach to quality or its current ten times [10] reduction goal for product development cycle times) quantum improvement goals, the achievement of which depends on massive competence development acceleration, provides important goalposts to target the effort. Finally, in-depth training of everyone involved, to foster the individual's ability to contribute is essential. Interestingly, the competence deepening and acceleration tools, the evening out of risks and returns in the face of uncertainty about the future value of specific competencies, and the setting of an ambitious strategic intent, also facilitate the ability and the willingness to diffuse and share competencies in the organization. Competence diffusion, though, raises some specific additional issues.

COMPETENCE DIFFUSION: APPRENTICESHIP VS. EXPLICITATION

Sharing and diffusing competencies do not come easily. While full articulation seems the simplest approach, it really applies only to the diffusion of fully packaged stabilized know how.[3] This may work well when the competence is tightly honed, and well known, e.g. McDonald's fast food operations, or the retail operations of a highly standardized bank, such as BCP's 'Nova Rede' network in Portugal or BancOne in the United States. A fully articulated approach is also most effective when creativity is not sought (e.g. routine operations, where safety may be important) and when fast deployment of a competence in multiple new branches developed quickly with new untested personnel, is more important than evolutionary learning. This premium on speed was the case both for

McDonald, at least internationally, and for BCP, after the liberalization of the Portuguese banking market provided the opportunity to cover the country quickly with new banking branches.

Most corporate competencies are not quite so articulated and well packaged as McDonald's or BCP's. They may not be so mature either. Management priority, therefore, may be more slanted towards further learning, and the deepening of competencies, rather than their full codification for easier transfer. Indeed, it has been observed that tight procedural articulation conflicts with deepening (Brown and Duguid, 1991). The current vogue for 'best practice' transfers reflects this difficulty: how to leave enough room for practices to improve, without making them so different from unit to unit that their transfer and sharing is made impossible. A careful differentiation, on the part of management, between what is left to evolve and what is made uniform is essential. Uniformity of format allows easier connections between various parts of an organization, while freedom of content, and differentiation of culture, allow innovation and selective evolution. Best practice exchanges act as a selection mechanism between evolution and innovative practice improvement efforts, and retention is facilitated by diffusion mechanisms, more or less formalized depending on the nature of the competence and on its ownership within the organization.

For less packaged competencies, and more constantly and unpredictably evolving ones, the full articulation and codification, and deliberate transfer may be even more difficult. For example, most innovative strategy consulting companies, such as McKinsey or Arthur D. Little, struggle with this issue. Competencies evolve with the learning of consultants, who then need to share their learning. Yet, what there is to share, and how to share it are not clear. To find out requires a substantial effort, leading to a tendency to undershare competencies. The same is true of R&D competencies, where what is to be shared is constantly evolving and being enriched (De Meyer, 1993). In such situations, informal emergent networking processes may be key, rather than explicit format transfers. Networks need to be supported by processes that encourage communication, awareness of the learning taking place in various parts of the organization, documentation, and incentives to collaborate. Nestlé, for example, has a very rich set of procedures to facilitate learning processes within its network of technical centres and 'research companies'. These range from the opportunities to develop face-to-face acquaintance via periodic internal conferences and frequent visits to the long-term mobility of key people between centres, fostering better deeper informal diffusion of competencies.

How competencies are held in the organization provides a second dimension along which to differentiate their diffusion. At one extreme, a competence can be totally individual, a unique know how possessed by one individual, alone. An orchestra's conductor might fit this case: although the conductor's and the orchestra's level of performance are both improved by mutual interaction, the performance of the orchestra is dependent on that of the conductor. A gifted software development engineer may have similar relationships with a development team to the conductor's relationship to the orchestra. At the other extreme, competence in a professional service organization may be everyone's property (Meister, 1982). Most often competence is lodged at some intermediate level: it is not the property of single individuals nor does it permeate the whole organization. Typically, it belongs to a small team, or a subunit in a large corporation. Perhaps competencies will emerge around a core process of the organization, or around a specific practice unit. Competence may thus reside more or less narrowly with individuals, small groups, teams, organizational subunits, specific functions (or groups of people involved in core processes) or the whole organization.

Processes that can be used to diffuse competencies depend both on the nature of the competence – or of its stage of evolution – and on the more or less collective or individual nature of its ownership. An individual formalized explicit competence is perhaps best diffused via formal training, tested by a period of apprenticeship or co-practice, and monitored via professional norms. Sharing the competencies of experienced chartered accountants, lawyers, or medical doctors probably comes closest to this type of process. A collective formalized competence can be transferred by a mix of formal training and informal teamwork and team integration. Arthur Andersen's famous CAPS programmes, at its St. Charles campus, provide an off-line training experience, but are designed to mimic client assignments, thus blending learning and action. An individual tacit competence is probably most difficult to share, except in a 'master–disciple' relationship, providing a monitoring and apprenticeship process not unlike that of the old guilds of the Middle Ages. Collective tacit competencies cannot be fully articulated, but a mix of articulation and apprenticeship provides a vehicle for transfer.

It is important to note that, within the same organization, various types of competencies need to be diffused differently, and the success of their diffusion also assessed differently. For example, Andersen Consulting has very different ways to transfer competencies at the junior associate level, at the senior partner level and at levels in between. How competencies are assessed also varies between a systematic, frequent, quantitative evaluation process at junior levels, and participation to a bonus pool, where each partner allocates 'points' to all other partners at senior levels.

Although we have so far differentiated and compared various approaches to competence diffusion these various approaches can also be blended to provide a balance between the acceleration of the development of competencies and the need to diffuse them quickly. IKEA, for example, resorted to an interesting dynamic approach to spearhead its rapid international expansion. New stores would be started by a specialized headquarters' team, who would plan the building, supervise its construction, launch the store (advertising, merchandizing, layout, etc.), operate it for its first year, and then hand over its management to a more permanent and more local team, and move on to the next store opening project. The store start-up teams were drawn from a small cadre of personnel, many of whom had been informally selected as high potential individuals in the IKEA culture. The approach had the advantage to concentrate and accelerate the deepening of store development and management competencies within a small group, and to diffuse these competencies to local teams in an apprenticeship process during the first year following the opening of each store. The management of each store could still decide to make adaptations to local circumstances, or to try innovative approaches once the start-up team had moved on, but as IKEA accumulated learning, the approaches followed by the various stores tended to converge and the differences between them to decrease. As the IKEA formula matured – at least in Europe – it became more important to diffuse existing competencies easily than to experiment to foster the development of competencies. In organizational learning terms, heuristics had been transformed into scripts, and the retention and diffusion of existing scripts became more important than the variation that would foster the development of new ones.

As for the acceleration of competence development, the commitment of the involved members of the organization is essential. Competence diffusion and institutionalization work only insofar as individuals who have skills are willing to share them, and those who benefit from the learning stay with the company, and continue cultivating these skills jointly. In other words, collective corporate goods are developed (Hogarth et al., 1991). Corporate rather than individual appropriation of newly developed competencies is facilitated by skill specialization, where complementarity and co-specialization are achieved only by the firm (a usual practice of consulting companies, and an implicit practice of many 'secretive' industrial companies such as Michelin as well as of classified programmes, such as the B2 project at Northrop). The existence of internal labour markets, rather than external ones, also facilitates competence diffusion, an argument often used to explain the greater emphasis put by Japanese companies on the development of their employees, in comparison to US companies. The lower the risk that an employee who has developed broad competencies, or gained an understanding for a wide range of competencies, will leave, the easier it is for the firm to allow the development of broad integrative competencies, rather than fragment competence development.

COMPETENCE INTEGRATION: SPECIFICITY VS. AGGREGATION

The heart of core competence management is the ability to integrate specific elements of know how, rooted in skills, technical systems and specific assets into wider value-creating competencies, through management systems and processes. Competitively valuable core competencies are rooted in integration between skills to create value for customers in ways that are not imitable by competitors. Fragmented narrow competencies are of little use. As stressed by researchers and practitioners alike, it is the constant striving for combination and blending of discrete elements of competencies that provide for opportunity creation and competitive advantage. Sony's miniaturization competence, for example, results from the integration of many different skills. AT&T's successful entry into the credit card business similarly results from the combination of many discrete competencies developed and cultivated over a long period of time in the telephone service business.

Customers value integrated competencies, yet integration is not valuable unless the elemental competencies are themselves outstanding. Top management is again caught in a dilemma between stressing elemental competencies and fostering the aggregation of competencies. Obviously, both are required, but where to put the priority may not be fully clear. British Aerospace, for example, is outstanding in wing aerodynamics, and keeps honing this competence via a whole series of partnerships (Airbus, Panavia, EFA, specific alliances like BAe's participation in the Swedish Gripen programme, etc.). To be outstanding at wing aerodynamics already requires a level of competence aggregation. In BAe's case, this is helped by advanced computer-based engineering systems, by a large on-line library of wing aerofoils test results, and by powerful simulation tools. These provide the basis for the aggregation of very specific competencies held by individuals or small teams of engineers. Indeed, effective aggregation starts at the individual level, with what Honda calls 'T-shaped' engineers, i.e. a lot of depth in a narrow field, to bring some valuable specific skills, but also some breadth across adjacent fields to allow 'connection' with specialists from other domains. Team processes also help integrate specific competencies, for example in product development, but in other areas as well. Focusing on business processes, rather than functional departments, also fosters core competence aggregation through joint learning, in addition to the customer responsiveness and cost reduction advantages that business process re-engineering usually brings.

The quality of programme and project management tools is another key determinant of aggregation competencies, at least in engineering-based firms, such as aerospace contractors. The ability to be a system and mission integrator, for example, hinges on the programme and project management competencies. Lockheed, for example, has won several major contracts with the US Department of Defense more on the basis of its programme management skills than on any specific technologies or elemental competencies. Similarly, it seems that its take-over of major competitors, such as General Dynamics' fighter aircraft division, is based on the expectation that Lockheed will bring superior programme management skills to improve the performance of the acquired units.

Competence integration itself may become a key competence of a firm. Indeed, beyond its aerospace equipment business, Lockheed has entered the airport operations business (where local authorities 'outsource' the operation of their airports to Lockheed) quite successfully, it seems, on the back of its integration competencies.

For most companies, however, integration competencies are difficult to dissociate from actual elements of competencies. Patterns and processes of competence integration are dependent on the tasks which led to their emergence. Communication channels, information filters, decision rules, and problem solving approaches are a reflection of the needs they emerged to address (Henderson and Clark, 1990). As such they are not domain-independent. To disentangle the integration competencies embedded in these channels, filters, rules and approaches is not what most firms succeed in doing. Quite to the contrary most become prisoners of set patterns, and are not able to reaggregate their competencies in a different pattern from that in which they emerged. This makes redeploying competencies to explore new opportunities more difficult.

COMPETENCE LEVERAGE: EXPLOITATION VS. EXPLORATION

Competencies develop and grow through practice. The more frequently and intensely a competence is practised, the more finely honed it becomes. Variations in the application of the same competency to new but related contexts, rather than repetitive practice, contribute to the development of that competency. Efficiency learning takes place through experience, effectiveness learning through enriching the repertoire of causal 'scripts' used in solving related but different problems (Brown and Duguid, 1991). This raises an additional dilemma for top management: to emphasize efficiency learning and the exploitation of mastered competencies in the existing business domain of the firm, or to emphasize effectiveness learning by stretching competencies to explore business domain extensions.

While efficiency learning takes place naturally, in following the natural inertia of the firm's competencies and product markets, effectiveness learning calls for an active management process. The first hurdle in that process is to discover new leveraging opportunities for the firm's competencies.

Opportunity discovery usually requires both creativity in identifying unmet needs and unserved market segments and/or flexibility in reconfiguring existing competencies. For example, while the credit card business was perhaps an obvious opportunity for AT&T, the reconfiguration of competencies from phone services to credit card markets was not just a straightforward transposition. Conversely, AT&T may have in hand all the competencies for a simultaneous translation phone service, worldwide, but to identify and assess the need for and price elasticity of such a service may not be easy. Core competence leveraging, thus, is an exercise both in external imagination and in internal flexibility.

External imagination does not come easily, most companies are prisoners of existing definitions of customers and markets (Levitt, 1975; Hamel and Prahalad, 1991). Imagination borders on corporate creativity. While the elements and sources of corporate creativity are known (Woodman *et al.*, 1993) their application to the discovery of new applications remains difficult.

There are no 'sure fire' solutions, but, it seems, practices which can improve the odds. First, the diffusion and sharing of competencies between businesses, in itself, seems to improve the likelihood of discovering new opportunities by exposing personnel to one another's competencies, and allowing a matching of competencies and possible opportunities. Applying the business logic of one product, or one industry to another may also help. Some observers would argue that Canon did not transform the photocopier industry through strategic brilliance but rather merely by applying to photocopiers the approaches and implicit logic it first developed in the camera business. Third, moving from the fixation on product-markets, to grasp underlying needs and functionalities, and the ways in which actual users assess value may also facilitate the discovery of new opportunities by identifying unmet or poorly served needs. This, in turn, is facilitated by direct linkages between technological product designers and users, allowing for a visceral sense of product integrity (Von Hippel, 1988; Hamel and Prahalad, 1991; Dougherty, 1992). More generally, metaphors and analogous reasoning may help unshackle the mindset of developers (Nonaka, 1991). Finally, fear of failure makes a learning approach to opportunity discovery and exploitation difficult. The cost of failure can be reduced both by reducing the cost of trials (e.g. through core platforms and variations, modularity, faster and less costly product development, more flexible manufacturing, decreasing economies of scale, and faster production ramp ups). For products or systems not amenable to this 'trial and error' learning approach (e.g. nuclear reactors or aircraft rather than walkmen or laptop computers) better simulation methods may offer similar advantages and allow the exploration of many engineering options at an affordable cost. Molecular modelling may come to play a similar role in the development of new pharmaceutical substances.

Beyond these technical approaches, organizational processes and cultural attitudes that depersonalize failure in discovery and exploration may also play a key role (Chakravarthy, 1990). Failure is seen as a collective tuition cost for finding new applications, not as the fault of a specific individual.

The second hurdle is to mobilize competencies in a new configuration. Internal flexibility to leverage competencies is equally difficult to achieve as the discovery of new opportunities towards which to mobilize them. New opportunities are likely to draw on a series of competencies which have been cultivated in various parts of the organization, and need to be combined in new ways. Accessing these competencies and getting the various subunits, wherever they are located, to contribute to the new opportunity may not be easy. Issues of subunit boundaries and possible misappreciation of the nature of the required competencies are likely to stifle the exploitation of new opportunities. For example, when VCRs were first introduced by Philips, their manufacturing was assigned to a video product group plant, (because VCRs were to be part of the video division marketwise), which lacked the required competencies, where an audio group plant, with the experience of audiotape decks, and the micromechanics competencies needed for VCRs, would have been a much better choice. Some companies, such as Sharp and Canon, in Japan, establish 'corporate priority' projects drawing personnel from many subunits to attempt to overcome subunit parochialism. Others, such as 3M in the USA try to build cultures and processes of sharing and opportunity developing.

Further, as we argued earlier, the pattern of competence aggregation may reflect the particular needs of its emergence, and not be easy to restructure and redirect towards new opportunities. The plasticity of competence deployment patterns is low. The quality of the match between competence and opportunity may be a third barrier to effective leverage. First, the company itself may define its served markets, or its strategic intent narrowly, thus ruling out a number of opportunities, or inadequately, hence missing more rewarding opportunities. For example, it has been argued that IBM's focus on mainframes and its concept of being a proprietary hardware company led it to define excessively narrowly, and for too long, the scope of opportunities available to the company (Ferguson and Morris, 1993). Similarly, Apple's concept of its business may have led the company to take less advantage of its operating system know how than it might, leaving an open opportunity to Microsoft (Rappaport and Halevi, 1991). Second, a company may push its reliance on core competencies too far. For example, the evidence is mixed on whether Minebea could effectively leverage the competencies developed in the manufacturing of miniature bearings to the production of semiconductor memories (Collis, 1991). The issue, in that particular case, is that although the high level of aggregation competencies (e.g. clean room operations) were similar, the disaggregated competencies were quite process- and material-specific, and steel is quite different from silicon.

Conversely though, the match between competencies and opportunities may also be too conservative. It is not just an issue of narrow market definition but also one of not using new opportunities to challenge the company to develop and test new competencies. Constantly exploiting the same set of competencies may lead to both complacency and vulnerability. The learning of existing competencies plateaus at a high, very acceptable level, but the organization members no longer feel a pressure for improvement. The set of competencies may become obsolete and not be renewed.

COMPETENCE RENEWAL: INCREMENTALISM VS. DISCONTINUITY

Exploration competencies, discovering new opportunities and creating the need to develop new know how is essential to the long term success of most firms (Hogarth et al., 1991) since the competitive value of any given competency is likely to decay over time (Dierickx and Cool, 1989) and/or to be curtailed by transilient or architectural innovations (Henderson and Clark, 1990). Elsewhere (Hogarth et al., 1991) we have argued that unbounded goals, simultaneous managerial attention to long term and short term, and the ability to acknowledge and manage the tensions created by a series of paradoxes are key to renewal competencies. It is also important, though, to recognize that the learning processes required for renewal competencies are quite different from those useful in cultivating existing competencies (Chakravarthy and Kwun, 1990). Unlearning existing competence 'enhancing' routines – or at least exempting the competence renewal processes from the discipline of these routines – so as to challenge dominant logics and bring new perspectives (Nonaka, 1991, Henderson, 1991). Internal variety is an enabling condition for renewal.

A few firms seem to develop a capability to manage both continuity and renewal. The constant practice of combining and recombining core technologies into new applications, and hence not to be locked into any particular set pattern of interaction between technologies, seems to have allowed Canon to master the transition from one product architecture to another, where other firms faltered (Henderson, 1994). Similarly, Canon's recent shift from laser printers to bubble printers may denote the same competence to master the transition between products and technologies which are deeply different.

Yet, renewal competencies are even more difficult to pin down, for analytical and managerial purposes, than performance competencies. Whereas the measurement of performance competencies can be quantitative – from 'learning curves' to 'time to 50% improvement' thresholds – the measurement of renewal competencies is much more difficult. Exploring also takes place mostly in a 'satisficing' mode, where performance expectations and thresholds play a key role, hence the importance of discrepancy creating strategic 'intents' which establish higher performance expectations. Further, 'learning by exploring' is not easily amenable to simple methods. Search and learning rules are not clear.

The development of renewal competencies in many organizations is also stifled by organizational processes. First, reasons for success may not be understood, and their continued validity not well assessed. Reasons for success may be missed[4] or successful approaches may not be replicable. Uncertain imitability prevails, even within the firm. This makes renewal threatening: what needs to change and what needs to be protected is not clear, and the feasibility of change is uncertain. Second, renewal threatens established businesses and individuals. Few companies willingly make obsolete the competencies of their own core businesses. More importantly, the 'unlearning' of past recipes is painful and generates anxiety (Schein, 1993). Third, top management, perhaps frustrated by the first two factors, often marginalizes renewal efforts into new ventures and 'skunkworks' the legitimacy of which remains vulnerable to corporate politics and financial fortunes. Acceptable performance may lead to risk avoidance (Bowman, 1980) and to an atrophy of renewal competencies, a 'failure of success' process. Fourth, which renewal competencies to cultivate is difficult to decide upon, in particular when the development of new competencies coincides with a deep change in business focus (e.g. Corning's repositioning into higher technology applications in the 1980s, such as optical fibres, or Intel's metamorphosis from memories to processors, or the current shift in mobile telephony towards consumer products).

Finally, renewal may not be possible. The aggregated competencies that would allow the redeployment of skills may not be possible. In the absence of high level aggregated competencies changes may not be addressed successfully. Henderson, for example, stresses that only Canon, among incumbent firms in the photolithographic equipment sector, was able to master the product architecture consequences of significant innovations in subsystems. Only Canon would master the systemic consequences of these changes.

CONCLUSION

Our argument so far has stressed the need for balance between inertial development and programmatic management of five key processes in the management of corporate competencies: competence development, competence diffusion, competence integration, competence leverage, and competence renewal. Although balance is the sought outcome, management efforts need to be devoted to pushing out, i.e. accelerating and deepening development, encouraging and facilitating diffusion, fostering integration, discovering and exploring opportunities for leverage, and complementing competence cultivation with competence renewal. The most important task for top management is to operationalize these efforts. Table 3.2 summarizes briefly the tools and approaches that top management can use to manage actively all five processes discussed above.

Although our sequential treatment of each process may not highlight the point, it is also obvious that the various processes are not independent. To some extent they do conflict and balance must also be achieved between processes. The key difficulty here is that not all processes are equally measurable. Competence development can be quite tangible, at least in some dimensions, such as quality, or cost and speed of operations. Competence diffusion is easy to measure, at least for some competencies, in particular the ones that can be routinized. Competence integration raises difficult issues, in particular that of disconnecting the capability to integrate competencies from the historical context in which they happened to have developed, and thus to reconfigure and redeploy competencies towards new opportunities, particularly when these new opportunities are not just to be served by existing subsystems of competencies and business processes, but need the recombination and reconfiguration of elemental competencies.[5] Measuring the success of leveraging is often an issue of opportunity cost, hence hard to assess. Finally, renewal competencies are even more difficult to assess. There may therefore be a natural tendency to pay attention to what is most easily measurable, i.e. progress along the development and diffusion dimensions, thus reinforcing the intrinsically conservative and inertial nature of core competencies.

Our brief inventory of management tools, in Table 3.2, also suggests that tools for development, diffusion, and leverage are both more numerous, more specified, and better routinized than tools for aggregation and renewal. These differences may in turn contribute to the observed inertial nature of competencies. It is easier to accelerate move-

Table 3.2 Management tools and approaches for core competence management

Development	Diffusion	Integration	Leverage	Renewal
Quality management	Articulation and transfer of procedures	T-shaped individual skill bases	Marketing imagination	Unbounded goals
Quality deployment	Best practice exchange	Programme and project management skills	Transfer of business logics, analogous reasoning	Multiple time frames
'Dialogue' processes	Selective uniformity, selective differentiation	Reconfiguration capabilities	Focus on underlying functionality, and 'value to cost' measures	'Exploring' skills
Business process reengineering	Networking processes (emergent and structured)	'Architectural' competencies	Direct linkages between technologists and customers	Unlearning
Collectivization of risks and returns within the firm	Professional norms and observability of performance		Modularity and flexibility in product design	
Strategic intent	Apprenticeships and co-practice		Simulation tools	
Competence development campaigns	Specialized, mobile accelerated competence development teams		Collectivization of risk of failure	
Professional training	Collectivization of risks and return		Internal flexibility	
	Internal labour markets		Transferability bases (?) of competencies	

ment on the existing competence trajectory of the firm than to reconfigure or re-invent and re-develop competencies.

The key management challenge, as the firm grows and matures, may well therefore be not to become a prisoner of one's own competencies. While for relatively new and young firms the development and diffusion of unique competencies may be the key priority, priorities may shift towards leverage, and later towards aggregation and renewal, as the firm, and its existing business domain mature. The nature of the top management priorities, therefore, may have to shift over time from developing to diffusing, to aggregating and leveraging, and finally towards challenging and renewing.

NOTES

1. A working paper in the INSEAD Working Paper Series is intended as a means whereby a faculty researcher's thoughts and findings may be communicated to interested readers. The paper should be considered preliminary in nature and may require revision.
2. Further, this emerging field suffers from the use of a few different terms in different ways, by different researchers. For useful attempts to clarify the language system being used, see Teece, Pisano and Shuen, 1990, and Nanda, 1992.
3. Leaving aside here the communication of scientific knowledge, for which full rigorous explicitation is essential, but which relates only indirectly to the development of know how and of corporate competencies.
4. It is striking, for example, to see how IBM masterfully achieved 'architectural' control over mainframes in the 1960s and 1970s and let Microsoft, and to an extent Intel, take such control away from IBM in personal computers in the 1980s.
5. It is more difficult for Canon to redeploy itself from generation to generation of photolithographic equipment than for AT&T to redeploy its transaction processing and billing subsystems towards the credit card market. Lockheed's success in airport management is probably an intermediate reconfiguration, which draws mostly on its integration skills (e.g. programme management and system integration) rather than on the elemental competencies of military systems and aircraft development and production.

REFERENCES

Barney, J. B., 1986, 'Organisational Culture: Can it be a source of sustained competitive advantage?', *Academy of Management Review*, 11(3), pp. 656–665.

Bowman, E. H., 1980, 'A Risk/Return Paradox for Strategic Management', *Sloan Management Review*, Spring 1980, pp. 17–31.

Brown, J. S. and Duguid, P., 1991, 'Organizational Learning and Communities-of-Practice: Toward a Unified View of Working, Learning, and Innovation', *Organization Science*, Vol. 2, No. 1 February, pp. 40–57.

Chakravarthy, B., 1990, 'Management Systems for Innovation and Productivity', *European Journal of Operations Research*, Vol. 47 (2).

Chakravarthy, B. and Kwun, S., 1990, *The Strategy Making Process: An*

Organisational Learning Perspective, Working Paper, Carlson School of Management, University of Minnesota.

Cole, R., 1989, *Strategies for Learning*, (Berkeley: University of California Press).

Collis, D. J., 1991, 'A Resource-Based Analysis of Global Competition: The Case of the Bearings Industry', *Strategic Management Journal* Special Issue, Vol. 12, pp. 49–68.

Cool, K. and Dierickx, I., 1994, 'Assessing Innovative Activity: The Pharmaceutical Industry, 1940–1989' in Y. Doz (Ed.) *Managing Technology and Innovation for Corporate Renewal* (Oxford: Oxford University Press).

De Meyer, A., 1993, 'Internationalisation of R&D as a means of Technical Learning', *Research Technology Management*.

Dierickx, I. and Cool, K., 1989, 'Asset Stock Accumulation and Sustainability of Competitive Advantage', *Management Science*, 35(12), pp. 1504–1511.

Dougherty, D., 1992, 'A Practice-Centered Model of Organisational Renewal through Product Innovation', *Strategic Management Journal*, Special Issue: Strategy Process: Managing Corporate Self-Renewal, Vol. 13, pp. 77–92.

Ferguson, C. H. and Morris, C. R., 1993, *Computer Wars: How the West Can Win in a Post-IBM World*, (Times Books: Random House Inc., New York).

Garvin, D. A., 1988, *Managing Quality*, (New York: The Free Press).

Gilson, R. J. and Mnookin, R. H., 1985, 'Sharing Among the Human Capitalists: An Economic Enquiry into the Corporate Law Firms and How Partners Split Profits', *Stanford Law Review*, Vol. 37, pp. 313–392.

Hamel, G. and Prahalad, C. K., 1989, 'Strategic Intent', *Harvard Business Review*, June, pp. 63–76.

Hamel, G. and Prahalad, C. K., 1991, 'Corporate Imagination and Expeditionary Marketing', *Harvard Business Review*, 69, 4, July–August, pp. 81–92.

Hedlund, G. and Nonaka, I., 1993, 'Models of Knowledge Management in the West and Japan' in *Implementing Strategic Processes*, (Oxford: Basil Blackwell).

Henderson, R., 1991, *Underinvesting and Incompetence as Responses to Radical Innovation: Evidence from the Photolithographic Alignment Equipment Industry*, Working Paper, WP 3163–90–BPS, MIT, Cambridge, Mass.

Henderson, R., 1994, 'Product Development Capability as a Strategic Weapon: Canon's experience in the Photolithographic Alignment Equipment Industry' in Toshi Nishiguchi (Ed.) *Managing Product Development*, (New York: Oxford University Press).

Henderson, R. and Clark, K. B., 1990, 'Architectural Innovation: The Reconfiguration of Existing Product Technologies and the Failure of Established Firms', *Administrative Science Quarterly*, 35, pp. 9–30.

Hogarth, R., Michaud, C., Doz, Y. and Van der Heyden, L., 1991, 'Longevity of Business Firms: A Four-Stage Framework for Analysis', INSEAD Working Paper 91/55/EP/SM.

Huber, G. P., 1991, 'Organizational Learning: The Contributing Processes and the Literatures', *Organization Science*, Vol. 2, No. 1, February, pp. 88–115.

Imai, M., 1986, *Kaizen: The Key to Japan's Competitive Success*, (New York: Random House).

Itami, H., 1987, 'Invisible Assets' in *Mobilizing Invisible Assets*, (Cambridge, MA: Harvard University).

Lave, J. and Wenger, E., 1990, *Situated Learning: Legitimate Peripheral Participation*, IRL Report 90–0013, Palo Alto, CA: Institute for Research on Learning.

Leonard Barton, D., 1992, 'Core Capabilities and Core Rigidities: A Paradox in Managing New Product Development', *Strategic Management Journal*, Special

Issue: Strategy Process: Managing Corporate Self Renewal, vol. 13, pp. 111–127.

Levitt, T., 1975, 'Marketing Myopia', *Harvard Business Review*, September–October, pp. 26 onwards.

Lippman, S. A. and Rumelt, R., 1982, 'Uncertain Imitability: An Analysis of Interfirm Differences in Efficiency Under Competition', *Bell Journal of Economics*, 13, pp. 418–438.

March, J. G., 1991, 'Exploration and Exploitation in Organizational Learning', *Organization Science*, Vol. 2, No. 1, February, pp. 71–87.

Marengo, L., 1992, 'Structure, Competence and Learning in an Adaptive Model of the Firm', *Papers on Economics and Evolution*, no. 9203, (Freiburg: European Study Group for Evolutionary Economics).

Meister, D. H., 1982, 'Balancing the Professional Service Firm', *Sloan Management Review*, Fall, 24 (1).

Miyazaki, K., 1991, 'Optoelectronics-related competence building in Japanese and European Firms', *Research Evaluation*, 1, 2, pp. 89–96.

Nanda, A., 1992, 'Resources, Capabilities, and Competencies', Working Paper, Harvard Business School.

Nelson, R. and Winter, S. G., 1982, *An Evolutionary Theory of Economic Change*. (Cambridge, MA: Belknap).

Nonaka, I., 1991, 'The Knowledge-Creating Corporation', *Harvard Business Review*, 69, 6, pp. 96–104.

Penrose, E. T., 1959, *The Theory of the Growth of the Firm*, (Oxford: Basil Blackwell).

Porter, M., 1980, *The Competitive Advantage of Nations* (New York: The Free Press), pp. 180–195.

Prahalad, C. K. and Doz, Y., 1987, *The Multinational Mission*, (The Free Press, New York).

Prahalad, C. K. and Hamel, G., 1990, 'The Core Competence of the Corporation', *Harvard Business Review*, May–June, pp. 79–91.

Quinn, J. B., Doorley, T. L. and Paquette, P. C., Winter 1990, 'Technology in Services: Rethinking Strategic Focus', *Sloan Management Review*, pp. 79–87.

Rappaport, A. S. and Halevi, S., 1991, 'The Computerless Computer Company', *Harvard Business Review*, July–August, pp. 69–80.

Rumelt, R., 1984, 'Towards a Strategic Theory of the Firm', in R. B. Lamb (Ed.) *Competitive Strategic Management*, (Englewood Cliffs, NJ: Prentice Hall).

Rumelt, R., 1991, 'How Much Does Industry Matter?', *Strategic Management Journal*, 12, 3, pp. 167–185.

Schein, 1993, 'How Can Organisations Learn Faster: The Challenge of Entering the Green Room', *Sloan Management Review*, 34, 2, pp. 85–92.

Schon, D. A., 1983, *The Reflective Practitioner: How Professionals Think in Action*, (New York: Basic Books).

Selznick, P., 1957, *Leadership in Administration*, (New York: Harper and Row).

Teece, D. J., Pisano, G. and Shuen, A., 1990, 'Firm Capabilities, Resources and the Concept of Strategy', Consortium on Competitiveness and Cooperation, Working Paper 90-9, University of California at Berkeley, Centre for Research in Management.

Von Hippel, E., 1988, *The Sources of Innovation*, (New York: Oxford University Press).

Wernerfelt, B., 1984, 'Consumers with Differing Reaction Speeds, Scale Advantages and Industry Structure', *European Economic Review*, 24, pp. 257–270.

Woodman, R. W., Sawyer, J. E. and Griffin, R. W., 1993, 'Toward a Theory of Organizational Creativity', *The Academy of Management Review*, Vol. 18, No. 2, April, pp. 322–354.

Part II

Competencies and corporate strategy

A key idea in the theoretical work on resources and competencies is that a firm's success depends on its unique and valuable capabilities. At the business level, theorists argue that capabilities are the source of competitive advantage and much of the current literature therefore focuses on identifying and exploiting a business's core competencies to improve business unit strategy.[1] At the corporate level, a competency perspective provides insights into the kinds of businesses in which the firm can compete successfully. Supporters of a competence approach to strategic management argue that it is the firm's capabilities which should guide decisions on portfolio building, diversification, acquisitions and divestments and resource allocation.

The current work on core competencies and firm resources as the basis of corporate strategy has roots going back to the 1960s. In *The Concept of Corporate Strategy*,[2] Kenneth Andrews of Harvard Business School wrote that corporate strategy 'defines the business in which a company will compete, preferably in a way that focuses resources to convert distinctive competence into competitive advantage'. In a similar vein, Igor Ansoff, in his 1965 book *Corporate Strategy*,[3] argued that firms should construct capabilities profiles of their strengths and weaknesses to help them assess their portfolio of business, and especially their diversification opportunities. A sound understanding of internal capabilities is necessary because 'The firm may not realize the full profitability potential or may even lose money unless it has the capabilities required for success in the new venture'. In 1990, C. K. Prahalad and Gary Hamel revived this theme in their influential article, 'The Core Competence of the Corporation'.[4] They advocated a rethink of the concept of the corporation. Instead of seeing the firm in terms of a portfolio of discrete businesses, Prahalad and Hamel urged managers to consider the corporation as a collection of competitively important competencies which could be used in different products and markets. One of the benefits of this approach, the authors argued, would be better decisions about resource allocation and diversification. The readings we have selected focus on these corporate issues, and how a competence perspective can be used in making decisions about a firm's overall strategy.

Gordon Conrad of Arthur D. Little, author of 'Unexplored Assets for Diversification', first published this article in 1963, at a time when many US firms were beginning to diversify. He briefly reviews different approaches to diversification: should firms diversify into related areas, or should they seek out growth opportunities in new industries? Should a company stick with products, markets and technologies that are familiar, or should it expand into different fields? Conrad's discussion of these issues anticipated much of the current thinking about capabilities as the basis of successful diversification.

Conrad observes that firms in the same industry often make similar diversification moves, identifying areas with technology or products similar to those of their existing businesses. The result is often intense competition and disappointing performance. To avoid these problems, the author advocates a different approach. He urges managers to broaden their understanding of their firm's core capabilities, to identify what makes their company different and unique. A company's core skills might be in particular functions, such as marketing, or they might be derived from long experience, such as an expertise in coping with unstable prices. Capabilities might also be based on the interaction of different functions, as in a company where the sales and research functions work closely together to solve customer problems; or, they might involve a complex set of skills, as in a capability in administering franchises. Every firm has its own history and experiences, and even firms in the same industries will have different sets of core skills. Conrad argues that a firm's capabilities can provide a guide to new areas of business, if it identifies businesses where it can exploit its core skills.

The second reading, by Constantinos C. Markides and Peter J. Williamson, both of London Business School, is 'Related Diversification, Core Competences and Corporate Performance'. Writing thirty years after Conrad, these authors also note that there is little agreement on the basis of successful diversification. The accepted wisdom, to be sure, is that related diversification enables the firm to exploit interrelationships across its businesses. Such interrelationships, based on economies of scale or scope, result in superior performance, at least in theory. However, Markides and Williamson point out that researchers have still not established that related diversifiers perform better than unrelated diversifiers, despite numerous empirical studies on this question. The problem, they argue, is in both the understanding and the definition of relatedness.

In common with Conrad, these authors argue that it is not product or market similarities that are the basis of successful diversifcation. Rather, it is the transfer of underlying capabilities from existing businesses to new ones that matters; this is the 'relatedness' that can be the source of competitive advantage. Markides and Williamson add an important proviso to this general argument. The capabilities, they argue, must be strategically important ones, meaning that competitors cannot easily imitate or acquire them. For example, a business may have developed a skill in managing a trucking fleet as part of its distribution system. It may identify another business that could also use its trucking fleet and decide that a merger would lower distribution costs for both businesses. But if rival businesses can buy trucking services that are just as efficient from specialist firms, then any cost advantage will be quickly lost. When capabilities can be easily matched by competitiors, they cannot be the basis of profitable diversification.

Markides and Williamson thus argue that even when businesses have similar underlying competencies or capabilities, this 'relatedness' does not necessarily create any economic advantage, or lead to superior performance. The authors suggest that both researchers and managers have too often overlooked this critical point in analysing diversification moves and the performance of diversified firms. The 'relatedness' that matters is the similarity in the underlying strategic capabilities among different businesses in corporate portfolios. In their article, these authors propose a new approach to measuring relatedness, one that more accurately captures these similarities. This approach, they argue, should provide a sounder basis for assessing the performance of firms which diversify in different ways.

A focus on capabilities can also contribute to decisions about allocating corporate resources, as explained by Amy Snyder and William Ebeling in 'Targeting a Company's Real Core Competencies'. The authors are both consultants with Braxton Associates, a management consulting firm specializing in strategic planning and strategy-related issues. Here they draw on their experience in helping international firms formulate strategy to argue that firms should define themselves in terms of their competencies. Snyder and Ebeling show how their competence approach differs from portfolio management techniques, where businesses are assessed in terms of market share and industry attractiveness. By focusing on core competencies, the authors argue, corporate managers can make better decisions about where to invest resources.

In this article, Snyder and Ebeling substitue the phrase 'key activity' for core competence. They do so because, in their view, managers often find the concept of core competence misleading. Frequently, managers define a core competence as a *characteristic* of a firm, such as its excellent reputation or its superior customer service. Such characteristics, they argue, emanate from the superior perfomance of key activities, and it is these key activities which managers need to identify and nurture. The authors acknowledge that achieving top management consensus on what are 'key activities' from a long list of skills, capabilities and competencies is not straightforward. They propose three criteria for establishing whether an activity is 'key'. First, it must offer significant added value. Second, it must be unique and offer lasting competitive advantage. Third, it must support multiple end products or services. Benchmarking, mapping employee and asset distribution, 'what if' scenarios (exploring actions implied by a particular decision) can all be used to achieve a managerial consensus on the key activities for the firm.

Snyder and Ebeling examine a particular business – slicing knives – in some detail to demonstrate how different approaches to portfolio decisions can lead corporate management to entirely different conclusions about the value of an under-performing business. Viewed from a product perspective, the business's small market share in an area of low growth would indicate a decision to dump the business. Viewed from a competence (activity-based) perspective, the business is seen to share key activities with sister businesses which presently enjoy a stonger market position. Growth is seen to be achievable, and the decision to keep it is indicated. The authors go on to explain the 'quadrant' tool which they have developed to help corporate managers decide how to direct resources towards the various activities in the portfolio. Key activities are arranged in a matrix according to the competitive advantage they bring and the value they add to end products. The completed matrix suggests where corporate resources should be invested to sustain, expand or acquire expertise in key activities. The ideal is to concentrate on activities which add high value and offer good competitive advantage. An activity which lacks both attributes can be outsourced. Activities lacking in one or the other can be targeted for improvement, by transferring learning across business units or acquiring it through alliances. The matrix of corporate activities is reminiscent of the growth/ share matrix of portfolio management, but the message here is that resource allocation decisions should be based on an anlysis of activities rather than businesses in the corporate portfolio.

Michael Goold, Andrew Campbell and Marcus Alexander, authors of 'Corporate Strategy: The Quest for Parenting Advantage', have developed yet a further perspective on the link between core competencies and corporate strategy. They argue that the existence of common competence areas in two or more businesses is neither a necessary nor a sufficient condition for a portfolio strategy. The key to clear thinking in this area, they argue, is to recognize the important role of the parent company in corporate strategy. If the parent company is able to create skill pools, linkage mechanisms and knowledge sharing between business units that have similar competencies, in a way that raises these competencies such that they become a shared source of advantage, then there is a logic for competence-based portfolio strategy. If the parent does not have the competence management skill then there is no logic for a competence-based portfolio strategy. It is the existence or not of relevant parenting skills that makes the competence concept relevant to corporate strategy, they argue.

In this framework, the focus is on the skills and competencies of the parent. Goold, Campbell and Alexander argue that many successful portfolio strategies are built on skills and knowledge that are not core to the businesses, but are core to the parent. For example, KKR has skills at financial engineering, deal making and creating management commitment to performance objectives. These skills justify KKR's involvement in a wide range of businesses that need a radical shake-up. RTZ, a British based mining company, has unique skills in financing mining projects so as to lay-off the currency, mineral price and operating risks. These skills have enabled RTZ to deal themselves into almost every one of the really profitable mining projects that have been set up in the last thirty years. Goold, Campbell and Alexander prefer their concept of parenting skills (the core skills of the parent organization) as being the key link between competence and corporate strategy. Their work explores the parenting skills of different corporate parents, and the ways in which these parenting skills add value to businesses in the corporate portfolio.

The readings in Part II show how a competence-based approach to corporate strategy can help managers address issues such as diversification, resource allocation and portfolio building. The authors included here offer a variety of approaches and frameworks, but each of them argues that managers need to understand their firm's valuable competencies, both existing ones and ones needed for future growth, in order to make sound decisions on key issues.

NOTES

1 Grant, Robert M., 'The Resource-Based Theory of Competitive Advantage: Implications for Strategy Formulation', *California Management Review*, Spring 1991, pp. 114–135; Hamel, Gary and Aimé Heene, eds., *Competence-Based Competition*, John Wiley & Sons, New York, 1994.
2 Andrews, Kenneth R., *The Concept of Corporate Strategy*, revised edition, Richard D. Irwin, Inc., Homewood, Illinois, 1980 (first published 1965).
3 Ansoff, H. Igor, *Corporate Strategy*, McGraw-Hill, 1965.
4 Prahalad, C. K. and Gary Hamel, 'The Core Competence of the Corporation', *Harvard Business Review*, May–June 1990, pp. 79–91.

Chapter 4

Unexplored assets for diversification

Gordon R. Conrad

Is something missing in the concepts of diversification we are being
taught these days? Take statements like the following:

- 'Diversify on the basis of what you know.'
- 'Don't fall victim to marketing myopia. Define your business broadly.
  If you're an oil company, you're in the energy business. If you're a
  railroad company, you're in the transportation business. . . .'
- 'A leading cause of serious marketing failure is diversification into
  product lines or distribution channels that have little or no similarity
  to the company's previous lines and channels.'

We hear statements like these a great deal. They are paraphrases of some of
the most respected and best-selling articles and books we know. Yet they
are inadequate, in my opinion. They can – and often do – lead to disap-
pointment. The metal pipe manufacturer who diversifies into plastic pipe,
or the magazine publisher who diversifies into printing, does not always
find the satisfying profits he expected. The old rule, 'Let the cobbler stick to
his last', does not say enough and is losing validity in modern business.

Why? I believe that in our enthusiasm for technology, research, and
particular markets or industries – even broadly defined ones – we tend
to overlook another more personal, more subtle level of competence in
an organization. This is the deeper level of talent and experience gathered within a company, a level that is independent of the products and
technologies making up the organization's business. This talent can be a
company's most valuable possession and can represent an essential
ability to operate successfully as a business. If looked at correctly, it
can suggest logical areas for diversification that would not come to light
when relying on more apparent abilities. It should be included in a
broadened definition of what a company 'knows'.

FALLACIES AND FAILURES

The present approach to diversification fails, in my view, for two reasons:

1 It leads management to look only at related fields – and often competition in these related fields has spread to the point where management cannot justify entrance now or in the foreseeable future.
2 It leads to a kind of 'group-think' in an industry about diversification opportunities – and this, in turn, leads to 'group-moves' which shrink the opportunities for all.

In many cases, the company seeking to change itself is one faced with maturity or obsolescence in its present business. This usually means that other companies in the industry have been feeling the same pinch or threat of pinch. As might be expected, they too are interested in getting into new fields. In fact, with the good communications existing today, whole industry segments can be observed thinking about and taking diversification action at roughly the same time. We have seen this happen, for instance, when supermarkets add on toiletries sections, auto dealers take on foreign car lines, and insurance companies and banks look toward the mutual fund business – and all in compressed periods of time.

As these examples suggest, companies operating in the same general types of business, faced with stagnation, and looking close to home for new opportunities, can obviously be expected to come up with similar answers as to what to do. They have corresponding raw-material positions and knowledge of their customers, as well as common production skills. These similarities of markets and technology lead each company logically to about the same conclusions concerning safe, nearby diversification opportunities as its competitors'. This is particularly true when everyone is looking for a 'growth industry' to go after. Chances become very strong that any 'growth industry' closely related to one company's present business will look attractive to the other firms, too.

Double trouble

What we wind up with is a 'double' concentration of diversification activity. Companies in like endeavors with similar problems and technologies begin looking at the same time for new places to expand close to home (not in a geographic sense but in the business and technological sense). Virtually all try to concentrate their efforts in 'growth' areas. The result is a rush into a restricted number of seemingly lucrative areas, with the prospect of fairly rapid overcrowding. To illustrate:

• We find virtually all the major oil companies moving into the petrochemicals field, which has been widely touted for years as a splendid growth industry. Concurrently, the chemical companies already in the petrochemicals business are further broadening their efforts. Likewise, companies manufacturing products that use petrochemicals have been integrating backwards and claiming 'diversification' into petrochemicals.

The result has been declining prices and significant overcapacity for major portions of the petrochemicals field. Some of those who have diversified here cannot see much hope for improvement in their situations.

- The plastics industry has lured many with prior product and raw-material connections in it. Chemical companies, oil companies, automobile companies, appliance manufacturers, building products manufacturers, whiskey distillers, and metal manufacturers, to name a few, have entered the area. The result for some of these companies was a period of rapid growth and high profit – but for a short period only. Now vast segments of the plastics industry – for example, plastic pipe, polyethylene film, molded housewares, and vinyl shower curtains – seem to be faced with a future of uninteresting profitability. And for many companies a solidly founded diversification for the future no longer exists as a possibility.

BROADER APPROACH

If the managers of an organization will examine it at its deeper levels and analyze the characteristics of its 'core' of talents and experiences, they may be able to diversify the company in directions that circumvent the problems just described. The broader view of the organization can provide a more *individual* picture of its strengths. And this added degree of individuality may be just the key needed to find a logical diversification route that is not as heavily traveled as those popular among one's competitors.

Of course, for some companies the core talents may not be significant enough to be relied on any more than are their acknowledged technological talents. This may be particularly so for very small companies and for those that have had a narrow scope in their operations or a short history of experience. However, for many others the core will be a highly individualized combination of abilities with real significance for strategy.

The talents I have in mind are, to some extent, individual, since they are based on the unique experiences of a company and of its key personnel. In addition, reactions of the organization's people to more general business problems contribute individuality. The types of solutions arrived at, and the types of mistakes made, all contribute to this body of essential business knowledge. Thus, even when the experiences an organization has had are not particularly unusual, they may have taught lessons not learned by many other organizations. For instance, management may have developed a sixth sense about taking calculated risks or 'leapfrogging' over the competition in introducing new products. Or it may have learned how to risk large capital sums.

My contention is that even in the *same* industry competitive companies may possess basically different knowledge, views, and experiences in many areas of their activities. Two companies in the appliance industry, for example, will take opposite positions on the use of franchise dealers, establishment of a brand-name image, the value of price discounts as opposed to low-margin list prices, use of advertising media, and other matters. Or two competing retailing firms may have developed divergent aptitudes for risking large capital sums or for investing in intangibles like personnel training as opposed to tangibles like plant and equipment. These positions may have been originally taken as a result of different core talents in the organizations; and, if not, certainly they will *lead to* different abilities and aptitudes over time. We are all familiar with instances of this happening. One that comes quickly to mind is the case of Minnesota Mining & Manufacturing:

At one point in its history '3Ms' would have been called an abrasives company with essentially the same characteristics as its competitors. As it grew in a multitude of directions, however, its character changed significantly, until today '3Ms' is not similar to its old competitors at all. Certainly this would not have happened but for a truly individual grouping of abilities in the company to begin with. And as these abilities have been tested and practised in unusual ways, they have doubtless grown more unique still.

It is such differences, alone and in combination, that companies may well turn to in order to find ideas and logical approaches for moving into new areas.

Skills to look for

What and where are the core skills that make so much difference? They may be found in the conventional functions such as marketing and production, which have developed as a result of the particular people and particular activities in the department. Or they may be the result of some unusual interaction of functions, as when marketing happens to use the research group in certain sales problems, or when purchasing develops a special proficiency for gathering intelligence on competitors' strategies. Uncovering these deeper capabilities requires an intimate look at not only the formal departmental structure in the company but also the specific ways in which groups combine to perform successfully. Let us look at some examples of what might be uncovered.

Dealing with tough unions

The ability to negotiate aggressively with unions is part talent and part long, painful experience. A company's management may have some uniqueness in this regard, particularly if tough and extremely powerful union elements have been dealt with. In such an instance, a management team might well be able to trust itself to operate effectively in an atmosphere of explosive union relations in an industry quite *un*related to its present business, viz., an industry where the critical success factor is labor relations rather than marketing, production, or research.

Living with unstable prices

Another business situation requiring peculiar talents and knowledge is that where there are erratic price fluctuations of raw materials and/or end products. Negotiating favorable short- and long-term purchase contracts for raw materials whose prices are tied in unique fashions to widely fluctuating published prices (e.g. tallow purchases for making soap or soybean purchases for making soybean oil) can be hazardous. It can also be the basic element in the success of a company.

Exploiting new product ideas

A further analysis of management could involve examination of its vigor and experience in rapidly capitalizing on new product ideas. Is this ability required in order to establish or maintain a competitive advantage? And has the organization learned the shortcuts and the roadblocks to this method of operation? If so, the talent could be very valuable – one that, standing by itself, could be applied successfully regardless of the type of business currently run. Thus, it might be desirable for a novelty toy manufacturer to look seriously at his chances in the field of 'fad' clothing for children and teenagers.

Sensitivity to customer needs

Whatever basic skills in marketing an organization has developed over the years can be another powerful weapon. I do not mean just selling ability or salesmanship, but rather the creative abilities possessed and the techniques applied in satisfying *any* customer's needs. Has your marketing organization learned to be sensitive to what customers expect in a product, how they use it, and how to deliver it? Knowing how to uncover *any* customer's real needs and then translating this knowledge into action is a creative asset applicable in solving difficult marketing problems in many industries. Having this skill could significantly remove restrictions that keep a company close to its present markets when diversifying.

Here the self-appraisal must be extremely objective and critical to discover whether the marketing talents are truly creative in the general sense or whether they are only creative within the framework of the company's present business and markets. The question becomes: are you and your marketing organization steeped in methods and techniques of use mainly in your present industry or of fairly general utility?

Administering franchises

Having a talent for selecting individuals who can be trusted in operating franchise dealerships is sometimes critical. It is part of a broader capability that encompasses knowledge of the mechanics of setting up, providing proper incentives for, and administration of, franchised dealer networks – the kind of sophistication that Singer Sewing Machine Company has developed. The same kind of skill could prove to be a prime asset having nothing to do with home appliances. For example, sale of termite-control systems has been established through franchised dealerships, and some food marketing also is done through franchise.

Negotiating in secret

The hard facts of business life have led many companies into channels of activity not unlike those that nations have to work in sometimes. The ability to deal 'under the table' or on a secret basis may be the whole key to one's marketing talent.

Along the same line, learning to gather intelligence accurately about competitors or customers can be essential. It may have to be done by dealing in politics, in bars, or in the drawing room.

'Do it yourself'

While delegation of responsibility can be an extremely important quality for executives in a well-established business, it may be a major *detriment* to success when entering some new and unrelated field. On the other hand, the will to learn 'from the ground up', to master sticky operating details, to be close to the man in the shop or on the sales route – traits like these, possessed by one or a few top executives, may be more useful in a new business than the formal 'organization-chart' approach generally advocated.

Making intuitive decisions

Dealing through committees, waiting for long, detailed studies to provide answers to unknowns, and putting questions to a vote are sometimes time-consuming thrashings that put companies at a disadvantage in operating competitively. A company with executives who can successfully circumvent these processes may have a genuine asset. In particular, ability to capitalize on the intuitive talents of practised, quick decision-makers may have great significance for a company's diversification.

Manipulation of technical service

I refer here not to the usual technical knowledge and customer-assistance ingredients of technical service, but to that hard core of experience often required in restricting technical service only to those places where its use leads to tangible new business for a company. Where technical service is a major part of over-all cost and a critical necessity for business survival, this skill takes on significant proportions. National Starch Products, Inc., for instance, owes part of its great success in the adhesives field to effective use of technical service.

What we are dealing with here is a certain kind of interaction between the sales and research departments:

- The sales manager is sometimes able to judge intuitively the worth of customers' technical service requests for generating new business or holding on to old business. He can work with the laboratory. He knows what it can and cannot accomplish in the time and budget allowable.
- Likewise, a real understanding on the part of the laboratory staff of the sales department's problems in keeping customers happy can be crucial in the efficient development of technical service answers. Note that the basic skill involved here is wholly divorced from the technical capabilities of the laboratory.

Investment know-how in distribution

In some businesses, investment in transportation equipment is a major capital cost, and the proper administering, maintenance, and minimizing of this investment *around the clock* – and under the pressure of constantly fluctuating operations – become fairly unique talents. The industrial gas field affords an illustration of this kind of know-how:

Investment in tank cars, tank trucks, and customer receivers for storing gas inventories is astronomical. In addition, complex distribution patterns must be developed to replenish regularly customers' supplies of gas where great distances and scattering of many small customers are involved. Knowledge in the traffic department of the hectic business of keeping tank cars and tank trucks in service around the clock is critical. How to balance the use of direct shipment to customers against the setting up of small independent distributors also becomes essential to success.

CHARACTERIZING THE COMPANY

The abilities I have discussed delineate part of what may be called the 'basic profile' of a company. Filling in all the details of this profile objectively and accurately – by examining each function in the organization for its core of talent and experience – is the next step in evolving a usable picture of the company. Management then has a checklist of skills for finding new directions for diversification and for establishing some logic in selection of alternate diversification routes.

Of course, implicit in the use of this profile is the matching of its important elements against the requirements for success in proposed areas of diversification. In fact, the whole process is a dangerous one unless the company gains a strong and penetrating insight into the ruling factors in the new areas, and this requires as careful an analysis as the one proposed here for developing the company's own basic profile. Analyzing these new areas can require fairly extensive market research. This might not be needed during the initial stages, when developing ideas of where to go, or in rough screening to establish their attractiveness; however, it becomes half of the equation in the final selection of a course of action.

Using the profile

To see how the profile can be used, let us take some examples. These are necessarily oversimplified, but they will suggest the value that such an investigation can have for management:

Opportunity for a railroad

A close look at a major railroad to uncover its basic profile might show that the following elements are crucial:

1 Ability to negotiate and manipulate complex rate schedules with federal agencies and industrial customers.
2 Experience in living under the close scrutiny of federal and state governments.

3 Facility in soliciting, and in negotiating for, large blocks of industrial business throughout virtually every subdivision of the economy.
4 Experience in inducing industries to locate and develop in new regions.
5 Sophistication in budgeting and financing of very large capital sums.
6 Experience in maintaining scattered consumer and industrial servicing locations.
7 Skill at complex scheduling on a mathematical basis of interrelated operations.

While not necessarily unique when taken separately, these elements do combine to yield a profile that would indicate some justification for this railroad to become an electric utility. It might conceivably set up a chain of electric utilities within its network of rail lines, where its contacts and knowledge of the geography and local politics would be unique.

Thus, Theodore Levitt's plea[1] that the railroads consider themselves transportation companies can be expanded to suggest that they use what they *have and know*, no matter in what direction it takes them.

Cigarettes to cosmetics

A single element may present itself and dominate a company's profile. Such could be the case for a cigarette manufacturer. Its *general* business acumen might not seem to suggest diversification opportunities, yet its extensive capabilities in advertising might hold an answer. Many companies would be afraid of the massive advertising techniques and budgets wielded in the cosmetics field, but this might be just what a cigarette company is basically suited to handle. Similarly, a cigarette manufacturer might do well in the razor-blade business, and a razor-blade manufacturer might succeed in the ball-point pen business – both of which have actually happened, of course, with Philip Morris and Gillette.

Strategy for a whiskey distiller

A distiller and national marketer of whiskies might possess an interesting profile of talents, including:

• Sophistication in natural commodity trading associated with its grain purchasing procedure.
• Knowledge of complex warehousing procedures and inventory control.
• Ability and connections associated with dealing in state political structures – i.e. state liquor stores, licensing agencies, and so on.

- Marketing experience associated with diverse wholesale and retail outlets.
- Advertising experience in creating brand images.

These characteristics might be of value in a company manufacturing and selling building products, e.g. wood flooring or siding, composition board, and so forth. The company would be trading in lumber or its by-products instead of grain; dealing with state political groups to gain building code acceptance and a position in state-controlled building projects; contributing effective marketing at both the wholesale level (e.g. construction supply houses) and the retail level (e.g. hardware stores and do-it-yourself centers).

Thus, the whiskey distiller might have some basic abilities for operating effectively in building products. These are two different businesses; yet success in both could depend on the same basic skills. Of course, the distiller would have a lot to learn, but this could come largely through acquiring a company in the building-products field. The whiskey distiller would at least be in the position of being able to talk the same basic business language with its acquired partner. It might also contribute some fresh approaches to the essential problems facing the building-products company in its own markets.

Concept at work

For a final illustration, let me turn again to the case of Minnesota Mining & Manufacturing. Here we have everyday proof of the power of core talents and aptitudes in making an unconventional diversification strategy successful:

While dramatically effective research and technology can be credited for part of '3Ms' success, underlying personnel strengths also were crucial. Without these, I suspect, little out of the ordinary would have happened to the company.

In the first place, research projects had to be screened and selected with some special point of view about expected commercial results. In running through a list of '3Ms' product additions (both internally developed and acquired), a conscious effort can be seen to select (1) highly specialized, (2) innovative products that required development of wholly new markets where no established need or slot existed. Into this category fell pressure-sensitive consumer and industrial tapes; film for packaging meals that were heated in the package; office copiers; reflective road signs; and stain repellents for clothing.

Success with such products called for special talents, some of them highly intuitive and hard to describe. In each case a latent need had to be uncovered, research had to be directed to fulfilling the need, and then the need had to be brought into the open and developed into a commercial reality. The company did not just direct its efforts to improving an existing product, making a minor variation on an old theme, or branching into related product lines and markets. Instead, it marshaled its basic abilities into an innovative research, product development, and marketing team for going after the really 'new', wherever it might turn up. *And these basic abilities had no strong ties to the company's older technologies.* This is evidenced by the breadth of its line now – decorative paper, office copiers, magnetic tapes, missile sealants, flat electrical cable systems, photographic film, cameras, and other kinds of goods.

CONCLUSION

For some companies the clearly marked diversification routes are fast disappearing; even those that seem obviously logical and smooth can prove dangerous in our increasingly competitive society. Yet diversification is still an important method of providing a company with protection from obsolescence in present products and with opportunities for future growth.

The situation seems to call for added tools that companies can use in assessing the suitability of various diversification routes and for suggesting additional logical prospects. These tools need to be designed to help companies find more individualized directions for diversification so that they will not lead or follow groups of their close competitors into the same new areas. Also, these tools should illuminate the basic strengths a company has and can rely on to diversify successfully.

The concept proposed in this article is intended to meet these needs by giving a company insight into its essential business talent and experience, its business way of life, its desires, and even its prejudices. It is a case of understanding what these are and putting them to work for the company just as technological skills are put to work.

APPENDIX: QUESTIONS TO CONSIDER

In the course of developing this article I have talked with a good many businessmen and close observers of the industrial scene. Here are some of the questions they have asked about my concept, together with my answers:

Q. How does the deeper level of skills you describe compare in importance with the more conventional technical and market skills when selecting diversification routes?

A. In every analysis of diversification alternatives, these deeper talents should be considered. For those companies lucky enough to have many obvious courses of action open to them (courses that relate to their technologies or market positions), these deeper skills play a lesser role. However, many others cannot discover any reasonable diversification opportunities based on their technologies or markets, and for them these skills may offer the only clues and be the most important strengths to rely on.

Q. Wouldn't some of the diversification failures you mention have been avoided simply with better management?

A. Certainly *some* of them could have been avoided. However, even the best managements are sometimes faced with drastic price declines and the other competitive pressures that come when their choices of areas for diversification become overrun by other companies. Such conditions can thwart the best management team and leave it with no course except withdrawal or sticking with a marginal situation. The point is to select a diversification area that will hopefully avoid these problems.

Q. How should management go about analyzing this subtler level of skills? Who in management should do it? How far down the ladder should the analysis go?

A. Executives in general management, staff management, and operating management should all look deeply into their own basic experiences and talents. They should look at each other's departments also, to detect what those on the inside may not see or see too much of. They should combine their separate analyses and be able to agree on what the company's 'basic profile' is.

As for how far down the ladder to go, include all groups or individuals who have an important role or noticeable effect on the character of the company. For instance, if the regional sales managers affect operations, have key skills or connections, or set local policy, they need to be included.

Q. Does a company's self-analysis become invalid every time there is a key management change?

A. It might. However, management succession is generally planned to perpetuate the present combination of skills and experiences that make the company able to go on in its present businesses. Thus, in the well-planned organization, the profile should not change materially with management change.

Q. Isn't there a strong tendency for a whole group of companies in one industry to derive the same basic profile?

A. This tendency is present, but remember that the profile need not be wholly unique in order to be effective. A shift in emphasis among elements of the profile or minor differences may be enough to set an individual direction for one of a group of similar companies. Thus, in the railroad example, even if its profile is like other railroads, its geographically unique structure can give it an advantage in a local area for establishing an electric utility.

Let me emphasize, however, that this tendency toward likeness is far from dominant. The important *differences* in talents and aptitudes of close competitors are likely to be quite striking.

NOTE

1. 'Marketing Myopia', *Harvard Business Review*, July–August 1960, p. 45.

Chapter 5

Related diversification, core competences and corporate performance

Constantinos C. Markides and
Peter J. Williamson

From 'Related Diversification, Core Competencies and Corporate Performance',
Constantinos C. Markides and Peter J. Williamson, *Strategic Management Journal*,
vol. 15, 1994, pp. 149–165, Copyright © 1994, Constantinos C. Markides and
Peter J. Williamson. Reprinted by permission of John Wiley & Sons, Inc.

ABSTRACT

Despite nearly 30 years of academic research on the benefits of related
diversification, there is still considerable disagreement about precisely
how and when diversification can be used to build long-run competitive
advantage. In this paper we argue that the disagreement exists for two
main reasons: (a) the traditional way of measuring relatedness between
two businesses is incomplete because it ignores the 'strategic importance' and similarity of the underlying assets residing in these businesses, and (b) the way researchers have traditionally thought of
relatedness is limited, primarily because it has tended to equate the
benefits of relatedness with the static exploitation of economies of scope
(asset amortization), thus ignoring the main contribution of related
diversification to long-run, competitive advantage; namely the potential
for the firm to expand its stock of strategic assets and create new ones
more rapidly and at lower cost than rivals who are not diversified across
related businesses. An empirical test supports our view that 'strategic'
relatedness is superior to market relatedness in predicting when related
diversifiers outperform unrelated ones.

A fundamental part of any firm's corporate strategy is its choice of what
portfolio of business to compete in. According to the academic literature,
this decision should reflect the 'superiority' of related diversification
over unrelated diversification (e.g. Ansoff, 1965; Bettis, 1981; Lecraw,
1984; Palepu, 1985; Rumelt, 1974; Singh and Montgomery, 1987). This is
because related diversification presumably allows the corporate center
to exploit the interrelationships that exist among its different businesses

(SBUs) and so achieve cost and/or differentiation competitive advantages over its rivals. But despite 30 years of research on the benefits of related diversification, there is still considerable disagreement about precisely how and when diversification can be used to build long-run competitive advantage (e.g. Hoskisson and Hitt, 1990; Rumanujam and Varadarajan, 1989; Reed and Luffman, 1986). In this paper we argue this disagreement exists for two main reasons:

1 Traditional measures of relatedness provide an incomplete and potentially exaggerated picture of the scope for a corporation to exploit interrelationships between its SBUs. This is because traditional measures look at relatedness only at the industry or market level. But as we explain below, the relatedness that really matters is that between 'strategic assets' (i.e. those that cannot be accessed quickly and cheaply by nondiversified competitors.[1] Therefore, to accurately measure whether two businesses are related, we need to go beyond broad definitions of relatedness that focus on market similarity; we need to look at the similarities between the underlying strategic assets of the various businesses that a company is operating in (see also Hill, 1994).
2 The way researchers have traditionally thought of relatedness is limited. This is because it has tended to equate the benefits of relatedness with the static exploitation of economies of scope. While we would not deny that economies of scope are an important short-term benefit of related diversification, we believe the real leverage comes from exploiting relatedness to create and accumulate *new* strategic assets more quickly and cheaply than competitors (rather than simply amortizing existing assets, i.e. reaping economies of scope). To predict how much a strategy of related diversification will contribute to superior, *long-run* returns it is necessary to distinguish between four types of potential advantages of related diversification.

   a the potential to reap economies of scope across SBUs that can share the same strategic asset (such as a common distribution system);
   b the potential to use a core competence amassed in the course of building or maintaining an existing strategic asset in one SBU to help improve the quality of an existing strategic asset in another of the corporation's SBUs (for example, what Honda learns as it gains more experience managing its existing dealer network for small cars may help it improve the management of its largely separate network for motorbikes);
   c the potential to utilize a core competence developed through the experience of building strategic assets in existing businesses, to create a *new* strategic asset in a *new* business faster, or at lower cost (such as using the experience of building motorbike distribution

to build a new, parallel distribution system for lawn mowers – which are generally sold through a different type of outlet);

d the potential for the process of related diversification to expand a corporation's existing pool of core competences because, as it builds strategic assets in a new business, it will learn new skills. These, in turn, will allow it to improve the quality of its stocks of strategic assets in its existing businesses (in the course of building a new distribution system for lawn mowers, Honda may learn new skills that allow it to improve its existing distribution system for motorbikes).

We term these four potential advantages of related diversification 'asset amortization', 'asset improvement', 'asset creation' and 'asset fission' respectively.

We will argue that the long-run value of a related diversification lies *not so much* in the exploitation of economies of scope (asset amortization) – where the benefit is primarily short-term – but in allowing corporations to more cost efficiently expand their stocks of strategic assets. Relatedness, which opens the way for asset improvement, asset creation and asset fission, holds the key to the long-run competitive advantages of diversification.

This means that in most cases, similarities in the *processes* by which strategic assets are expanded and new strategic assets are created are more important than static similarities between the strategic assets that are the *outcome* of those processes. Firms that are diversified across a set of 'related markets' where the strategic assets are either few, or the processes required to improve and create them are context-specific cannot be expected to out-perform unrelated diversifiers.

THE MEASURE OF RELATEDNESS

The strategy of related diversification is considered superior to unrelated diversification because it allows the firm to exploit interrelationships among its different business units. Specifically, the corporate center in related diversifiers is expected to *identify* important assets residing in any one of its SBUs and then *transfer* these assets and *utilize* them in another SBU. Canon's deployment of technology from its camera SBU in developing its photocopier business is a good example.[2]

Even though the advantages of the strategy of related diversification are usually cast in terms of the cost of differentiation benefits that arise from the cross-utilization of the firm's *underlying assets*, the actual measurement of relatedness between two businesses often does not even consider the underlying assets residing in these businesses. Relatedness has been traditionally measured in two basic ways (e.g. Montgomery, 1982; Pitts and Hopkins, 1982): (i) using an objective index like the entropy index of SIC count (e.g. Caves *et al.*, 1980; Jacquemin and Berry, 1979; Palepu, 1985) which assumes that if two businesses share the same SIC they must have common input requirements and similar production/technology functions; and/or (ii) using a more subjective measure such as Rumelt's (1974) diversification categories which consider businesses as related 'when a common skill, resource, market, or purpose applies to each.' (Rumelt, 1974: 29).

We do not doubt that the traditional measures could be acceptable proxies for what they are trying to measure. In fact, if these measures did not suffer from any *systematic* bias, one would consider them as a 'good enough' way to substitute for a costly and time consuming ideal measure. However, they do suffer from one systematic bias. Consider a firm using the strategy of related diversification so as to exploit the relatedness of its SBU-level assets. Suppose, however, that the SBU-level assets that the corporate center is trying to exploit are not 'strategically important' (as defined below). For example, suppose that the asset services that Firm X provides to an SBU by cross-utilizing the assets of a sister subsidiary are such that any other firm can easily purchase on the open market at close to marginal cost. In that case, even if Firm X achieves short-term competitive advantage through exploitation of economies of scope, it will not really achieve any sustainable competitive advantage *over time*; other firms will quickly achieve similar positions by purchasing similar asset services. The opportunity for a diversified firm to amortize the costs of running a trucking fleet by sharing it across two SBUs is often a case in point. If nondiversified firms could buy similar trucking services from a common carrier (which itself achieves the economies of scope across customers) at close to marginal cost, then there would be no competitive advantage to diversification even though the two markets were closely 'related' according to traditional measures like SIC similarity.

This implies that any measure of relatedness should take into consideration not only whether the underlying SBU-level assets of a firm are related, but also consider whether these assets are a potential source of competitive advantage. Even if the traditional measures of relatedness do a good job in capturing the relatedness of the underlying assets, they *consistently* ignore the evaluation of whether these assets are 'strategic' assets; and they do so because in measuring relatedness, they do not *explicitly* consider the underlying assets.

Strategic assets

To win competitive advantage in any market, a firm needs to be able to deliver a given set of customer benefits at lower costs than competitors, or provide customers with a bundle of benefits its rivals cannot match (Porter, 1980). It can do so by harnessing the drivers of cost and differentiation in its specific industry. For example, if scale is an important driver of cost leadership then those firms that operate large-scale plants will out-perform their subscale competitors. However, to effectively exploit these cost and differentiation drivers, the firm needs to access and utilize a complex set of tangible and intangible assets. For example, to reap the benefits of scale economies in production, it may require the services of tangible assets like a large-scale plant and intangible assets like the skills to manage this scale facility effectively and distributor loyalty to support a constant high volume of sales.[3]

Given that a particular set of asset stocks is necessary to allow a firm to exploit cost and differentiation advantages, the crucial question for a firm is: 'How can I access these assets?' A firm can secure these required asset services in a number of ways. It may obtain them with the *endowment* which establishes the business. A company established to exploit a proprietary technology, for example, often receives a valuable patent asset from its founder. It may *acquire* the assets on the open market, or contract directly for the services of an asset (as in the case of an equipment lease). It might access the required asset services by *sharing* the asset with a sister SBU or an alliance partner. Finally, it may *accumulate* the required asset through a process of combining tradeable inputs with existing asset stocks and learning by doing (Dierickx and Cool, 1989).

Firms that possess assets which underpin competitive advantage will earn rents (Rumelt, 1987). To the extent that competitors can identify these rent producing assets, they can decide between two alternative ways in replicating this competitive advantage: they may seek to imitate the assets through one of the four mechanisms above, or they may try to substitute them with other assets which can earn similar rents by producing equivalent or superior customer benefits. *The assets on which long-term competitive advantage critically depends (strategic assets) are, therefore, those that are imperfectly imitable and imperfectly substitutable* (Barney, 1986; Dierickx and Cool, 1989).

The importance of asset accumulation processes

The conditions above imply that assets which are readily tradeable cannot act as sources of long-term competitive advantage (Williamson, 1975). Similarly, assets which can be quickly and/or cheaply accessed through endowment, acquisition or sharing can only provide competitive advantage which is short-lived. In the long run, internal accumulation is likely to be the most significant source of imperfectly imitable and imperfectly substitutable assets. This is because most assets will be subject to erosion over time (see e.g. Eaton and Lipsey, 1980). Customer assets like brands, for example, will decay as new customers enter the market or former customers forget past experience or exit the market. The value of a stock of technical know-how will tend to erode in the face of innovation by competitors. Patents will expire. Thus, assets accessed through initial endowment or an initial asset base shared with another SBU will tend to lose their potency as sources of competitive advantage over time unless they are replenished by internal accumulation processes.

Moreover, even when an asset can be accessed through acquisition, alliance, or sharing, it is quite likely that the existing assets available will not perfectly fit the requirements of the market they will be used to serve. Existing assets generally need some adaptation to a specific market context and integration with existing asset bundles. Internal asset accumulation processes therefore play a role in molding assets which an SBU accesses externally into a competitive, market-specific bundle.

Regardless of whether the initial stock of strategic assets within an SBU is obtained by endowment or acquisition, or accessed through sharing, therefore, the long-term competitive advantage of a firm will largely depend on its ability to continuously adapt and improve its strategic assets to meet market-specific demands and to create new strategic assets that it can exploit in existing or new markets.

If these asset accumulation processes were frictionless and firms could speed them up at little cost, then it would be difficult for a firm that gained an initial advantage in respect of a set of assets (e.g. through endowment, sharing or first mover experience in a new, growing segment of the market) to maintain this lead. In practice, however, there are many impediments which prevent laggards from replicating or surpassing the asset positions of the leaders. Dierickx and Cool (1989) identify four separate categories of these impediments to asset accumulation: time compression diseconomies, asset mass efficiencies, asset interconnectedness and causal ambiguity.[4] These impediments also lie behind the concept of barriers to mobility (Caves and Porter, 1977) and Rumelt's 'isolating mechanisms' which include property rights on scarce resources, lags, information asymmetries and other sources of friction in processes of asset imitation (Rumelt, 1987).

When the process necessary to accumulate an asset suffers from one or more of these impediments, all firms will face higher costs and time delays in building it. This will restrict their ability to satisfy their market by offering the differentiation or cost advantages that the elusive asset would underpin. Impediments like time compression diseconomies, asset mass efficiencies and asset interconnectedness, however, will impose higher costs on later entrants to a business, making it more difficult for them to catch up with first movers and established firms who have had longer to accumulate nontradeable assets. Diversifiers entering a market for the first time against established firms would therefore suffer a handicap from late arrival, other things being equal.

It may be, however, that by deploying its existing core competences a diversifier can overcome some of these frictions. By drawing on its existing competence pool, such a corporation may be able to imitate valuable, nontradeable assets, or accumulate new, substitute ones, or create entirely new strategic assets more cheaply and quickly than competitors who lacked access to similar core competences: to grow new trees more rapidly and more cheaply by drawing on a common, existing root stock. Likewise, by properly deploying core competences between business units, a diversified corporation may also be able to maintain or extend its competitive advantage in its existing businesses through its ability to augment its nontradeable, market-specific assets more quickly and cheaply than its competitors. This is especially important in market environments that are undergoing significant change. Even firms with massive asset bases will lose their competitive advantage if they are unable to develop the new, strategic assets necessary to serve a changing market.

Core competences as catalysts in the 'production function' of strategic assets

If strategic assets are the imperfectly imitable, imperfectly substitutable and imperfectly tradeable assets necessary to underpin an SBU's cost or differentiation advantage in a particular market, then core competences can be viewed as the pool of experience, knowledge and systems, etc. that exist elsewhere in the same corporation which can be deployed to reduce the cost or time required either to create a new, strategic asset or expand the stock of an existing one. Compentences are potential *catalysts* to the process of accumulating strategic assets. If the firm knows from past experience how to efficiently build the type of distribution network which will improve the competitiveness of its product (i.e. the 'competence' in building a suitable type of distribution network exists), then it will be able to put the necessary asset in place more quickly and cheaply than a firm which lacks this competence. Competences may also act as catalysts to the processes of adapting and integrating assets that an SBU has accessed through acquisition, alliances or sharing. Prahalad and Hamel (1990), for example, cite the case of NEC's competency in managing collaborative arrangements as an important factor in their ability to access and then internalize technological assets and skills from their alliance partners.

This catalytic role of competences in the 'production function' for building assets which are nontradeable, nonsubstitutable and difficult to accumulate is illustrated in Figure 5.1. Inputs include time, readily tradeable assets, existing nontradeable assets and the catalyst to the construction process: competences.

The obvious next question is: where can a firm get hold of the competences that would allow it to speed up its rates of asset accumulation, adapatation and integration? The first place to look is the open market.

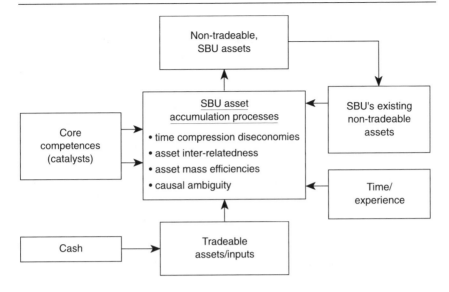

Figure 5.1 Core competences and the 'production function' for assets

But competences themselves often have characteristics which render markets inefficient as a mechanism for exchange. Characteristics such as information impactedness and scope for opportunism make competences, like other intangible assets, difficult to sell at arms-length (Williamson, 1973; Caves, 1982, Ch. 1). This leads to excess capacity in competences which cannot be easily utilized by seeking buyers in the open market. Unique competences developed by an SBU through learning by doing therefore risk becoming 'imprisoned' in that unit, even though they could be potentially valuable catalysts to the process of asset accumulation in other businesses (Prahalad and Hamel, 1990).

Compared with the problems associated with trading competences in the open market, it is often more efficient to transfer competences between businesses using conduits *internal* to a single organization (Williamson, 1975). Such internal mechanisms include posting staff from one business unit to another, bringing together a corporate task force with individuals from a number of businesses to help solve a problem for one of them, and passing market intelligence or other information between SBUs which could act as catalysts to asset accumulation.

Not all of the competences of a corporation which can act as catalysts in expanding the asset base of a new or existing SBU, however, will make an equal contribution to improving the competitive advantage of an SBU. Honda's competence in building networks of dealers for consumer durables may speed up the rate and improve the cost at which it can build an effective, specialized distribution network for its new lawn mower product. But if a competitor could effectively substitute this by a distribution agreement with one or two national retail chains, the Honda Corporation's competence may afford its lawn mower SBU little or no competitive edge. Likewise, if a rival could acquire a suitable network at a competitive price, or obtain access to one through a strategic alliance, access to Honda Corporation's competence might provide its related SBU with little or no competitive advantage. In both of these cases, while the competence is both available and transferable, it does not lead to the creation of a strategic asset that is both hard to substitute and difficult to imitate.

By contrast, Honda's competence in small petrol engines may enable its lawn mower SBU to quickly and cost effectively bring a superior product to market, backed by a superior production process. If competitors had no way of matching the resulting buyer benefits, except by spending a great deal of money over a long period of time, Honda's engine design organization and the combination of its manufacturing hardware and software would represent extremely potent strategic assets for the lawn mower SBU once they were in place. So access to Honda's engine competence would be a very significant source of competitive advantage for its lawn mower SBU.

We therefore have two conditions which must be satisfied for internal transfer of competences between SBUs to create advantage for the corporation:

1 it must be more efficient to transfer the competence internally between businesses in the same group than via an external market;
2 the competence must be capable of acting as a catalyst to the creation of market-specific assets which are nontradeable, nonsubstitutable and slow or costly to accumulate, thereby acting as a source of competitive advantage for the recipient SBU.

The larger the efficiency advantage of internal transfer, and the more costly the resulting asset is to accumulate, the greater the advantage to be gained from shifting a competence from one business unit to another existing or new SBU.[5]

A DYNAMIC VIEW OF RELATEDNESS

So far we have established that an SBU's competitive advantage depends importantly on its access to strategic assets. We have also discussed how core competences can be used as catalysts in the processes of expanding an SBU's stock of strategic assets. The real, long-run benefits of relatedness should therefore lie in opening up opportunities to quickly and cheaply create and accumulate these strategic assets. It is then possible to distinguish five different types of relatedness.[6] These distinctions help pinpoint exactly when and how related diversification will lead to competitive advantage for a corporation (and when it will not).

The first category, we term 'exaggerated relatedness'. This is where the markets served by two SBUs share many similarities, but there is little potential to exploit these similarities for competitive advantage. The relatedness is 'exaggerated' in the sense that looking at the overall similarity (which traditional measures of market-relatedness tend to do, as we explain below), overstates the likelihood that a corporation will achieve superior performance by diversifying across both markets. This exaggeration may arise under any of a number of different conditions. It may be that while the diversified firm can quickly and cheaply build the asset stocks necessary to supply the market, so can any other firm, because most of these assets are easily imitable. Even if other, nondiversified firms cannot replicate the assets built by the diversifier, they may be able to substitute some other, readily available asset at no disadvantage to their competitiveness. In short, the assets that that relatedness helps a diversifier build may be *nonstrategic*. A manufacturer of fashion knitwear in Europe or North America, for example, may have the competence to bring a local production facility for knitting standard, men's socks on-stream quickly and efficiently. But such a facility may prove a nonstrategic asset against competitors who rely on off-shore sourcing for this type of nontime sensitive, nonfashion product. This type of relatedness, therefore, would not create an opportunity for profitable diversification.

Similarly, exaggerated relatedness may arise when the market-specificity of the strategic assets and the competences that can help build them, are underestimated by the indicators a diversifier chooses to consider. Diversification by Levis from jeans into men's suits, for example, was recognized as a failure. The two businesses may appear highly related on many dimensions from production through to marketing and distribution, but the strategic assets and competences required to build competitive advantage turned out to be very different.

The second type of relatedness arises where the strategic assets in one SBU can be shared with another to achieve economies of scope (e.g. Porter, 1987; Teece, 1982). This type of relatedness underpins what we term 'amortization advantage', by allowing related diversifiers to amortize the cost of an existing asset by using it to serve multiple markets. This type of relatedness can offer important, short-term advantages in the form of reduced costs and improved differentiation. But, for most corporations, diversification is a long-term step that could be costly to reverse. And simply exploiting its *existing* stock of assets (even if they are the 'right' assets) cannot be enough to create *long-term* competitive advantages (e.g. Prahalad and Hamel, 1990). The truly successful firms

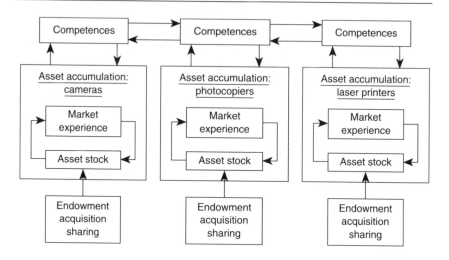

Figure 5.2 Core competences and asset accumulation at Canon

over the long term will be the ones that continuously *create new* strategic assets.

The third category of relatedness is where the strategic asset itself cannot be shared or transferred between two SBUs (because it is market-specific), but the competence gained in the process of building or maintaining an existing strategic asset in one SBU can be used as a catalyst to help improve the quality of an existing strategic asset in another SBU. This role of competences in asset accumulation is illustrated with the example of Canon's camera, photocopier and laser printer divisions in Figure 5.2.

Consider the position at Canon at the point where the company has successfully established itself in both the camera and photocopier businesses. Many of the strategic assets which underpin these respective SBUs cannot be shared directly. The dealer networks and component manufacturing plans are largely specific to each SBU. But in the course of its operations producing and marketing cameras, the camera division has extended this initial asset stock by a mix of learning-by-doing and further purchases of assets in the market. As a by-product of this asset accumulation process, the camera business also developed a series of competences like knowledge of how to increase the effectiveness of a dealer network, how to develop new products combining optics and electronics and how to squeeze better productivity out of high-volume assembly lines.

Because Canon is in two businesses, cameras and photocopiers, where the processes of improving dealer effectiveness, speeding up product development or improving assembly-line productivity are similar, it can improve the quality of the strategic assets in its photocopier business, by transferring competences learned in its camera business and vice versa. This type of relatedness, similarities in the *processes* required to improve the effectiveness and efficiency of separate, market-specific stocks of strategic assets in two businesses, opens up opportunities for what we call 'asset improvement' advantages for related diversifiers.

The fourth type of relatedness emerges where there is potential to utilize a core competence developed through the experience of building strategic assets in existing businesses, to create a *new* strategic asset in a *new* business faster, or at lower cost. For example, in the course of operating in the photocopier market, and building the asset base required to out-compete rivals, this SBU also accumulated its own, additional competences that the camera SBU had not developed. These may have included how to build a marketing organization targeted to business, rather than personal buyers, and how to develop and manufacture a reliable electrostatic printing engine.

When Canon diversified into laser printers, this new SBU started out with an endowment of assets, additional assets acquired in the market and arrangement to share facilities and core components. But even more important for its long-term competitiveness, the new laser printer SBU was able to draw on the competences built up by its sister businesses in cameras and photocopiers to create new, market-specific strategic assets faster and more efficiently than its competitors (illustrated by the arrows pointing to the right in Figure 5.2). This kind of relatedness, where the competences amassed by existing SBUs can be deployed to speed up and reduce the cost of creating new market-specific strategic assets for the use of a new SBU, we term the 'asset creation' advantage of related diversifiers. Again, only where the processes required to build the particular strategic assets needed by the new SBU are 'related' in the sense that they can benefit from existing core competences, will this type of diversification advantage be available.

The fifth, and final, type of relatedness is where in the process of creating the new strategic assets required to support diversification into a new business (like laser printers), the corporation learns new competences that can then be used to enhance its existing SBUs. For example, in creating the assets required to support the design, manufacture and service of the more sophisticated electronics demanded by the laser printer business, Canon may have developed new competences that could be used to improve its photocopier business. Alternatively, by combining the competences developed in its photocopier and laser printer businesses, may have helped it to quickly and cheaply build the strategic assets required to succeed in a fourth market: that for plain paper facsimiles. This kind of advantage over single-business firms or unrelated diversifiers, we term 'asset fission' advantage.

It is these last three types of relatedness that are likely to offer the greatest advantages from related diversification over the long-run. As the label suggests, exaggerated relatedness offers little or no scope for a strategy of related diversification to deliver superior performance, despite what may be a high degree of similarity between two markets. Related diversification designed to reap economies of scope, helping to amortize existing assets, is likely to provide only ephemeral advantage. Only relatedness that allows a corporation to access asset improvement, asset creation and asset fission promises long-run competitive advantage to related diversifiers. The problem is that traditional measures of relatedness have not been designed to distinguish between these profitable and unprofitable types of diversification.

Extending traditional measures of market relatedness: towards strategic relatedness

As we have seen above, it is not broad market-relatedness that matters. Two markets may be closely related, but if the opportunity to rapidly build assets using competences from elsewhere in the corporation does no more than generate asset stocks which others can buy or contract in at similar cost, then no competitive advantage will ensue from a strategy of diversification between them. 'Strategic relatedness' between two markets, in the sense that they value nontradeable, nonsubstitutable assets with similar production functions, is a requirement for diversification to yield super-normal profits in the long-run. By failing to take into account differences in the opportunities to build strategic assets offered by different market environments, the traditional measures suffer from the 'exaggeration' problem described above. They will wrongly impute a benefit to related diversification across markets where the relatedness is primarily among nonstrategic assets.

In order to operationalize the concept of strategic relatedness, we need to develop indicators of the importance of similar types of nontradeable, nonsubstitutable and hard-to-accumulate assets in different market environments. These types of assets may be divided into five broad classes (Verdin and Williamson, 1994):

- *customer assets*, such as brand recognition, customer loyalty and installed base;
- *channel assets*, such as established channel access, distributor loyalty and pipeline stock;
- *input assets*, such as knowledge of imperfect factor markets, loyalty of suppliers and financial capacity;

- *process assets*, such as proprietary technology, product or market-specific functional experience (e.g. in marketing or production) and organizational systems;
- *market knowledge assets*, such as accumulated information on the goals and behavior of competitors, price elasticity of demand or market response to the business cycle.

Thus, if our indicator suggested that channel access and distributor relationships were likely to be very important to competitive advantage in each of two markets, we would identify them as 'strategically related' on this dimension. We would then be more confident that core competences in building networks of channel relationships would be applicable to both. If, on the other hand, the second market involved a product that was most effectively sold directly to a small number of buyers, we would class the markets as having lower strategic relatedness on the channel dimension. Although these markets may be closely related in some other way, such as use of similar raw materials, the opportunity to benefit from transfer of competences in building a third-party distribution network would not be available. Meanwhile, if all competitors could buy raw material inputs at a similar price, relatedness on the input dimension would not offer a source of competitive advantage. The relatedness between this second pair of markets would be 'non-strategic'.

We could then develop an overall picture of the degree of strategic relatedness between pairs of markets by using a portfolio of indicators, each one seeking to measure the extent to which competence in building the same class of strategic asset could add to competitive advantage in both environments. The higher the level of strategic relatedness between two markets, other things equal, the larger would be the expected gains from diversification of firms from one to the other.

We are the first to acknowledge that the structural indicators we use in the empirical investigation that follows are not direct measures of how similar the processes required to build strategic assets are between two markets. We are not able to develop a direct, quantitative measure of the degree to which core competences are transferable across SBUs serving each set of markets where our sample firms operate. However, we would contend that by going beyond the standard variables used to capture industry structure (like advertising and R&D intensity), to include indicators such as whether the product lines in each market are made-to-order or sold from stock, or how many of the product lines require after-sales service, we have taken an important step towards this goal. Specifically, we believe that our measures come closer to capturing the extent to which two markets share similar nontradeable, nonsubstitutable and imperfectly imitable assets (often intangibles), with potential to draw on the same root-stock of competences, than traditional measures (especially since these have largely ignored the distribution, marketing and service requirements as well as the need for customization during manufacture, that our measures emphasize).

In what follows, we discuss the structural indicators used for three of the main classes of strategic assets on which we have data: customer assets, channel assets, and process experience assets.

Customer asset indicators

The first set of indicators seeks to capture the fact that the nature of interactions with the customer is an important determinant of the types of assets necessary to effectively serve a market.

1 *Customer concentration/fragmentation.* This indicator, FEWCUST, measures the degree to which each manufacturer deals with few, large customers rather than interfacing with a fragmented base of accounts. FEWCUST, is defined as the percentage of product lines for which there were less than 1,000 customer accounts at the manufacturer level. If the manufacturer deals through resellers, it will reflect the number of distributor accounts which it must manage. To the extent that the manufacturer also deals directly with users, these additional accounts are also included in computing this measure.

Our objective is to capture the extent to which there is scope for manufacturers to build deep and sustained relationships with their account base: dedicating a member of sales staff to individual customers; responding to customer's specific commercial and information needs; developing proprietary IT interfaces; using consignment stocks and so on. To the extent that a corporation's portfolio of markets shares these similar sales management requirements, we would expect there to be greater opportunities for building and sharing core competences in these areas. Conversely, if a corporation's portfolio were strategically unrelated on this dimension, including a mix of businesses some with a concentrated account base and others facing account fragmentation, we would expect fewer opportunities for building and sharing core competences in sales and customer service.

2 *Service requirement.* Good customer relationships (service reputation) and organizational capital (to provide quality service), both largely nontradeable assets, are likely to be more important in industries characterized by a high level of service requirement. Access to core competences in rapidly establishing an organization capable of providing quality service to the customer will offer greater advantage in such markets. To the extent that a corporation's portfolio of markets shares these similar service management requirements, we would expect there to be greater opportunities for building and sharing core competences in these areas. The service requirement in the industry is measured by the

percentage of product lines requiring a 'moderate to high' degree of after sales or technical service (HSERV).

Channel asset indicators

A second class of indicators refers to the importance of imperfectly tradeable, channel-related assets as a basis for competitive advantage. Such assets are likely to be more important in industries where a large portion of the products are sold through intermediaries: opportunities for a related diversifier to share competences in delivering products, information and service to the customer will then be high.

3 *Channel dependence.* Our indicator of the degree of third-party channel dependence, CHANNEL, is the percentage of products which pass through an intermediary before reaching the final user, rather than being sold direct to users by the manufacturer.

Distribution relationships are a critical asset in many businesses dependent on third-party channels. They are also difficult to trade on a free standing basis. Skills in building and managing distribution and dealer networks form the basis of a potentially important core competence. Where market economies dictate that that dependence on third-party channels is high, competences in dealer recruitment and overcoming 'shelf space' restrictions (Porter, 1976) will be valuable in assisting an SBU to accumulate the assets it requires to compete effectively. Strategic relatedness will also tend to be higher among markets that share similar levels of channel dependence.

Process experience asset indicators

In most industries it is important to build up relevant process experience and associated assets in order to underpin competitive advantage. We use two measures to indicate the degree of similarity between the types of process experience assets that SBUs require: the proportion of products which are made to order and the average skill level of employees.

4 *Product customization (products made to order) vs. standardization.* Successful made-to-order supply depends on a variety of asset bases to facilitate two-way communication with customers, the design and management of flexible manufacturing systems, and the reduction of lead times. Efficient supply of products from stock requires a different set of tangible and intangible assets which underpin effective stock, control, demand forecasting, and batching and run-length efficiencies, etc. In both cases, nontradeable assets play a potentially important role, but the nature of the assets and the competences required to accumulate them differ. Strategic relatedness between businesses will therefore tend

to be high when they share a common focus on either made-to-order production or supply from stock.

Our measure of relatedness on this dimension is the percentage of product lines supplied by the business which are made to order based on customer specifications (*TORDER*).

5 *The average skill level of the labor force.* In businesses where groups of skilled staff are an important source of advantage, human capital and the associated systems to generate and manage will be even more critical to advantage than in businesses with high labor intensity, but low skill levels. Again, businesses which share the need to develop an effective base of skilled staff with experience working together will have higher strategic relatedness than a pair of businesses, one requiring highly skilled staff and the other, a base of cost effective, low skilled workers.

Our indicator, SKILL, measures the proportion of 'high-skilled' jobs in the industry as a percentage of total employment.

HYPOTHESES, DATA AND METHODOLOGY

Hypotheses

So far we have argued that the traditional way of measuring relatedness between two businesses is incomplete; to be meaningful, relatedness needs to consider: (i) the 'strategic importance' of the underlying assets of these two businesses (i.e. are these assets nontradeable and nonsubstitutable?); and (ii) whether these assets are related. Only firms that exhibit this type of 'strategic relatedness' will perform well in the long term. This implies that if we were to measure the performance of firms classified as 'related' in the traditional (Rumelt) way and again according to whether their underlying strategic assets are related, we should be able to show that the latter way of looking at relatedness is superior. Therefore:

> *Hypothesis 1:* Related diversifiers will outperform unrelated firms only where they compete across a portfolio of markets where similar types of accumulated assets are important.

In addition, the above discussion suggests that even within the population of related–diversified firms (defined as such in the traditional way), some related firms will do better than other related firms. Specifically, those related firms that compete across a portfolio of markets where similar types of accumulated assets are important should outperform the related firms that compete in a portfolio of markets where accumulated assets are less important or the types of strategic assets required differ widely across the firm's portfolio. Therefore:

> *Hypothesis 2:* Related firms that compete in a portfolio of markets where similar types of accumulated assets are important will outperform other related firms.

Data and methodology

To test these hypotheses, a sample of 200 firms was randomly selected from the 1981 *Fortune* 500 list. The population of *Fortune* 500 firms was selected for study because it contains many diversified firms. The sample firms were classified according to Rumelt's (1974) diversification categories (i.e. Single-business; Dominant-business; Related-business; and Unrelated-business), using data from the TRINET tapes as well as their annual reports. Since this is a study on diversification, the Single-business firms were excluded from the sample. Hence, the final sample consists of 164 diversified firms.

To test Hypothesis 1 we first measure relatedness in the traditional (Rumelt) way as a (0.1) dummy (RELATED): those firms classified as Related or Dominant take the value of 1, while firms classified as Unrelated take the value of 0. The following equation is then estimated

$$\text{ROS}_i = \alpha + \beta_i \ (\text{RELATED}) + \sum_{i=2}^{4} \beta_i \ (\text{IND})_i + \varepsilon \qquad (1)$$

where ROS is the profitability of the sample firms, measured as return on sales, and IND are industry control variables. We use three standard variables to control for industry effects: R&D intensity (RDSLS), measured as the total expenditure on R&D as a percentage of sales in a given industry; advertising intensity (WXAD), measured as expenditure on media advertising as a percentage of sales in an industry; and capital intensity (CAPX), measured as capital expenditures as a percentage of sales in an industry.[7] We decided to use return on sales (ROS) rather than return on assets (ROA) as our profitability variable for a specific reason: as explained by Ravenscraft and Scherer (1987), depending on the accounting method that a firm uses to account for an acquisition (pooling of interest vs. purchase accounting), profitability measures such as ROA end up *systematically* smaller under purchase accounting than under pooling of interest accounting. To avoid this potential bias we use ROS which is not affected by the accounting policies of acquisition recording. Finally, even though it is possible that profitability affects the industry variables as much as it is affected by them, we decided to treat the system as recursive rather than endogenous because we believe that feedbacks in the system occur at sufficiently long lags to allow us to pull out individual equations for separate treatment (e.g. Cowling, 1976).

After estimating Equation (1), we replace the RELATED variable by our structural indicators of relatedness to reestimate the above equation, i.e.

$$\text{ROS}_i = \alpha + \sum_{i-1}^{5} \beta_i K_i + \sum_{i-1}^{3} \beta_j \ (\text{IND})_j + \varepsilon \qquad (2)$$

where K_i are the five structural indicators described in the previous section. In order to test our hypotheses about strategic relatedness, we express each K_i as the weighted average of each structural indicator 'i' divided by the weighted variance of the indicator across the businesses in each diversified firm's portfolio (A/V).[8] The reason for this transformation is best explained by example. Suppose we have two diversified firms, Firm X has 70% of its sales in a business requiring a high level of after-sales service, but has diversified the remainder of its sales into businesses where the products do not require any after-sales service. The indicator HSERV will therefore have a high variance for Firm X, suggesting little scope for sharing competences in building a service network. By dividing our average indicator by this variance, we are effectively discounting for the fact that any competence Firm X has in building an after-sales service network cannot be exploited in its other businesses (it is 'imprisoned'). Compare this with Firm Y which has all of its sales in two businesses, both of which require high after-sales service. Firm Y will score in two ways on our indicator K_i (compared with Firm X). It will start out with a high weighted average on HSERV. And the fact that both its businesses share a requirement for high after-sales service means that the variance of HSERV is very low for Firm Y, so the value of its competence in building effective service networks will not be discounted as it was for the unrelated diversifier, Firm X.

To calculate the weighted average of each structural indicator we first obtained an industry breakdown of the indicator from Bailey (1975). Next, each sample firm's sales by SIC were obtained from the TRINET tapes and the percentage of the firm's sales in each SIC was calculated. The industry-weighted average of each indicator was then calculated by multiplying the share of a firm's sales in each SIC by the corresponding value of the indicator in that SIC, and adding the results.

To calculate the weighted variance of each indicator, we used the following formula:

$$\text{variance } (x) = \sum (s\, x^2) - \bar{x}^2$$

where $\bar{x}^2$ = weighted average of the indicator x; and s = percentage of each industry (SIC) in total sales.

A priori we would expect that the coefficient of RELATED in Equation (1) is positive and significant, consistent with previous studies on related diversification. In addition, for Hypothesis 1 to be supported we should find: (a) the R^2 of Equation (2) significantly higher than the R^2 obtained from Equation (1), implying that Equation (2) does a better job in explaining the profitability differences between Related and Unrelated firms; and (b) the coefficients of the structural indicators in Equation (2) to be *positive* and significant.

To test Hypothesis 2 we simply estimate Equation (2) again, but only

Table 5.1 Means, standard deviations and intercorrelations[a]

Variable	Mean	S.D.	1	2	3	4	5	6	7	8	9
1. ROS	11.904	4.69	—								
2. A/V CHANNEL	0.732	2.34	0.014	—							
3. A/V TORDER	4.321	21.65	0.128	-0.819	—						
4. A/V FEWCUST	0.66	1.42	0.145	0.245	-0.029	—					
5. A/V HSERV	0.58	1.11	-0.015	-0.309	0.126	-0.528	—				
6. A/V SKILL	220.6	375.4	0.18	-0.336	0.495	-0.051	0.217	—			
7. CAPX	6.543	3.93	0.416	-0.051	0.064	-0.197	0.038	0.101	—		
8. WXAD	3.229	2.19	0.215	0.037	-0.019	0.139	-0.096	-0.133	0.0002	—	
9. RDSLS	1.851	1.14	0.204	-0.057	0.023	-0.031	-0.108	-0.119	-0.046	0.240	—

[a] $N = 164$: Correlation coefficients greater than 0.19 are significant at $p < 0.05$, those greater than 0.25 are significant at $p < 0.01$, and those greater than 0.32 are significant at $p < 0.001$.

on the subsample of firms classified as 'related' in the traditional way (N = 109). The hypothesis will be supported if Equation (2) does a good job (as measured by its R^2) in explaining the variability in the profitability of related firms.

Data for calculating the five structural indicators and the three industry-control variables were derived from the following sources: The variables FEWCUST, CHANNEL, HSERV and TORDER, as defined above, were drawn from a US survey of marketing expenditures (Bailey, 1975); the variables ROS, CAPX and WXAD come from Compustat; RDSLS was taken from the National Science Foundation (1978); and SKILL was computed from job classifications contained in the Census of Population (1980).

RESULTS

Table 5.1 presents descriptive statistics and correlations for all the variables in the study. The low intercorrelations among these variables suggest no problems with multicollinearity. The low correlations imply that there is sufficient independent variation among the variables used in this study to allow discrete effects to be estimated.

The estimated coefficients from Equation (1) are reported in Table 5.2. Consistent with previous studies, we find that Related diversification is positively correlated with profitability. Consistent with IO theory, we also find that the proxies for industry structure (advertising, capital and

Table 5.2 Relatedness measured by Rumelt categories[a]

Variable	Dependent variable = ROS81	
	(A)	(B)
Constant	11.828	5.674
	(26.98)***	(6.06)***
RELATED	1.239	1.370
	(1.52)	(1.94)**
WXAD	–	0.378
		(2.55)***
RDSLS	–	0.788
		(2.72)***
CAPX	–	0.510
		(6.33)***
	$N = 160$	$N = 159$
	adj. $R^2 = 0.008$	adj. $R^2 = 0.26$
	$F = 2.30$	$F = 15.05$

[a] t-statistics reported in parentheses
* significant at the 10% level (two-tail test)
** significant at the 5% level (two-tail test)
*** significant at the 1% level (two-tail test)

Table 5.3 Relatedness measured by strategic indicators

Variable	Dependent variable = ROS81	
	(A)	(B)
Constant	5.437	5.773
	(3.55)***	(1.69)*
A/V FEWCUST	0.812	0.906
	(3.13)***	(3.14)***
A/V HSERV	0.712	0.676
	(2.17)**	(1.89)*
A/V CHANNEL	0.549	0.542
	(2.24)**	(2.12)**
A/V TORDER	0.054	0.048
	(2.01)**	(1.72)*
A/V SKILL	0.002	0.002
	(2.07)	(2.12)**
WXAD	0.286**	0.165
	(2.05)**	(0.70)
RDSLS	10.4	1.178
	(3.75)***	(3.56)***
CAPX	0.556	0.572
	(7.24)***	(6.31)***
	$N = 164$	$N = 109$
	adj. $R^2 = 0.36$	adj. $R^2 = 0.41$
	$F = 12.25$	$F = 10.13$

* significant at the 10% level (two-tail test)
** significant at the 5% level (two-tail test)
*** significant at the 1% level (two-tail test)

R&D intensity) are also positively correlated with profitability. The equation is statistically significant at the 99% level and explains about 26% of the variation in the dependent variable.

The comparative results obtained from Equation (2) when relatedness is measured by the five strategic indicators are presented in column (A) of Table 5.3. Again, the equation is statistically significant at the 99% level. Two results stand out: First, the adjusted R^2 of this equation (0.36) is significantly (at the 1% level) bigger than the adjusted R^2 obtained from Equation (1). This is strong support of Hypothesis 1 in that compared with the traditional definition of relatedness, our measures of relatedness do a far superior job in explaining the variation in the dependent variable. Second, the five structural indicators that we used to capture strategic relatedness exhibit the expected sign and are statistically significant, again strongly supporting Hypothesis 1.

Our results with respect to the structural indicators imply the following:

• Operating in a portfolio of markets with high service requirement (HSERV) allows the firm to benefit from customer relationship skills and accumulated competences in working with the customer and providing quality service. Other marketing competences can be most effectively developed and exploited when the firm operates in a portfolio of markets where a few large customers exist.

- When a manufacturer can operate by serving a few large accounts – FEWCUST – (i.e. its direct customers are not fragmented), it will be able to build up deep and sustained relationships with these customers, and so develop its core competences in managing sophisticated customer interfaces.
- Operating in markets where products have to pass through intermediaries before reaching the final user (CHANNEL) allows the firm to build up its dealer recruitment skills and channel management competences.
- Operating in markets where products are custom-made (TORDER) enables the firm to build up and exploit competences in the exchange of complex information with its customers and/or develop flexible manufacturing.
- Operating in markets where labor skill is high (SKILL) allows the firm to build up competences in managing knowledge-based activities which can be transferred to other businesses. It may also help the firm improve its competences in human resource management.

These results are in general conformity with Hypothesis 1. Similarly supporting results were obtained for the second hypothesis. These results are presented in column (B) of Table 5.3 and are the estimates of Equation (2) when only the subsample of Related firms is used. The five strategic indicators are able to explain more than 41% of profitability differences among the population of related firms. This suggests that even within the population of related–diversified firms (defined as such in the traditional way), some related firms will do better than other related firms. Specifically, since all five of the strategic indicators come out positive and significant, we can argue that those related firms that compete across markets where certain types of assets (nontradeable, nonsubstitutable and slow and costly to accumulate) are important, outperform the related firms that compete in markets where these accumulated assets are less important.

SUMMARY AND CONCLUSIONS

In this paper, we argued that the traditional way of measuring relatedness between two businesses is incomplete because it ignores the 'strategic importance' and similarity of the underlying assets residing in these businesses. A firm may be in a set of related businesses without deriving a significant advantage from the potential links between its

SBUs. Relatedness will be of little advantage when it does not assist the firm in accumulating nontradeable, nonsubstitutable assets efficiently. This, in turn, implies that it is relatedness of strategic assets between SBUs that is important, not the market-level relatedness between businesses.

But simply exploiting strategic assets will not create long-term competitive advantage. In a dynamic world, only firms who are able to continually build new strategic assets faster and more cheaply than their competitors will earn superior returns over the long term. Core competences have a pivotal role to play in this process. By transferring core competences between its SBUs, a corporation is able to accelerate the rate and lower the cost at which it accumulates new strategic assets. These opportunities for benefitting from core competences underpin the dynamic advantage of related diversification and define the types of relatedness that a firm should seek to exploit (asset amortization, asset improvement, asset creation and asset fission).

This analysis led us to hypothesize that 'strategic' relatedness is superior to market relatedness and that related firms outperform unrelated ones *only* in markets where accumulated assets are important. These hypotheses were supported by our empirical tests. Specifically, we found that firms operating in portfolios of businesses which shared similar opportunities to exploit brand building: marketing and channel management; and process skills in customization and management of skilled teams gained significant benefit from related diversification.

ACKNOWLEDGEMENTS

We would like to thank Harbir Singh, Julia Liebeskind, Robert Hoskisson, two anonymous reviewers and especially Gary Hamel for many helpful suggestions on earlier drafts.

NOTES

1. It is important here to clarify the difference between 'strategic assets' and 'core competences'. Strategic assets are assets that underpin a firm's cost or differentiation advantage in a particular market and that are imperfectly imitable, imperfectly substitutable and imperfectly tradeable. These assets also tend to be market-specific. An example would be Honda's dealer network distributing and servicing its motorbikes. On the other hand, core competences are the pool of experience, knowledge and systems, etc. that exist elsewhere in the same corporation and can be deployed to reduce the cost or time required either to create a new, strategic asset or expand the stock of an existing one. Thus Honda's experience in building competitive dealer networks for a particular class of consumer durables would be an example of a core competence. Each of these networks (one for motorbikes and another for lawn mowers, for

example) would be a separate strategic asset: 'different trees, sharing the same (core competence) root stock.'

2. An extension of this argument has been proposed by Hill (1988): the corporation will be in a better position to exploit the interrelationships among its businesses if it is *structured* appropriately. Hill finds that related diversifiers are better served by the CM-form organizational structure than the M-form structure.

3. See Verdin and Williamson (1994) for a fuller discussion of the link between Porter's cost and differentiation drivers and the assets on which exploitation of these drivers depend.

4. *Time compression diseconomies* are the extra cost associated with accumulating the required assets under time pressure (the cost of compressing an activity in time). For example, it may take more than twice the amount of marketing to achieve in 1 year the same level of brand awareness as an established competitor may have been able to develop over a period of 2 years (other things equal). *Asset mass efficiencies* refer to the fact that some types of assets are more costly to accumulate when the firm's existing stock of that asset is small. It is more difficult, for example, to build the customer base of a credit card when it has few existing users. *Asset interconnectedness* refers to the fact that a lack of complementary assets can often impede a firm from accumulating an asset which it needs to successfully serve its market. *Causal ambiguity* refers to the impediment associated with the uncertainty of pinpointing which specific factors or processes are required to accumulate a required asset (the precise chain of causality is ambiguous).

5. The role of organizational structure in allowing a firm to exploit the benefits of related diversification is explored in more detail in Markides and Williamson (1993).

6. We would like to thank Gary Hamel for his contribution in the formulation of these ideas.

7. Given the multiindustry nature of the sample firms, these three variables were industry-weighted. As an example of how this was achieved, consider how we industry-weighted WXAD (a firm's *industry* advertising intensity): First, a Compustat program was used to identify all the firms assigned to each 2-digit SIC, and to calculate their advertising intensity. Then, using their sales as weights, the average advertising intensity of every SIC was estimated. Next, each *sample* firm's sales by SIC were obtained from the TRINET tapes, and the percentage of the firm's sales in each SIC was calculated. The firm's industry-weighted advertising intensity was then calculated by multiplying the share of the firm's sales in each SIC by the corresponding advertising intensity of that SIC, and adding the results.

8. We'd like to thank an anonymous reviewer for suggesting this to us.

REFERENCES

Ansoff, H. I., 1965, *Corporate Strategy*. McGraw-Hill, New York.

Bailey, E. L., 1975, *Marketing Cost Ratios of U.S. Manufacturers*. Conference Board Report No. 662. Conference Board, New York.

Barney, J. B., October 1986, 'Strategic factor markets: Expectations, luck and business strategy', *Management Science*, 32, pp. 1231–1241.

Bettis, R. A., 1981, 'Performance differences in related and unrelated diversified firms', *Strategic Management Journal*, 2(4), pp. 379–393.

Caves, R. E., 1982, *Multinational Enterprise and Economic Analysis*. Cambridge University Press, Cambridge, MA.

Caves, R. E. and Porter, M. E., 1977, 'From entry barriers to mobility barriers: Conjectural variations and contrived deterrence to new competition', *Quarterly Journal of Economics*, 91, pp. 241–262.

Caves, R. E. and Porter, M. E., Spence, M. A. and Scott, J. T., 1980, *Competition in the Open Economy: A Model Applied to Canada*. Harvard University Press, Cambridge, MA.

Cowling, K., 1976, 'On the theoretical specification of industrial structure-performance relationships', *European Economic Review*, 8(1), pp. 1–14.

Dierickx, I. and Cool, K., December 1989, 'Asset stock accumulation and sustainability of competitive advantage', *Management Science*, 35, pp. 1504–1514.

Eaton, B. and Lipsey, R., 1980, 'Exit barriers are entry barriers: The durability of capital as a barrier to entry', *Bell Journal of Economics*, 11, pp. 721–729.

Hill, C. W. L., 1988, 'Internal capital market controls and financial performance in multidivisional firms', *Journal of Industrial Economics*, XXXVII(1), pp. 67–83.

Hill, C. W. L., 1994, 'Diversification and economic performance; Bring structure and corporate management back into the picture'. In R. Rumelt, D. Schendel and D. Teece (eds.). *Fundamental Issues in Strategy*. Harvard Business School Press, Boston, MA, pp. 297–321.

Hoskisson, R. E. and Hitt, M. A., 1990, 'Antecedents and performance outcomes of diversification: Review and critique of theoretical perspectives', *Journal of Management*, 16, pp. 461–509.

Jacquemin, A. P. and Berry, C. H., 1979, 'Entropy measure of diversification and corporate growth', *Journal of Industrial Economics*, XXVII(4), pp. 359–369.

Lecraw, D. J., 1984, 'Diversification strategy and performance', *Journal of Industrial Economics*, XXXIII (2), pp. 179–198.

Markides, C. C. and Williamson, P. J., 1993, 'Corporate diversification and organizational structure: A resource-based view', Working paper, London Business School.

Montgomery, C. A., 1982, 'The measurement of firm diversification: Some new empirical evidence', *Academy of Management Journal*, 25(2), pp. 299–307.

National Science Foundation, 1978, *Research and Development in Industry*, Technical Notes and Detailed Statistical Tables, Washington, DC.

Palepu, K., 1985, 'Diversification strategy, profit performance, and the entropy measure', *Strategic Management Journal*, 6(3), pp. 239–255.

Pitts, R. A. and Hopkins, H. D., 1982, 'Firm diversity: Conceptualization and measurement', *Academy of Management Review*, 7(4), pp. 620–629.

Porter, M. E., 1976, *Interbrand Choice, Strategy and Bilateral Market Power*, Harvard University Press, Cambridge, MA.

Porter, M. E., 1980, *Competitive Strategy: Techniques for Analyzing Industries and Competitors*, Free Press, New York.

Porter, M. E., May–June 1987, 'From competitive advantage to corporate strategy', *Harvard Business Review*, pp. 43–59.

Prahalad, C. K. and Hamel, G., May–June 1990, 'The core competence of the corporation', *Harvard Business Review*, pp. 71–91.

Ramanujam, V. and Varadarajan, P., 1989, 'Research on corporate diversification: A synthesis', *Strategic Management Journal*, 10(6), pp. 523–551.

Ravenscraft, D. J. and Scherer, F. M., 1987, *Mergers, Sell-offs and Economic Efficiency*. The Brookings Institution, Washington, DC.

Reed, R. and Luffman, G. A., 1986, 'Diversification: The growing confusion', *Strategic Management Journal*, 7(1), pp. 29–35.

Rumelt, R., 1974, *Strategy, Structure and Economic Performance*. Division of Research, Harvard Business School, Cambridge, MA.

Rumelt, R. P., 1987, 'Theory, strategy and entrepreneurship'. In D. Teece (ed.), *The Competitive Challenge*. Cambridge, Ballinger, MA, pp. 137–158.

Singh, H. and Montgomery, C. A., 1987, 'Corporate acquisition strategies and economic performance', *Strategic Management Journal*, 8(4), pp. 377–386.

Teece, D. J., 1982, 'Towards an economic theory of the multiproduct firm', *Journal of Economic Behavior and Organization*, 3, pp. 39–63.

U.S. Bureau of Census, 1980, 'Job classification statistics', *Census of Population*, U.S. Government Printing Office, Washington, DC.

Verdin, P. J. and Williamson, P. J., 1994, 'Core competences, market analysis and competitive advantage: Forging the links'. In G. Hamel and A. Heene (eds), *Sustainable Competitive Advantage through Core Competence*, Wiley, New York, forthcoming.

Williamson, O. E., May 1973, 'Markets and hierarchies: Some elementary considerations', *American Economic Review*, 63, pp. 316–325.

Williamson, O. E., 1975, *Markets and Hierarchies*, Free Press, New York.

Chapter 6

Targeting a company's real core competencies

Amy V. Snyder and H. William Ebeling, Jr.

ABSTRACT

By recognizing its core competencies, a company can clearly define organizational boundaries and focus resources for maximum advantage. The authors outline an approach for identifying those competencies that can provide a company with the best chance to achieve long-term competitive advantage.

The twin concepts of core competence and business processes figure prominently in most discussions of corporate strategy.[1] The core competence concept helps top managers answer the fundamental question 'What should we do?' and the business processes perspective addresses the question 'How should we do it?'

Both concepts are indispensable in guiding firms to achieve enduring competitive advantage and superior profitability, and both are founded on a simple notion: that the firm is a system of activities, not a portfolio of individual products or services. Some activities are performed so much better than the competition and are so critical to end products or services that they can be described as core competencies. When a series of activities are organized into a system that works better than the sum of its parts, this business process can also create competitive advantage, even if component activities by themselves do not.

While business process reengineers have achieved significant success in decreasing costs while simultaneously improving service levels, relatively few firms claim to have correctly identified and fully exploited their core competencies or key activities. (Throughout this article, we will use the terms *core competency* and *key activity* interchangeably.)

Business process reengineers have developed an analytically rigorous discipline that can be systematically applied and plainly communicated to others. For the core competency concept to achieve this same success, it must be linked to the underlying business economics that drive competitive advantage, and it must be applied in the same systematic manner as the business process concept.

In the mid-1970s, corporate planners began to question whether the product-centered business unit was the most appropriate unit of strategic analysis. In work undertaken for a global chemical company in 1977, Braxton Associates redefined the unit of analysis from product-centered business units to *activities* and developed insights about how competitive advantage is created in the long run.[2]

In the course of our work with the chemical company, we demonstrated that gaining a strong relative share in key value-added activities is more relevant to competitive position than gaining share of the related product market. In the 1970s, we used the slicing knife schematic to demonstrate that assessing competitive advantage from a product perspective can lead to erroneous conclusions (see Figure 6.1). The insight that underlies the activity perspective is that a firm can not be viewed only as a collection of individual products or services – this merely describes the revenue-generating side of the firm. Equally important, the firm is a system of activities that must be organized and managed to maximize the value of its offerings while minimizing their cost – that is, to create competitive advantage.

The slicing knife example makes an important point, but a key question remains. Once it is determined that a firm enjoys a comparatively strong activity position, the next logical question is 'So what?' Achieving strong activity position is critical to competitiveness only when the particular activity adds significant value to the end product or service.

In the 1980s, Michael Porter documented the concept of the value chain and used it to show how a series of activities could be viewed as a system designed to create competitive advantage.[3] Porter's work was instrumental in popularizing the activity perspective and the importance of activity linkages.

However, the popular version of Porter's value chain does not consider the value-added[4] concept in sufficient depth. This is unfortunate, because the value-added structure determines which activities are critical to success and which are not.

It is usually a mistake to invest heavily in activities that represent only a small fraction of the overall value of a firm's products or services. The company that produced the page you are now reading would be better off with a competency in printing and page setup than in packaging, even though the printed journal was delivered in a protective package, because packaging does not represent a significant fraction of the overall value of the delivered journal.

Classical business-unit approach

Activity perspective

Business interrelationships

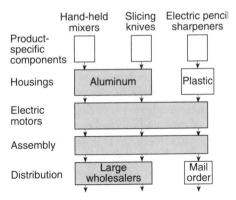

Product-based growth–share matrix

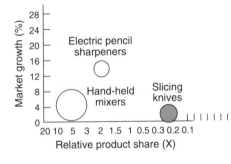

Relative product share (X)

Activity-based growth–share matrix

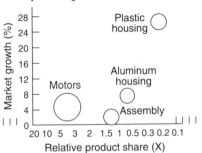

Relative product share (X)

Observations/implications

- Slicing knife business suffers from low growth and low market share

- Business is a 'dog' according to classical analysis, and it is not likely ever to attain a low-cost position

Observations/implications

- Slicing knife business shares key activities with other businesses (see shaded areas above)

- Thanks to sharing, these core activities are relatively strong and enjoy a low-cost position

- Slicing knife business should be able to generate cash, despite low *product* share

Conclusion: LIQUIDATE

Conclusion: HOLD/GROW

Figure 6.1 Slicing knife example

CLEAR THINKING TURNS MUDDLED

Activities are now being called core competencies. A subtle but important shift happens when the word *activity* is replaced by *core competency*:

the key characteristic moves from something the organization does (evoked by activity) to a characteristic the organization possesses (evoked by core competency).

There is a disturbing tendency today to identify characteristics such as 'quality products' and 'a good reputation' as core competencies, when these characteristics are really the result of performing discrete activities well. In failing to associate specific, underlying activities with these claimed competencies, managers are unable to focus on preserving and strengthening the building blocks that create quality products in the first place. Business analysts must dig deeper. When they do, they will find that real core competencies are tangible value-added activities that are performed more effectively and at lower cost than that of the competition. These unique and enduring activities constitute a firm's core competencies.

When a firm fails to correctly identify its core competencies, it misses attractive opportunities and chases poor ones. In the US, electric utilities diversified into businesses such as real estate and coal mining with mixed success.

The desk–chair example shown in Figure 6.2 demonstrates where these diversification efforts went wrong. The exhibit depicts the activities required to manufacture desks and chairs. This diagram shows the relative value-added contribution of each activity and the amount of activity-sharing between desk and chair products (fabrication and finishing constitute high value-added activities, while assembly and warehousing contribute less value to the final product).

In this case, low value-added activities enjoy more sharing between desks and chairs than high value-added activities. Since most of the value added consists of separate and distinct activities (not shared activities), one should conclude that the desk and chair businesses, while

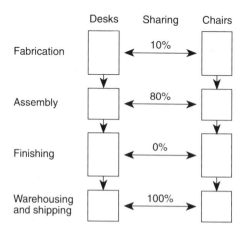

Figure 6.2 How related are these businesses?

related, are distinct and separate businesses. Evaluating activity synergies between electric utilities and the real estate business would have led utilities to a similar conclusion.

Properly identified and exploited competencies can be powerful competitive weapons. The success of Honda Motor Co. during the past twenty years can be attributed to its focus on a single core competency: small engine manufacture. From its initial position in motorcycles, Honda transferred its small-engine manufacturing expertise into small cars, pumps, lawn mowers, and other products where engines were a significant value-added element, all the while moving down the activity-based experience curve. Had Honda determined that its core competency was in supplying motorcycles and related products, lawn mower manufacturers around the globe might be a lot better off today.

In the late 1970s, the General Electric Co. learned a hard lesson about nurturing and organizing around core competencies. Figure 6.3 is a simplified view of the value-added structure of a segment of the consumer electronics industry at that time; the shaded areas show how competitors chose to participate. While GE focussed on marketing and built a strong brand image, this was not enough. Competitors like Panasonic (Matsushita) and Radio Shack beat GE because they chose to nurture activities that represented greater value added – Panasonic in components and Radio Shack in retailing.

GE's lesson is summarized in Figure 6.4, which shows the way a portfolio of activities should be managed against business realities. If competitive advantage (often driven by relative cumulative experience) in a given activity is low, but the activity adds substantial value to the end product, then learning should be accelerated and volume increased – for example, by joint ventures or acquisitions (upper left-hand quadrant). Alternatively, if competitive advantage is high but the activity represents a small fraction of the overall value of the offering, then management must protect the activity strength through maintenance investments, while avoiding overinvestment.

Obviously, the best situation would be for all activities to be in the upper right-hand quadrant, where competitive position is high and these activities represent a large portion of overall value added. In general, activities in the lower left quadrant (where both competitive position and value added are low) should be outsourced.

FOUR IMPERATIVES OF CORE COMPETENCIES

The GE and Honda examples demonstrate the importance of organizing around 'real' core competencies or activities and the implications of failing to do so. Once senior management develops the strategic intent to identify, nurture, and organize around activities that can be made

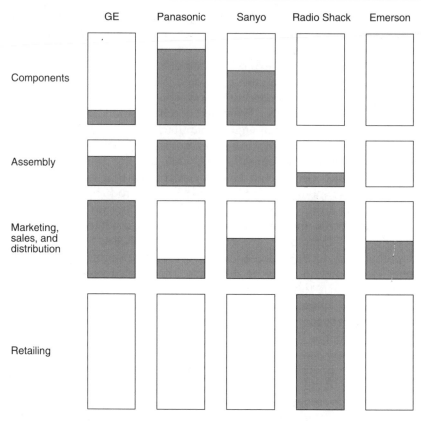

Figure 6.3 Segment of consumer electronics industry in the 1970s

unique and enduring, a few rules must be followed to transform this commitment into competitive success.

Rule 1: avoid laundry lists

If senior management settles on more than a handful of key activities or core competencies, it is probably over-reaching and certainly ignoring the intent of the word *core*. Many successful companies have targeted either one or two key activities.

Identifying key activities is one of the most important contributions senior management can make. In our view, proposed core competencies should:

• Contribute significantly to the ultimate value of the end product or service.

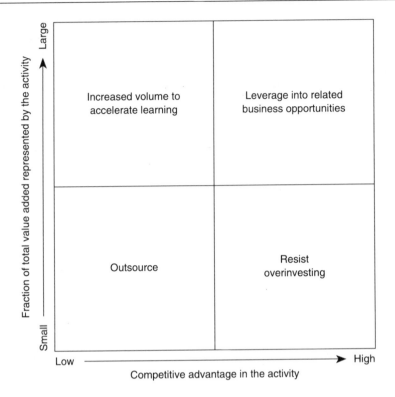

Figure 6.4 Portraying the corporate activity portfolio

- Represent a unique capability that provides enduring competitive advantage.
- Have the potential to support multiple end products or services.

Rule 2: achieve senior management consensus on core competencies (What business are you really in?)

Evaluating potential core competencies using the previously described screening approach is a necessary but insufficient step in building a competency-driven organization. If competencies are to be nurtured and shared widely throughout the firm, senior management must reach consensus on which these are and act on the results of their selection process.

In working to build senior management consensus on key activities, we have achieved good results using the following approaches (among others):

- Activity-based benchmarking.
- Employee and asset distribution.
- 'What if' scenario development.

Activity-based benchmarking is a technique that can steer debate away from subjective opinions and toward hard facts. For example, if the vice president of operations claims that order processing and fulfillment is a core competency, he could develop a persuasive argument by demonstrating an enduring competitive advantage in order-processing speed, cost, and customer satisfaction.

A compelling argument can also be built by answering some simple questions about an organization's internal configuration, for example: 'What do your employees do? Where are your assets?' If 80% of a company's employees are on the plant floor, the marketing vice-president must argue persuasively to convince his colleagues that marketing and sales is really a key activity. After all, *people* embody the collective learning so extolled today, and learning becomes a formidable competitive weapon when it is built up and shared among a large number of employees.

'What if' approaches are also useful in working with a group to select core competencies. A senior-management deadlock can often be broken by working out the implications of selecting a single core competency as a guide for future actions.

In a deadlocked situation, one might ask, 'What actions are implied by the adoption of core competency "X"? What products and markets are most attractive given this core competency? What will the company look like five years from now if competency "X" guides our actions?'

These same questions should be answered for each proposed core competency. While this approach may seem simplistic, it can be combined with other, more analytical approaches to help the group reach consensus on a core competency (or two) that makes the most sense for the corporation.

Rule 3: leverage core competencies inside the organization

Once senior management identifies and agrees on the firm's core competencies, it must work zealously to ensure that competencies are continually strengthened, shared widely throughout the corporation, and managed in a way that best preserves the competitive advantages they create. The importance of this mandate cannot be stressed enough – if senior management fails to organize around key activities, they will disappear.

Recall the slicing knife example: while the electric motor manufacturing activity enjoys a strong relative activity share, motor costs will not necessarily be lower than that of the competition. Only if this company organizes and conducts its operations so as to capture the collective learning taking place in the motor manufacturing activity will it drive costs down as cumulative experience increases.

Actions that may be necessary to best exploit identified competencies run the spectrum from physically reconfiguring disparate manufacturing processes to simply communicating more effectively. Consider the case of a leading international manufacturer of electrical products. Division A developed expertise in the design and manufacture of surface-mounted printed circuit boards and used this skill to reduce the costs of its products. Division B had an outmoded, expensive production process, in part because it was several generations behind in printed circuit-board design. Division B could have benefitted from Division A's surface-mount expertise and in return could have driven down costs for both divisions by increasing overall volume. Instead, Division A jealously guarded its capabilities, and Division B continued to struggle.

This behavior cannot be tolerated if key corporate skills are to be exploited to their fullest potential. New approaches to project coordination and interdepartmental communication can help to break down the barriers. Today, corporate planners are applauding 'adaptive organizations', which: 'retain some vestiges of the old hierarchy and maybe a few traditional departments . . . [but rely on] . . . a pattern of constantly changing teams, task forces, partnerships, and other informal structures.'[5]

The goal of the adaptive organization is to ensure that the best core competencies, whether embodied in technologies, processes, or employees, are linked to the most promising market opportunities so that learning is maximized and travels quickly throughout the corporation.

Rule 4: share core competencies outside the corporation as well

Sometimes sharing and nurturing core competencies within a corporation is not enough. As markets evolve, new activities may be required. Moreover, in today's global marketplace, even giant corporations blanch at the cost of launching new products and entering new markets. With product lifecycles shrinking and R&D costs skyrocketing, some companies find it easier to embrace their competitors rather than fight them.

Collins and Doorley have studied multinational alliance behavior and observe that 'The corporation of the future will need to take a more dynamic view of its business. . . . There is often insufficient time to switch from one mode of operation to another as markets evolve [through their product lifecycles]. From the very start of a new business, companies must find ways of building competence in each area of competitive advantage – even if they are not well placed to do so on their own.'[6]

Thinking about alliances from the perspective of key activities that can be shared adds clarity to a complex and difficult partner-identification process. As senior executives have begun to focus on maximizing the value of the core competencies they identify, alliance activity has increased substantially.

REDEFINING CORE COMPETENCIES

Identifying core competencies and inspiring the organization to nurture and organize around them is one of the most important contributions senior management can make. The reverse is also true: selecting the wrong competency or too many core competencies is one of the worst conceivable management errors.

It is our experience that an effort like this should be undertaken every three to five years, as part of a periodic review of corporate strategy. However, when an industry undergoes a fundamental change in its value-added structure, a reassessment is critical. Often management cannot respond fast enough and heavy losses result.

Western Union could not make the transition into the information age because it failed to recognize the growing importance of the transmission infrastructure; it eventually fell into bankruptcy. However, when the core check printing business of Deluxe Check Printers became threatened by electronic funds transfer (EFT), Deluxe correctly perceived that it had to cultivate new skills to preserve its historical performance. Senior management redefined its core competency – from printing checks to facilitating financial transactions – and built a successful EFT and data processing business.

In redefining its business, Deluxe recognized that its role in check clearing and processing and its financial institution marketing expertise might offer more enduring value to its customers than printing checks. Deluxe combined these enduring skills with acquired skills in computer automation, and it moved successfully in a new direction.

Companies with a widely shared understanding of their unique and enduring capabilities and the evolving value-added structure of their industries will rise above the competition, just as Deluxe and Honda did. By whatever name (activities, core competencies, or value-chain elements), firms that define their competitive advantage based on structural superiority in the discrete activities they perform are more often than not long-term winners; these companies turn their core competencies into competitive weapons, not competitive traps.

NOTES

1. For a discussion of how core competencies can be used to focus corporate activities, see C. Prahalad and G. Hamel, 'The Core Competence of the Corporation,' *Harvard Business Review* (May–June 1990). For a discussion of the business process approach, see M. Hammer, 'Reengineering Work: Don't

Automate, Obliterate,' *Harvard Business Review* (July–August 1990). These two approaches were contrasted and compared in an article by G. Stalk, P. Evans, and L. Schulman, 'Competing on Capabilities: The New Rules of Corporate Strategy,' *Harvard Business Review* (March–April 1992).

2. Since the mid-1970s, Braxton has applied the activity perspective to a broad range of strategic decisions. For example, see H. Ebeling, Jr. and T. Doorley III, 'A Strategic Approach to Acquisitions,' *Journal of Business Strategy* (Winter 1983).

3. M. Porter, *Competitive Advantage: Creating and Sustaining Superior Performance*, (New York: The Free Press, 1985).

4. *Value added* is often defined as the selling price less the cost of all purchased inputs. Under this definition, when selling price cannot be determined because a market for intermediate goods does not exist, the total cost of the activity is used as a proxy for value added, with profit shown as a separate value element. But cost is not always the most accurate measure of value added. Consider a quality control function that saves millions of dollars without incurring much cost. In this case, value added represents the cost of *not* performing the activity. The most appropriate method for determining value added should be selected on a case-by-case basis.

5. *Fortune* (June 17, 1991), p. 36.

6. T. Collins and T. Doorley, *Teaming Up for the 90s* (Homewood, IL: Business One Irwin), 1991, pp. 44–45.

Chapter 7

Corporate strategy: The quest for parenting advantage

Andrew Campbell, Michael Goold and Marcus Alexander

As they craft corporate-level strategy, most chief executives today fail to address two crucial questions: What businesses should this company, rather than rival companies, own and why? And what organizational structure, management processes, and philosophy will foster superior performance from its businesses?

We are not saying that chief executives intentionally avoid or ignore those questions. They simply lack the tools and processes for the job. Most planning processes focus on developing business-level, rather than corporate-level, strategies. Even more important, the planning frameworks that corporate-level strategists have commonly used have proven inappropriate or impractical.

The growth/share matrix, introduced in the 1970s and adopted by two-thirds of all US corporations within a decade, encouraged companies to balance their business portfolios with a mix of stars, cash cows, and question marks. But the poor performance of companies using the portfolio-management technique, and disillusionment with diversification, have discouraged all but a handful of companies from using it today.

For the past five to ten years, increasing numbers of companies have been trying to stick to their knitting, as Tom Peters and Bob Waterman first advised in the book *In Search of Excellence* in 1982. Companies have been shedding the businesses they acquired as diversifications in order to focus instead on core businesses, relying for guidance on the core competence concept. In introducing the concept (The Core Competence of the Corporation, *HBR* May–June 1990), C. K. Hamel and Gary Prahalad proposed that companies should build portfolios of businesses around shared technical or operating competencies and should develop structures and processes to enhance their core competencies.

Despite its powerful appeal, the core competence concept has not provided practical guidelines for developing corporate-level strategy. Many companies have tried to define their core competencies, but, lacking reliable analytical tools, few have achieved the clarity they sought. Furthermore, the core competence model does not account for the success of companies such as ABB Asea Brown Boveri, BTR, Emerson Electric, General Electric, Hanson, and Kohlberg Kravis Roberts, whose businesses have limited technical or operating overlap.

The framework we propose – the parenting framework – fills in the deficiencies of the core competence concept. It provides a rigorous conceptual model as well as the tools needed for an effective corporate-level planning process.

Based on research with some of the world's most successful diversified companies, the parenting framework is grounded in the economics of competitive strategy. Multibusiness companies bring together under a parent organization businesses that could potentially be independent. Such parent companies can justify themselves economically only if their influence creates value. For example, the parent organization can improve the businesses' plans and budgets, promote better linkages among them, provide especially competent central functions, or make wise choices in its own acquisitions, divestments, and new ventures.

Multibusiness companies create value by influencing – or parenting – the businesses they own. The best parent companies create more value than any of their rivals would if they owned the same businesses. Those companies have what we call *parenting advantage*.

Previous strategic frameworks have focused on the businesses in the portfolio and searched for a logic by examining how they relate to one another. The underlying assumption has been that portfolios of related businesses perform better than portfolios of unrelated ones. The growth/share matrix implies that businesses are related if their cash, profit, and growth performance create a balance within the portfolio. The core competence concept says that businesses are related if they have common technical or operating know-how. The parenting framework, in contrast, focuses on the competencies of the parent organization and on the value created from the relationship between the parent and its businesses.

The parent organization is an intermediary between investors and businesses. It competes not only with other parent organizations but also with other intermediaries, such as investment trusts and mutual funds. Corporate-level strategies, therefore, make sense to the extent that the parent creates sufficient value to compete with other intermediaries. That occurs when the parent's skills and resources fit well with the needs and opportunities of the businesses. If there is a fit, the parent is likely to create value. If there is not a fit, the parent is likely to destroy value. The parent, we have found, is highly influential, and its impact is rarely neutral.

Demerger decisions, such as the one facing Imperial Chemical Industries (ICI) in 1992, dramatically illustrate the importance of fit between the parent and its businesses. To split a large and venerable organization that had been built up over decades demanded a powerful rationale. (See Geoffrey Owen and Trevor Harrison, 'Why ICI Chose to Demerge,' *Harvard Business Review*, March–April 1995.)

Divestment decisions, such as the exit of oil companies from the minerals business, also illustrate the logic of the fit. Companies such as British Petroleum (BP), Exxon, and Shell entered minerals in order to diversify. They believed they had the appropriate skills for that business because, like oil, it involved exploration, extraction, government relations, and large, technically complex projects. Minerals and oil seemed to share competencies.

However, after more than ten years of experience, oil companies are getting out of the minerals business. BP sold its minerals businesses to the RTZ Corporation in 1989, and Shell recently sold its operations to Gencor in South Africa. Why? Because their minerals businesses have consistently underperformed those of minerals specialists. The minerals businesses of Atlantic Richfield, BP, Exxon, Shell, and Standard Oil had an average pretax return on sales of −17% during the mid-1980s, while independent metal companies achieved a 10% return. One reason for the disparity is the influence that managers in oil-company parents exercised over decisions made in their metals businesses. As a manager in BP's minerals businesses explains, 'The problem was that the BP managing directors could not really come to grips with the minerals business or feel they understood it. There was always that vestige of suspicion that led to a temptation to say no to proposals from the business or, alternatively, if they said yes, to say yes for the wrong reasons.' In other words, the influence of the parent managers on the minerals business was faulty because of insufficient understanding – an insufficient fit – between the parent and the business.

The oil companies' diversification into minerals failed because, despite similarities, some success factors in minerals are different from those in oil. Exploration, for instance, is not as critical. Finding new mineral deposits is not necessarily a passport to profit. More important is access to low-cost deposits because only those deposits make profits in cyclical downturns. For minerals businesses, forming joint ventures with companies that already have low-cost mines can be more profitable than searching for new deposits. Pressure from oil-company managers to spend more on exploration was therefore counter-productive. RTZ, the new parent of BP's minerals businesses, has not had that problem, however. 'It has been easy to add value,' Robert Adams, RTZ's planning director, explains, 'because we have some specialist expertise in mine planning and operations and a natural affinity for the investment and exploration decisions and trade-offs that you face in cyclical minerals businesses.'

The oil-company examples show that fit between parent and businesses is a two-edged sword. A good fit can create additional value; a bad one can destroy value. Bad parenting causes business-unit managers to make worse decisions than they would otherwise. In one company, the managers in the minerals business had taken bad advice about exploration techniques from their oil-company bosses. When asked why, they replied, 'They had acquired us so we thought they must know something we didn't.'

Our framework for developing corporate-level strategy is based on assessing the nature of the fit between the corporate parent and its businesses. Is there a match that will create value, or a mismatch that will destroy value? By answering that question, corporate strategists can consider which changes – either to the portfolio of businesses or to the parenting approach – will improve fit.

ASSESSING FIT

Few corporate-level managers find it easy to assess the fit between the corporate parent and its businesses. The reason, in part, is that they seldom openly address the question. But even if they do, it is a tough question to answer. It is like asking whether a particular manager fits a particular job. One must understand a great deal about the manager and the job to judge well.

To aid those judgments, we have developed a structured analytical approach. It begins with an assessment of the businesses. First, we examine the critical success factors of each business. We need to understand those factors in order to judge where the parent's influence is positive and where it is negative. Second, we document areas in the businesses in which performance can be improved. Those are areas in which the parent can add value. They represent the upside potential.

Armed with those analyses, we then review the characteristics of the parent, grouped in a number of categories. That analysis ensures that managers will consider all the main characteristics of the parent when they judge whether its influence is likely to fit the business's opportunities and needs. The final step is to test the judgments against the results that the businesses achieve under the influence of the parent.

Critical success factors: understanding the businesses

The concept of critical success factors is familiar to most managers. In every business, certain activities or issues are critical to performance and to the creation of competitive advantage. However, success factors differ among and even within industries. For example, those in bulk chemicals are not the same as those in specialty chemicals.

Most businesses-level plans define the critical success factors as part of the rationale for the actions proposed. A special analysis of critical success factors is not, therefore, usually necessary to develop corporate-level strategy. However, it is a good idea to summarize critical success factors, confirm their importance with business-level managers, and check whether circumstances in the business have changed – for example, whether its costs have risen. (See Table 7.1.)

Critical-success-factor analysis is an important base for assessing fit. It is useful in judging whether friction is likely to develop between the business and the parent. A parent that does not understand the critical success factors in a business is likely to destroy value. It is also useful for judging how similar the parenting needs of different businesses are. In the food-company example, the restaurant and retail businesses are more similar than the hotel, property, and food-products businesses. Finally, critical-success-factor analysis is a prerequisite for a parenting-opportunity analysis.

Parenting opportunities: gauging the upside

To add value, a parent must improve its businesses. For that to be possible, there must be room for improvement. We call the potential for improvement within a business a *parenting opportunity*.

Many kinds of parenting opportunities may present themselves. For example, a business may have excessive overhead costs that its managers are unaware of. For the right parent, the high overhead is an opportunity. Or two businesses might be able to gain economies of scale by combining their sales forces. The businesses' managers may find such consolidation difficult because of personal animosities or loyalties, or concerns about control. The combining of sales forces is, therefore, an opportunity for the right parent. In another example, a business may have good, but not world-class, manufacturing and logistics management skills. A parent company that has world-class expertise in those areas can help that business. (See Table 7.2 for a checklist of circumstances in which parenting opportunities can arise.)

Most businesses have parenting opportunities and could improve their performance if they had a parent organization with exactly the right skills and experience. The purpose of a parenting–opportunity analysis is to document those opportunities and estimate their significance. The analysis can be a major challenge, though, because the parent often needs a depth of expertise in the business to identify the opportunities. For example, a parent that is not expert in manufacturing might not know that a business lacked world-class manufacturing skills. Or a parent without detailed knowledge of a business's market may not be aware of the opportunity to combine sales forces.

Table 7.1 Critical success factors for a diversified food company

Success Factors	Food products	Property	Restaurant A	Restaurant B	Retail	Hotels
Product branding	★					★
Selling	★					★
Product mix management	★					
Scale and capacity utilization	★					
Business development skills		★				
Formula branding			★	★	★	
Positioning to match locality		★	★	☆	★	
Site selection		★	☆	★	★	★
Property development costs		★	☆	★		☆
Value engineering			★	★		★
Detailed operating controls			★	★	★	★
Management selection and training			★	★	★	★
Supply chain logistics	★		★	★	★	★
Low overheads	★	★	★	★	★	★

Table 7.2 Ten places to look for parenting opportunities

Size and age	Old, large, successful businesses often accumulate bureaucracies and overheads that are hard to eliminate from the inside. Small, young businesses may have insufficient functional skills, managerial-succession problems, and insufficient financial resources to ride out a recession. Are those factors relevant to the business?
Management	Does the business employ top-quality managers compared with its competitors? Are its managers focused on the right objectives? Is the business dependent on attracting and retaining people with hard-to-find skills?
Business definition	The managers in the business may have an erroneous concept of what the business should be and may consequently target a market that is too narrow or broad, or they may employ too much or too little vertical integration. The trend of out-sourcing and alliances is changing the definitions of many businesses, thus creating new parenting opportunities. Is each business in the portfolio defined to maximize its competitive advantage?
Predictable errors	Does the nature of a business and its situation lead managers to make predictable mistakes? For example, attachment to previous decisions may prevent openness to new alternatives; business maturity often leads to excessive diversification; long product cycles can encourage excessive reliance on old products; and cyclical markets can lead to overinvestment during the upswing.
Linkages	Could the business link more effectively with other businesses to improve efficiency or market position? Are linkages among units complex or difficult to establish without parental help?
Common capabilities	Does the business have capabilities that could be shared among businesses?
Special expertise	Could the business benefit from specialized or rare expertise that the parent possesses?
External relations	Does the business have external stakeholders, such as shareholders, government, unions, and suppliers, that the parent company could manage better than it does?
Major decisions	Does the business face difficult decisions in areas in which it lacks expertise – for example, entering China, making a big acquisition, or dramatically extending capacity? Would the business experience difficulty getting funding for major investments from external capital providers?
Major changes	Does the business need to make major changes in areas with which its management has little experience?

Three types of analyses can help strategists identify parenting opportunities. First, strategists list the major challenges facing a business, which are normally recorded in the business plan. Then they examine each challenge to see whether it contains a parenting opportunity. For example, one business faced two major challenges: to expand capacity in order to meet the demands of a growing segment and to lower costs by improving purchasing. The first challenge did not contain a parenting opportunity, because the business-unit managers had already successfully expanded capacity many times and would likely be able to do so again without parenting influence. However, the second challenge did contain a parenting opportunity: the business-unit managers had weak purchasing skills and had never recruited a top-ranking purchasing manager. A parent with suitable skills would be able to coach the business managers, helping them avoid pitfalls, such as offering a salary too low to attract someone with the expertise they need.

In the second type of analysis, strategists document the most important influences the parent has on the business and then judge whether those influences are addressing parenting opportunities that were not identified in the first analysis. For example, at one parent company, the central engineering function develops the technical procedures and standards for all its chemical businesses. Conversations with business-unit and central-engineering managers confirmed that having a central department develop standards addressed a parenting opportunity. The business-unit managers lacked the skills and time to become expert in technical and engineering standards. Moreover, the businesses were sufficiently similar so that technical lessons learned in one situation could be applied to others. Central engineering was able to create value by helping the businesses raise technical standards.

A third kind of analysis looks at the influence different parent companies have on similar businesses to see whether they have discovered still other parenting opportunities. This step requires that managers learn about rival parent companies through public documents, individuals in those companies, or consultants and industry observers. Frequently, rivals share information about their parenting activities, believing it to be of low commercial value.

Characteristics of the parent: assessing fit

The next step in developing a corporate-level strategy is to decide how closely the parent organization fits with the businesses in the portfolio. That involves documenting the characteristics of the parent organization, then comparing them with the critical success factors and parenting opportunities in each of the businesses.

Parenting characteristics fall into five categories:

1 the mental maps that guide parent managers;
2 the corporate structure, management systems, and processes;
3 the central functions, services, and resources;
4 the nature, experience, and skills of managers in the parent organization; and
5 the extent to which companies have decentralized by delegating responsibilities and authority to business-unit managers.

The five categories are lenses through which one can view the influences of the parent. Although the categories have obvious links and overlaps, analyzing each one separately ensures a comprehensive understanding of the parent. (See the Appendix for a fuller description of the categories.)

With a good grasp of a parent's characteristics and hence of the influence it exercises, strategists can then ask two key questions:

1 Does the parent have characteristics – that is, the skills, resources, management processes, and so forth – that fit the parenting opportunities in the business? Can the parent exploit the upside potential of the relationship?
2 Is there a misfit between the parent's characteristics and the business's critical success factors? What is the potential downside of the relationship?

The 1989 acquisition of Champion International Corporation, the spark-plug company, by Texas-based manufacturer Cooper Industries illustrates the importance of the two questions. Cooper uses a distinctive parenting approach designed to help its businesses raise their manufacturing performance. New acquisitions are 'Cooperized' – Cooper audits their manufacturing operations; improves their cost accounting systems; makes their planning, budgeting, and human resource systems conform with its systems; and centralizes union negotiations. One business manager observes, 'When you are acquired by Cooper, one of the first things that happens is a truckload of policy manuals arrives at your door.' Such hands-on parenting has been effective in transforming the cost and quality of certain kinds of manufacturing businesses.

The issue facing Cooper was whether Champion would fit with that parenting approach. For example, would Cooper's manufacturing-services department be able to add value to Champion? Manufacturing at Champion fell short of best practice, offering a major opportunity for Cooper's parenting skills. But there were some worries. Spark plugs involve ceramic manufacturing, an area about which Cooper's manufacturing-services department knew little. Moreover, Champion's factories produced millions of spark plugs annually in high-volume processors, while Cooper's manufacturing staff was most knowledgeable about slower, cell-based or batch-process operations. In addition, Champion had a number of operations outside the United States, while Cooper had less experience working in foreign countries.

To judge Champion's fit, Robert Cizik, Cooper's CEO, had to examine his company's parenting characteristics and assess the potential and risks for each one. What would be the impact of centralizing union negotiations, imposing Cooper's cost accounting processes, and so on? Cizik had to judge the net effect of all those influences.

In addition, he had to consider whether Cooper's parenting influence would be better for Champion than that of rivals. Dana Corporation, another manufacturing-oriented parent company, also spotted the opportunity at Champion. Would Cooper's impact on Champion be greater than Dana's and hence justify the premium Cooper had to pay to acquire the business in direct competition with Dana?

Impact on results: validating the judgments

One can test a company's judgments about how well its parenting characteristics fit with its businesses by examining the company's track record with different sorts of businesses. A technique we call *success and failure analysis* is a useful way of summarizing a parent's track record. The analysis involves listing important decisions and classifying each as a success, a failure, or neutral. It is often useful to group decisions by type: for example, key appointments, major capital investments, new product launches, or acquisitions. By identifying the influences of the parent and by searching for patterns of success and failure, one can identify types of situations in which the parent's influence is positive or negative. (See Figure 7.1.)

Performance analysis is yet another way of validating managers' judgments about fit. It involves reviewing the performance of each business in comparison with its competitors. Businesses with comparatively poor results are probably not benefiting from, and may be hobbled by, the parent's influence. However, strategists must exercise care in reaching such conclusions. A business may be performing well or poorly without the parent having any significant influence on it. One must be sure that the performance is due to the parent's influence before using such evidence to assess fit. The real question is whether the business is performing better or worse than it would as a stand-alone, independent company. One way to make that judgment is to compare the performance of different businesses in a company's portfolio with their par return on investment, as predicted by the Profit Impact of Market Strategies (PIMS) methodology. PIMS is a research database of detailed information on thousands of business units, submitted by participating companies. One of the uses of the database is to provide par perfor-

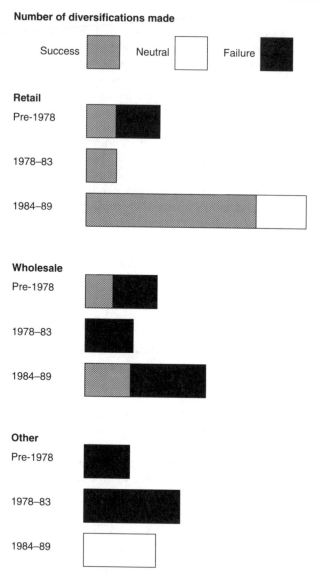

Figure 7.1 Success and failure analysis

mance statistics for a business, based on responses to a questionnaire about its structural and strategic characteristics.

Profitability that is much higher or lower than par levels is a strong indication that the parent has had an impact. However, even then, strategists must understand to what extent the unusual performance is due to the influence of the parent.

THE FIT ASSESSMENT AT BTR

BTR, one of Great Britain's most successful companies, illustrates the importance of the fit between a parent and its businesses. In the industrial manufacturing businesses that make up the bulk of BTR's portfolio, the company's characteristics fit well both with the parenting opportunities that the company is targeting and with its businesses' critical success factors. BTR has gone from strength to strength, often achieving margins on sales in the 15–20% range, while competitors settle for 5–10%.

Sir Owen Green, managing director of BTR from 1967–87, identified certain parenting opportunities in industrial manufacturing businesses. Particularly in mature niche areas, he found that businesses often underperform. Their financial information on product profitability may not tell them where they are making money and where they need to improve productivity. Their fear of losing customers may cause them to underprice, especially with larger customers. They may adopt a fill-the-factory mentality and pursue marginal sales, particularly in a recession. In an attempt to move away from mature product areas, they often diversify in a way that is wasteful.

Green learned from experience that BTR could improve those businesses' performance dramatically. For instance, by imposing a more rigorous budgeting and financial-reporting system, he encouraged business managers to pinpoint their richest profit sources, cut unnecessary costs, and achieve higher productivity. By pushing for price increases in line with or ahead of inflation, he showed managers how they could get higher prices from good customers. By focusing managers' attention on margins rather than sales, he helped managers shed the fill-the-factory mentality. By insisting on a tight business definition focused around the skills of the factory, he dissuaded managers from diversifying wastefully.

Over the years, BTR has developed parenting characteristics that fit its businesses, as described in the Appendix. Green's insights, his commitment to giving managers responsibility for meeting profit targets, and his understanding of the critical success factors in industrial manufacturing businesses are now written into the *mental maps* that guide BTR's parenting.

BTR's *structure* comprises a large number of small, tightly defined, autonomous profit centers, each with its own management team. The company's renowned profit-planning *process*, which demands detailed cost and profit information for every product line in every business, shapes its management systems. The process permits parent managers to challenge and stretch the profit targets of the businesses, to press for price increases and margin improvements, and to raise the standards of financial management throughout the company. The profit-planning process has become a powerful tool in the hands of the BTR parent managers, who have accumulated vast experience in interpreting the plans and comparing the performance of many similar profit centers.

BTR does not believe in large *central staffs* or *functional resources*. As Alan Jackson, BTR's current CEO, explains, 'It is very important to remember that each business remains separate. We certainly do not have any nonsense like central marketing or group marketing directors. We do not blunt the edges of clear business-unit focus. That would be criminal.' Corporate headquarters is small and concentrates mainly on financial control, with only 60 employees in London and similarly small groups in the corporate offices in the United States and Australia. The headquarters building is modest, and its furnishings seem to have changed little since it was built in the 1960s. The inscription on the boardroom clock epitomizes the company's culture: 'Think of rest and work on.'

The primary *skills* of the people in the parent organization involve motivating and controlling profit center managers and using the profit-planning process to improve their performance. Nearly all the BTR senior managers have long personal experience with industrial manufacturing businesses.

Finally, the *decentralization contract* gives profit center managers the freedom to make their own decisions, as long as their profit-planning ratios and bottom line are satisfactory. The parent interferes in running its businesses only when it sees ways to enhance performance.

'Our game is really in industrial manufacturing,' Jackson comments. 'We know how to set up a plant. We know how to get productivity improvements. We know how to downsize and squeeze when volumes fall.' In such businesses, BTR is good both at seeing the parenting opportunities and at understanding the critical success factors.

BTR's approach, however, fitted less well with some of the distribution businesses it obtained as part of larger acquisitions. That is not because there are no parenting opportunities to be found in cost reduction, productivity improvement, or pricing, which are BTR's forte. Rather, distribution businesses have some critical success factors that do not fit BTR's approach. 'We have found that it is much harder to downsize distribution businesses when volumes fall,' Jackson explains. The BTR approach seeks to maintain margins even when volumes decline, which is often possible in industrial manufacturing because true fixed costs are a small percentage of the total. In some distribution businesses, the approach does not work because of the relatively high fixed costs associated with maintaining a distribution network. 'As volumes fall,' Jackson says, 'we press for cost reductions, and that can be achieved only by closing depots. But closing depots causes further volume losses and weakens the rest of the network.'

The financial results also indicate a poor fit between the parent and its businesses. BTR's distribution businesses have not outperformed competitors in the same way that its manufacturing businesses typically do. In manufacturing, BTR's return on sales is frequently double that of the average competitor, while margins in distribution are closer to industry norms. 'We have been less successful away from industrial manufacturing,' Jackson says. 'Distribution businesses need a different sort of philosophy.' So he decided to divest some of BTR's distribution businesses, such as National Tyre Service in Great Britain and Texas-based Summers Group. The parenting opportunities in distribution businesses were not great enough to warrant a change in BTR's parenting approach.

The BTR example shows that fit assessments require difficult judgments about the parent's positive and negative influences. A structured analytical approach to making those judgments can help by breaking the problem into smaller elements and ensuring that analysts take all relevant aspects of the parent and the businesses into account. But analysis cannot replace judgment. Parent managers must be honest with themselves about their own strengths and weaknesses. Most companies will find they have a good fit with some portfolio businesses and a poor one with others. The challenge for the corporate strategist is to decide which changes in parenting are appropriate.

MAKING CHANGES TO IMPROVE FIT

To pull the judgments about fit together and rank a company's businesses, it helps to summarize the assessments into a matrix (Figure 7.2).

The horizontal axis of the matrix records how well the parent's characteristics fit the business's parenting opportunities – the first set of judgments made in the fit assessment. The vertical axis records the extent of any misfit between the parent's characteristics and the business's critical success factors – the second set of judgments made in the fit assessment. A good fit reduces the danger of destroying value in a business.

Each portfolio business can be located on the matrix. The matrix in our illustration plots the businesses of the diversified food company described in the table of critical success factors. Each position on the matrix has implications for the company's corporate strategy.

Heartland businesses

Businesses that fall in the top right corner should be at the heart of the company's future. Heartland businesses have opportunities to improve that the parent knows how to address, and they have critical success factors the parent understands well.

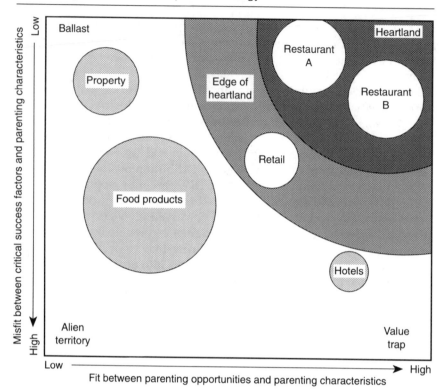

Figure 7.2 Parenting–fit matrix for a diversified food company

In the case of the two restaurant businesses in the graph, the parent provides high-quality services in property development, food purchasing, menu management, and staff scheduling. The parent also has skills in formula branding, in setting performance targets that generate above-average restaurant margins, and in designing flat structures for chain operations that keep overheads per unit to a minimum. Furthermore, the parent does not have any characteristics that will destroy value; none of its characteristics conflict with the businesses' critical success factors.

Heartland businesses should have priority in the company's portfolio development, and the parenting characteristics that fit its heartland businesses should form the core of the parent organization.

Edge-of-heartland businesses

For some businesses, making clear judgments is difficult. Some parenting characteristics fit; others do not. We call those businesses, such as the retail business in the food-company example, *edge of heartland*. The parent's skills in staff scheduling, brand management, and lean organizational structures appear to add value to the business. However, the added value is partly offset by critical success factors that fit less well with the parent. For example, the retail business requires skills in site selection and property development that are different from those required for the restaurants. The parent's influence in those areas is probably negative. With edge-of-heartland businesses, the parent both creates and destroys value. The net contribution is not clear-cut. Such businesses are likely to consume much of the parent's attention, as it tries to clarify its judgments about them and, if possible, transform them into heartland businesses.

Many edge-of-heartland businesses move into the heartland when the parent learns enough about the critical success factors to avoid destroying value. Sometimes that means changing the parent's behavior or the business's strategy, but often the solution is for the parent to learn when not to intervene and when to be sensitive to special pleas from the business.

When Unilever acquired Calvin Klein's perfume business, it adjusted its usual parenting approach to increase the potential for value creation. For instance, Unilever did not impose its famous human resource management processes on Calvin Klein, because it recognized that its managers and Calvin Klein's would not mix easily. Unilever also did not impose its marketing policies, which would have conflicted with Calvin Klein's. Calvin Klein, for instance, does not use market research to launch its upmarket perfumes in the same way Unilever does to launch mass-market products. Unilever treated Calvin Klein as a global business, while its own personal-products businesses are national or regional. To accommodate the differences between Calvin Klein and its other businesses, Unilever changed or neutralized many of its usual parenting influences and channeled most contact between the two companies through a single person.

Ballast businesses

Most portfolios contain a number of *ballast businesses*, in which the potential for further value creation is low but the business fits comfortably with the parenting approach. That situation often occurs when the parent understands the business extremely well because it has owned it for many years or because some of the parent managers previously worked in it. The parent may have added value in the past but can find no further parenting opportunities. In the food-company example, the property business fits that category. The business owns a large number of sites that are leased to third parties. The company has little potential for adding value to the business operation because it has identified no parenting opportunities. It also has little potential for destroying value because the parent managers are so familiar with the property-business issues.

Most managers instinctively choose to hold on to familiar businesses. Sometimes that is the right decision, but it should always be examined. Ballast businesses can be important sources of stability, providing steady cash flow and reliable earnings. But ballast businesses can also be a drag on the company, slowing growth in value creation and distracting parent managers from more productive activities. Moreover, there is a danger that changes in the business environment can turn ballast businesses into what we call *alien territory.*

Managers should search their ballast businesses for new parenting opportunities that might move them into heartland or edge-of-heartland territory. If that effort fails or if the parenting opportunities that are discovered fit better with a rival's characteristics, companies should divest the ballast business as soon as they can get a price that exceeds the expected value of future cash flows. Not surprisingly, that advice is difficult for most managers to take. Profitable businesses requiring little parent attention seem ideal. However, the risks of holding on to them may be substantial. Companies with too many ballast businesses can easily become targets for a takeover.

Alien-territory businesses

Most corporate portfolios contain at least a smattering of businesses in which the parent sees little potential for value creation and some possibility of value destruction. Those businesses are alien territory for that parent. Frequently, they are small and few in a portfolio – the remnants of past experiments with diversifications, pet projects of senior managers, businesses acquired as part of a larger purchase, or attempts to find new growth opportunities. But, in the food-company example, the largest business – food products – fits partly into alien territory, even though it is the company's original core business. The industry has become international, so the national business has become less competitive. The parent's managers have little international experience and have mostly come up through the restaurant side of the company. Their influence is more likely to destroy than to create value in the business.

Managers normally concede that alien-territory businesses do not fit with the company's parenting approach and would perform better with another parent. Nevertheless, parent managers often have reasons for not divesting them: the business is currently profitable or in the process of a turnaround; the business has growth potential, and the parent is learning how to improve the fit; there are few ready buyers; the parent has made commitments to the business's managers; the business is a special favorite of the chairman; and so forth. The reality, however, is that the relationship between such businesses and the parent organization is likely to be destroying value. They should be divested sooner rather than later. The company in our example should sell its food-products business to an international food company.

Companies need to be clear about their heartland before they can recognize alien territory. They also need to be clear about their alien territory in order to recognize their heartland. Hence, as companies describe their heartland businesses, they will give as many negative criteria – which are alien-territory criteria – as they do positive ones. For example, here is how managers at Cooper Industries describe their heartland: manufacturing businesses, metal-based manufacturing in particular rather than service or assembly; businesses with proprietary products and strong technology; cell-based manufacturing, not continuous process; businesses whose marketing and distribution costs are less than manufacturing costs; businesses with strong market positions; businesses large enough to support Cooper's overhead; and businesses with no intractable environmental or union problems. The criteria help Cooper strategists sort among heartland, edge-of-heartland, and alien-territory businesses and improve their acquisition and divestment decisions. Cooper has exited a number of businesses that did not fit its criteria. Most recently, it proposed divesting its original business – oil tools.

Value-trap businesses

Parent managers make their biggest mistakes with *value-trap businesses*. They are businesses with a fit in parenting opportunities but a misfit in critical success factors. The potential for upside gain often blinds managers to the misfit – that is, downside risks.

In the food-company example, the hotel business is a value trap. The parent believed its restaurant and retail skills would bring success in the hotel business. Management initially saw it as an edge-of-heartland experiment, with parenting opportunities in food purchasing, property-development costs, and performance benchmarking. But value was destroyed in other vital areas. Hotel businesses require selling skills, referrals from other businesses, and specialized site selection. The parent's influence in those areas proved highly negative, and, five years after its acquisition, the business is probably worth half the capital invested in it.

The logic of core competence can push parent managers into value traps as they strive for growth through diversification. In Europe, many privatized utility companies have created engineering consultancies and construction companies on the basis of their competence in engineering and managing large construction projects. But the parent organizations' bureaucratic policies, planning systems, and decision processes, which are geared to their capital-intensive base businesses, proved to be severe disadvantages for the new businesses. The parents burdened their businesses with unreasonable overheads, restrained them from paying appropriate salaries, encouraged them to overspend on balance-sheet items, and prevented them from grasping market opportunities in a timely manner. What sounded like a synergistic core competence has led the parents into a value trap.

CHANGING PARENTING CHARACTERISTICS

Faced with a spread of businesses across the parenting–fit matrix, as in the graph, managers might assume that they should change the skills and resources of the parent organization in order to move all their businesses into the top right corner. Our research suggests, however, that parenting characteristics are built on deeply held values and beliefs, making changes hard to implement. Good parents constantly modify and fine-tune their parenting, but fundamental changes in parenting seldom occur, usually only when the chief executive and senior-management team are replaced.

It is also difficult for parent organizations to behave in fundamentally different ways toward different businesses in their portfolios. The interlocking nature of parenting characteristics, pressures for fair and equal treatment of all businesses, and deeply held attitudes all mean that a parent tends to exert similar influences on all its businesses. Alan Jackson's recognition of the difficulties likely to arise from treating BTR's distribution and manufacturing businesses differently persuaded him to sell the distribution businesses rather than compromise the corporate philosophy.

Companies are coming to understand that it is often easier to change the portfolio to fit the parent organization than to change the parent organization to fit the businesses. That realization accounts for the rise in demergers and corporate-level break-ups. ICI, for example, chose to divide into two portfolios rather than attempt to be a good parent to businesses with widely different parenting needs.

The process we have described is a structured means of creating corporate-level strategy. Critical-success-factor analysis identifies areas in which the parent's influence is inappropriate. Parenting-opportunity analysis focuses attention on the upside potential. The parenting–fit matrix ranks the businesses, exposing those with lower levels of fit.

The most immediate benefit that companies receive from such analyses is identifying misfits. With that knowledge, they start to reduce the impact of bad parenting techniques and exit alien-territory businesses.

Additional value creation comes from focusing on the best parenting opportunities and developing the parenting skills to match. But it is a long-term challenge requiring the parent to learn new skills. Moreover, maintaining fit is a dynamic process. As the needs of the businesses change, the parent organization must continually review its behavior and its portfolio of businesses.

Companies without sound corporate-level strategies gradually lose strength and fall prey to hostile predators or become emaciated from periodic downsizing and cost cutting. Excessive overhead consumes profits, businesses that do not fit lose ground to competitors, and decisions are guided by the wrong criteria. Management fads, cash availability, or business-level performance – rather than parenting fit – influence acquisition decisions. Bureaucratic tidiness, arbitrary cost targets, or organizational politics – rather than value creation – influence changes in the parent.

Companies with sound corporate-level strategies create value from a close fit between the parent's skills and the businesses' needs. The best companies, however, do more. They strive to be the best parents for the businesses they own – to create more value than rivals would. They are on a quest for parenting advantage.

Just as the concept of competitive advantage has been one of the greatest contributors to clearer thinking about business-level strategy, we believe the concept of parenting advantage can achieve the same for corporate-level strategy. Parenting advantage not only drives planning; it also helps executives make decisions. Will an acquisition, divestment, corporate function, coordination committee, reporting relationship, or planning process enhance parenting advantage? If not, it should be reexamined and new ideas generated.

APPENDIX: UNDERSTANDING THE PARENT

To understand the parent organization, we recommend a systematic review of its characteristics in five categories:

1. The parent's *mental maps* are the values, aspirations, rules of thumb, biases, and success formulas that guide parent managers as they deal with the businesses. Mental maps shape the parent's perception of opportunities to improve business performance. They embody its understanding of different types of businesses. They underlie the knee-jerk reactions and intuitive assumptions of the parent. Usually, they reflect deeply held attitudes and beliefs and are based on managers' personal experiences. A manager with 20 years of experience in commodity chemicals will have very different maps from one who has spent 20 years in fashion retailing.

2. The parenting *structures, systems,* and *processes* are the mechanisms through which the parent creates value. The number of layers in the hierarchy, the existence of a matrix, the appointment processes, human resource systems, budgeting and planning processes, capital-approval systems, decision-making structures, transfer-pricing systems, and other coordination or linkage mechanisms are all important aspects of parenting. The design of structures and processes is important, but more particular to each company is how managers interact within the structure or process.

3. Corporate *staff departments* and *central resources* should support line management's efforts to create value. Some parents have large central functions, some as few as possible. Resources, such as patents held by the parent, the corporate brand, special government relationships, or access to scarce property or financial assets, can also be important characteristics. The potential for central staffs and resources to create value depends on the circumstances in each business: a large manufacturing-services staff may be helpful for one business but completely unnecessary or damaging for another.

4. Parents often create value because they have *people* with unique *skills*. The parent's mental maps will likely overlap with the expertise in functions and services. Yet neither of those characteristics sufficiently emphasizes the importance of key individuals in parent companies. Some corporate parents are dominated by managers, such as Jack Welch at General Electric or Allen Sheppard at Grand Metropolitan, whose personalities and skills make a critical difference. But a skilled division head or technical director can also be the parent's greatest source of value, provided his or her style, beliefs, and skills address parenting opportunities in the portfolio.

5. The *decentralization contract* between parent and business defines which issues the parent normally influences and which it delegates to business managers. It contains the authorization limits, job descriptions, and formal statements of due process. However, it is typically embedded in the culture of the company rather than fully explicit. The decentralization contract should direct the parent's attention toward those business issues to which it has something to contribute and away from those for which its influence is likely to be damaging.

Part III

Managing core competencies across business units

Core competencies and organizational capabilities are increasingly familiar concepts to managers, and the value of these ideas in strategic management is now widely recognized. With regard to multibusiness companies, the sharing of competencies and capabilities across businesses can clearly provide a justification for the existence of a multibusiness portfolio. A firm can create economic value across its portfolio of businesses when it uses its core competencies in new areas or transfers competitively important capabilities between sister businesses. In reality, few firms have proven themselves able to identify their competencies or leverage them across their businesses, and there is little practical guidance to help managers with these tasks. Much of the literature on competencies, organizational learning and skill sharing is still at the theoretical stage, with researchers only beginning to explore the validity of this approach in practice. In a recent *Harvard Business Review* article, Cynthia Montgomery and David Collis acknowledged this dilemma when they wrote 'How many companies have developed a statement of their core competencies and then have struggled to know what to do with it?'[1]

To help fill this gap, our aim has been to find readings which help managers understand 'what to do' with these concepts. In this section, we have chosen readings which explore the practical tasks of managing and communicating skills across business units. The articles included here are based on research at many companies, including exemplars such as Canon, Matsushita, and 3M. Each of the authors aims to provide guidance on how competencies can be nurtured and shared across business units within the same organization.

'Building Core Skills' is by Andrew Campbell and Michael Goold, founding directors of the Ashridge Strategic Management Centre. The Strategic Management Centre's research and consulting work has been especially concerned with the role of headquarters in managing large diversified businesses. In this piece, the authors address an issue which is central to leveraging competencies: how can diversified, decentralized companies – the most common model for Western firms – manage the corporation's skill base effectively? Beginning in the 1980s, many firms downsized and even dismantled corporate functions, delegating more responsibility to business units. Campbell and Goold explore how this restructuring has changed the role of the corporate centre in managing competencies, and provide a framework to help headquarters' managers understand different approaches.

Campbell and Goold's work is based on their research at companies such as Mars, Shell, Unilever and 3M. In this article, the authors use the phrases 'core skills' and 'key business skills' rather than 'competence' or 'capability', but the concepts are similar.[2] Like core competencies, key business skills are important in delivering a chosen strategy and succeeding against competitors. Key business skills are also ones which are relevant across a portfolio of businesses. The first problem of corporate management is deciding which business skills are key. The authors argue that broadly defined skills such as 'marketing' or 'coating technology' are too general to be useful. They advocate breaking down each key business skill into its components and subcomponents. The 'skill tree' is a tool managers can use to identify the critical components of skills, and to recognize how superior know-how in specific areas can lead to competitive advantage. The corporate centre must have this depth of understanding to help the businesses develop and share their competitively important know-how.

Once the centre has identified key skills and their underlying components, the question becomes how best to encourage the development of superior know-how and transfer it across business units. In their research, Campbell and Goold discovered that firms have various approaches to sharing competencies. They discuss five generic approaches: stimulating the network, promoting central developments, co-ordination of common solutions, imposing best practice and creating a company way. Decisions about which approach to use depend on a company's own culture and also on its commercial imperatives. For example, in a company where business unit independence is highly valued, the most appropriate approach to transferring best practice may be to stimulate the network, ensuring that local managers are aware of developments elsewhere in the firm. In cases where standardization of routines is critical, the centre may take a more active role, imposing best practice on the business units. Often, Campbell and Goold observe, companies use a variety of approaches, managing different competencies in different ways.

Campbell and Goold support the contention that the corporate centre must take responsibility for managing competencies across business units, but they argue that there is no 'one best way' to do this. In seeking to manage core skills successfully, corporate managers must focus on two tasks: identifying correctly the critical know-how that is relevant in different businesses and selecting a suitable approach to ensure this know-how is leveraged across business units.

The role of the corporate centre in managing competencies is also investigated by Anil K. Gupta and Ilkka Eerola in 'Knowledge Creator vs. Knowledge Broker: Corporate Roles in Technology Development in Diversified Firms'. The authors focus on technology development, but they argue that this is an important issue for every company because no industry today can be considered technologically mature. Gupta and Eerola reiterate some of the main themes in the literature on core competencies: they urge managers to perceive their firms as portfolios of technologies as well as portfolios of businesses, they encourage managers to find ways of exploiting similar technologies in different products and businesses, and they see the development of future capabilities as a critical management task. Their paper explores the ways in which a headquarters carries out its responsibilities in technology development and in leveraging technologies across different business units.

The traditional structural choice for diversified firms is between centralisation and decentralisation. Gupta and Eerola describe the advantages and disadvantages of these organizational structures in terms of their effect on overall business performance and on the development of new technologies. Decentralization means that a business has greater control over its resources and it is often easier to target its development efforts at market needs. Centralization, though, can accelerate technology development because of economies of scale, critical mass and a longer-term outlook. The authors argue that managers should not perceive corporate structure as a stark choice betwen these two alternatives. Instead, they propose a combination of approaches. By selecting the organizational approach most appropriate to the circumstances, managers can capture the benefits of both centralization and decentralization. The role of the headquarters can thus vary, with it functioning as a 'Knowledge Broker', or an intermediary in the dissemination of know-how across different businesses, or as a 'Knowledge Creator', when the headquarters assumes direct responsibility for technology development through centralized research labs. The authors encourage corporate managers to abandon 'either–or' thinking when considering the role of the corporate centre in developing and leveraging critical technologies.

In 'Intra-Firm Transfer of Best Practices', Gabriel Szulanski of INSEAD reports on the findings of a research project on the transfer of learning and competencies within organizations. Szulanski observes that many firms have opportunities to exploit internal knowledge by transferring strategically important learning from one unit to another within the firm.

His research aims to identify just how such transfers occur, and the potential problems that may impede the transfer of learning across an organization. Participating companies included Banc One, British Petroleum, Rank Xerox and Burmah Castrol.

In his study of specific best practice transfers, Szulanski identifies various stages in the process, beginning with the awareness that one unit can improve its performance by adapting a practice from another unit. Subsequent milestones are the decision to effect the transfer, the actual transfer of a practice, and the achievement of satisfactory performance by the unit adopting the new practice. For each stage in the transfer process, Szulanski identifies the mechanisms used by firms to facilitate these transfers of best practice, such as central experts or advisors, consultants, informal visits and workshops. Often, the same mechanisms are used at different stages of the transfer process. For example, firms frequently use project teams to identify the feasibility of transfers, to plan and implement transfers, and also to help integrate the practice within a unit.

Szulanski's framework helps managers understand the complexity of the transfer process, and the kinds of managerial interventions required to make such transfers successful. This research also identifies some of the barriers that prevent organizations from leveraging their existing knowledge and competencies across different units. The characteristics and motivation of both the source and recipient of the practice, the relationship between the two units, and the organizational context can all contribute to – or undermine – the transfer of learning and best practice within an organization.

The remaining readings in this section are case studies on how learning and competencies are managed in specific companies. Much of the detailed research in this area has focused on cross-functional learning and multi-site skill sharing. This research is relevant to multibusiness companies as well, inasmuch as the findings help us to understand how capabilities are developed and diffused in an organization. We have, therefore, included a case study of Chaparral Steel by Dorothy Leonard-Barton of the Harvard Business School because it provides an excellent description and analysis of organizational learning. The author's special interests are in issues of corporate learning in technology transfer situations, and in learning as a competence. In 'The Factory as a Learning Laboratory', included here, Leonard-Barton explores the development of a new method of producing steel beams at Chaparral Steel. Chaparral succeeded in this invention because it was able to integrate its own expertise with that of five different companies around the world. This innovation is just one of many achievements at the company, which has a world-class reputation for quality, technological leadership and high productivity.

Chaparral's success at innovation is all the more remarkable because the company has no research laboratory or development function: the factory itself fulfils these functions. All employees, from the shop floor to administration, assume responsibility for continuous improvements, innovations and learning. Leonard-Barton describes how learning at Chaparral Steel is reinforced by management practices and strong company values. The management hierarchy is flat, and egalitarianism is an important value within the company. Employees are expected to be problem-solvers and innovators. The company demonstrates its commitment to these values in concrete ways. All workers are on a salary rather than hourly rates, and lay-offs are avoided by a degree of under-staffing. There are opportunities for on-the-job study and apprenticeships, and a generous travel budget allows many employees at all levels to attend conferences, visit suppliers and make benchmarking visits to other manufacturers. The company's informality and its purposefulness encourages internal networking and the diffusion of knowledge. Chaparral also supports external networking and continuous environmental scanning, to ensure its knowledge of products and processes is completely up to date.

Chaparral's learning system cannot simply be imitated by other companies; indeed, the CEO comments that he can take competitors around the plant and show them almost '*everything* and we will be giving away *nothing* because they can't take it home with them'. Leonard-Barton argues that, while the details of Chaparral's learning capability are unique, the underlying principles are relevant to other corporations, including those much larger than Chaparral. She concludes that international competition and the need for speedier innovation will force many more companies to improve their learning capabilities, and that this can be done by integrating learning skills, management procedures and values.

The following reading, 'Creating Knowledge in Practice', is by the Japanese academics Ikujiro Nonaka and Hiro Takeuchi. The reading is a chapter from their book, *The Knowledge-Creating Company*.[3] In this chapter, the authors explore the development of a bread-making machine at Matsushita Electric Industrial Company to illustrate how an innovation is created within a business, the impact of the innovation on other businesses in the portfolio and indeed on the overall corporate strategy.

Nonaka and Takeuchi's research at Matsushita provides insights into how competencies are built in the first instance. They call the process of building new competencies 'knowledge-creation', and it involves organizational structure and processes, corporate culture and values as much as technological change and product innovation. In the 1980s, several of Matsushita's home appliance businesses, including rice cookers, food processors, toaster ovens and hot plates, were competing in mature markets with low growth. The company combined three of these businesses to gain some economies of scale and also to encourage innovation by combining the technology and know-how of the different businesses. This restructuring was not immediately successful, as each of the businesses had its own culture and perspectives. As the authors explain, 'It almost seemed as though they spoke different languages'. To overcome these problems, Matsushita strove to improve communications through planning conferences, newsletters and committees. The authors characterise these efforts as 'enabling conditions' that set the stage for product innovation. The new Cooking Appliances Division eventually decided to develop a bread-making machine, which depended on combining existing technologies from the businesses and on developing a new technology for kneading bread dough. One of the team members apprenticed herself to a master baker in order to learn the 'secrets' – or tacit knowledge – of kneading dough, and then conveyed her knowledge to the divisional engineers who were successful in creating a mechanism which duplicated the actions of kneading.

The bread-making machine was a great success, in both Japan and America, and this accomplishment had an impact on other divisions of the company. The authors explain how the development processes and values of the Home Appliance Division were transmitted to other parts of the company, inspiring product innovations in TV sets, audiovisual equipment and other areas. At the corporate level, Matsushita worked to establish a new vision for the company, based on the concept of 'human electronics' and setting challenging performance goals. There were also organisational changes. Matsushita eliminated its business group system, whose purpose was to co-ordinate product development and marketing across divisions, because it interfered with the autonomy necessary for innovation. Once the group layer was abolished, the divisions themselves took more initiative in co-ordinating their activities, through interdivisional project teams.

Nonaka and Takeuchi describe the process of developing and leveraging capabilities at Matsushita as a series of spirals, with each innovation stimulating changes elsewhere in the organization, and these changes in turn contributing to new knowledge creation. Their case study illustrates that the corporate centre must establish the 'enabling conditions' that lead to the creation of new capabilities, and also be responsive to the innovations which occur within the businesses to ensure that new capabilities can be fully leveraged across other business units.

The final reading, 'Leveraging Competencies across Businesses' is taken from *Corporate-Level Strategy* by Michael Goold, Andrew Campbell and Marcus Alexander.[4] The book examines how multibusiness companies add value to their portfolio of businesses, and also the ways in which parents destroy value through inappropriate influence on the business units. In the reading included here, the focus is on one aspect of value creation: leveraging competencies. The detailed case studies of Canon, Cooper and 3M show how corporate values, structure and processes support both the development and sharing of capabilities in these multibusiness companies.

Canon is frequently cited as one of the most successful practitioners of competence-based strategic management. Its structure is best described as a corporate 'hub' with product division 'spokes'. Most resources are considered to be owned by the company as a whole. The company uses taskforces, job rotation and other devices to sustain communication across the divisions and between the centre and the businesses. Through its organizational structure, and its large administrative and R&D staffs, Canon aims to exploit its resources fully. In particular, the company is able to combine its technologies in different ways, examplifying the idea that core competencies are ones which support various products and are relevant in different businesses. Its products cover a broad spectrum, including cameras, photocopiers, bubblejet printers, X-ray equipment and calculators.

Goold, Campbell and Alexander emphasize that Canon's success is based on more than shared technologies in its businesses. While Canon has many different businesses in its portfolio, the company's largely organic growth has meant that the centre has developed a sound understanding of these different businesses. Furthermore, the businesses share not only core technologies but other key characteristics as well, such as the use of multiple sales channels, and these similarities simplify the management task of the corporate parent. Canon has therefore largely avoided the value destruction that often occurs when the corporate parent lacks a feel for its businesses. It is Canon's proficiency in developing and sharing core technologies, combined with its skill and experience in managing a diverse portfolio, that underpin the company's success.

The case studies of Cooper Industries and 3M demonstrate that Western companies can also successfully manage competencies across business units, albeit using a different approach. As Goold, Campbell and Alexander explain, Cooper and 3M rely on powerful central functions to leverage their capabilities across autonomous divisions. At Cooper, the corporate Manufacturing Services department is a centre of excellence, with expertise in different manufacturing technologies. The Manufacturing Services department acts as an internal consultant to existing businesses, sharing its knowledge and improving manufacturing practice throughout the company. The department is also active in assessing and improving newly acquired businesses. Cooper further leverages its manufacturing capabilities through its divisional structure, which groups together businesses which can share resources and know-how.

At 3M, it is the technical function that ties together the divisions and disparate businesses. Each division has its own laboratories which are responsible for product development, and the central technical function ensures that these divisional labs are well managed. A laboratory audit process not only maintains standards, but contributes to the exchange of know-how throughout the company. The central function ensures that the divisional labs have sound procedures for new product introduction, and that there are sufficient candidates for technical posts throughout the company. 3M's Technical Forum, which includes all the company's technical staff, keeps its members up-to-date on new developments and issues. The central technical function is also responsible for ensuring that know-how and innovations are shared throughout the company, a goal which is well supported by the company's values and culture.

The case studies of Matsushita, Canon, Cooper and 3M provide many insights into how successful multibusiness companies develop their core competencies and exploit them in their different businesses. It is clear from these detailed studies that it is not just the distinctive skills or competencies themselves that are important. Managing capabilities requires appropriate organizational processes, structures and values. Sharing capabilities across businesses is a complex process, and the challenge for corporate managers is to find or create approaches that will work in their own organizational context.

NOTES

1 Collis, David J. and Cynthia A. Montgomery, 'Competing on Resources: Strategy in the 1990s,' *Harvard Business Review*, July–August 1995, pp. 118–128.
2 Other writers who use the work 'skill' in a similar way include McKinsey consultants Irvin and Michaels ('Core skills: Doing the right things right', *McKinsey Quarterly*, Summer 1989) and Tom Peters ('Strategy Follows Structure: Developing Distinctive Skills', *California Management Review*, vol. XXVI, No. 3, Spring 1984). Consultants Klein *et al.* (Skill-Based Competiton', *Journal of General Management*, vol. 16, issue 4, Summer 1991) have coined the word 'metaskill' to emphasize that core competence is a dynamic phenomenon – i.e. the deployment of skills results in a cycle of continual learning and improvement.
3 Nonaka, Ikujiro and Takeuchi, Hiro, *The Knowledge-Creating Company*, Oxford University Press, New York, 1995.
4 Goold, Michael, Campbell, Andrew, and Alexander, Marcus, *Corporate-Level Strategy*, John Wiley & Sons, Inc., New York, 1994.

Chapter 8

Building core skills

Andrew Campbell and Michael Goold

INTRODUCTION

Decentralized companies are currently wrestling with the problem of how to manage skills and competencies across their portfolio of businesses. This paper describes how managers at the centre can define which skills they should focus on and what role the centre should take in managing them.

Prior to the 1980s, companies handled skills that were important to more than one business unit through strong central functions. Many companies had large central functions such as marketing, engineering or information technology (IT). British Petroleum, for example, had a central engineering function of more than 1,500 people as recently as the mid-1980s. These central functions set policies and standards throughout the corporation. They also controlled most of the recruitment, in particular the graduate intake, organized training and acted as skilled reservoirs for their companies.

In the 1980s, companies started to decentralize these central functions and reduce the size of corporate headquarters. Where functions were retained, their policy-making role was reduced and their service role emphasized.[1] At BP, for example, a previously strong IT function was set up as an internal consulting service, selling its expertise to the business units. Over a short period the function shrank by more than half its former size because the business units chose not to use its services.

There were a number of reasons why these changes took place. First, nimble *niche competitors* focused on specific segments of the market and took away market share from the established competitors. In response, the larger companies had to segment their business into market-focused and competitor-focused units, giving the managers of these business units the freedom to take whatever action was necessary to compete in the new environment. The increased competition from focused businesses caused large companies – most recently IBM is an example – to give more autonomy to their business unit managers and reduce the size and influence of central functions.

Second, there was a growing *perception of mismanagement by the centre.* The central functions were frequently seen as bureaucratic and unresponsive to the needs of the businesses. One business unit chief executive told us: 'The problem with central marketing is that they are always right. It is always someone else's fault. You would think we existed to serve them rather than the other way round.'

Often the centre was criticised for imposing inappropriate skills. We were told by the head of a record retailer: 'We have a completely different security problem to that of our sister company, yet we were forced to use the central security service. Their problem is mainly about shrinkage caused by customers. Our problem is staff. You can't use the same security principles to solve both problems.'

In other cases, central functions were criticized for using the wrong methods or mechanisms: they imposed central standards in situations where businesses needed flexibility to meet customer needs; they set up coordination committees between managers who had few common interests; they ran expensive conferences for managers with little to learn from each other; and they centralised the development resources and budgets in situations where variety of development efforts would have been more suitable.

A third reason for decentralization was that *skills became less scarce.* Historically, central functions had existed in part because of the scarcity of skills. But, over time, the business units were more able to do their own work in areas like engineering and IT, and external suppliers were more available in everything from catering services to corporate strategic planning. The availability of skills and competent external suppliers made central functions less necessary. They could no longer benefit the organization by acting as a skill reservoir.

Skills management neglected

The decentralization trend has undoubtedly produced net benefits. Greater freedom and accountability have promoted initiative at the business unit level, and this has resulted in increased performance. But decentralization has also had a cost. As companies decentralized and reduced the control exerted by the corporate centre, they have used 'lateral linkages', such as informal networking and corporate-wide projects, to replace the central functions.[2] For example, when Electrolux acquired businesses in the white goods industry with the intention of developing an international strategy, it did not centralize any functions. Instead it set up formal coordination in four product areas, networking mechanisms to encourage cross-fertilization, and five corporate-wide projects designed to improve operating performance.

However, for many companies, these lateral linkages have proven harder to operate than expected. 'Horizontal planning', as Michael Porter calls it, has frequently been crowded out by vertical, strategic business unit (SBU) planning.[3] Coordinating committees and networking mechanisms have often proved time-consuming and delivered little value.[4] Business unit managers have developed an aversion to corporate projects, which they see as a distraction from their real priorities. And most personnel functions have not taken on the functional training or functional recruitment activities of the old central functions. The result of all these changes is that some important corporate skills are no longer being adequately managed.[5]

In this paper, we attempt to show that companies pursuing decentralization do not need to lose control of the management of these key skills. Based on our interviews with a sample of exemplar companies (Appendix 1), we describe a systematic approach to the management of skills that involves: (i) identifying the company's 'core skills' in detail; (ii) understanding the different roles the centre can play in developing and transferring those core skills across the business units; (iii) choosing an approach that makes commercial sense and takes into account the company's capability and natural way of working.

IDENTIFYING CORE SKILLS

The first problem facing managers in decentralized companies is to decide what skills to try to build. At one level this may be a trivial question. If the businesses in the portfolio are mainly consumer packaged goods, as in Unilever, then one of the important core skill areas is marketing. If most of the businesses are connected by common technologies, such as precision coatings and polymers, as in 3M, then a core skill area is the technology itself.

But at the level of detail needed for taking management action the identification of core skills is not straightforward. For example, within the marketing function at Unilever it is necessary to decide which marketing skills are core and which are not. For example, is consumer research a core skill area that needs to be managed? Is new product testing? Is advertising agency selection? Is product positioning? Is product packaging? And, outside of the marketing area, is sales force management a core skill that Unilever's central management should be focusing on? Is industrial selling? Is the management of multi-country retailers? Central managers need to develop a way of identifying the skill areas that will benefit the most from some central involvement in developing and transferring best practice.

To do this central managers need to understand the connection between skills and competitive advantage and the difference between the centre's role in managing the skills of a single business unit and managing core skills across business units.[6]

Understanding skills

Skills are important to competitive advantage. To succeed against competitors, each business unit needs to have a strategy for gaining advantage in the market place. Without some kind of advantage in meeting market needs a business unit cannot expect to out-perform its competitors.

Advantage can come from many different sources. Location can be a source of advantage, for example, due to lower labour costs in a particular area. Size can be a source of advantage due to economies of scale. But most sources of advantage are rooted in superior skills: the business makes better quality products, markets them better, has better salesmen and looks after the customers better, because of some superior know-how.

Few businesses have superior skills in all functions but successful businesses have a skill advantage in some functions important to the business unit's strategy. If the strategy is about quality, the unit is likely to have an advantage in manufacturing skill or in total quality management. If the strategy is about service, then the business will need to have some advantage in service skills either through designing better systems or easier to service products.

With this understanding of skills, we can draw a 'skill tree' for a business unit that links the 'key business skills' with the needs of the market place (Figure 8.1).[7] A key business skill is an activity the business needs to do particularly well to succeed with its strategy. Most strategies involve a cluster of key business skills. The confectionery businesses at Mars needs to have strong skills in volume manufacturing, quality management, product branding and new product development to succeed with their strategy of being the brand leader in the mass-market, countline-dominated, snack-food sector of the confectionery market.

Each key business skill in the cluster can be analysed further into 'components' and 'sub-components'. Components are the factors needed to perform the key business skill to a high standard. Components can be broken down into sub-components and to even finer levels of detail. Figure 8.2 is an illustrative 'Skill Component Analysis' of an important skill area in Whitbread Restaurants – delivering delightful service.

Figure 8.2 illustrates the broad range of components that make up a business skill. Some components are inanimate, such as the quality of the parking facilities or the quality of the ambience. Others depend on the

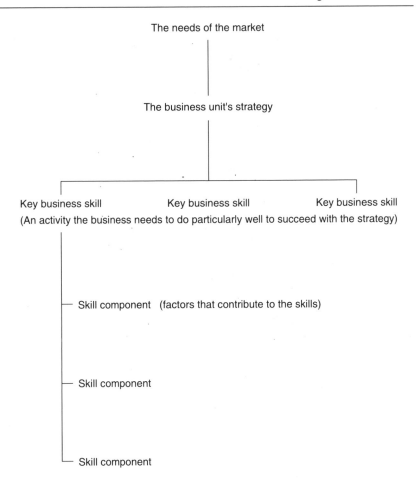

Figure 8.1 Skill tree

skills of individuals or teams such as the greeting of guests or the waitering. The way we are using the phrase business skill is, therefore, slightly different from the normal use of the work skill. A business skill is something the business, as a whole, does well whether it is because of the skills of the employees or because of inanimate factors such as the layout of the work floor or the quality of the materials being used.

Each component of a business skill depends on know-how. If the component is a skill such as waitering, the know-how may be embedded in the individual waiters or waitresses. If the component is inanimate like the size of the menu, the know-how is likely to be codified as recorded knowledge (e.g. a menu becomes daunting if it has more than 25 items on it). In any business skill there are a large number of components each of which depend on elements of know-how. It is,

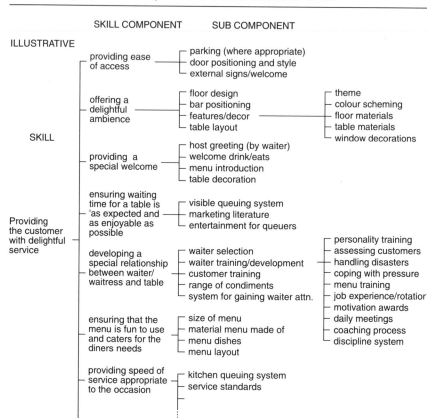

Figure 8.2 Skill component analysis

therefore, the management of the know-how that is critical to success-fully managing business skills.

Some components are more important than others: they have a greater impact on the overall performance of the business skill. We can call these key components: components where the quality of the know-how can have a big impact on the overall performance. It is through these key components that a business can gain competitive advantage. By developing know-how that is superior to competitors a business can gain advantage.

At this point it is worth taking stock of the new language we are developing to understand skills. It consists of 'key business skills', 'skill components and sub-components', 'key components' and 'superior know-how'. The last two terms need further explanation.

Key components are those components which are critical to the building of a superior skill. Key components are the components where the company has or can develop some proprietary know-how, some superior ability or knowledge that is not widely used by its competitors. Most of the components of a business skill will be performed to a reasonable standard by most competitors. For example, most family restaurants serve reasonably good food on clean plates on clean tables in a restaurant that is not overcrowded. The difference between unusual service and the average does not lie in these standard components. It is the key components such as the behaviour of the waiter that distinguish between average and excellent service.

Of course businesses can have weaknesses even in standard components and part of the management task is to reduce the impact of weaknesses. However, as we will make clear later, it is through focusing on key components and on creating superior know-how that a group of companies can build competitive advantage across its portfolio of businesses.

The thesis that we are presenting is, therefore, that understanding skills at a business unit level involves defining 'key business skills' and pin pointing the 'key components or sub-components' where 'superior know-how' can give the business a competitive advantage.[8]

Managing skills from the centre

In many companies the strategic planning process is used to clarify the key business skills and to give the centre an opportunity to assess how the business unit is planning to develop its skills. In more advanced companies strategic controls are being developed to measure a business unit's performance in key areas.[9] The centre can, therefore, use a combination of planning processes and control procedures to make sure that the business units are devoting the necessary attention to their key business skills. The centre can audit the business unit's plan to make sure it will keep them ahead of competitors.

The management and building of 'core skills' across the portfolio of business units is a different process which requires a different role from the centre. 'A core skill' is a key business skill that is 'relevant' in a number of businesses in the portfolio (say at least a third) – property development in Whitbread Restaurants, component purchasing in Philips UK, colour mixing of paints in Courtaulds Protective Coatings, site selection in Shell's Automotive Retailing businesses. These are all key business skills for individual business units.

These skills are 'relevant' to sister companies in the portfolio, because they have 'key components' in common. It is rare that a key business skill is identical across a number of businesses: if the businesses are in different countries the markets and cultures are different; if the businesses are in the same country but in different products, then the technologies and customers will be slightly different. As a result, it is not common for a skill to be relevant in its entirety. A skill is normally relevant because it has key components in common and, in particular, because the superior know-how developed in one business can be used in the other businesses.

Where core skills exist, in other words where the businesses have key components in common, the centre has a role in managing the superior know-how that the businesses share. In these circumstances (Appendix B) the centre has a role that goes beyond just making sure that each business has a work plan for keeping ahead of competitors. The centre has a role in helping the businesses work together to speed up the development of know-how and ensure that the benefits are spread to the other business units.

THE CENTRE'S ROLE IN BUILDING CORE SKILLS

Building core skills involves managing the development and transfer of best practice in key skill components that are common across business units. Success comes from focusing on transferable best practice and the know-how that lies behind it. Skill trees and skill component analysis, defined in the previous section, are useful tools to help managers identify key skill components that involve transferable know-how.

The management of these key components involves making choices about how to develop proprietary know-how and how to transfer the benefits across the business units. In our fieldwork we observed that companies chose different central roles for different components. These different roles are based on different levels of involvement in both the *development process* and the *transfer process*, and we were able to define five *generic approaches to managing core skills*.

The development process

Proprietary know-how is the basis of superiority in a business unit's key business skills. It is normal, therefore, for business units to invest in the development of the know-how involved in the key components. With a portfolio of businesses with similar key components, development of know-how can be occurring in all of the businesses simultaneously. The centre's role in this development process is to decide whether to interfere with the decentralised decision making of the separate business units.

At one extreme the centre can decide to remain detached from the development process allowing business units to carry out local development work against their local agendas and priorities. At the other extreme the centre can choose to take charge of development to gain from the benefits of economies of scale, to eliminate duplication or to ensure that sufficient money is spent. In between these extremes are many intermediate positionings in which the centre seeks to coordinate the work being carried out in different units. For example, in a company with a portfolio of retail businesses, development work on retail operating systems could be carried out centrally through a central systems unit; it could be done separately by each business developing enhancements to their existing systems; it could be done by a lead business with the intention of transferring the developments to other businesses; or it could be done by a combination of businesses working together or working with the centre.

In practice there are many variations and combinations. In some cases, the resources are located in the centre, reporting to a central functional manager, yet many of the development projects are commissioned and directed by the business unit managers. In other cases, the development work is carried out in the business units, but under the direction of a central development manager. By judging which manager had final authority over both the size and direction of development work we are able to develop a classification of the degree of centralization of the development process.[10]

The transfer process

The way in which the benefits of know-how are transferred across business units depends upon the nature of the know-how. If the know-how is embedded in the innate skills of individuals or teams, then the benefits of the know-how can be transferred by creating a central service built round these innate skills, by developing and transferring skilled individuals or by transferring the know-how involved in selecting, training and developing the skilled individuals. If the know-how is in the form of codified knowledge, it can be transferred by simple communication.

What we have observed is that the main concern of the centre is not so much the choice of mechanisms for transferring the benefit, but rather the choice of the degree of pressure the centre should exert to ensure that the transfer occurs.

The minimum level of pressure is where the centre seeks to make the less competent units aware of the know-how and skills available elsewhere, allowing the business unit managers to decide for themselves which mechanisms of transfer to use and how far to take advantage of the know-how. This can be done by creating networks of managers in different units, by newsletters and face to face communication and even by offering expert help or services from the centre.

The maximum level of pressure is where the centre demands that the business units use the benefits of the available know-how and act quickly to discipline managers who are slow to respond. This can be done by issuing policy instructions, insisting on certain performance standards, removing reluctant managers and setting up central functions to carry out the activities concerned.

In between these two extremes, there are many other positionings. The centre can exert pressure to transfer the benefits of know-how by vigorously challenging the managers in business units, applying peer pressure through committees or task forces and supplying performance data and benchmarks to embarrass the poor performers.

Five generic approaches to managing core skills

To simplify the data we collected, we developed a matrix: one axis represents the degree of central control in the development process, the other represents the level of pressure used by the centre in the transfer process (Figure 8.3).[11] As we plotted company examples on

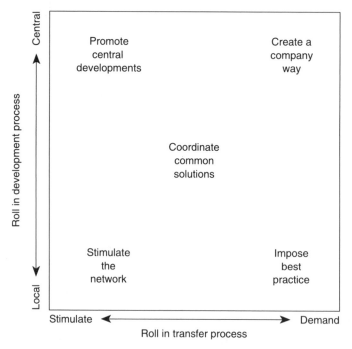

Figure 8.3 The role of the centre in managing core skills

this matrix, we identified five generic roles for the centre in managing core skills: 'stimulate the network', 'promote central developments', 'coordinate common solutions', 'impose best practice' and 'create a company way'.[12]

- *Stimulating the network* is the central role that requires least involvement. Development is decentralized and uncoordinated. The centre may stimulate development by encouraging business units to spend money on the area. But it does not attempt to control either the size of expenditure or the direction of development. Know-how is transferred between units through formal and informal networks. The centre will stimulate these networks by sharing information and creating opportunities for managers to meet each other. But the centre will not put pressure on individual businesses to take up know-how or best practice developed in other parts of the group. In decentralized companies the majority of key skill components are managed in this way because stimulating the network is the role that involves the least interference from the centre.
- The centre may decide to *promote central developments* in order to encourage the transfer of know-how that has been developed centrally. Even though the centre will have decided the size of the development budget and directed individual development projects, central managers may prefer to allow business unit managers to make their own decisions about whether to use these developments in their own businesses. It is common for the centre to take on this role for key components that involve scientific research and central laboratory work. For example, 3M has Technical Centres which are centrally controlled laboratories focusing on a technology with group-wide relevance. These laboratories have responsibility for advancing the technology. But they have no power to pressure divisions to use the technology they develop.
- *Coordinating common solutions* is a central role that involves working closely with business units on both development and transfer. Many cases fit this middle ground, where development efforts are jointly conceived and directed and the centre puts pressure on businesses that are slow to take up the new developments. The know-how advances that resulted in the deodorant Axe were developed by the French subsidiary of Unilever Personal Products as a result of a product concept brief defined by the centre. The centre then worked closely with other European countries to roll out the benefits of this know-how and attempted to persuade countries to stick closely to the original AXE concept. The centre and the French subsidiary continue to work together to refine the 'product instructions' based on experience and further know-how developments throughout Europe.

We noted that it is unusual for the centre to attempt to coordinate development work without also seeking to pressure businesses to implement the results of the development. It is also unusual for the centre to pressure businesses to accept skills and know-how from other business units without also seeking to influence the development efforts. As a result 'coordinating common solutions' is a role that covers all of the central ground in our matrix.

- *Imposing best practice* is not a common role. We did however identify a few cases where the centre imposed know-how when it had not directed the development work. Companies adopt this approach when the centre discovers big discrepancies in performance in a skill area that is easily documented. For example, at Whitbread Restaurants, the centre noted that its Pizza Hut subsidiary was benefiting from have clearly defined quality standards for customer service. So it imposed this practice on the other restaurant chains. The centre did not impose particular standards. It imposed the policy that each restaurant should have defined standards. In other words it imposed a management process that was easy to document. We have found that this role – imposing best practice – is most common in manufacturing and operating areas, particularly where the know-how is in the form of codified knowledge.
- The final approach, *creating a company way*, involves the centre controlling development work and imposing methods and standards on the organization. It is a common role for the management of know-how in the finance and personnel functions and it is also widely used on issues where there is an additional benefit from consistency and standardization – for example in the know-how connected with brand names. The use of the Shell logo is centrally controlled by managers in the marketing division. They issue policy guidelines on what is allowed and what is not allowed and they control development work on how to improve the logo and the way it is used.

In many skill areas such as marketing or process engineering it is not possible to document policies and standards that can be written down and imposed. Nevertheless, we found many examples in these less easily documented skills areas where the centre had 'created a company way' of doing things. For example, one of 3M's key skill components is the way managers, passionately committed to their ideas, bootleg resources to pursue projects that have not been funded in the development budget. This is not a skill that can be documented in methods and standards. Yet it has become a 3M company way, jealously guarded by central management and symbolized by the 15% rule – managers are allowed 15% of their time to pursue projects of their own choosing. The 'company way' has been created by managing values and cultural norms rather than through policy statements and instructions.

As we documented company examples, we noticed that the centre can take on different role for different key business skills and even for different key skill components (Figure 8.4). The central role at 3M differs for different skills. New product marketing skills are highly decentralised: the centre 'stimulates the network'. Coating technology is more centralized: the centre 'promotes central developments' in certain areas where it has designated a Technology Centre. Even within a key business skill such as the management of development laboratories the centre takes on a different role for different components. The way the centre becomes involved in the know-how concerned with the process of defining projects could be to promote central developments. The know-how involved in monitoring projects could be managed by imposing best practice. At each further level of detail the choice of how the centre manages know-how can differ by sub-component.[13]

CHOOSING A CENTRAL ROLE FOR EACH KEY COMPONENT

Having identified the key skill components and understood the different options, the company can set about choosing the most suitable central role for managing each component. During our research we had hoped to be able to specify what central role would be most appropriate for each type of skill component. However, the evidence from our research sample indicated that there was no stable link between the type of skill component and choice of central role. The choice of central role seemd to depend more on the culture of the company than the component. Both Mars and Unilever have brand management skills; yet they manage similar skill components in very different ways with equal effectiveness. In Mars the know-how involved in selecting advertising agencies is managed by stimulating the network. In Unilever Personal Products, on the other hand, it is managed by creating a company way. We realized that each company has an established way of working and an established role for the centre on most issues. It is not that one is better than the other. Both companies have found ways to make their system work well.

We realized, therefore, that companies need to ensure that the approach they choose takes account of the established ways of working – what we have called *cultural constraints*. These constraints needs to be balanced with the *commercial needs of the business* and *tensions* that occur between the two need to be managed sensitively.

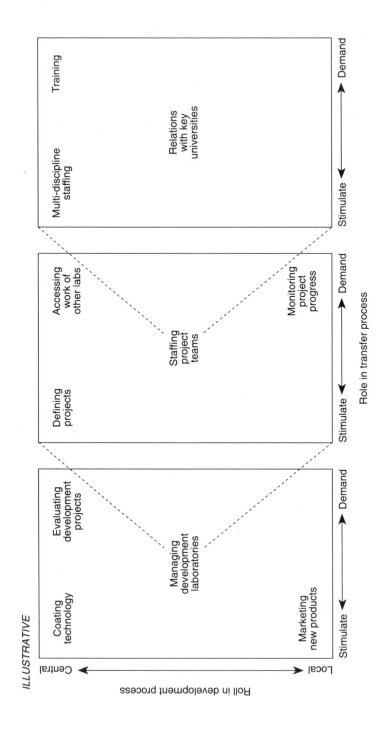

Figure 8.4 The role of the centre

Cultural constraints

The centre's established roles are influenced by the policies it has taken in the past on decentralization and involvement. The established roles are mainly informal, based on understandings that have developed between managers over time and precedents that have been set in the past. When taken together, the centre's established roles amount to an informal 'decentralization contract'.[14] If it were possible to write them all down, these established roles would define in detail the way the centre is expected to get involved in or remain detached from all aspects of the business.

We realized that it is this decentralization contract that is the most potent force in the choices managers make about how to manage a particular skill component. Instinctively managers in Mars or Shell or Whitbread ask themselves 'if I interfere on this issue will it contravene the principles of decentralization and autonomy we subscribe to', or 'what is the usual way that we handle this kind of an issue?'.

Moreover, these instincts appear to make sense. From looking at cases of failure, cases where attempts to centralize development or impose know-how had been blocked, we noted that a major cause was resistance by unit managers who believed that the centre was 'interfering'. These decentralization contracts appear to exist in the minds of managers, and unless explicitly renegotiated, the existing contract acts as a barrier to changes in the central role. The current decentralization contract is a 'constraint' of the organization that should be taken into account when choosing the centre's role.

Commercial imperatives

But we also noted other influences on the choice of central role, influences relating to the market place, technology and competitive dynamics. These influences we have called 'commercial imperatives' – commercial reasons that make it imperative that either the development process or the transfer process is managed in a particular way. For example, the amount of money needed for research to advance know-how is frequently much greater than any one business unit can afford. By centralizing development work the company can afford bigger projects and gain from economies of scale. Information technology is one area where the need to centralize development is increasing as the costs of writing software rise. Perversely, the pressure to centralize software development is increasing at a time when many IT functions are being decentralized. The tension being created by these two trends is likely to slow down know-how development in one of the functions that has the greatest potential for creating new core skills. For companies where IT is a potential source of advantage, choosing the appropriate development approach is vital to future competitive success.

Commercial imperatives can also exist for the transfer process. In situations where standardization is important to commercial success the transfer of know-how must be imposed by the centre. Accounting firms, for example, need to be able to offer identical services from different country partnerships to large multi-national companies. Standardization is particularly important in the audit service. As a result, international accounting firms such as Price Waterhouse have standard audit manuals used by each of the different partnerships, and a central technical function whose role is to approve changes to the manuals and support development initiatives. The central technical function imposes know-how transfer in order to ensure common audit standards in different partnerships.

Appendix C provides a list of the factors that managers should consider when deciding whether there are any commercial imperatives that limit the choice of central role. Thus for each skill component, management must choose a central role based on any commercial imperatives that relate to the component; and, any restrictions arising from the cultural constraints. Figure 8.5 is a model designed to help managers focus on these two dimensions – commercial imperatives and cultural constraints.

Managing tensions

In many situations the centre can choose a role that meets the needs of the commercial imperatives and does not clash with its cultural constraints. In these situations the decision about how to manage the skill component is easy to make.

But in some situations the imperatives and the constraints point towards different solutions – there is a tension between the role the centre should take to maximise performance and the role the centre should take to fit in with the established organization rules of behaviour. The trite answer to this tension is for central managers to change the rules. In practice, a much more politically astute solution needs to be found because, without the support of business unit managers, all efforts to manage skill components will fail.

Tensions between imperatives and constraints occur in a limited number of predictable situations (Appendix D). To illustrate the challenge of managing these tensions we will examine one situation in detail – product internationalization. In this situation the product is becoming more international, making product and marketing know-how in one country more relevant to other countries. But in prior years, companies in different countries will have operated independently and frequently the

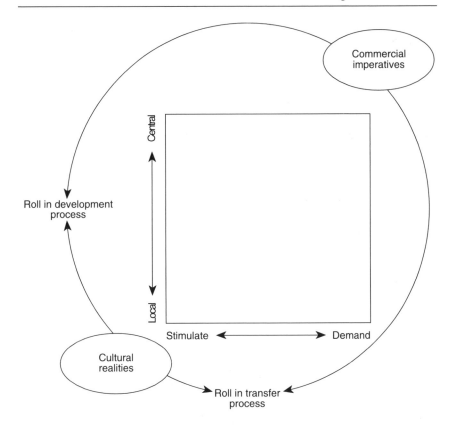

Figure 8.5 Choosing a management approach: Imperatives and Realities Model

companies may not have been part of the same organization. Where independence has been high, the established decentralization contract will only allow the centre a minimal role: development will have been decentralized and few networks for transferring know-how will exist.

But the commercial forces of internationalization are making it necessary to centralize development, coordinate marketing decisions and standardise some product features. Assuming the trend to internationalization continues, the centre will need to move, over time, into a dominant role, creating a company way for most of the key skill components. The management challenge is to find a way of going from a situation where the centre has been uninvolved in know-how management to a situation where the centre dominates the management of certain critical know-how components.

We have noted three successful responses to this challenge. The first response is to avoid the problem by de-emphasizing or exiting that part of the business where the skill components need managing. This is in many cases a rational response. If the dominant organization behaviour in other parts of the company is one of high levels of decentralization, the centre may not be able, even in the medium term, to win the support of business unit managers to a change in behaviour in this product area. The company will be unable to manage the critical skill components well and will be likely to lose ground to competitors over time. Rather than follow a second best solution which could lead to loss of competitive position the company will do better to de-emphasize or exit the business.

The second response is to seek to make major changes in the existing decentralization contract by formulating a new strategy, changing the organization structure, renegotiating roles and changing managers who resist the new order. When done with determination and a grasp of the detail at the skill component level, this solution can be effective. But it is risky and highly disruptive. The centre frequently does not have sufficient grasp of the detail, individuals with unique skills or knowledge can be sidetracked or sacrificed, and the organization will take some years before it will settle into the new relationships. The track record for changes of this kind is poor.[15] While we were working with Unilever Personal Products, we were told that a major reorganization and change in the central role for the detergents businesses in Europe under the flag of 'Lever Europe' had been unsatisfactory and a new attempt to coordinate the businesses in Europe was being made only 18 months after the first attempt was announced.

The third solution to the challenge is to change gradually. The initial step in gradual change is to identify the key skill components and start managing each component in the best way possible, given the restrictions of the existing decentralization contract. These 'toe-in-the-water' initiatives serve two purposes. They help to clarify the skill component giving managers the opportunity to judge its relevance. They also begin to develop a groundswell of support for more involved management. Because the toe-in-the-water initiatives do not threaten the existing decentralization contract they do not attract political attention.

The next step in gradual change is to increase the involvement of the centre as the support for involvement develops. The centre responds to pressure from the business unit managers rather than the other way round. In Unilever Personal Products, we identified a groundswell of support from younger marketing directors and product managers for greater coordination by the centre. The need to transfer know-how quickly, to roll out new product ideas before competitors in as many countries as possible, and to standardise some product attributes to aid international recognition is apparent to these managers. Until recently the forces in favour of decentralization and independence have slowed up the transfer process and encouraged not-invented-here attitudes.

Now many of the old style managers have retired and a new breed of globally aware managers are taking their place. It is now appropriate for the centre to play a stronger coordination role in both the development of know-how and the transfer of its benefits.

The final step in gradual change is to pull together the many small changes in a new statement of the centre's role and strategy. In gradual change the definition of the strategy and appropriate working relationships come near the end of the change period rather than at the beginning.[16]

It is apparent that some situations do not allow managers time for gradual change. Major change or an exit from the business are the only choices. However, in many situations there is time: four or five years is not too long a period to make the changes. In these cases, an understanding of the existing decentralization contract and a sensitive attitude towards winning support from business unit managers will help to avoid the expensive mistakes made by so many companies.

CONCLUSION

In reality, many recent attempts by decentralized companies at building and sharing know-how have been disappointing. At Philips UK, for example, the Organisation and Efficiency (O&E) function set out to build skills in total quality management, just-in-time manufacturing and fast product development. These skill areas were clearly important to many of the business units in the UK. Yet little was actually achieved, despite the vigorous efforts of the O&E managers, and eventually the function was disbanded.

The reasons for this lack of success are instructive and by no means unusual. First, the O&E managers did not break down the skill areas mentioned into enough detail to define the key components or pinpoint the components that were relevant across the businesses. Since Philips UK business units are highly diverse, ranging from consumer products to professional products and from high-tech areas like semi-conductors to mature areas like light bulbs, few skill components were in fact relevant to the majority of business units. Second, Philips' switch from a geographic structure to a product structure during the 1980s made the role of the national organisation unclear and sapped the determination of the UK centre to take an active role in managing know-how. Without the determination of the centre the existing decentralization contract was unlikely to change. Finally the O&E managers were unable to win the attention of business unit managers to their initiatives: the business unit managers were reluctant to commit time to working with UK-based functional managers as long as the degree of control likely to be exercised by the Dutch-based division bosses was unknown. Because the business unit managers did not accept what the O&E function was trying to do little could be achieved.

The Philips example illustrates the three conditions necessary for success in building core skills: whichever role it chooses; the centre must be determined, the business unit managers must have accepted the centre's role; and the effort must be focused on key components that are relevant across business units.

At Philips today, faced with a profit crisis, nothing immediate is being done to find another way of building core skills across the UK business units. The danger is that the profit revival about to come from decentralization and increasing accountability may lead managers to believe that the centre does not need to play an active role in building core skills. If this happens, Philips will find it hard to hold its place in the world electronics industry.

Our research suggests, however, that companies pursuing decentralization do not need to lose control of the management of their core skills. To succeed in the task, managers must start by carefully analysing the components that make up core skills and that are relevant across business units. As Eero Lumatjarvi, Senior Marketing Member of Unilever Personal Products Coordination, said, 'The key is to decide which elements of the product package know-how are critical and relevant across countries. Should we focus on the colour of the bottle, the shape of the label, the brand name, etc? That is what we are trying to decide'.

Once the skill components have been chosen, the centre needs to decide how much control to retain over the development of know-how and the transfer of best practice. Heavy-handed initiatives can be worse than complete inaction. By examining the commercial forces at work and remaining sensitive to the organization's natural ways of working, the centre can choose a role that will speed up the building of core skills.

In some cases this role may involve the creation or retention of a central function to set policies and manage development budgets. In other cases it may involve no more than organizing a conference to stimulate the informal networks between managers. The choice of mechanism (e.g. central function versus functional conference) is less important than the choice of central role. In fact, for each central role a broad range of mechanisms can be effective.

In short, building core skills in an increasingly decentralized environment demands painfully detailed analysis of skill components as well as full acceptance by both the centre and the business unit managers as to how the skill components are best managed. Companies who are prepared to meet these conditions will be able to build their core skills faster than their competitors and thus maintain their competitive edge.

APPENDIX A: RESEARCH SAMPLE AND METHODS

Sample

A sample of companies were chosen on three criteria. First, companies where management were prepared to give us broad interviewing access. Second, companies where management believed they were good at transferring skills and capabilities across the portfolio. Third, companies we had reason to believe were well managed. The companies in the sample were:

- Courtaulds – Protective Coatings Division
- Mars – Confectionery Division
- 3M – Technical Division
- Philips – UK Division
- Shell – Automotive Marketing Division
- Unilever – Personal Products Division
- Whitbread – Restaurants Division

Methods

At each site we focused our interviews on one or two functional areas, choosing, in each case, a function of critical importance to the business.
   Interviews aimed to achieve three outputs:

1 Document linkage benefit stories: situations where a business unit had benefited from learning from another part of the group.
2 Record the linkage mechanisms being used by the companies to encourage skill development and transfer.
3 Understanding the commercial and organizational context in which the linkages were happening.

APPENDIX B: WHEN WILL CORE SKILLS EXIST?

The strategy of the business units are sufficiently similar that they have some key business skills in common:

- either, the same businesses in different countries;
- or, similar businesses in different markets in the same country;
- or, similar markets being served with different products.

The key business skills are sufficiently similar that they have some key components in common:

- superior know-how exists (or the potential for superior know-how) enabling at least one business unit to outperform competitors in the key business skill;

- the proprietary know-how can be used to advantage in the other businesses.

APPENDIX C: FACTORS LIKELY TO CREATE COMMERCIAL IMPERATIVES

Development process

1 Rarity of skill/resources needed for development – if rare centralization of development effort is likely to be better.
2 Economies of scale of tasks needed for development – if high then cooperative or central development is likely to be better.
3 Importance of market interaction in the development process – if it is important then decentralized processes are likely to be better.
4 Stage of know-how life cycle – in early stages a decentralized approach that encourages diverse developments are likely to be better.

Transfer process

1 Degree of further development or application work needed to use the new know-how in the local environment – if it is high then imposing know-how is likely to be inappropriate.
2 Size of performance gap between the company and its competitors – if the company's performance is substantially worse than competitiors then imposition may be necessary to retain competitiveness.
3 Degree to which standardization has commercial value – if standardization is valuable in its own right then imposition is appropriate.
4 Stage of know-how life cycle – in the maturer stages of the cycle imposition may be more appropriate.

APPENDIX D: FORCES CREATING TENSIONS

- The trend for customer needs or products to become more alike (globalization)
- Know-how developments that affect
  - economies of scale
  - size of development needed
  - availability of skill (know-how innovation)
- The process of know-how maturing (know-how S-curve)
- Changes to the need for coordination from
  - convergence of de-coupling

– globalization
– customer demand for one-stop shopping (coordination)

NOTES

1. Rosabeth Moss Kanter has been one of the most prominent recorders of the process of corporate headquarters slimming. In *When Giants Learn to Dance*, Simon and Schuster, 1989, she describes the jargon; 'Inside companies, down-sizing (cutting employment), demassing (eliminating middle management positions), and decentralising corporate staff functions are among the tactics used by companies eager to be seeking and destroying wealth dissipators (improving profits)' (p. 57).

2. Rosabeth Moss Kanter has also been in the forefront of academics studying the new mechanisms companies are using to replace the old central functions, Chapter 4, in *When Giants Learn to Dance*, title 'Achieving Synergies: Value Added, Value Multiplied', describes many of the changes taking place.

   Michael Porter's book *Competitive Advantage*, Free Press, 1985, also has a useful chapter on mechanisms – chapter 11 'Achieving Interrelationships'. The section from p. 393 – organizational mechanisms for achieving interrelation-ships – provides a useful classification.

   C. K. Prahalad and Yves Doz also describe horizontal mechanisms in *The Multi-National Mission*, Free Press, 1987. In chapter 11, 'Managing Interdependencies Across Businesses', they show how data management tools, manager management tools and conflict resolution tools, can be used to manage without central functions.

   Christopher Bartlett and Sumantra Ghoshal, *Managing Across Borders*, HBS Press, 1989, also describe the new style of management in an excellent chapter entitled 'Managing Complexity: Developing Flexible Coordination'.

3. Michael Porter, *Competitive Advantage*, Free Press, 1988, Chapter 10.

4. All of the authors in note 2 above also comment on the difficulty management have had in making lateral mechanisms effective. Michael Porter opens his chapter on interrelationships with the sentence 'Achieving interrelationships has in practice proven to be extraordinarily difficult for many firms.'

   In the conclusion to *When Giants Learn to Dance*, Moss Kanter describes two 'principal problems' getting in the way of 'synergies'. The first is 'top management typically over estimates the degree of cooperation it will get and under estimates the costs.' (p. 345).

   Bartlett and Ghoshal examine the successes and failures of the companies in their sample and conclude 'perhaps the most difficult task is to coordinate the voluminous flow of strategic information and proprietary knowledge required to operate a transnational organisation', p. 170, *Managing Across Borders*.

   In the opening sentences on their chapter on interdependencies Prahalad and Doz comment 'few companies seem to have found an approach to manage the evolving interdependencies across businesses successfully'.

5. Gary Hamel and C. K. Prahalad have made this point eloquently in a famous *Harvard Business Review* article 'The Core Competence of the Corporation', *Harvard Business Review*, May/June 1990 No. 3. The point has also been made by Rosabeth Moss Kanter in her criticism of 'mindless downsizing' and 'management cowboys'. The focus on capability, competence and skills is resurfacing under the title 'the resource based view of strategy' (see note 6

below). The reality is that the earliest writings of Chester Barnard and Kenneth Andrews clearly underlined the importance of building capability.

6. There is a growing school of literature called the 'Resource-Based Theory of Competitive Advantage', Robert M. Grant, *California Management Review*, Spring 1991. It is also referred to in a number of different articles in the *Strategic Management Journal*, Summer 1991 Special Issue on Global Strategy edited by Christoper Bartlett and Sumantra Ghoshal. David Collis' article 'A Resource-Based Analysis of Global Competition' is an excellent example of the research which this school is now spawning.

7. In essence this tool is identical to the value chain tool of Michael Porter, the business system tool of McKinsey & Co and the activity based analysis tool of Braxton Associates. It differs in being much more detailed than the value chain and focused on skill elements rather than activity elements.

8. A solid article on benchmarking as a tool of analysis is 'Benchmarking World Class Performance', Walleck, O'Hallaron and Leader, *McKinsey Quarterly* 1991: 1. Another good piece is *The Power of Best Demonstrated Practice*, Bain & Co.

9. Michael Goold and John J. Quinn's book *Strategic Control: Milestones for Long-Term Performance*, London, Financial Times/Pitman Publishing, reissued 1993, describes best practice in this area.

10. All the authors who have researched interrelationships acknowledge the existence of strong barriers to accepting know-how from other parts of the organization. Michael Porter summarizes the 'impediments to achieving interrlationships', pp. 385–393 of *Competitive Advantage*. The most interesting piece of direct research has been done by Tom Allen, an MIT professor who studied the degree of technical know-how exchanged within laboratories. He found that technicians preferred to go outside for information and know-how, even though it was more readily available inside the laboratory, because of the perceived costs of working with colleagues – *Managing the Flow of Technology*, Thomas Allen.

11. Sumantra Ghoshal develops a categorization of innovation processes within multi-national companies that is similar. He identifies central, local and global innovations p. 47. 'The Innovative Multinational', unpublished PhD thesis, Harvard University No. 8617980. The same categorization is described in *Managing Across Borders* by Bartlett and Ghoshal.

12. Norman Blackwell, Jean-Pierre Bizet and David Hensely all of McKinsey & Co develop a similar categorization in 'Shaping a Pan-European Organisation', *McKinsey Quarterly*, July 1991. McKinsey & Co sponsored the research that this paper is built on and the exchange of thinking helped to bring our view and theirs into some proximity.

13. Christopher Bartlett and Sumantra Ghoshal produced an exhibit similar to Figure 8.4 in *Managing Across Borders*, p. 97. Our research has confirmed a conclusion of theirs that we were initially most uncomfortable with – namely that adjacent issues could be managed with different levels of coordination and differentiation.

14. Christopher Bartlett and Sumantra Ghoshal use the term 'administration heritage', chapter 3, *Managing Across Borders* to describe a concept similar to our decentralization contract. We have found the latter term more useful because the idea of a contract leaves managers more aware of their power to change the contract so long as they can persuade the business unit managers to agree to the changes. The administrative heritage language is too passive because it implies that the past is a drag on the speed of change.

Another reason for preferring the contract idea is that we identified situations where the contract changed when new managers from outside were appointed to the business units. These managers carried with them administrative heritage from their previous organizations that was just as strong as the administrative heritage of their new employer. The discussions that followed changed the previous decentralization contract as the centre managers adjusted to the desires of these new business unit managers.

Bartlett and Ghoshal refer to the work of Hannan and Freeman 'Structural Inertia and Organisation Change', *American Sociological Review*, Vol. 49 (1984). Hannan and Freeman talk about 'normative agreements' and explain why these agreements are resistant to change. The ideal of 'normative agreements' is, we believe, closer to the concept of a decentralization contract.

15. We collected all the case studies of major organization change for coordination and skill reasons produced by Harvard and Insead. Only one (Henkel) was a story of success. The others either documented failed efforts or described bold changes which, with the passage of time, proved not to work.

16. Recent work on mission and mission statements (*A Sense of Mission*, Andrew Campbell, Hutchinson, 1990), demonstrates that written statements are most powerful after the change has been achieved rather than beforehand. Because change is a political process, clear statements of intention or vision can provide the ammunition needed for those managers determined to undermine the change. We have observed that it is not unusual for the explanation to follow the action by months or even years.

Chapter 9

Knowledge creator vs. knowledge broker: Corporate roles in technology development in diversified firms

Anil K. Gupta and Ilkka Eerola

In many corporations, a radical flattening of the corporate hierarchy has been accompanied by a near-complete decimation of the corporate role – except, of course, for financial consolidation. Complete decentralization can make each SBU very market-focused and it does reduce the complexity of corporate headquarters' task. However, before one can conclude that this is the most effective way to manage the multi-business firm, some important questions need to be asked. From a technology development perspective, these are: does technological strength constitute part of the corporation's core competence? Will the upgrading of these technologies occur more speedily through complete decentralization or should the corporate office play any kind of a proactive role? If so, what might this role be?

Based on a field study of and discussions with senior executives in several large corporations, we argue that, for most diversified corporations, neither complete centralization nor complete decentralization will prove to be satisfactory organizational solutions. The former runs the risk of becoming a university-like think tank whereas the latter runs the risk of an excessive focus on today's products, today's technologies, and today's markets. We also propose that a shift away from 'binary' thinking requires a sequence of three steps: (i) accepting the need for selectivity in choosing between centralization vs. decentralization for different activities; (ii) learning how to make centralized technology management more responsive to SBU needs while keeping it centralized; and (iii) learning how to leverage decentralized technology capabilities across SBUs while leaving them under the control of SBUs.

We conclude the paper by suggesting that the correct approach for managing technology development must be tailored to the specific strategic context and requirements of each corporation. Towards this end, the paper discusses the characteristics of and key guidelines for managing two different archetypes of corporate headquarters' role: 'knowledge creator' vs. 'knowledge broker'.

INTRODUCTION

One of the most dramatic and far-reaching trends sweeping large diversified corporations today is the move towards a flattening of the corporate hierarchy and a radical decentralization of corporate functions to various divisions/SBUs. The basic logic underlying such decentralization generally has been both clear and persuasive. One, decentralization pushes profit responsibility deeper into the organization. Two, product life cycles are getting shorter and most markets are increasingly characterized by greater technological and competitive turbulence; in such a context, shorter response times can be important bases for competitive advantage. Therefore, it is seen as critical that control over all key functions be moved to those who are closest to the customer.

Our study of several corporations indicates, however, that managers can easily get carried away in the zeal to erase any and all traces of their top-heavy pasts – as if choices regarding how to organize came only in an 'either–or' form and that if centralization had made the company too ponderous and slow, then the only option was to move to its exact opposite. While such binary thinking[1] might be somewhat valid for downstream functions such as marketing and customer support, we contend that it is particularly risky for the organization of a critical upstream function viz. technology development. The experience of many corporations that have managed through radical decentralization for a long time (e.g. Johnson and Johnson) as well as those which have moved towards such decentralization more recently (e.g. Caterpillar and Vickers) indicates that, while a corporate technology center can easily fall prey to the 'ivory tower syndrome', *complete decentralization runs a different but equally grave risk viz. an excessive commitment to current products and current technologies leaving the SBUs vulnerable to the threat of technological leapfrogging by competitors and new entrants.*

For companies that recognize the risks associated with either of the two extremes, execution of the corporation's technology development agenda poses a particularly difficult organizational challenge. What, if any, technology development activities should the parent keep centralized at the corporate level? Should the company have a chief technology officer and, if so, what should his/her role be? If technology activities must be kept centralized, how can the company prevent the development of an 'ivory tower syndrome'? Similarly, if technology activities must be decentralized to SBUs, is it still possible to obtain system-wide benefits by leveraging know-how from one SBU to another? Based on an analysis of the experience of some of the largest industrial corporations in the US, this paper aims to clarify and provide guidelines pertaining to these and related questions.

The core themes underlying our arguments are:

(i)   no industry can be regarded as technologically mature and that, implicitly or explicitly, every company has a technology strategy;
(ii) the diversified corporation needs to be managed not just as a portfolio of SBUs but also as a portfolio of technologies since many critical technologies may cut across SBUs;
(iii) for some technologies, the corporate headquarters role may be that of 'knowledge creator' whereas, for others, it may be that of 'knowledge broker;'
(iv) formal structure is just one of several important organizational mechanisms that determine the effectiveness and efficiency with which any corporation's technology agenda is executed; other important mechanisms are budgetary control, physical location of technology development activities, and the use of formal and informal mechanisms for lateral coordination across functions and across SBUs.

THE CORPORATION AS A PORTFOLIO OF TECHNOLOGIES

Every product (or service) can be looked at from multiple perspectives. For the customer, it represents a means of fulfilling his or her needs and desires. For the accountant, it represents a bundle of costs intertwined into a cost structure. However, from the perspective of the designers and the manufacturers, the product also represents a bundle of embedded product and process technologies. Thus, for example, Kodak's blood analyzer can be viewed as a bundle of coating technology, colorimetrics, instrumentation, and biotechnology. Similarly, General Electric's CT scanner represents a bundle of X-ray, data processing, and video display technologies. Even a relatively 'simple' product such as Gillette's new Sensor razor system is a bundle of sophisticated materials science, advanced mechanical analysis, and microlaser welding technologies.

The key advantage in looking at products as bundles of technologies is that it highlights several important facts:

(i)   the apparent maturity of a product often reflects the maturity of the current combination of technologies embedded in it. Incorporation of new product or process technologies often changes product characteristics (including cost and quality) and even product life cycles in dramatic ways. Witness, for example, the advances in tennis rackets, golf clubs, athletic shoes, cordless power tools, and even Japanese rice cookers over the last decade;
(ii) competitive advantage in particular product-markets generally

derives from competitive advantage in one or more of the underlying technologies – either singly or in combination;

(iii) over time, the number of technologies relevant, indeed critical, to
most products is proliferating e.g. the incorporation of electronic
chips into washing machines, of robotics into forest logging
machines, and of optics and electronics into hospital lab equipment;

(iv) from an evolutionary perspective competitive advantage derives
not just from the technological edge that the company might have
today but also, perhaps more so, from the rate at which the company is able to keep upgrading its technological competence.

Thus, *while the short-term focus of the company may rightly be on the
exploitation of today's technologies through today's products, the long-term
focus must be on the preservation, advancement, and development of the
technology portfolio – the corporate crown jewels – that will be needed
tomorrow.*

It is clear that even a single business firm must generally manage a
portfolio of multiple technologies. Interestingly, however, because
many technologies tend to be common to very different products and
SBUs, the technology portfolio of the typical multi-business firm generally may not be very much larger than that of any one of its SBUs.
Take the case of a Fortune 500 company which makes defense equipment (e.g. transportation vehicles), specialized industrial machinery
and products (e.g. street sweepers and airplane loaders), and petroleum industry equipment along with other products. In this company,
while some technologies are indeed unique to particular SBUs, certain
critical technologies such as materials science, electronics, computer
modelling and simulation, and advanced mechanical analysis are
seen as cutting across most, if not all, SBUs. Thus, as depicted in Figure
9.1, the corporation as a portfolio of technologies might cut a very
different picture from what it looks like as a portfolio of SBUs.

Irrespective of how the corporation chooses to manage its portfolio of
technologies, the fact remains that, from an evolutionary perspective, the
ability of any of its SBUs to maintain a competitive edge in its particular
market will be a function of the speed with which the particular SBU is
able to keep upgrading and exploiting its technological base. Thus, a
central question for corporate headquarters becomes: how should the
parent manage the corporate-wide portfolio of technologies so that (i)
the seed of technological upgrading remains high, (ii) the costs of this
upgrading are kept low, and (iii) the company and its SBUs are able to
commercially exploit technological developments and do not fall into the
trap of technological advancement for its own sake – a task more appropriately left to universities and research institutes.

THE DILEMMA FACING DIVERSIFIED FIRMS

A useful starting point to understand the dilemma facing diversified firms is to look first at the case of single business firms. For *the single business firm*, the fundamental strategic questions can be stated as follows:

- Give the particular industry and the company's competitive strategy, what is the portfolio of critical technologies (e.g. product, process, and information technologies) that the firm must manage and master?
- What should be the firm's competitive posture (e.g. pioneer vs. follower) for the various technologies in this portfolio?
- What is the firm's strategy (e.g. internal development vs. external sourcing) regarding the future development and upgrading of these critical technologies?

Even within the same industry, many of the answers could well vary across technologies and across companies. For example, different firms within the same industry might choose to be pioneers and/or followers in different technologies – as in the case of the minicomputer industry where, historically, Digital Equipment has sought to be the leader in product design and Data General has sought to be the leader in process technologies. The organizational challenges facing the single business firm derive from its technology strategy and deal with ensuring (i) that the company is successful at developing the desired pioneering technologies, (ii) that its pioneering technologies can be successfully commercialized and exploited in the marketplace, and (iii) that the company is able to learn from and absorb/adapt the pioneering technologies of others so as to nullify the latter's potential edge.

It is important to note that, while American and European firms generally have done well at technology development, their record at converting new technologies into commercial successes has been less glorious. The well-known cases of Xerox's inability to capitalize on its technological leadership in personal computers and Philips' mishaps in exploiting its leadership in VCR technology illustrate this phenomenon most starkly. American and European firms have also suffered from a lop-sided emphasis on product as opposed to process research; thus, Japanese firms, which have suffered less from the 'not invented here' syndrome and which have paid greater attention to the development of process technologies have found it relatively easy to appropriate the technological advantage originally held by American or European firms. As Ralph Gomory, former senior vice-president of science and technology at IBM, observed recently, 'The United States is learning only now the hard lesson it taught the rest of the world earlier this century:

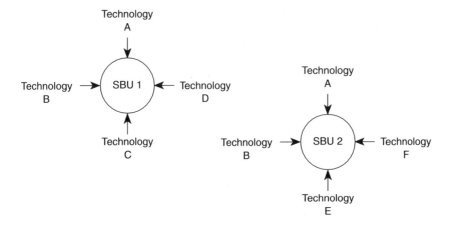

Figure 9.1 The corporation as a portfolio of SBUs vs. a portfolio of technologies

Product leadership can be built without scientific leadership if companies excel at design and the management of production.'[2]

The above observations regarding the challenges facing the single business firm are consistent with some of the core conclusions of research on successes and failures in exploiting technological developments: (i) a tight coupling between research centers and markets/marketing people is essential for successful product development; and (ii) a tight coupling between research centers and manufacturing/process engineers is essential for ensuring that the product designs can be manufactured at a competitive cost. Without tight coupling between R&D,

manufacturing, and marketing, the risks of repeating the Xerox experience in the PC industry become quite high.

The *diversified firm* faces all of the strategic and organizational challenges in technology management that the single business firm faces except that these get multiplied several times over – across the multiple SBUs. Every SBU within the diversified firm makes and sells a distinct set of goods and services to a distinct set of customers. Thus, for every SBU, there is likely to exist a portfolio of critical technologies which must be identified correctly and managed effectively and efficiently. However, over and beyond these SBU-level issues, the diversified firm also faces some fundamental organizational challenges unique to it: to the extent that there do exist commonalities in the technologies critical to multiple SBUs, should the development of these technologies be managed centrally in a corporate technology center or should this responsibility be left decentralized to the individual SBUs?

The case for decentralization

The major advantages of decentralization to SBUs can be identified as follows:

- *Tighter integration of R&D with manufacturing and marketing functions and greater customer orientation*: Giving each SBU direct control over its technology development efforts does not guarantee that the needed integration between R&D, manufacturing, and marketing will occur. However, it does ensure (i) that the existence of a common superior will necessitate frequent interaction at least among the various functional heads, and (ii) it now becomes possible for the SBU head to use his/her formal authority to force the needed integration.
- *Faster response to market needs*: Since R&D activities are funded directly out of the SBU budget, the pressure on SBU labs to keep their research activities targeted towards the SBU's specific needs is likely to be high. Also, given the profit-oriented evaluation system used in most companies to monitor and control SBU performance, SBU-level R&D efforts are more likely to be geared towards incremental improvements rather than technological breakthroughs. The net result should be a greater willingness on the part of SBU labs to respond more quickly to market needs than in the case of a centralized corporate technology center. The speed of market response should also be affected positively by the improved inter-functional coordination that results from decentralization to SBUs.

It is precisely these potential advantages that persuaded Caterpillar in 1989 to shift from a functional to an SBU-based structure, to decentralize many product development responsibilities to the SBU level, and to significantly increase the SBUs' budgetary control over the activities of the corporate research and engineering group. It is the same reasoning that led Vickers Corp. in the early 1980s to completely shut down the corporate research center and to devolve all research responsibilites to newly created global business units. This is also the logic that has supported Johnson and Johnson's decision to keep R&D efforts decentralized at the divisional/operating company level through most of its history.

The case for centralization

Given the criticality of tight inter-functional coordination and speedy market response, one might wonder as to why R&D activities should ever be centralized at the corporate level. However, it is important to note that centralization of R&D is also associated with some major benefits:

- *Economies of scale in technology development efforts*: To the extent that certain critical technologies are common across many SBUs, a centralized technology development effort would clearly enjoy the benefits of scale economies. For example, at Caterpillar, despite decentralization of responsibility for product development to SBUs, the fact remains that many core technological issues cut across SBUs. For example, given the changing composition of labor force, the control systems in not just one product category but the entire product family may need to be redesigned so that a 100 lb. woman could drive a heavy machine with almost the same ease as driving a car. Similarly, the challenge of making welds that are as strong as the core metal, of extending the life of transmission systems, of incorporating robotics into products, and of moving to FMS-based cellular manufacturing may not be confined to just one SBU. Thus, decentralization of these core technology projects may lead to redundancy, inefficiency, and ultimately slowness in technology advancement.
- *Critical mass and the ability to hire more talented personnel*: Being human, the willingness of talented scientists and engineers to join a technology center would obviously be affected by potential rewards – both intrinsic and extrinsic. The magnitude and challenge of projects in a corporate technology center would typically be higher than that of projects in SBU-based technology cells. Also, given a bigger overall scale of operations in a corporate technology center, the prospects for career advancement should typically be better. Both of these factors should give the corporate technology center an edge in hiring more talented personnel.
- *Stronger inter-disciplinary focus*: As noted earlier, the number of tech-

nologies relevant to any product is proliferating. Thus, the importance of inter-disciplinary focus is increasing steadily. To the extent that technology development responsibility is decentralized to SBUs, the risk would increase that potentially complementary technologies could remain buried within the separate SBUs.

- *Longer-term orientation and greater willingness to pursue riskier projects*: Two factors increase the likelihood that a corporate technology center would pursue longer-term and riskier projects more readily than would SBU-based technology cells. One, the portfolio of technology projects at the corporate-level is likely to be much broader; thus, the corporate technology center can more easily spread the risks across a number of projects. Two, given the profit-oriented evaluation system for SBUs prevalent in most corporations, the risk-propensity of SBU managers is likely to be lower than that of corporate executives.
- *Better prospects for utilizing technology as the basis for entry into new business arenas*: SBUs typically will have well-defined product-market charters. Thus, a decentralized technology organization is less likely to consider and pursue opportunities for exploiting the existing technology base for entry into new business arenas.

The dilemma facing diversified corporations in the organization of technology development is obvious: 'DAMNED IF YOU DECENTRALIZE AND DAMNED IF YOU DON'T.' Not surprisingly, more and more companies are now realizing that they no longer have the luxury of choosing between centralization and decentralization. Corporations with a history of centralized technology managment (such as AT&T, Caterpillar, and ICI) now find themselves struggling with the question of how to increase SBU control over technology development. At the same time, corporations with a history of extreme decentralization (such as Johnson and Johnson for decades and Vickers more recently) are now making adjustments to provide a proper counter-balance to decentralization lest they end up mortgaging their corporate futures to short-term oriented 'here and now' thinking. In essence, companies can ill afford to continue thinking of organizational options in binary '0-1' terms.

BEYOND CENTRALIZATION VS. DECENTRALIZATION

The shift away from simplistic centralization vs. decentralization thinking requires a sequence of three steps:

(i)   Accepting the need for selectivity in choosing between centralization vs. decentralization for different activities.
(ii) Learning how to make centralized technology management more responsive to SBU needs while keeping it centralized.

(iii) Learning how to leverage decentralized technology capabilities across SBUs while leaving them under the control of SBUs.

The need for selectivity

The first step in moving beyond binary thinking is to accept the premise that the costs and benefits of centralization vs. decentralization may differ radically from one technology activity to another. Within the same company and for even the same technology, the cost–benefit comparison may also change across time. Thus, at a minimum, the move to selectivity will require that the parent must engage in corporate-wide technology assessments on a periodic basis and remain flexible with respect to the organization of its technology management activities.

Caterpillar's experience in shifting from a functional to an SBU-based structure illustrates the need for selectivity. After carefully studying the organizational histories and experiences of several leading corporations, Caterpillar concluded that the search for simple structural solutions was essentially futile and that the logic of corporate and SBU strategies and the presence or absence of scale economies dictated different organizational approaches for different functions and activities. This selectivity is reflected well in the reorganization of the former Research and Engineering department which had historically commanded a budget of about $400 million. Virtually all engineering and product development work which includes product development has now been decentralized to the SBUs and is funded and managed by the SBU chiefs. In direct contrast, virtually all research – which, in Caterpillar's case, means technology development rather than basic research – continues to be funded and managed by the parent. Working on a time-frame of 7–10 years or longer, the mission of this centralized effort is the advancement of critical technologies that cut across SBUs. As Bernard Sorel, the company's chief technology officer, explained: 'Caterpillar's strategy is to be differentiated in products. That means being differentiated in components. Ultimately, that boils down to being differentiated in terms of the underlying technology.' The company has chosen yet another approach to the management of the product testing center. Given the common needs of the SBUs and inherent scale economies in this activity, it did not make sense either to let each SBU build its own testing center or to let each SBU own a fraction of the existing facilities. Thus, the test center continues to be managed centrally; however, unlike the case with research, the entire costs of the test center are charged out to SBUs based on level of usage.

Without doubt, selectivity in organizing different activities makes the task of managing more complex and more challenging for corporate as well as SBU managers. The challenge is analogous to that of successfully running a global business where managers no longer have the luxury of choosing between a purely local vs. a purely global orientation. In most cases, organizational complexity is the essential price for succeeding as a multi-business company just as it is for succeeding as a multi-national company.

Making centralized activities responsive to SBU needs

The decision to centralize certain technology development activities should generally ensure the benefits of scale economies, critical mass and interdisciplinary focus for these activities. However, centralization does not also have to imply that the central research labs will spend most of their resources on pursuing 'star wars' technology with little commercial relevance. Our investigation reveals that companies can use at least two different approaches to make corporate technology centers more responsive to SBU needs:

- *SBU involvement without budgetary control*: This approach involves giving the SBUs representation on a 'corporate technology council' with approval and oversight responsibilities for corporate-level technology projects. The funding may still come directly from corporate budgets without any allocation or charge-back to SBUs. This is the approach presently used by Caterpillar for its centralized research activities. Direct corporate funding should ensure a greater willingness to pursue riskier long-term projects. At the same time, SBU involvement in the approval of projects should have double benefits: (i) keep these projects more targeted towards SBU needs, and (ii) enhance SBUs' awareness of and sense of responsibility towards corporate-level technology projects.
- *SBU budgetary control*: This approach involves giving SBUs direct funding control over at least a part of the corporate technology center's budget. For instance, in the case of Matsushita Electric, the central research labs get only half of their budget through direct funding; the rest comes from projects commissioned by the divisions. Over the last decade, many companies (e.g. General Electric, Philips, and others) have begun to adopt this approach. It seems clear that, if the corporate technology center literally is required to 'sell' technology development projects to SBUs, it would have no choice but to be responsive to SBU needs.

We believe that, while partial SBU control over the corporate technology center's budget might be a desirable goal for many companies that choose to centralize certain technology activities, it does require SBU general managers to be inherently long-term oriented in their strategic planning and to have high appreciation for the role of technology in competitive advantage. For companies whose historical approach to controlling SBUs has been largely 'financial' rather than 'strategic' or which are just embarking on the road to divisionalization, the 'SBU involvement' approach is more likely to be a better first step.

Leveraging capabilities across SBUs despite decentralization

Should the parent choose to decentralize some or all of the corporation's technology activities, it may still be advisable to foster leveraging of capabilities across SBUs. 3M Corporation is a well-recognized master at such lateral leveraging. While the concrete opportunities for technological leveraging across SBUs often may be obvious (as in the case of corporate attempts to transfer know-how from defense-related SBUs to those serving non-defense markets), it need not always be so. Within Procter & Gamble, the transfer of skills at making colloidal solutions from the liquid detergents business to the orange juice business (which was struggling with the question of how powdered calcium could be made to stay suspended in orange juice) is one interesting example of serendipitous leveraging.

Thus, technology leveraging across SBUs can be both 'planned' and 'serendipitous'. Planned leveraging will typically require active involvement (i.e. direct brokering) by the parent. However, by definition, serendipitous leveraging cannot be planned. The appropriate corporate role here will be indirect brokering i.e. to create smoothly functioning horizontal networks so that the prospects for serendipitous technology transfer are maximized. Later in this paper, we discuss the management of such 'knowledge broker' roles in greater detail.

Alternative corporate HQ roles

Building on the above analysis, three archetypes of corporate headquarters roles can now be identified:

- *Total decentralization*: Technology management is totally decentralized to the SBUs. There is no corporate role in technology management.
- Parent as *'knowledge broker'*: Technology development responsibilities are decentralized to SBUs. however, a specialized corporate office actively monitors technology developments and SBU needs and acts as broker for (i) the internalization of outside technologies, and (ii) the transfer of technologies among the various SBUs.
- Parent as *'knowledge creator'*: SBUs rely on corporate labs for technology development. In budgetary terms, there are two alternative funding approaches: (i) the corporate-level technology activity is funded directly by corporate HQ as a 'cost center'; (ii) corporate technology

activities are contracted and paid for by SBUs on the basis of internal market mechanisms.

The pursuit of selectivity in centralization vs. decentralization will often imply that the actual corporate role in many companies will be a mix of the three archetypes; at the same time, it is possible, however, that, in many cases, one or the other role may dominate.

MANAGING THE 'KNOWLEDGE BROKER' ROLE

We define the 'knowledge broker' role as one where there may not exist any central research lab or corporate technology center and yet corporate headquarters chooses to play a proactive role in technology advancement within SBUs. The goal here is to leverage to the fullest extent the know-how that alrady exists both outside and inside the corporation without corporate headquarters taking a direct responsibility for knowledge creation. In a knowledge broker role, the corporate technology group acts strictly as a go-between. The primary decision-making authority continues to rest with the SBUs. Thus, the adoption of a 'knowledge broker' role at corporate headquarters should ideally have no effect on the autonomy of the SBUs. The leveraging of technologies typically includes both 'brokering in' (i.e. bringing outside technologies into the corporation) as well as 'brokering across' (i.e. proactively fostering technology transfer across SBUs).

Management of 'brokering in': The two most important requirements for successful 'brokering in' are:

- The corporate technology group should expend its efforts and resources at emphasizing breadth (rather than depth) of knowledge. They will probably never understand the SBUs' operations and markets as deeply as the SBUs do; nor will they understand the emerging technologies as deeply as would the potential external developers of these technologies. Instead, the corporate technology group should realize that their 'value added' will lie primarily in arbitrage i.e. in establishing the potential SBU-level relevance of emerging technologies sooner than what may otherwise be true. Thus, their capabilities at monitoring both emerging technologies and SBU needs must be outstanding.
- The primary strategy for embedding new external technology into a host SBU should be to let it be pulled in by 'champions' within the SBU. Without local champions, there is little likelihood that SBUs would assume ownership of the new technologies. Without such ownership, the new technology is likely to remain at best an academic curiosity for the SBU and have no effect on the SBUs' products, processes, or external competitive position. In short, without local

champions, trying to take external technology to an SBU may be more difficult than pushing a rope.

The experience of Marriott's Technology Advancement Group (TAG) is instructive in terms of the importance of local champions within host SBUs (see Appendix for a brief look at some of the reasons behind TAG's success as a knowledge broker). In its full-service hotel business, Marriott prepares tens of millions of bills annually. In cooperation with a leading computer manufacturer, TAG wanted to experiment with simultaneous laser-print of billing details as well as the logo and graphics so as to save on the cost of pre-printed billing forms. However, the project ran into at least two roadblocks. One, the current vendors of forms got concerned and started applying counter-pressure. Two, the hotel people became concerned that this technology may slow down the customer check-out process. As Richard Schroth, corporate vice-president and the head of TAG, explained: 'We did a backtrack and tried to see if we could find a champion somewhere else. This project is now doing well in our Residence Inn operations. There, guests stay for a month or so, have 4–5 page bills at checkout and, when leaving, are not in as much hurry as in the full-service hotels. We learned a lot from this experience. One, don't get stuck to your original vision of how a technology might be used by a particular SBU. Two, either cultivate or find a champion within the SBU and then work through the champion.'

Management of 'brokering across': The corporate technology group's goal here is to ensure technology transfer from leading edge SBUs to other SBUs where the particular technology may be relevant. It is entirely conceivable that, reflecting their peculiar histories, industry characteristics, and competitive strategies, different SBUs may have developed leadership positions in different technologies. In such a case, the potential for technology transfer is likely to be particularly rich. In many American corporations, a widely recognized need also exists for technology transfer from defense-related SBUs to other SBUs serving non-defense markets. For most companies, ensuring technology transfer across SBUs has proven to be enormously frustrating. As one chief technology officer in a prominent defense and industrial equipment corporation told us: 'After several years, I can count on one hand the number of technology transfers from our defense business to other SBUs. This has been one of my biggest frustrations.'

Assuming that there exists genuine potential for technology transfer across SBUs, the most common reason for failure in actually ensuring such transfer lies in an erroneous assumption on the part of would be knowledge brokers. The assumption is that if they can help the host SBUs become aware of technological capabilities available in other SBUs, the needed technology transfer would begin to occur. Of course, the establishment of lateral communication links among various SBUs is critical and some companies (e.g. 3M and Monsanto) have reportedly achieved considerable sophistication in establishing internal technical forums for the exchange of know-how among SBUs. Nonetheless, the fact remains that awareness of what technology can be borrowed from where is merely the starting point of successful technology transfer. Two other critical factors, which determine the likelihood of successful inter-SBU technology transfer, are: the motivational context within which the SBUs operate and, assuming motivation, the types of organizational mechanisms that are used to effect the transfer of technology.

In general, potential host SBUs are more likely to be eager and pro-active in pulling technology from sister SBUs if the evaluation and reward system for SBU managers emphasizes innovation and growth in addition to current profitability. While the logic behind this statement might appear obvious, it is regrettably true that, in many companies, hopes for an innovative culture where SBUs would be eager to borrow technology from sister SBUs continue to co-exist with purely ROI-based evaluation and reward systems. In such cases, the ensuing frustration should come as no surprise.

The creation of appropriate transfer mechanisms also requires a deep understanding of precisely what kind of technology it is that needs to be transferred. Some types of knowledge (e.g. a design blueprint or a chemical formula) may exist in a codified form; in these cases, knowledge transfer may require nothing more than an exchange of documents and some discussion. However, other types of knowledge (e.g. many types of process technologies) tend to be more tacit and are embedded either in individual people or in whole organizational systems. If the technology is embedded in *individual people,* then the only effective way to ensure technology transfer may be to transfer the appropriate personnel who are walking carriers of the technology from the provider SBU to the recipient SBU. However, if the technology is embedded in *a whole organizational system,* then transferring even a key person will prove fruitless. In such a case, the best option would be to transfer a team of people from the recipient SBU to the provider SBU so that the former can immerse themselves into the latter's organizational system, acquire the necessary know-how and then go back to their own SBUs as a near complete team. Such an approach is illustrated rather well in the case of L. M. Ericsson which, in the 1970s, transferred a whole 40-man Italian team to Sweden for a period of 18 months to learn about electronic switching.[3]

To conclude, the key tasks for a corporate technology group in operating as a successful knowledge broker for technology transfer across SBUs are:

(i)   influencing corporate-level executives in creating evaluation and reward systems for SBUs that emphasize innovation and growth in addition to current profitability;

(ii) creating lateral communication mechanisms among SBUs so that they are more likely to become aware of the potential to pull in and utilize leading technologies from sister SBUs;

(iii) designing and implementing transfer mechanisms that take into account the extent to which the technologies to be transferred are codifiable vs. embedded in individuals or organizational systems.

MANAGING THE 'KNOWLEDGE CREATOR' ROLE

We define the 'knowledge creator' role as one where corporate headquarters takes direct responsibility for technology development. Of course, as discussed earlier, in most corporations, the knowledge creator role would generally be appropriate only for a subset of the company's total technology agenda. Specifically, these would be technologies that are critical to and cut across many SBUs and where significant scale economies exist in managing the technology development centrally.

By definition, the execution of a knowledge creator role would require the presence of central research labs or a corporate technology center. The question of how such central research facilities should be managed has already been the focus of a vast body of literature on R&D management. Accordingly, in this section, we will highlight only some of the key factors that need to be kept in mind in managing the knowledge creator role effectively:

- *The need for political backing*: The greater the commonality in critical technologies across SBUs, the greater would be the necessity for technology strategy to be regarded as a core component of the overall corporate strategy. In order that this requirement be met effectively, it would generally be important that the chief technology officer have the necessary status and political power in the corporation to affect the formulation of the overall corporate strategy. In the extreme, this is illustrated in the case of Apple Computer where the chief executive officer has also formally adopted the title of chief technology officer.

- *Management of technological discontinuities*: The knowledge creator role would also require skills at the management of organizational conflict that is likely to accompany technological discontinuities. The jump from one generation of technology to another has the potential to produce clashes within the R&D organization as well as between the R&D organization and the manufacturing and marketing functions.

- *Monitoring and managing links with the external scientific community*: As technology proliferation has continued, even the largest, most technology intensive corporations have begun to realize that they must depend increasingly on technology developments outside the corporation. For instance, a study of the Swedish telecommunications giant L. M. Ericsson concluded that, in 1985, the company was sourcing 70–80% of its technology externally – a complete reversal from 1975 when internal R&D had accounted for 70–80% of the company's needs.[4] Along the same lines, Issac Barpal, Vice-President, R&D for Westinghouse Corp. estimated in 1988 that the company created only about 10% of the technology contained in its products.[5] The increasing need to rely on technology developments external to the corporation implies that even those corporate technology officers who are deeply committed to a knowledge creator role for corporate headquarters must see the 'brokering in' of external technology as one of their critical tasks.

- *Building tight coordination with divisions and their markets*: As was discussed earlier, the risks of an R&D unit becoming an ivory tower are much greater in the case of a corporate technology center than in the case of SBU-based R&D units. Some approaches to mitigate this risk are: SBU involvement in and/or budgetary control over corporate technology projects, movement of personnel from research to engineering to production along with the project, and routinized contact between R&D personnel and customers. The need for a pro-active stance by the chief technology officer in ensuring customer contacts is evident from the following observations by Motorola's CEO, George Fisher: 'We've established a massive program of increasing customer visits at all levels of the organization . . . [However] our technologists are still not visiting as many customers as we would like. I don't think it's a lack of desire on their part. People who don't give speeches aren't comfortable giving speeches. People who don't visit customers aren't comfortable visiting customers.'[6]

To sum up, while effective management of the 'knowledge creator' role does require an ability to hire and motivate competent personnel to staff the corporate technology center, the success of CTC depends crucially also on the extent to which it monitors external technology trends and is integrated into the SBUs' needs.

THE CORPORATE TECHNOLOGY OFFICE: AN IVORY TOWER OR A PROTECTOR OF CROWN JEWELS

Scholars as well as executives have long recognized the fundamental linkage between a company's technological base and its strategic health. As Kenneth Andrews, one of the founding fathers of the strategy field, observed in 1971: 'Technical developments are not only the fastest

unfolding but the most far reaching in extending or contracting opportunity for an established company.[7] More recently, Michael Porter has
argued that 'there is, in fact, no such thing as a low technology industry
. . . Viewing any industry as technologically mature often leads to strategic disaster.'[8] Consistent with these perspectives, a mid-1980s survey
of 700 top managers of major West European industrial corporations
indicated that they saw technology as the thorniest management problem for the 1990s and regarded it as a key top management strategic
responsibility.[9]

Technological trends over the last five years certainly do not provide
any reason to doubt these predictions; if anything, the pace of technological evolution has picked up and the proliferation of technologies
relevant to any product or process continues to increase. In such a
context, it becomes critical that every diversified company look upon
itself not just as a portfolio of SBUs but also as a portfolio of technologies. Sophistication in managing the SBU portfolio is essential for
exploiting current competitive advantage in today's markets; however,
it is sophistication in managing the technology portfolio that will determine the company's ability to sustain its competitive advantage over
time.

In some companies, the portfolio of *critical* technologies may well be
different across SBUs. In these cases, the wise decision will be to leave
technology development exclusively within the hands of SBU general
managers with corporate headquarters acting as no more than a technology cheerleader. However, given the proliferation of technologies
relevant to most products and processes, for most companies, there
will exist commonalities in the different SBUs' portfolios of critical
technologies. Wherever such commonalities exist, corporate headquarters must play more than a cheerleader role. It must get involved more
directly in the development of the SBUs' technology strategies. For those
common technologies where significant scale economies exist, there
might be merit in centralizing technology development in a corporate
technology center; in doing so, it is critical to remember that the ivory
tower tendencies of a corporate technology center can be countered
through SBU involvement in and/or partial budgetary control over
the center's activities. On the other hand, for those common technologies
where scale economies are insignificant, it may still be wise to leave
technology development decentralized within the SBUs; however,
decentralization can be made to coexist with active corporate brokering
to leverage technological capabilities across SBUs.

In conclusion, we propose that companies treat their technology portfolios as the equivalent of corporate crown jewels. While creating ivory
tower central research labs would often be a waste of shareholders'
capital, it might be equally irresponsible for corporate headquarters to

abdicate their responsibility for the preservation and enhancement of these crown jewels. Undoubtedly, the concrete approaches adopted by each corporation will need to be tailored to its own unique strategic, technological, and historical context. While the principles might be universal, the solutions must be unique for each company.

APPENDIX: CORPORATE HQ AS A 'KNOWLEDGE BROKER': THE MARRIOTT EXPERIENCE

The Technology Advancement Group (TAG) at Marriott Corporation – a 'knowledge broker' par excellence – consists of five people serving a nearly $8 billion company. TAG's agenda does not include developing any basic technology themselves. Instead, their value-added lies in serving as 'proactive' technology brokers, in customizing external technology for Marriott use through the development of prototypes, and in serving as custodians for such technology. Despite recent corporate restructuring and disbanding of several corporate functions, TAG has continued to receive support up and down the hierarchy. Here are some concrete approaches that TAG appears to have found as particularly useful:

Work through champions within SBUs – TAG believes that external technology must be pulled in by SBUs rather than pushed from the top. Thus, besides monitoring emerging technologies and SBU needs, corporate role is defined primarily as educating and cultivating technology champions within SBUs. This ensures direct line funding of new projects without appealing to corporate headquarters. It also ensures a rapid assimilation of new technologies as well as a speedy rejection of potentially 'hare-brained' ideas. Also, given a show-case within one SBU, technology transfer to other SBUs becomes relatively easier.

Maintain a balanced technology portfolio – TAG believes that it is important to maintain a balanced portfolio of long- and short-term technology projects. A sufficient number of short-payback projects ensures that there would always remain enough political support to persuade SBUs to take chances with longer-run and riskier technology assimilation projects.

Remain visible – Without any concrete technology development agenda, it is easy to succumb to the 'out of sight, out of mind' syndrome. Two approaches which help TAG remain visisble are: (i) a Technology Briefing Center for showcasing a steady stream of emerging technologies and how they have been used for competitive advantage by companies in closely related industries; and (ii) an in-house technology newsletter 'Bits and Pieces'. The newsletter, which features not only external but also internal developments, is supported purely by subscriptions from SBUs – forcing TAG to remain relevant.

Build technology alliances with leading vendors – On several projects, TAG has been successful at persuading one or more SBUs into becoming product/service development partners with some of the world's leading high technology corporations. The latter are constantly in need of concrete applications to fine-tune and showcase their emerging technologies. Marriott SBUs which might take on a collaborative role in such ventures are able to get cutting-edge technology customized to their needs ahead of their competitors at a fraction of the cost. TAG acts as an interim owner of the technology during the customization and prototyping phase.

Other approaches include encouraging operations people to do technology sabbaticals with TAG. Even the name itself was changed from Advanced Technology Group to reflect a more pro-active stance on the part of this hardy band of technology arbitrageurs.

NOTES

1. We are grateful to Mr. Bernard Sorel, Vice-President, Technical Services Division, Caterpillar Inc., for suggesting the term 'binary 0-1 thinking'.
2. Gomory, R. E. From the 'ladder of science' to the product development cycle. *Harvard Business Review,* November–December 1989: 99–105.
3. As reported in Bartlett, C. A. and Ghoshal, S. 1988. Organizing for Worldwide Effectiveness: The Transnational Solution. *California Management Review,* Fall: 54–74.
4. Granstrand, O. and Sjolander, S. 1990. Managing innovation in multi-technology corporations. *Research Policy,* 19: 35–60.
5. Barpal, Isaac 1988. New roles for research administrators. *SRA Journal,* Winter: 19–23.
6. Avishai, D. and Taylor, W. 1989. Customers drive a technology-driven company: An interview with George Fisher. *Harvard Business Review,* November–December (p. 108).
7. Andrews, K. R. 1971. *The concept of corporate strategy.* Homewood, IL: Dow-Jones Irwin (p. 60).
8. Porter, M. E. 1985. *Competitive advantage.* New York: The Free Press (p. 165).
9. *International Management Review.* The thorniest management problem – technology. January 1985.

Chapter 10

Intra-firm transfer of best practices

Gabriel Szulanski

The Intra-Firm Transfer of Best Practices Project started in July 1992 and concluded officially in October 1994. Participating companies included:

- AMP
- AT&T Paradyne
- Banc One Corporation
- British Petroleum
- Burmah Castrol
- Chevron Corporation
- EDS
- Kaiser Permanente
- Rank Xerox
- Sprint

This project was designed and conducted by Gabriel Szulanski in partial fulfillment of the requirements for a Ph.D. in Strategic Management at INSEAD, the European Institue of Business Administration. In line with practice in most top US business schools, this dissertation project was devised as a serious research effort aiming to advance the theory and practice of management.

The research design consisted of three phases. During the first phase, a broad field survey of 45 firms and benchmarking specialists provided the language to discuss the phenomena and helped calibrate the theoretical framework of the study. In a second phase, research case studies were written to document clear instance of success and failure in transferring best practices within three selected US and European companies. Finally, guided by theoretical considerations, field survey, and clinical work, a specialized questionnaire was prepared and administered in eight companies to test the validity of the conceptual framework.

The research was supervised by a committee of distinguished academics in the fields of Strategic Management and Organizational Behavior. The committee was chaired by Sumantra Ghoshal and composed by Michael Brimm, Karel Cool, and Richard P. Rumelt.

About the report

This report aims to provide a map for thinking about the transfer of best practices inside the firm, as well as some concrete suggestions about how to make it work. The findings of the study are used to profile a typical transfer to help the reader develop a feel for how a transfer happens and what problems are likely to be encountered in the process. The profile includes a brief discussion of the main actors and entities, some important milestones, the activities between those milestones, and the most prevalent difficulties that the firms in the sample experienced during the process. This profile is then used as a canvas on which to summarize the results of the statistical analysis of the barriers to transfer best practices inside the firm. The presentation ends with a review of the mechanisms most frequently used by the participating firms to transfer best practices.

The statistical analysis revealed four main sources of difficulty. In decreasing importance, these were the lack of absorptive capacity[1] of the recipient, lack of understanding of the practice, poor relationship between the source and the recipient, and the lack of motivation of the recipient. A more fine-grained analysis revealed also that during specific stages of the transfer, other sources of difficulty could be as significant or even more significant than those four. In the review of mechanisms used to transfer best practices, it was found that there is not one single mechanism to transfer best practices, but that the choice requires a more fine-grained analysis of the transfer to choose the proper mix of mechanisms for the tasks at hand. Furthermore, it was found that a same mechanism could often be used to accomplish more than one task.

The report is organized as follows. First, a brief discussion of the connection between the transfer of best practices and a firm's overall performance is followed by a test of intuition about the transfer of best practices inside the firm. Next, the findings are presented in three steps: the profile of a typical transfer, the summary of the analysis, and the mechanisms used to transfer best practices. At the end of this document, brief statements by the participating companies are given on why they decided to join in this project.

BEST PRACTICES AND FIRM PERFORMANCE

The transfer of best practices inside the firm is, conceptually speaking, a different phenomenon than the transfer of best practices between firms – or as it is also known, competitive benchmarking. One might guess that confidentiality is less of an issue for intra-firm transfers than it is for benchmarking with other firms. However, the crucial difference is that the transferred practice already exists and has proven itself inside the firm. It is for that same reason that the transfer of best practices is a

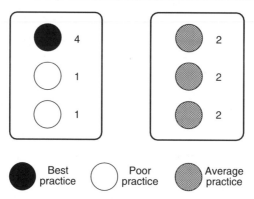

Figure 10.1 Best, poor and average practice

different phenomenon than the implementation of practices developed through Research and Development (R&D) or acquired by licensing new technologies. The point is that firms that manage to successfully transfer best practices are not acquiring new knowledge, but are exploiting better their existing stock of knowledge.

To illustrate this difference with an example, ponder the picture in Figure 10.1. The two rectangles represent two firms, each composed of three roughly comparable manufacturing plants (the inner circles). A white circle represents poor manufacturing practice that yields one unit of profit; a gray circle represents average practice that yields two units of profit, and a black circle represents best practice that yields four units of profit. The numbers to the right of the circles represent the profits produced by each of the firm's plants. In their annual reports, both firms will declare a profit of six (4+1+1 and 2+2+2). If the investigation stops at the gates of these two firms, both will appear similar.

Looking inside both firms reveals a very different picture. While the firm on the right is making the most out of its knowledge, the one on the left is not. To improve its performance, the firm on the right will have to bring new knowledge from the outside by licensing a superior technology or by benchmarking with another firm. Alternatively, this firm may improve its performance by developing new knowledge through R&D.

The firm on the left, however, does not need new knowledge to improve its performance. It could double its profits by replicating existing knowledge. If this firm manages to transfer the practices from the best-practice plant that produces four units of profit (the black circle) to the two poor-practice plants that produce only one unit of profit (the white circles), it will double its overall profits – from six (4+1+1) to 12 (4+4+4).

If this example appears artificial or unrealistic, be assured that the results of a typical internal benchmarking study are very similar in nature. It is not uncommon in these studies to find gaps worth several million dollars in the performance of otherwise comparable units.

This was a recurring finding of the Intra-Firm Transfer of Best Practices Project – one that explains why the transfer of best practices is becoming such an important managerial responsibility. By stressing management by fact, initiatives on quality, benchmarking, and reengineering ferret-out stunning gaps in performance (2:1 is not uncommon). Once the economic importance of these gaps in performance is understood, actions naturally follow to close these gaps. The transfer of best practices inside the firm is one important way to reduce these avoidable deficits in performance.

TEST YOUR INTUITION

To test your intuition about the transfer of best practices inside the firm, please answer the following two tests. Completing this short exercise will stimulate you to collect and assemble all you know about the transfer of best practices. As you read the report, you will find answers to these exercises derived from the actual findings of the study.

Test #1 Which transfer will be easier?

On one extreme, a transfer could be 'mandated' by senior management. On the other extreme, a transfer could be 'spontaneous', emerging from the grassroots of the company without any direct managerial intervention. In between these two extremes, a transfer could be 'strongly suggested' rather than imposed, just 'favored', or simply made known as 'optional'.

All other things being equal, how would you rank, based on your own experience and observations, the degree of difficulty of these five kinds of transfer?

Table 10.1

Type of transfer	Level of difficulty				
	LOW				HIGH
Mandated	1	2	3	4	5
Strongly suggested	1	2	3	4	5
Favored	1	2	3	4	5
Optional	1	2	3	4	5
Spontaneous	1	2	3	4	5

Test #2 Not invented here (NIH) syndrome

The Not Invented Here[2] (NIH) syndrome refers to the frequently observed narcissistic inclination of organizational subunits to reject ways of doing things not of their own making. After all, who could possibly know their business better than they do themselves?

This syndrome is one of the most often cited difficulties to transfer best practices inside the firm. The findings of this study corroborate that. Indeed, the term NIH has become an integral part of the vocabulary and of the accepted wisdom about the transfer of best practices inside the firm. Yet, it was also found in this study that wisdom may sometimes obscure as much as it illuminates.

The purpose of this intuition test is to illustrate the limits of the conventional wisdom about the NIH syndrome. Please complete the graph in Figure 10.2 based on what you know about the NIH syndrome. The horizontal axis of the graph refers to the self-assessed status of the recipient. Thus, for example, 'superior' means that the recipient unit evaluates itself as a superior unit among those of its kind within the company. In turn, the vertical axis indicates the observed level of motivation of the recipient to accept a best practice from another unit.

As predicted by the NIH syndrome, it was found that the higher the

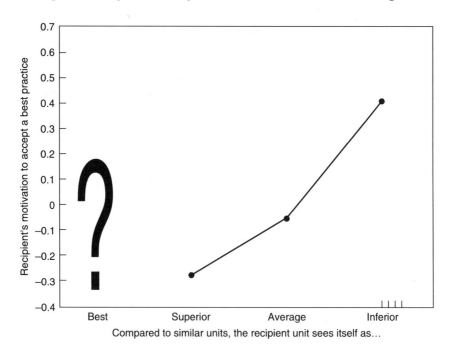

Figure 10.2 The not invented here syndrome

subunit's self evaluation, the lower its motivation to accept a best practice. Thus an 'average' unit is less motivated to accept best practice than an 'inferior' unit is. Likewise, a 'superior' unit is less motivated to accept best practices than an 'average' unit is.

In your opinion, how motivated to accept a best practice will a unit be that evaluates itself as 'best'?

THE FINDINGS

In this section, the findings of the study are used to profile a typical transfer to help the reader develop a feel for how a transfer happens and what problems are likely to be encountered in the process. This profile is then used as a canvas on which to summarize the results of the statistical analysis of barriers or sources of difficulty to transfer best practices inside the firm. The presentation of the findings ends with a review of the mechanisms most frequently used by the participating firms to transfer best practices.

Profiling a typical transfer

Ponder the following two assertions. All transfers are different. All transfers are alike. Both assertions could be right depending at which level of abstraction one chooses to describe transfers. If we limit the description of a transfer to merely verifying the existence of a starting and ending point, then all transfers are alike. They start and then they end.

Conversely, if we describe every single detail of a transfer, however miniscule, then it is very likely that all transfers are different because participants may vary, the chronology may be different, the practices transferred may vary and so on. Neither of these two levels of abstraction is likely to be of much use to provide a general map to manage transfers.

One may choose, however, an intermediate level of detail that permits a description general enough to apply to a wide variety of transfers, yet nuanced enough to provide a useful map for managers to navigate and analyze transfers of best practices inside the firm. Choosing such an intermediate level of detail enables one to profile a typical transfer.

In this section, the findings of the study are used to generate such a profile for a typical transfer. The profile includes a brief discussion of the main actors and entities of some important milestones, of the activities between those milestones, and of the most prevalent difficulties that the participating companies experienced during the process.

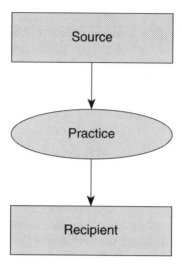

Organizational context

Figure 10.3 Organizational context

Main actors and entities

The main actors in a transfer are the source unit, the recipient unit, and the organizational context in which the transfer takes place. An important entity is the practice that is being transferred (Figure 10.3).

The source unit is another division, company, or subunit within the organization. The recipient unit will generally perform tasks that are similar in some way to those performed by the source or will at least share some business processes.

The organizational context is comprised by all the other parts of the firm that are neither source nor recipient in the transfer. Thus, for example, a regional quality office, a corporate benchmarking department, other subunits, or even external consultants can all be considered as part of the organizational context when thinking about a transfer.

Milestones

Imagine the timeline of a transfer. One of the findings of the study is that for most transfers, however disparate, respondents could almost always identify four milestones along the timeline. These milestones are: (1) the formation of the transfer seed, (2) thumbs up, (3) flicking the switch, and (4) end of ramp-up.

Formation of the transfer seed

The earliest possible time in which a transfer can begin is when both a need and the best practice suitable to fulfill that need appear within the organization. The order of their appearance is not important. The fact that both appear, of course, is. The formation of the transfer seed happens typically when the best practice first enters the organization or when a potential recipient discovers its existence. In this project we asked respondents the date of both events, taking the most recent one to indicate the date when the seed was formed. More than 70% of the respondents could trace back in time the month and the year in which the practice entered the company. More than 85% of the respondents could trace back in time the month and the year when they became aware of the existence of the best practice that was later transferred.

Thumbs up

The second milestone that most respondents could identify is the date when the decision to proceed with the transfer was actually taken – the date when the blessing of 'thumbs up' was given to the transfer. This event could have been just a simple handshake, yet in most cases the 'thumbs-up' event was a task team meeting, the approval and signing of a formal document, or a presentation to senior management. More than 86% of the participants could trace back in time the month and the year when the 'thumbs-up' decision was taken.

Flicking the switch

The third milestone that most respondents could identify was the date when the best practice became operative at the recipient unit. The date when the switch was flicked. The actual event could be the start-up of a manufacturing plant, the roll-out of a new process, or cut-over to a new system. More than 78% of the participants could trace back in time at least the month and the year when the switch was flicked.

End of ramp-up

The fourth milestone that most respondents could identify was the date when the recipient, after ironing out initial problems, achieved a satisfactory level of performance. The nature of this event tends to depend on the nature of the practices in a particular industry. For example, a steel mini-mill is considered to have achieved a satisfactory level of performance when it reaches break-even. A semiconductor 'fab' is said to achieve this point when it is certified. A bank reaches this point when it can balance its operations with its own personnel. More than 70% of the participants could trace back in time at least the month and year of the 'end of ramp-up'.

Figure 10.4 summarizes the presentation of the milestones indicating the time period that elapsed, on average, between the different milestones. The timing is based on close tracking of several unfolding transfers and on information collected from 271 questionnaires on 122 transfers of 38 practices.[3]

Activities between the milestones

Intra-firm transfer of best practice could be viewed as an unfolding process where the relative conspicuousness of organizational activities fluctuates in-between the milestones. For example, an activity that is prominent before 'thumbs-up', such as studying the feasibility of a particular transfer, may fade to the background or just stop after the 'thumbs-up' decision is taken. Based on the fieldwork and a thorough literature review, this section describes which activities are likely to be salient in the period of time defined by two consectuive milestones.

In between the formation of the seed and the 'thumbs-up' decision, four principal activities seemed predominant. Efforts to identify best practices coexisted with efforts to identify unmet needs, efforts to understand and to share understanding about best practices, and efforts to assess the feasibility of particular transfers. The order in which these activities occur is not always clear – nor need it be. Indeed, sometimes the 'thumbs-up' decision resulted from an orderly systematic process and sometimes in response to a chaotic sequence of events. However, in successful transfers, evidence could be found for the existence of the four types of processes.

Once the 'thumbs-up' decision was taken, efforts to bridge the communication gap between the two units and the technical gap of the recipient did become noticeable. After the 'thumbs-up' decision and before the 'flicking of the switch', both the source and the recipient identified and linked key individuals for the transfer from each unit. A more detailed planning of the transfer was followed by efforts to develop and implement the recipient's infrastructure to make it suitable to support the new practice. Efforts to train the recipient's personnel were also apparent. Not all of these actions are likely to be necessary. If the source and the recipient unit had a pre-existing working relationship, the communication gap may not exist. Similarly, if the transfer is merely a transfer of information, there may be no need to develop the infrastructure of the recipient.

With the technical gap closed, the recipient is ready to 'flick the switch'. This done, unexpected problems always emerge. This is also

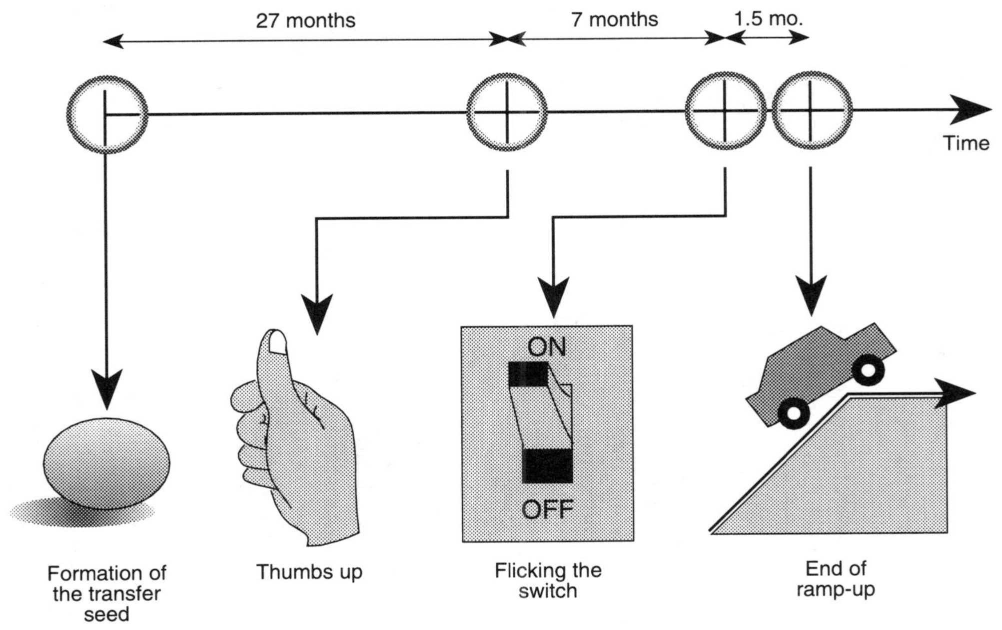

Figure 10.4 Milestones

known as Murphy's Law: if something can go wrong, it will. Thus, in most transfers immediately after 'flicking the switch', the performance of the recipient is lower than expected. In some cases much lower. The main activity is simply problem solving if the necessary expertise is readily available within the recipient. If not, an active search for this expertise and consultations with the source unit are likely to increase significantly during this part of the transfer. Meanwhile performance ramps up until it reaches a satisfactory level. This is important because special provisions for the ramp-up period may be discontinued past this point.

Having achieved satisfactory performance, the recipient sets up to integrate the practice into its routine operation. The practice will slowly shed its status of novelty to become integrated into the recipient's fabric of practices. This is a gradual but important process that is frequently overlooked. Indeed practices must be kept alive. If unsupported, practices peter out. Continuous improvement efforts and occasional radical enhancements to the practice may be necessary to keep the practice aligned with the evolving needs of the recipient. When conditions change, a practice will persist only if people continue to know how to do their job and if they continue to consent to do it. In any case, the half-life of a best practice is rarely longer than a few years.

A typical transfer

A typical transfer was either mandated or strongly suggested by senior management. Transfers of both technical and administrative practices were equally likely. The most frequent justification for a transfer was to reduce costs in the recipient unit. Yet, it could also be initiated to transfer new capabilities, to improve quality, to reach world-class level of performance in an existing capability, to fulfill a demand from an important customer, or to achieve companywide standardization of a particular organizational approach.

A typical transfer involved, on average, 15 people and cost roughly $90,000 to the source, close to $30,000 to the recipient, and about the same amount to a third party – typically a corporate office or a regional office. These actual costs were generally anticipated by both the source and by the recipient.

With respect to timing, nine months elapsed, on the average, from the moment the decision to transfer was taken ('thumbs-up') until the recipient achieved a satisfactory level of performance ('end of ramp-up'). Relative to the initial planning, the beginning of the transfer was typically delayed by less than one month as well as the date in which the practice finally became operational at the recipient unit. Likewise, support to the recipient unit had to be extended slightly beyond the initial provisions. Nonetheless, after gaining experience with the practice, recipients typically revised upwards their pre-transfer expectations and were fairly satisfied with both the quality of the practice and the quality of the transfer. In most successful cases, the recipient slightly outperformed the source and its version of the practice differed somewhat from that of the source.

In about a third of the transfers studied, the 'thumbs-up' decision was formalized in a document. This document specified the timing of the transfer, its scope, and the responsibilities of the recipient unit.

The main difficulties experienced to reach the 'thumbs-up' milestone were the ranking of the performance of different subunits on the practice, the limited ability of the source units to isolate the key components of the practice, and to explain how they achieved superior results.

The most frequently observed vehicle to transfer best practice was training materials. In decreasing order of occurrence, recipients also relied on blueprints of the practice furnished by the source, on sending some of their people to be trained at the source or on help of personnel from the source who came to give support on-site. In about a third of the transfers, recipients installed new systems and hired new staff (see Figure 10.5).

The main difficulties experienced during the exchange of information and knowledge between the source and the recipient could be traced to a breakdown of transfer-related communication within the recipient, to inadequate planning of the exchange (which impaired the recipient to free personnel from regular operations to be properly trained in the new practice), and to unnecessary modifications to the practice made by the recipient.

Once the recipient started operating with the new practice, i.e. after 'flicking the switch', unexpected problems arose because the recipient had different working conventions than the source. Difficulties also arose because, in some respect, the documentation furnished by the source was deficient. Unexpected problems also arose when the practice had unsatisfactory side effects that had to be corrected, and when the recipient's environment was different from that of the source in unexpected ways. People left the recipient after having been trained or were found to be poorly qualified for their new role once the recipient unit started operating with the new practice. In both situations, a replacement had to be found quickly. In most transfers, the personnel from the recipient was cooperative – even enthusiastic in some instances. However passivity, foot dragging, and feigned acceptance were apparent as well.

After satisfactory performance was obtained, the recipient typically changed some of the procedures, increased the scale, or placed new demands on the practice. In 5% of the cases the practice was discontin-

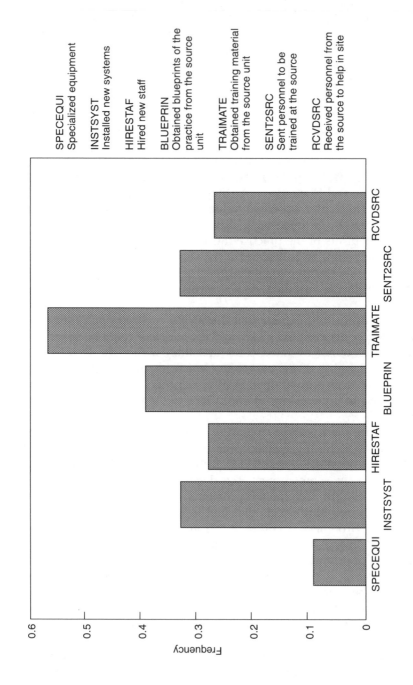

SPECEQUI
Specialized equipment

INSTSYST
Installed new systems

HIRESTAF
Hired new staff

BLUEPRIN
Obtained blueprints of the
practice from the source
unit

TRAIMATE
Obtained training material
from the source unit

SENT2SRC
Sent personnel to be
trained at the source

RCVDSRC
Received personnel from
the source to help in site

Figure 10.5 Vehicles of best practice

ued, and in 2.5% of the cases it was replaced by a superior alternative. Integrating the practice within the recipient's routine operation was more difficult when roles weren't well defined and when the personnel was not content to play their roles in the new practice. Difficulties also were experienced when individual values disfavored performing the practice, when it wasn't clear why the recipient needed that practice or when, even though clear, the justification did not make sense. The percentage of people who could have used the practice and were actually using it depended to some degree on continued support from the organizational context and from the source. In all cases, this percentage declined as more time elapsed. The average rate of decay was about 2.5% per year.

WHERE DO DIFFICULTIES COME FROM?

In the previous section a typical transfer was sketched. This was used as an opportunity to introduce and describe succinctly the most often observed difficulties. In this section we move from the difficulties themselves to focus on the predictors or sources of difficulty.

Origins of difficulty

Difficulties during a transfer may stem from the characteristics of the source, of the recipient, of the practice, and of the organizational context where the transfer takes place. Thus, one could plausibly expect a transfer to be more difficult if the source is not motivated to support the transfer or is not perceived as a reliable source of best practices. Difficulties can also occur if the recipient is not motivated or does not have the knowledge and skills necessary to absorb the new practice, if the relationship between the two units is difficult, and if the practice is not well understood or is not robust to work smoothly in different settings. Finally, more difficulties can be expected if the organizational context does not offer the necessary climate and support.

Principal origins of difficulty at each stage

The statistical analysis intended to identify and measure which of the potential sources of difficulty enumerated above will be most important and whether their relative importance would fluctuate before and after the main milestones were reached.

Overall, the four most important predictors of difficulty were the absorptive capacity of the recipient, i.e. its ability to identify, value, and implement the best practices, how well the practice was understood,

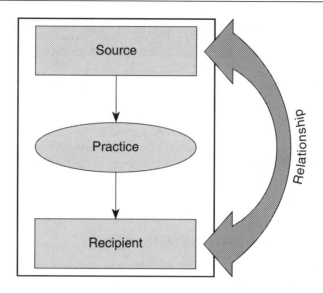

Figure 10.6 Organizational context

the quality of the relationship between the two units, and closely related to that, the level of motivation of the recipient unit.

As can be seen from Figure 10.7, the relative importance of the predictors of difficulty did vary before and after the main milestones. For example, the statistical analysis revealed the most important predictors of difficulty between 'seed' and 'thumbs up' were the lack of perceived reliablity of the source unit, the lack of robustness of the practice, and poor understanding of the practice. On the other hand, between 'thumbs up' and 'flicking the switch', the most important predictors of difficulty were the lack of absorptive capacity of the recipient, a difficult relationship between the source and the recipient, and a low level of motivation of the source.

Figure 10.7 summarizes the results of the statistical analysis. The numbers represent the rank-order of the three most important sources of difficulty for each portion of the transfer.

WHICH MECHANISMS DO PEOPLE USE TO TRANSFER BEST PRACTICES?

The tasks of best practice transfer

Several activities stood out for each stage of the process. Before the thumbs-up decision, efforts to identify best practices, identify unmet needs, share identified best practices, and examine the feasibility of

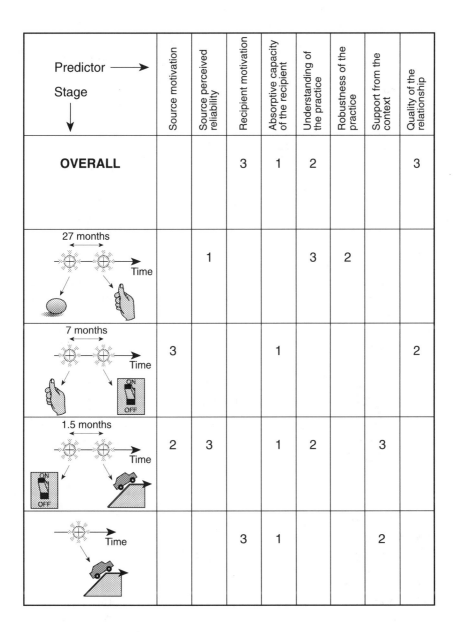

Predictor → Stage	Source motivation	Source perceived reliability	Recipient motivation	Absorptive capacity of the recipient	Understanding of the practice	Robustness of the practice	Support from the context	Quality of the relationship
OVERALL			3	1	2			3
27 months		1			3	2		
7 months	3			1				2
1.5 months	2	3		1	2		3	
			3	1			2	

Figure 10.7 Predictors of difficulty

transfers were apparent. Before flicking the switch, efforts to foster communication between the units, to plan the transfer, to implement it, and to train the recipient's personnel gained the foreground. After the switch was flicked, several acitons were noted to get up to speed – principally solving unexpected problems. Finally, after the end of the ramp-up period, several actions were detected aiming to integrate the new practice within the routine operation of the recipient.

The mechanisms of choice for each task

The respondents to the survey were asked to enumerate which mechanisms they used to accomplish each of these tasks. Specifically, they were asked which mechanisms they used to identify best practices, to identify unmet needs, to share best practices, to study the feasibility of a transfer, to communicate, to plan a transfer, to implement a transfer, to train the recipient, to help the recipient get up to speed, and to integrate the practice in the recipient's routine operations.

The frequency of choice of a particular mechanism was then tabulated and rank ordered. For example, it was found that the most frequently used mechanism to identify best practices was a central advisor/expert, next were newsletters, and third were operational reviews. Table 10.2 summarizes the findings. It should be noted also from Table 10.2 that the same mechanism may be used to accomplish more than one task.

MANAGING THE TRANSFER OF BEST PRACTICES

This section suggests how to use the findings presented in this report to plan and help manage transfers of best practice inside your organization. Four practical steps are outlined.

1. First, *familiarize yourself with the phenomenon*. Good management will be more likely with a richer, deeper and more nuanced understanding of what is being managed. Develop a feel for how a transfer happens by reading carefully the description of a typical transfer, and paying special attention to the milestones, actors, and entities, and also to the difficulties that are most likely to emerge at each stage.

2. Next, *use the list of questions in the appendix to assess which sources of difficulty are likely to prevail in your particular case*. When assessing the level of motivation of the source unit, be conservative about your assessment of the actual level of motivation that the source unit will actually display (Figure 10.8). Indeed, source units carried on average three times as much financial burden as recipients or third parties did – a fact that was not always anticipated. As a result, some source units, although initially well predisposed to support the transfer, found themselves unable or unwilling to see the transfer to its conclusion. On average,

Table 10.2 Mechanisms of choice

	Identify best practices	Share best practices	Identify unmet needs	Study feasibility of transfer	Communicate	Plan transfer	Implementation	Train the recipient	Help recipient get up to speed	Integrate the practice
Central advisor/ expert	1		2	2			3	2	2	
Company newsletters	2	2								3
Operational reviews	3									
Presentations		1		3	3	2				
Informal visits		3			1			3	3	
Audit teams			1							
Continuous improvement			3							
Project team recommendation				1		1	1			2
Conferences					2					
Start-up team						3	2			1
Workshops								1		
Central consultants								3		
Help from other units									1	

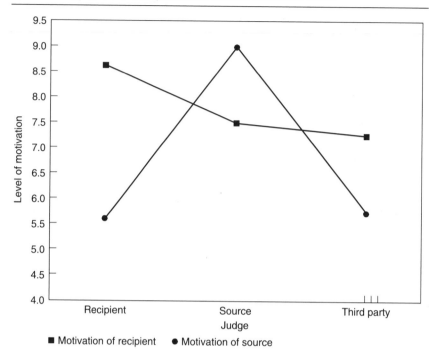

Figure 10.8 Motivation of source and recipient, as judged by source, recipient and third party

their self-assessed motivation appeared exaggerated when contrasted to the perceptions of recipients and third parties. Conversely, the recipient's self-assessment of motivation was largely corroborated by the source units and by the third parties.

3. Once the main sources of difficulty for a particular transfer are established and the expected motivation of the source unit is calibrated, *use Figure 10.7 to identify which stage(s) of the process are likely to demand more managerial attention*, i.e. where more difficulties are to be expected given the sources of difficulty that you have identified. For example, if you conclude that the source unit does not appear sufficiently motivated to support the transfer, difficulties are to be expected during the implementation of the transfer (between thumbs up and flicking the switch) and also during the ramp-up period of the recipient (between flicking the switch and the end of ramp-up). Likewise, if the recipient is not motivated to support the transfer, the highest level of difficulty is going to be experienced during the integration of the new practice in the recipient's operations (after the end of ramp-up).

4. Once you have identified the stage where most attention is to be devoted, *determine which task, from those characteristics at that stage, has to*

be accomplished. For example, if most problems are expected during the integration stage (after the end of ramp-up), the required task is to support the integration of the practice into the operations of the recipients. To determine how to accomplish the required task, you could get ideas from Table 10.2 for which organizational mechanisms to use. For example, if the key task is to integrate the practice in the recipient, Table 10.2 suggests that the most prevalent way to accomplish this task is to secure the presence of a start-up team past the end of the ramp-up period to help smooth the integration of the practice. Alternatively, if other mechanisms prevail in your company, you could check Table 10.2 to see if mechanisms that already exist are used in general to accomplish the required task.

Having completed steps 1–4, you should have developed a feel for when to expect the highest level of difficulties, what the likely sources of those difficulties are, and what could be done to overcome some of those difficulties.

At this stage of the analysis, two questions typically emerge. The first question that pops up is whether the transfer should be mandated, just suggested, made optional, or left to unfold spontaneously (Figure 10.9).

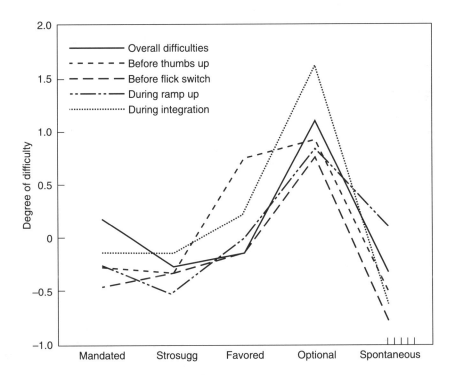

Figure 10.9 Which transfer is more difficult?

The findings suggest that transfers that are 'strongly suggested' or those that are entirely 'spontaneous' seem to experience the lowest degree of difficulty. In contrast, transfers that are 'optional' seem to experience the highest level of difficulty (see your response to the intuition test #1).

In cases when more than one potential recipient exists and the transfer will proceed in a staggered way, a second question is likely to arise: to which of the many possible candidates to receive the practice should the transfer be attempted first, so as to increase the chances of a success (Figure 10.10)? The findings suggest that units that rate themselves as best are likely to be the most motivated recipients, closely followed by units that rate themselves as inferior (see your response to the intuition test #2). Because the best units also are likely to be the most resourceful and able ones, they are probably the best choice as recipients for the first transfer. If those units turn out to be willing recipients and actually realize gains from the transfer, the NIH barrier is likely to collapse for later transfers of the same practice. If the best unit of the organization accepted the practice and gained from it, its success will be visible and any other unit following suit will be in good company.

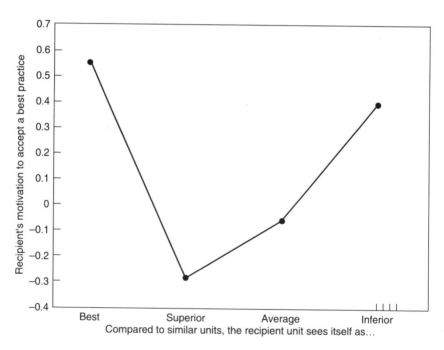

Figure 10.10 The not invented here syndrome

SUMMARY AND CONCLUSION

As you might have guessed, the transfer of best practices inside the firm is a complex phenomenon. No simple formula exists for making it work. The right 'thing to do' should be in harmony with the unique characteristics of your organization.

This report meant to provide a map for thinking about transfers of best practices inside the firm as well as concrete suggestions on how to make it work. The description of a typical transfer purported to help develop a feel for how a transfer happens and what problems are likely to be encountered at each stage. The statistical analysis revealed four main sources of difficulty. In decreasing importance, these were the lack of absorptive capacity[4] of the recipient, lack of understanding of the practice, poor relationship between the source and the recipient, and the lack of motivation of the recipient. A more fine-grained analysis also revealed that during specific stages of the transfer, other sources of difficulty, such as the lack of perceived reliability of the recipient unit, could be temporarily as significant or even more significant than those four. Finally, the survey of mechanisms that are most frequently used to transfer best practices revealed that different mechanisms are used to accomplish the different tasks required to successfully complete a transfer. The survey also revealed that the same mechanism could in many cases be used to accomplish more than one task.

Some findings from the survey are striking. For example, it was interesting to discover some of the limits of accepted wisdom about the transfer of best practices. It was counter intuitive, keeping the predictions of the NIH syndrome in mind, to find that units that evaluated themselves as best turned out to be the most motivated recipients. It also was striking to note how long it took, on the average, to recognize the existence of an opportunity to transfer best practice inside the company (27 months) when compared with the time it took to implement the transfer of that practice (9 months) once the transfer was decided. Taken together, these findings suggest that a primary way to stimulate the transfer of best practices might be to increase the level of awareness to the existence of best practices and to shorten the time it takes to get past the thumbs-up event. Benchmarking may play an important role in that. In turn, the level of awareness can probably be most effectively increased by stimulating a transfer in which the best units of the organizations act as recipients.

Any conclusion drawn from this study should be properly qualified with an explicit acknowledgment of its limitations. The study encompassed only a selected group of companies. Furthermore, in some cases, the number of valid observations was relatively limited. For example, out of the 126 recipients of best practices studied in the survey, 11 ranked inferior, 42 ranked average, 67 ranked superior, and only six units ranked best. Thus, the finding about the motivation of the best units, which calls into question the accepted wisdom about the NIH, although it is statistically significant and confirmed by the fieldwork, should be taken not as an unquestionable universal fact, but rather as food for thought and as a strident warning against any simple recipe derived from accepted wisdom. Yet limitations non-withstanding, this study is the largest systematic study of transfers of practices within organizations and the first to seek explicitly a balanced perspective by combining the perspectives of the source of the best practice, of the recipient of the best practice and of a third party.

It should be noted that the sources of difficulty are likely to respond only gradually to influence. Short-term quick gains are usually costly and ephemeral. Thus, for example, senior management could conceivably boost swiftly the motivation of both the source and of the recipient by vigorously endorsing a particular transfer. Yet this approach has obvious limitations because senior management could not possibly endorse all transfers equally. More importantly, senior management may not even be aware that the possibility to endorse a transfer does exist. It would require unusual and persistent attention for that particular transfer to be perceived in a large company as anything more than a passing fad or flavor of the month. Overcoming the principal barriers to the transfer of best practices, i.e. developing the absorptive capacity of recipients, gaining better understanding of practices, and enhancing the quality of the relationship between organizational subunits is likely to require concerted effort and a non-negligible period of time.

Thus, it appears that an effective approach to improve an organization's ability to transfer best practices will start with a careful assessment of the sources of difficulty and a selective and concerted intervention on the most significant ones. This report may be useful to guide and support such an effort. This could begin by stimulating the most plausible kind of transfer, the 'low hanging fruits', and by learning from the outcome where the actual obstacles lie to transfer best practices within your organization. Attention to the suggested sources of difficulty, milestones, and actors could provide a useful common framework for the organization to begin exploring itself. As argued, there is no one best way, but there might be a best way for your organization.

Recently, much attention has been paid to the idea of the learning organization. When an organization transfers internal best practices successfully, it is broadening its learning by putting to use knowledge it has already acquired. Thus, the recommendations in this report, to the extent that they help stimulate and manage the transfer of best practices, are also pointing to concrete ways to progress towards the holy grail of the learning organization. Specifically, they are pointing out ways in which organizations can better themselves by learning from what they already know.

Why did the companies participate in the project and what have they learned from the process apart from the findings of the project? Listen to the coordinators.

AMP saw a great opportunity to participate in the INSEAD Project:

As is the case with most organizations, we realize the potential achievements that can be gained from the sharing and implementation of recognized practices within an organization. Being both a multi-divisional and multi-national company, we can identify endless opportunities from internal sharing. As such, we were particularly interested in learning how to most effectively transfer these practices, learning not only from or own experiences but also from other participating companies as well.

AT&T Paradyne believed that the results of this study will prove to be very beneficial, especially to multi-national corporations:

In numerous instances, we've found it difficult to transfer excellence from one plant or division to another. Involvement in this study has already improved our ability to conduct similar international studies.

British Petroleum took part in this project for a number of reasons:

A company of this size, with tens of thousands of employees spread all around the world, has to do all it can to avoid reinventing wheels. Anything that can help us minimize that has to be to our advantage. We have a small team who is working on this issue, and early discussions with INSEAD showed that our thinking was going along similar lines. We have been able to add the INSEAD work into our own organization research to identify some key hurdles and facilitating factors in the process of transfer.

The division of Burmah Castrol that took part in the INSEAD study faces a fragmented and highly competitive marketplace:

The division operates through a highly decentralized structure with largely autonomous operating units located in individual territories. This is a key strength in facilitating rapid response to local market opportunities. However, historically this structure has inhibited the sharing of best practice, particularly in such areas as marketing concepts. The division has identified increased sharing of experience between individual units as one of its strategic objectives. Participation in the study helped in highlighting awareness of the problem, although the difficulties had already been well aired at international conferences. The main lesson we've learned by taking part in this project, outside the conclusions drawn by the researchers, was that the sharing of best practice is a discrete activity in its own right, even in such areas as marketing where the experience relates to concepts rather than hardware. The process needs appropriate central and unit management attention in the same way as any other element of international business.

Chevron Corporation decided to participate in the Intra-Firm Transfer of Best Practices Project because the issue of sharing best practices has emerged as a key corporate strategy and will continue to be of great importance in the future:

The oil and gas industry continues to be a very competitive one. A corporation like Chevron must continue to cut its cost in order to survive. We can no longer afford the luxury of continually 'reinventing the wheel'. We also are becoming more devoted to developing a 'Committed Team' of empowered employees as one of our key corporate strategies. We believe that one of the characteristics of such an empowered workforce is their ability to openly share best practices within the corporate boundaries and adopt best practices of others.

EDS was interested in finding out the complexities of intra-firm transfer of best practices:

The process used in the INSEAD study was enlightening and informative. The results will be used to improve the way information (more specifically, benchmarking information) flows across the corporation.

Kaiser Permanente participated in the Intra-Firm Transfer of Best Practices Project to expand its understanding of methods for exchanging knowledge and successfully transferring practices across its numerous sites:

We feel it is imperative to do this because of health care reform pressures and increasing demands by customers to rapidly improve outcomes, reduce utilization, and improve member and patient satisfaction. During our participation in the project, many interesting issues inherent in the exchange process became uncovered. Mr. Szulanski's framework provided us with a common model and language with which to discuss these issues. His framework also helped us anticipate the barriers and problems we might face during the transfer process and has facilitated our understanding of organizational and cultural challenges needed to bring about change.

As a company with operating units in every European country, Rank Xerox has for some time been aware of the need and benefits for successfully transferring best practices within its organization:

The INSEAD study presented an excellent opportunity to learn and assist in making the transfer of practices successful, i.e. fully implemented, with benefits realized and lasting. At the time of the study, the company was about to embark upon a project of identifying and transferring revenue-generating best practices. By participating in the study and identifying past practices for close analysis, it was hoped that learning could be gained that would aid the current work. A small number of past transfers were selected varying between national and international transfers and between management processes, systems transfers, and marketing. The project demonstrated to us the need to inspect very rigorously how successful the transfers had been. In the spirit of learning, we always intended to go back and learn from our own experience. Participating in the process propelled us to actually go back and inspect the transfers, thus making the mere fact of participating in the project useful in itself.

APPENDIX: PREDICTING THE LEVEL OF DIFFICULTY – A CHECKLIST

The following checklist is meant to help gauge the level of difficulty that might be experienced when transferring organizational practices in your organization. The higher the number of negative answers, the more likely that a source of difficulty will manifest itself during the transfer.

Assessing the absorptive capacity of the recipient

- Does the recipient have a clear division of roles and responsibilities to implement the transfer?
- Does the recipient have the necessary skills to implement the practice?
- Does the recipient know who can help solve problems associated with the new practice?

Assessing the level of understanding of the practice

- Are operating procedures for the practice readily available?
- Is there a precise list of skills, resources, and prerequisites necessary for successfully performing the practice?
- Do existing work manuals and operating procedures describe precisely what people working according to the canons of the new practice *actually* do?

Assessing the quality of the relationship between the source and the recipient

- Is communication between the source and the recipient easy?
- Is collaboration between source and recipient sought actively by the source, or at least well received?
- Is collaboraton between source and recipient sought actively by the recipient, or at least well received?

Assessing the support in the organizational context

- Would a unit not lose status by exposing needs it's unable to meet?
- For performance improvement, does your company see copying and adapting practices from other units as legitimate as devising original solutions?
- Are existing performance measures of the practice detailed enough to be meaningful?

Assessing the motivation of the source

- Is the source willing to make the effort to communicate with the recipient?
- Is the source willing to train the recipient's personnel?
- Is the source willing to help the recipient solve unexpected problems when these occur?

Assessing the motivation of the recipient

- Is the recipient willing to analyze the feasibility of adopting the new practices?
- Is the recipient willing to implement the systems and facilities needed for the new practice?
- Is the recipient willing to assign personnel to be trained in the practice?

NOTES

1. The term 'absorptive capacity' refers to the preparedness of the recipient unit to recognize the value of a practice, assimilate it, and apply it to commercial ends. Cohen, W. M., and D. Levinthal, 1990. 'Absorptive capacity: A new perspective on learning and innovation.' *Administrative Science Quarterly* 35(1), 128–152.
2. We found that the term NIH is used with many different meanings. For a rigorous definition of the term NIH, see Katz R. and T. J. Allen, 1982. 'Investigating the Not Invented Here (NIH) Syndrome. A look at the performance, tenure, and communication patterns of 50 R&D Project Groups.' *R&D Management* 12(1) 7–19.

3. To confirm the precision of the dates supplied by the respondents, they were asked also to assess how much time in months they thought elapsed between the decision to initiate the transfer and the end of ramp-up.
4. The term 'absorptive capacity' refers to the preparedness of the recipient unit to recognize the value of a practice, assimilate it, and apply it to commercial ends. Cohen, W. M., and D. Levinthal, 1990. 'Absorptive capacity: A new perspective on learning and innovation.' *Administrative Science Quarterly* 35(1), 128–152.

Chapter 11

The factory as a learning laboratory

Dorothy Leonard-Barton

What is the next production frontier? The author argues that it is operating factories as 'Learning Laboratories.' These are complex organizational ecosystems that integrate problem solving, internal knowledge, innovation and experimentation, and external information. Chaparral Steel is the model example, and the experiences of its managers and employees are used throughout the article to show how the learning laboratory works.

Just after 2:00 am on 26 March 1991, the night crew at the Chaparral Steel minimill in Midlothian, Texas, cast the first production run of 'near netshape' steel beams in the United States. General Manager Lou Colatriano grinned with tired satisfaction and headed home for his first break in forty-four hours. From a sketch on a paper napkin to the first red-hot slab of metal that emerged from a patented mold to streak down the new mill line, the elapsed time was twenty-seven months. That included design, mold development, modeling, pilot runs, and construction, and it represented expertise from five companies on three continents. 'One of our core competencies,' explained CEO Gordon Forward, 'is the rapid realization of new technology into products. We are a learning organization.'

Every manufacturing company in the United States would like to be able to make that statement. Yet a steel mill seems an unlikely place to look for lessons on the quick commercial realization of inventions. In fact, so does any factory, as innovation is generally associated with research laboratories and development organizations. Moreover, we usually assume that the pressure to get product out the door conflicts with learning. But as speed to market becomes an increasingly important criterion of competitive success, we need to rethink our concept of what a factory is. Factories *can* be learning laboratories.

For decades, US factories were passive service organizations to the rest of the company, churning out products designed without benefit of manufacturing input and burying product and process defects under mountains of inventory. The past decade has seen a transformation of many of these operations into low-inventory organizations dedicated to total quality and to active participation in new product development. What is the next frontier for production? In this article I suggest that it is running operations as learning laboratories.

WHAT IS A LEARNING LABORATORY?

A learning laboratory is an organization dedicated to knowledge creation, collection, and control. Contribution to knowledge is a key criterion for all activities, albeit not the only one. In a learning laboratory, tremendous amounts of knowledge and skill are embedded in physical equipment and processes and embodied in people. More important, however, are the nontechnical aspects, the managerial practices and underlying values that constantly renew and support the knowledge bases.

In this article I put Chaparral Steel under the microscope as an example of a highly successful learning laboratory; its leadership has put tremendous effort into creating a consistent learning system. Many of Chaparral's practices are found piecemeal (often experimentally) in other US organizations. As my references suggest, scholars studying best practices among Japanese manufacturers have made strikingly parallel observations, and Chaparral's policies are consistent with prescriptions by organizational learning theorists. Whether you are managing a fabrication shop or claims processing in an insurance office, Chaparral's management system offers a potentially useful model.

TAKING AN ORGANIC SYSTEM VIEW

Chaparral is the tenth largest US steel producer. Its high-quality standards have been rewarded by the market, and it consistently sets records for productivity, compared to both US and Asian competitors (see Appendix: The Evidence on Chaparral Steel). Clearly, whatever it is doing works.

A close look at the company reveals an organic learning system so tightly integrated that Forward says he can tour competitors through the plant, show them almost '*everything*, and we will be giving away *nothing* because they can't take it home with them.' His confidence derives from the fact that the learning laboratory cannot be constructed piecemeal. It is comprehensible only as an organic whole; close scrutiny is required to appreciate its delicacy. To complicate matters, such a corporate ecosystem is in continuous flux, constantly regenerating itself. Even if a competitor identifies important elements of the system, emulation will require time. By then, Chaparral managers trust they will have moved on to the next innovation. The Chaparral system has evolved in response to a turbulent competitive environment, as Forward observes: 'We have to go like hell all the time. If the price of what we sell goes up too high, . . . all of a sudden lots of folks will be jumping in. And they can get into business in eighteen months or so . . . We constantly chip away the ground we stand on. We have to keep out front all the time.'[1]

A learning laboratory does not occur spontaneously but is designed, created, and maintained through constant managerial attention to communicating the underlying values, checking the management systems' smallest details for consistency, and adapting any inharmonious elements. Thus managers designing a learning laboratory need to adopt holistic, systems thinking. They will have to acknowledge the practical utility and bottom-line impact of corporate values. They may have to confront chronic underestimation of the interdependence between incentive and education systems and corporate strategy. Moreover, such systems thinking must permeate the organization's every level. Everyone in the firm must appreciate the self-reinforcing nature of knowledge-creating activities. Only by comprehending the whole system can one understand why, when a fragment of the learning laboratory is pulled out to be examined (a particular project, a specific learning activity), it comes out vinelike, trailing roots back to deeply held values and widely observed management practices. It is this intense interconnectedness that makes such systems difficult to imitate and fragile – but effective.[2]

Learning requires creation and control of both external and internal knowledge for both current and future operations. Therefore, four distinguishing activities are critical to a learning laboratory: (1) problem solving (in current operations); (2) internal knowledge integration (across functions and projects); (3) innovation and experimentation (to build for the future); and (4) integration of external information flows (see Figure 11.1).[3] Each activity is the operational expression of an underlying value and is strongly supported by a compatible managerial system of procedures and incentives. Thus each activity, value, and managerial system functions as an internally consistent subsystem. Although I will describe each subsystem separately, the four are mutually aligned and interrelated; that is, values and managerial systems underlying one subsystem also support the other three. An in-depth look at the four subsystems at Chaparral suggests some of the principles that distinguish a learning laboratory.[4]

Before exploring these subsystems, however, we need a brief explanation of Chaparral's near net-shape project, an innovative foray directly into the traditional territory of 'Big Steel' that illustrates the company's knowledge creation and control subsystems.

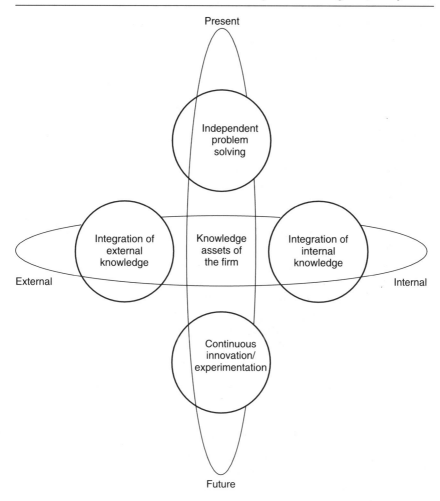

Figure 11.1 Knowledge creation and control activities in a learning laboratory

THE NEAR NET-SHAPE PROJECT

One way to push equipment performance and ensure learning is to set goals for each project considerably beyond current capabilities.[5] Chaparral managers set a very ambitious goal for the near net-shape project: to produce large (eighteen- and twenty-four-inch wide) structural steel I-beams for the same per-pound cost as the simple round reinforcing bars ('rebars'), the company's first product. 'We knew what it took to make rebar,' explains General Manager Duff Hunt. 'The challenge was to produce a more difficult product for the same cost. . . . We decided on the twenty-four-inch because we wanted to explore the most technically challenging product. Because there may be some idiosyncrasies about the process that we need to learn, we also chose a second size . . . based on the amount of North American consumption.' Reaching this cost objective (half of Big Steel's) required drastically reducing the energy costs (roughly 25% of total) of rolling the steel into the required end shape. The nearer to the final ('net') shape the molten steel could be cast, the less rolling required.

The only known processes for casting steel to its near net shape were far too capital and labor intensive for Chaparral, which views large investments in either capital or labor as a threat to future flexibility. The steel-making molds and processes developed for the near net-shape project therefore embody knowledge beyond anything available on the market and, in fact, beyond anything the leading vendors of steel-making molds thought possible. The approximately four-foot copper alloy tube through which the molten steel passes to emerge in nearly I-beam shape is deceptively simple in appearance. However, the mold is patented, which suggests that the combined expertise of Chaparral designers and Italian and German mold fabricators endowed it with cutting-edge knowledge. The mold is contoured so the hot metal won't bind as it shrinks going through, and the fabrication methods produce an absolutely smooth finish on the sides, to lessen chances of rending the thin skin surrounding the molten steel as it emerges. It is difficult to imagine how Chaparral could have succeeded in this knowledge-intensive project had the company not been run as a learning laboratory.

THE LEARNING LABORATORY SYSTEM

Some of the activities, values, and managerial practices described below characterize any high-quality organization. Others are very unusual – at least in the United States. Since they operate as a system, we have to look at the whole operation to understand why emulating just some parts may never produce true learning laboratories.

Subsystem one: owning the problem and solving it

The first critical learning subsystem is the triad of (1) the independent problem solving required for continuous improvement of current processes, (2) egalitarianism as an underlying value, and (3) shared rewards as the reinforcing incentives system (see Figure 11.2). Empowered individuals, who command respect in the organization and who feel ownership in the system, have the self-confidence, freedom, and motivation to continuously solve problems. The principle involved here turns the old production saw of 'if it ain't broke, don't fix it' on its head and maintains: 'if it ain't being fixed continuously, it's broke.'

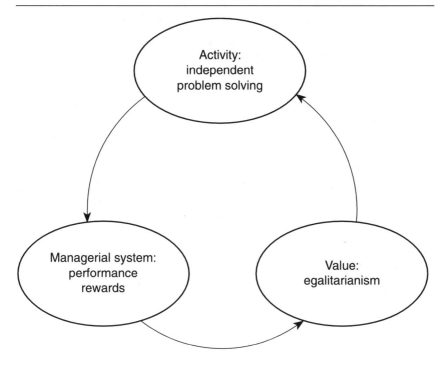

Figure 11.2 Subsystem one: Owning the problem and solving it

Activity: independent problem solving

Learning starts with empowered individuals who can identify and solve problems independently because they have a clear sense of operating objectives. The often-articulated vision at Chaparral is to lead the world in the low-cost, safe production of high-quality steel. This resembles the mission of many other companies that are not learning organizations. For a learning lab, the test of a vision is the extent to which it permeates the whole organization, guiding every micro and macro decision. Unless the vision can be directly translated into operational principles, that is, into guidelines for running the factory lines, it may have little effect on actual shop-floor behavior. Chaparral's goal of leading the world requires innovation beyond the current cutting edge of production techniques. Maintaining a cost advantage requires constant improvements in productivity. The vision dictates that those improvements cannot come at the expense of quality or employee safety. Therefore the goal for every hour, the criterion for every person's activity, is crystal clear: make ever more steel – increasingly better than anyone else. 'We never stray far from the market,' says Hunt.

In a learning environment, progress has to be everyone's business – not just that of a few specialists. At Chaparral, who owns a production problem and responsibility for its solution? An incident during the first few weeks of operating the near net-shape caster, when cooling hoses were bursting, provides some insight. 'When something like that comes up, and there seems no immediate solution,' explains a senior operator, 'you go see what the problem is. You don't say, "That's not my area," or "I don't know that much about it." You just show up.' In this case, a group of operators, a welder, some foremen, and a buyer spontaneously gathered to discuss the problem and just as spontaneously scattered to seek solutions. 'Everybody telephoned some person they thought might know how to fix the problem – vendors, experts – and within three to four hours we were getting calls back,' says the senior operator. 'Service people were showing up, and we worked the problem out. If it had been just one guy, probably a foreman, and everyone walked out, . . . it would have taken him ten times longer to find a solution.'

Because the performance goal is very clear, supervisors do not need to micromanage the line, and the organization runs lean. For instance, two months after the first run of the near net-shape casting, the pulpit controls operator is carefully checking the timing on the line with a stopwatch. The red-hot beams pass through the rolling mill stand once, then stop, reverse, and go through again. Meanwhile, the flow of steel behind the beam being rolled is diverted. Every second of unnecessary diversion costs money because the diverted steel will have to be reheated to be rolled. Therefore the operator wants to achieve split-second timing. Asked who suggested he perform this function (which is often given to a process engineer elsewhere), he is surprised at the question: 'No one.' He considers it obvious that improvement is always a part of his job: 'We're still learning, but we will get it. You just take it upon yourself to roll as much steel as you can whether you are the pulpit operator, the roller, the furnace operator: . . . We want to do the best we possibly can. Everybody here has the attitude to pick up the pace.'

One of the greatest advantages of this attitude, as a maintenance foreman points out, is that 'ideas come from just about everybody. The operators working on the equipment have a lot of input because they see the exact problems when they happen.' Moreover, potential improvements are immediately enacted with no wait for management approval or standardization of 'best practices'. If it works, it is the *de facto* standard. If it improves performance, everyone will imitate it. 'Whoever can come up with an idea on how to fix it, from the millwrights or myself right on up to the top, . . . does it right then,' explains a foreman. At Chaparral, there is no formal requirement, as at some Japanese companies, for a certain number of improvement suggestions from each employee. Everyone is involved in some process improvement projects, and, as the foreman explains, 'We are all out here to make it run. Probably 90% of the problems never even make it to the morning meetings [held among everyone on the shift to discuss problems]. They are fixed in the field.'[6]

The downside to this intrapreneurial attitude is that although managers set the goals, no one has the authority to tell another employee *how* to accomplish a task. Process engineers and supervisors who know a better procedure often have difficulty convincing operators on the line – much less their peers. 'You can't tell them how to do it,' Administration Vice President Dennis Beach admits somewhat ruefully, 'and they don't do it the way you would.' The engineers concur. They are not called upon enough, in their opinions. However, the benefits from general ownership of all problems are that it is not possible to 'pass the buck' and no one expects a steady-state manufacturing process – ever.

Value: egalitarianism and respect for the individual

A learning environment is premised on egalitarianism, the assumption that all individuals have potential to contribute to the joint enterprise (if they are willing to develop competence). Forward has observed, 'We figured that if we could tap the egos of everyone in the company, we could move mountains.'[7] Outward symbols of values are important because they convey meaningful messages to all employees. At Chaparral there are no assigned parking places, no different colored hard hats or uniforms reflecting title or position, and the company dining room is a local diner. More unusual, a scant two levels separate the CEO from operators in the rolling mill; a visitor is surprised when an operator stops Forward on a walk through the plant to discuss a new product's problems. A millwright notes: 'If you have tact, you can tell anybody from Mr. Forward on down exactly what is on your mind. There is no problem in expressing your opinion here.' Repeated requests to interview a particularly knowledgeable project manager are politely rebuffed with a shrug and an explanation from a vice president: 'Sorry, he just doesn't want to. I can't *make* him.' However, respect for the individual does not mean equality of responsibility, lack of discipline, or even consensual decision making. Chaparral managers believe that a supervisor should be a leader, trained to make good decisions – including hiring and firing.

Managerial system: performance rewards

Positive thinking and slogans alone cannot create genuine employee investment in innovation and in identifying and solving problems.[8] Chaparral has taken unusual steps to ensure that performance and incentive systems back up management's belief in egalitarianism. In 1986–87, when employment leveled off, and management confronted potential stagnation, the pay structure was overhauled to reward accumulation of skills as well as performance. Even more radical (especially for a steel mill) was the switch from hourly wages to salary for everyone. There are no time clocks at Chaparral. Forward explains, 'When I am ill, I get a day off. Why shouldn't everyone else?' He is fond of saying that the management system was designed for the 97% who are 'conscientious people who want to put in a full day's work.' The 3% who abused the system were let go. Beach summarizes the philosophy: 'We manage by adultery. We treat everyone like an adult.' Moreover, the pain and pleasure of work are spread around. For instance, in contrast to many factories, operators are not assigned to shifts according to seniority. Everyone rotates into night shift, a practice that fosters knowledge accumulation twenty-four hours a day and guards against a possible disproportionate accumulation of skills and knowledge in the most favored hours. The reward for seniority is thus not greater comfort, but more challenges. How do senior employees feel about that? 'During the summer in Texas,' one foreman rationalizes with a grin, 'you'd *rather* work at night.'

Steel-making is hot, dirty, demanding work; the pace of innovation and the constant pressure to produce more, better, and more safely in this organization exacerbate the brutal conditions imposed by the technology. What keeps the workforce from burning out? One factor is the incentive systems that have evolved.[9]

Bonus schemes are linked to company profits – for everyone. 'We think janitors and secretaries are important in our success, too, and they should share in the rewards,' observes Forward. An operator comments, 'The more money the company makes, the more I make. The profit-sharing system creates built-in pride.' Further, 93% of the employees are stockholders and together own 3% of the stock. In 1988, each employee received one share for every year worked at the company; 62% buy additional shares every month through payroll deductions. Although the monetary implications are small, this policy is consistent with the rest of the rewards structure, and some employees find it symbolically important. A furnace controls operator comments, 'I feel like this company partly belongs to me. Owning part of the company makes you care. I take better care not to waste anything because I feel like I am paying for it.'

These could be just words, of course. Scholars studying the relationship between such incentive systems and productivity have not reached consensus about the benefits of employee shareholding (partly because shareholding agreements vary widely). However, there is strong support for the notion that profit sharing generally does raise productivity.[10]

At Chaparral, the dual incentives of employee profit sharing and share-holding seem a natural complement to the rest of the learning laboratory system.

Subsystem two: garnering and integrating knowledge

The second subsystem revolves around knowledge accrual (see Figure 11.3). In the learning laboratory, knowledge is highly and visibly valued. Management invests in educating the whole person, not just the technical side, and knowledge flows freely across boundaries. The principle is this: every day, in every project, add to the knowledge resources.

Activity: integrating internal knowledge

In a learning laboratory, one would expect to see visible embodiment of knowledge creation and control in highly innovative physical systems. Chaparral boasts of such cutting-edge equipment as an automobile shredder that they believe is the fastest and most efficient in the world, a horizontal (instead of vertical) caster, and some of the most advanced

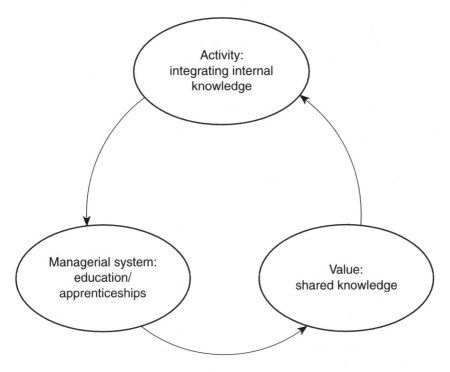

Figure 11.3 Subsystem two: garnering and integrating knowledge

digital furnace controls anywhere. Because of the constant push to improve production, Chaparral managers have to design what they need, rather than purchase the best available equipment off-the-shelf. Why design in-house? 'To keep the knowledge here,' a mill manager explains. Moreover, managers assume that the performance of *any* purchased equipment can be improved. Some improvements are novel enough to be patented. Rolling mill equipment that its vendor believed was limited to eight-inch slabs is turning out fourteen-inch, and the vendor has tried to buy back the redesign. The two electric arc furnaces, designed originally to melt annual rates of 250,000 and 500,000 tons of scrap metal, respectively, now produce over 600,000 and 1 million tons, respectively.

The physical processes following the molding step are also knowledge intensive. Only one other steel mill in the world does the hot-link rolling employed in the near net-shape casting project, whereby hot cast steel is sent directly into the rolling mills. Using this technique was a big risk because no one knew exactly what the properties of the thinner cast steel would be. The hot link meant less subsequent rolling than usual and hence less 'working' of the steel to obtain the desired crystalline structure. The risk paid off when the combination near net-shape casting and hot link turned out to produce steel with exceptionally good metallurgical characteristics. Chaparral processes seem clear out-growths of skill, yet how does such expertise and knowledge accumulate?

Just as continuous processing has great advantages for manufacturing over most batch processing, so the unimpeded flow of information aids learning more than fragmented, batch-processed information.[11] Most organizations are physically structured to emphasize vertical (hierarchical) and horizontal (functional) boundaries. In contrast, Chaparral management emphasizes homogenizing the level of knowledge throughout; few pockets of information are isolated by position, function, or working shift.[12]

Information flow at Chaparral is obviously aided by its size, deliberately held to under a thousand employees. An individual garnering knowledge on a trip, at a conference, or from an experiment can readily transmit it, as all employees are located in the same place and know each other. The company was also designed to facilitate knowledge flows by encouraging as many accidental meetings as possible. The plant layout accommodates the hands-on style of management favored at Chaparral; even Forward's office is just steps away from the furnaces and mills. The locker room is located here also, so that at least once a day employees cycle through the one-story headquarters building.[13] Consequently, meetings are as likely to be held in the halls as in the conference rooms. Since many decisions go unrecorded and memos are anathema, it is important that people see each other frequently.

Hierarchical boundaries are minimal. This is a do-it-yourself company with no acknowledged staff positions and only a few positions that seem stafflike, such as personnel. There are fifty graduate engineers and technicians, all with line duties. In fact, everyone has line responsibilities, most of them tied directly to steel production, and decision making is pushed down to the lowest possible supervisory level, 'where the knowledge is.' Lead operators are selected for their knowledge-transmitting as well as knowledge-creating skills, because much knowledge flows horizontally among peers. Work is structured with the objective of disseminating knowledge. For instance, in commissioning the new mill that receives the near net-shape product (that is, ramping it up to problem-free production), only two teams of operators are being trained. Each team works a twelve-hour shift (with paid overtime). After the initial eight weeks of this grueling schedule, these operators will be dispersed among the rest of the crews to diffuse the knowledge they have created and assimilated about the new process's idiosyncrasies.

Chaparral has also proven that traditional horizontal boundaries can be redrawn and expectations altered. The quality control department is responsible for reacting to quality problems identified by operators on the line – not by separate inspectors. Production workers do 40% of maintenance tasks. A maintenance foreman notes that 'at Chaparral, we get involved with the whole process. We are not just tied to one area.'

Although the company has a marketing department, everyone is considered a salesperson. Every employee from CEO to receptionist has a business card to use with customers. Security guards do data entry while on night duty and are trained paramedics as well. Such multifunctional experience is encouraged not only to make the organization more flexible but because management believes it discourages territorial possessiveness over information.

No research and development (R&D) department exists separate from production. Forward maintains that 'everybody is in research and development. The plant is our laboratory.' This statement has implications beyond the obvious that there is no research function. Some of the problem solving and experimentation that are done in the midst of production involve research. However, interfacing with the possessors of the latest scientific knowledge is not restricted to an elite group of specialists. Knowledge accumulation in a learning lab cannot be the responsibility of a few special people. Forward describes the large, separate research centers in some companies as 'lovely, really nice. But the first time I went into one of them I thought I was entering Forest Lawn [Cemetery]. After you spend some time there, you realize you *are* in Forest Lawn. Not because there are no good ideas there, but because the good ideas are dying there all the time.'[14]

At Chaparral, even operators participate in R&D activities. When the world's leading supplier was constructing the patented mold for the near net-shape project, the three-person team that shuttled back and forth to the site in Germany, learning about the fabrication process and serving as a source of information about the intended production process, included an operator. As described later in Subsystem Four, Chaparral employees at all levels are constantly tapping into the latest, most current knowledge banks around the world.

Value: shared knowledge

Since performance drives everything in this company, and individual incentives are tied to performance, employees seem engaged in a marathon relay race, where winning as a company team takes precedence over individual ownership of ideas, and knowledge is liberally shared. There are acknowledged experts, such as the director of operations who is an 'equipment whiz', and the mold expert who was largely responsible for the near-net shape design, and the organization does not lack for large egos. However, Vice President of Operations Dave Fournie says that 'you don't *have* to have credit for particular ideas to be thought good at your job. Lots of innovations take more than one good idea. They go through a gestation period, and lots of people figure out how to make sense of it. The point is to focus on the good of the *whole*. That's why we don't have suggestion boxes, where you hide ideas so someone else won't steal them.'

Chaparral employees are often unable to identify the source of production innovation. Production Manager Paul Wilson explains, 'It is hard to say who fathers an idea. It doesn't make any difference. Everybody shares in the pride of doing, and if the experiment fails, everyone shares in the failure. In other places, a few people do a lot of innovating. Here a lot of people do little bits that add up.' A millwright makes similar observations: 'No one is looked down upon. If I am supposed to know more than somebody else but that other person catches [an oversight], well that's fine – he just bailed me out. I am more than likely going to help him out a different time.'

Managerial system: apprenticeships and education

An organization that values knowledge must provide mechanisms for continuous learning. Chaparral management has sent some employees to school to obtain advanced degrees, but it also invests heavily in an unusual formal apprenticeship program for everyone in the plant, which it developed with the Bureau of Apprenticeship and Training in the US Department of Labor. (Most apprenticeships are run by unions.) As

Forward notes, 'Expertise must be in the hands of the people that make the product.'

The roughly three-and-a-half-year program allows apprentices to progress to the level of senior operator/craftsman by successfully completing 7,280 hours of on-the-job training and designated formal schooling. The foremen of individual crews schedule the on-the-job training and evaluate the candidate's systematic progression through various tasks in the factory. For example, 2,200 hours in steel-pouring operations is one qualification in the ladle metallurgy apprenticeship. In addition, all apprentices complete study programs in safety, operating processes across the entire company, mathematics as related to operations, metallurgy, and basic mechanical maintenance 'in an effort to give all operators a solid basic understanding of the equipment used and the operating processes.' Scheduling this study, which requires four hours of unpaid work a week, is left up to the individuals, who have five options: home study with manuals and videos; in-plant study in instructor-monitored study rooms; formal classes; personalized tutoring by instructors; and study in work areas as operations permit. (Operators may also get credit for prior experience by proving knowledge on the job.) Courses include basic engineering knowledge such as conduction in liquids and gases, as well as very specific skills such as ladder logic programming for understanding programmable controllers and lubricant storage and handling. Perhaps more surprising are such sessions as 'working with other people' under 'troubleshooting skills.'

The most unusual aspect is the instructors. Selected foremen rotate in from the factory floor to teach. 'It creates a lot of credibility for the education program on the factory floor,' explains one instructor. 'What's more,' he adds wryly, 'I have to live with what I teach. So I'd better do a good job.'

Chaparral also invests in outside courses of all types, tending to train its own people rather than hiring those with a particular skill. A maintenance foreman attended a special engineering course because 'no one knew anything about vibration analysis so I was asked to go study it.' External education includes nontechnical courses as well. In few factories would a furnace controls operator attend a Dale Carnegie-type course to help him enhance the interpersonal skills critical to smooth teamwork. Line managers are expected to be technical experts, constantly up-to-date with cutting-edge technology – whether that be some aspect of metallurgy or human resources. Therefore every manager attends conferences and cultivates a professional network of information sources. The manager of the scrap shredding operations, for instance, has just attended a conference on recycling – in the future, Chaparral's expertise in recycling may be an important corporate capability.[15]

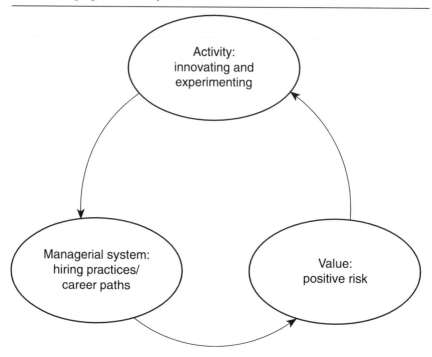

Figure 11.4 Subsystem three: Challenging the status quo

Subsystem three: challenging the status quo

The third subsystem in a learning laboratory involves constantly pushing knowledge frontiers (see Figure 11.4). The company must select employees for their desire to challenge their own and others' thinking. They must see risk as positive, because it comes with the experimentation critical to innovation. The company must select suppliers for their superior capabilities – and for their willingness to be pushed beyond the bounds of their current knowledge. The principle involved is this: always reach beyond your grasp.

Activity: continuous experimentation

Learning requires constant pushing beyond the known, and Chaparral employees are skilled experimenters. A visitor was surprised to find that extensive overhead slides explaining the formal Taguchi experimental designs that were guiding the development of the horizontal caster had been prepared for the board of directors. This extremely technical presentation was to help directors understand the methodical knowledge-creation process, enable them to identify critical decision points, and thereby better equip them to evaluate the risk. Another example of knowledge-creating experimentation more often found in research laboratories than factoriess is the one-sixth scale model of the near net-shape caster, which uses water to approximate the flow of steel. Standing alongside the rolling mill, close to a water source, this model allowed testing of several types of baffles and lengths of mold. Resulting observations guided much of the eventual mold design decisions.

Innumerable large and small experiments are more of the 'cut-and-try' variety. 'We aren't always as systematic about our learning as we could be,' Forward admits. Many creative simulations are conducted right on the production line. The advantage is that the more closely the experimental environment approximates the final production environment, the more immediately relevant is the information generated. The disadvantage is the obvious potential to disrupt production – which is why most factories prefer to isolate experimentation. In one of many projects leading to the near net-shape casting, a prototype of metal splashboards was first constructed out of plywood. By continuously soaking the wood in water, the crews were able to keep it from being consumed by molten steel just long enought to prove the concept. 'We were the local hardware store's favorite plywood customers for a while,' one employee recalled. Similarly, during the design of the near net-shape caster, several prototype molds of almost pure copper were used to determine if casting a dog-bone-shaped slab was possible. The soft molds held together just long enough to show this new casting process's feasibility.[16]

The operating role is this: if you have an idea, try it. Line managers authorize tens of thousands of dollars for experiments without higher authority. Hunt explains, 'We use products to do research. We can close the feed-back loop between researchers and users by using new methods and new materials within our facility.' Wilson agrees: 'In other companies, the word is – don't rock the boat. Here we rock the hell out of the boat. We don't know the factory's limits. We want it to change, to evolve.'

Not every suggestion is instantly suggested. When a maintenance operator at a conference spied new digital furnace pulpit controls, he then had to convince his supervisor to invest. For almost two years, the supervisor remained uninterested in visiting the Mexican vendor and a site using the controls. Yet the operator persisted. Finally, his supervisor understood the potential of these state-of-the-art controls and agreed to their installation and customization to Chaparral operators' specifications.

During the development of the near net-shape beams, Chaparral frequently disconcerted development partners by its innovation speed. One innovation followed so hard on the heels of the previous one that they almost overlapped. When the German mold developers finished a prototype on schedule and called to ask how they should ship it, they were astonished to be told, 'Don't ship it at all; cut it up and make it look like this.' The designers had already learned enough from the prototyping process to improve the design. A new mold would be required. What surprised partners was that Chaparral did not appear to begrudge the 'wasted' $40,000 per mold, since the knowledge engendered by each prototype enabled the next step in innovation.

Value: positive risk

In a research laboratory, risk is accepted as the norm, since the cutting edge is always fraught with uncertainty. In contrast, risk is usually anathema in a production environment. Managers of a learning factory must tolerate, even welcome, a certain amount of risk as a concomitant of knowledge acquisition. Chaparral managers avoid riskless projects because a 'sure thing' holds no promise of competitive advantage – no opportunity to outlearn competitors. Says Forward, 'We look at risk differently from other people. We always ask what is the risk of doing *nothing*. We don't bet the company, but if we're not taking some calculated risks, if we stop growing, we may die.

This positive attitude toward risk permeates the company. If everyone experiments, learns, and innovates, then neither success nor failure can be heavily personalized. If individuals are singled out for praise, then they have an incentive to protect ideas as intellectual property rather than seek embellishment from friendly critics and codevelopers. If individuals are singled out for blame, then the risk of failure may overwhelm the impulse to innovate. What happens when you try something and it doesn't work? What is the penalty? 'Everybody makes mistakes,' a Chaparral foreman responds. 'You don't have to cover up a mistake here. You just fix it and keep on going.' The philosophy appears to apply even when the failed experiment is very expensive. In 1986, when Fournie was medium section mill superintendent, he championed the installation of a $1.5 million arc saw for cutting finished beams. Not only did the magnetic fields attract any small unattached pieces of metal for yards around, including pens and watches, but the engineers were never able to refine the equipment to the point of effective operation. Since promoted to vice president of operations, Fournie is somewhat amused to find that visitors 'can't believe you can make a mistake like that and not get crucified.' He tries to take the same attitude toward those who work for him: 'You don't start them out on $1.5 million projects, but you have to give them freedom to make mistakes. The reward for having ideas is getting to carry them out. You give them bigger and bigger chunks and evaluate.' Operators on the line have a consistent view of the atmosphere for innovation.: 'You have an idea – good, bad, indifferent – just spit it out and we'll talk about it. Someone may laugh [at it] but you'll laugh back next week.'

A potential hazard of this positive attitude toward risk is that no one wants to admit a mission is impossible. 'Once we say we will do something,' Fournie explains, 'we hang on and try like nobody's ever tried before. Tenacity makes lots of projects work here that don't work other places – but when it just can't be done, it's hard to call the project off.' One of his key criteria for determining if people are ready for promotion is whether they know when to ask for help, when to admit that they are in over their heads: 'It's a tough call . . . the hardest decision to learn to make.' He speaks from experience. He not only set up the arc saw project; he killed it.

Managerial system: hiring practices and career paths

The most important managerial system in a learning laboratory is selecting and retaining the right employees. Because employees must be innovators, constantly challenging the status quo, they are selected as much for their potential, their attitude toward learning, and their enthusiasm as for a specific background. Although top managers and a few specialized 'gurus' at Chaparral have extensive steel experience, when Chaparral was first set up, management decided not to look for workers with industry experience. Beach explains: 'We were looking for bright, enthusiastic, articulate people, and we preferred people who had not been exposed to other companies' bad habits.' The company therefore hired (and continues to hire) from the immediate geographic area, seeking ranchers and farmers with mechanical ability but no steel experience. Chaparral looks for 'a twinkle in the eye, a zest for life,' for 'basically conscientious people who can put in a strong day's work and enjoy what they're doing.' This love of work is critical in an organization that deliberately runs somewhat understaffed to avoid laying people off during market downturns. A learning laboratory is not a good match for someone who works solely for a paycheck or who equates promotion with increasingly easy work.

Chaparral's original applicants went through six weeks of intensive training with daily evaluations and faced stiff competition. Top performers were given their choice of jobs and an immediate 20% pay rise. Highly selective hiring procedures continue to reflect concern that new employees fit into the Chaparral culture, that at least one supervisor be personally committed to their training and progress, and that the team have a stake in their success. Although personnel does some preliminary screening, current applicants undergo one or more days of demanding interviews with at least five employees, including two foremen, before they join Chaparral. Only one out of ten applicants selected for interviews can expect to be hired, and the final decision belongs to the foreman with direct responsibility. These very cautious, resource-intensive selection practices may account in part for the extremely dedicated workforce, which boasts an absentee rate about one-fourth that represented by the National Association of Manufacturers.

Since people are the key resource in a knowledge-intensive organization, keeping them is critical.[17] Beach explains: 'From the very beginning, we designed this organization with Maslow's hierarchy of needs in mind [i.e. that once people's basic needs for food, shelter, and belonging are satisfied, they will aspire to a fourth level of need, self-esteem, and finally, the fifth, self-actualization.] I know it's not stylish, but we really believe in that hierarchy, so we constantly look at what will help people become self-actualized, at their ego needs. . . . People like a challenge and a well-defined goal out there.'[18]

A strong aid in motivating continuous innovation is a clear path for advancement, not just in salary but in position. Asked what he looks for in a job, a millwright responds: 'As long as I am moving forward, I can think for myself, and I feel that I am contributing, I will be happy.' Chaparral managers believe that skilled, innovative people will leave an organization if they see no possibility for personal growth. During the 1986–87 reorganization to address possible stagnation, some maintenance and shipping operations were reorganized into autonomous, self-directed teams with rotating leadership. Management regards this change as an organizational experiment that may provide a model for other parts of the company.

The company invests in crosstraining at a number of levels. Management has learned the necessity of training in advance of the need because of problems experienced early in the company's history, when operators who were automatically moved up into lead and then supervisory positions as vacancies opened proved underprepared. In response, Chaparral management established such idiosyncratic practices as 'vice-ing'. In other companies, when a foreman or supervisor is absent, usually the foreman from a prior shift stays on in that position. When a similar absence occurs at Chaparral, the prior foreman works the extra hours, at his usual pay level, but in a *subordinate* role. The most senior operator or craftsman is then temporarily promoted to 'vice foreman' to cover the supervisory position. Thus the company retains operating experience in the form of the prior shift foreman and simultaneously trains the senior operator for future work as a foreman. A supervisor explains, 'You get a little pay increase and a whole lot more responsibility. I got a chance to see whether I really wanted to be a foreman or not, and it gives you a little respect for the boss's job.'

Managers are similarly prepared for the future. Recently the production managers for the three mills were given the title of general manager

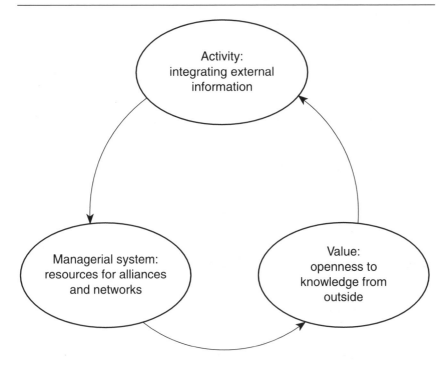

Figure 11.5 Subsystem four: Creating a virtual organization

and asked to learn each other's jobs and to cover for each other. This crosstraining is intended to prepare them for general management of an entire operation, when Chaparral starts up another site.[18]

Subsystem four: creating a virtual research organization through networking

A learning laboratory obviously needs access to the latest knowledge, embodied in the best minds and best equipment available. However, not all companies can afford an internal research organization. Moreover, no company can cover all the technological advances, worldwide, that may affect its future. Therefore the principle behind the fourth and final subsystem is this: create a virtual research organization through extensive networking and alliances – for learning and for economic reasons (see Figure 11.5).

Activity: integrating external knowledge

At Chaparral, employees constantly scan the world for technical expertise that others have already invested in. Managers never hesitate to invent when necessary but only after assuring themselves through extensive searches that no available system will suit their needs. While building the horizontal caster, they made repeated trips to the few other world sites that had somewhat similar equipment. Chaparral also constantly benchmarks its capabilities, not just against immediate competitors but also against best-of-class companies, even those from totally different industries. Three on-site laboratories support production through chemical and physical product analysis, but the company has created a virtual research organization through extensive networking and alliances. Information obtained externally is rapidly incorporated through development projects, flowing through the created network almost as readily as it does inside the walls of the learning laboratory, because in both cases people working directly in production transmit the knowledge.

The network was heavily used in the near net-shape project. At its outset, a team of managers and foremen visited Japan and determined that one firm had the most advanced 'profile' casting process in the world. Yet it was inflexible, would cost more than the entire company', and was more labor intensive than desired. Chaparral therefore enlisted the help of German and Italian suppliers. At first extremely skeptical of this small company from the middle of Texas and hence unwilling to try to make the radical mold design, the German supplier began to believe that seemingly impossible goals could be achieved only when it saw how far Chaparral had progressed with the help of the Italians. Chaparral employees visited the German vendor every few weeks, and ultimately Chaparral's expertise combined with the German's cutting-edge knowledge to produce a patented mold that neither company could have made alone.

Concerned that the relatively thin cast steel emerging from this mold might have undesirable metallurgical qualities, Chaparral reached again into its network for testing. Since it had not yet built its own rolling mill, and none existed anywhere that could receive the novel shape, managers identified a production laboratory in Mexico with very flexible equipment. Chaparral's superindendent of steel-melt technology went to Mexico to direct the simulation of the future mill design, using Mexican equipment and workers. To their delight, Chaparral managers discovered that the samples demonstrated superior characteristics.

The development and testing laboratories in the German and Mexican firms served as virtual extensions of the corporation, for they possessed special equipment and skills that complemented Chaparral's design capabilities. However, knowing such sources of expertise exist would be useless if the factory were not able to tap them, to jointly create more knowledge, and then to absorb that knowledge into the production system.

Chaparral's collegial knowledge network seems more characteristic of a research laboratory than of a factory. Possibly because of Forward's early career as a research metallurgist, the company aggressively pursues the latest knowledge. Chaparral sought the coveted Japanese certification for steel, not because managers thought they would ever sell much steel in Japan, but because they believed the Japanese would go through the company's process carefully – and Chaparral would learn much from the exercise. Forward takes a distinctly nontraditional view of environmental scanning for a factory: 'By the time you hear about a technology in a paper at a conference, it is too late.' This philosophy explains why Chaparral invests in unorthodox knowledge-gathering mechanisms, for instance, by cosponsoring a research conference with the Colorado School of Mining about a new alloy under investigation. Forward himself treks back regularly to his alma mata, MIT, to consult with university experts.[20]

Very occasionally, this method of R&D has failed the company. The most notable example is the previously mentioned electric arc saw. No one in the plant or in its network of experts, including the vendor, was able to solve the technical difficulties. The mill manager left the saw in place for almost a year to allow time for everyone to attempt solutions and to accept failure, while he sought an alternative technology. It is not clear that an in-house R&D facility would have helped in this case because the required invention lay in the unfamiliar realm of electromagnetic fields. Managers at Chaparral believe that through their virtual R&D organization, they can actually tap a larger variety of knowledge bases than they would be able to support internally, given their size. Still, they will have to continue investing in internal expertise in order to integrate the externally obtained knowledge.

Value: openness to knowledge from outside

Knowledge garnered through such networks can flourish only in an environment that rejects the 'not invented here' mentality. At Chaparral, 'not reinvented here' is the operative slogan. There is no value in recreating something – only in building on the best existing knowledge. People in a learning laboratory value the capability to absorb and use knowledge as much as to create it. They understand that all invention is a process of synthesis. As its practices suggest, a key Chaparral value is global outreach – openness to innovation, whatever its origin. Knowledge is valued not so much for the pedigree of its source but for its usefulness.

Managerial system: resources for alliances and networks

To support information gathering and reinforce global outreach, the company invests heavily in employee travel (and regards the expenses as just that – investments), often sending a team, including foremen and technical staff as well as vice presidents and operators, to investigate a new technology or to benchmark against competitors. Newly acquired knowledge need not filter down through the ranks, because the people who absorbed it are the ones who will apply it. In 1990, seventy-eight people from production, several of them operators, visited a customer site at least once. They also visit other minimills. Asked why he visited a sister plant, an operator states: 'To see if I could pick up any new ideas to use here.' And did he? 'Yes, several.' And he points out some small operational changes. Forward elaborates: 'We send the people who can best tell us what's going on – whoever they are.' Chaparral managers also invest in long-term relationships with suppliers to extend the network. In 1985, while seeking Japanese suppliers, they identified a high-quality company that was not doing much development. As a general manager explains, although it was clear that initially the supplier 'would learn more than we' from the alliance, Chaparral spent the money to send employees over to 'hand hold' so as to develop a capability that would be useful in the future.

This constant dispersal of mixed employee teams to customers, competitors, and suppliers throughout the world serves a dual purpose. The visits are regarded as learning sabbaticals that keep life 'exciting' for employees. They are a source of information for the company as a whole. 'We want them to . . . come back with new ideas about how to make improvements or new ways to understand the problem.'[21]

CONCLUSION

The factory, in fact any backroom operation, is not usually regarded as an arena for experimentation and learning. Chaparral Steel challenges this concept of operations. Factories *can* function as learning laboratories (see Table 11.1). The most important characteristic of such organizations is that they are totally integrated systems. They are difficult to imitate because every employee, from CEO to line operator, is technically capable and interested in learning. Moreover, the whole organization is designed around the creation and control of knowledge. The four subsystems described above are not only internally linked but tremendously dependent upon each other. Continuous education depends upon the careful selection of willing learners. Sending workers throughout the world to garner ideas is cost effective only if they are empowered to apply what they've learned. The organization is unlikely to be open to outside knowledge if it does not place a strong value on sharing knowledge or does not give rewards for bettering the whole company's performance. Thus continuous learning depends upon the sense of ownership derived from the incentive systems, upon the pride of accom-

Table 11.1 Comparison of traditional factory with factory as learning lab

	Traditional factory	Learning lab
1. Research and development function	Separate and distant from production.	Merged with production (everyone does development).
2. Experimentation on factory floor	Rare, feared.	Constant, welcomed.
3. Innovation	Exclusive province of engineers.	Everyone's business (but their own methods).
4. Equipment and processes	If it works, don't fix it.	Design your own; constantly improve.
5. New technology	Reject: not invented here.	Never reinvent here.

plishment derived from special educational systems, upon values embedded in policies and managerial practices, as well as upon specific technical skills. The line operator appears to take the same perspective on the conduct of daily activities as the CEO. Chaparral is tremendously consistent.

Paradoxically, the system's interdependence is also a potential weakness, as competencies often are.[22] A learning laboratory may have trouble recreating itself. Any organization is likely to be somewhat limited by its 'congenital knowledge' and by the stamp placed upon it by its founders.[23] A significant challenge for Chaparral is how to grow. Forward has noted that 'to stand still is to fall behind', and the company's credo to provide growth for its skilled people requires some forward momentum. Therefore, it must either grow larger where it is or clone itself in a new location. How will it transplant the deep worker knowledge, the motivation, the commitment, and the informal systems of knowledge sharing?

For other companies interested in creating factories as learning laboratories, the questions are: can it be done in a plant within a large corporation, where many of the managerial systems have already been set corporatewide and therefore are not at the plant manager's discretion? Can an existing plant be transformed when plant managers may not have the luxury of selecting people as freely as Chaparral did? Can a company less geographically isolated hope to reap returns on investing in its employees' intellectual advancement, or will they be lured away by other companies?

Similar questions were raised a decade ago when US manufacturers first began to understand how Japanese companies were competing on the basis of quality. Initially overwhelmed by the difference in activities, values, and managerial systems implied by the total quality approach, many US managers were pessimistic about their ability to change their operations to the extent needed and reluctant to invest in employee education. Yet today, many US-based factories achieve quality levels never even aspired to in 1980.[24]

For many of these improvements, the Japanese were our teachers, having learned from Deming and Juran.[25] According to some researchers, Japanese managers may also be ahead of their US counterparts in creating learning laboratories, since 'Japanese companies are usually adept at organizational learning.'[26] As the references at the end of this article suggest, many of Chaparral's managerial practices and values also characterize best practices in Japan, such as investing extensively in formal and informal education; searching worldwide for the best technology and methods and absorbing that knowledge into home operations; and valuing employee empowerment, problem solving, and risk taking.[27] Apparently, such learning systems are not uniquely Japanese.

Of course, creating a learning laboratory in a 'green-field' site is easier than in an existing plant. As not all US factories can start up from scratch, creating a learning laboratory implies big changes. But do we really have any choice? No financial formulas, corporate reshuffling of departments, or exhortations by corporate management to integrate across functions will foster the creativity and productivity needed for international competition.

Experts on change management suggest that three critical elements are required for altering current practices: (1) dissatisfaction with the status quo; (2) a clear model of what the changed organization will look like; and (3) a process for reaching that model, that vision of the future.[28] Examples such as Chaparral can aid all three. One way of stimulating dissatisfaction with current practices and hence motivation to change is to observe other companies where an alternative management style appears to be yielding superior results. By benchmarking against such companies, managers can derive principles to incorporate into their own particular visions. Chaparral offers a model of a factory as a learning laboratory, and if the specifics are not transferable, the principles underlying the Chaparral vision are.

The precise process for implementing these principles will differ markedly from company to company. It is possible to interrupt a factory's current systems by introducing new equipment, new learning skills and actitivies, new knowledge-creating management systems, or new values. But interrupting a current system is only the first step. As the Chaparral example demonstrates, learning skills, management procedures, and values are interrelated. Values unsupported by management systems are vapid; management systems that run counter to values are likely to be sabotaged; learning activities unsupported by values and management practices will be short-lived. If a learning capability is to be developed, the whole system must eventually be addressed.

APPENDIX: THE EVIDENCE ON CHAPARRAL STEEL

Chaparral has been setting records in steel production almost since its inception in 1975. In October 1982, it set a world record by producing 67,666 tons in one month – then the highest monthly tonnage produced from a single electric furnace/continuous casting combination. By 1984, the company was listed in *Fortune's* May 28 cover story on the ten best-managed factories in the United States.

Chaparral's pace of improved performance continues unabated. Compared to a Japanese average output of 600 tons per worker-year and a U.S. output of 350 tons, Chaparral put out 1,100 tons of steel per worker-year in 1989. Its 1990 productivity figures of 1.5 worker-hours per rolled ton of steel compared to an overall U.S. average of 5.3 (including integrated steel mills), a Japanese average of 5.6, and a German average of 5.7. Chaparral is currently the largest supplier of steel rod for the oil industry and the largest supplier of rod for mobile home frames in the United States.

The company has won significant international recognition for quality as well. In spring 1989, Chaparral was awarded the right to use the Japanese Industrial Standard certification on its general structural steel products. It was the first U.S. steel company and only the second company outside Japan given that privilege. Out of approximately fourteen U.S. companies producing hot-rolled carbon bars and shapes, the company claims to be the only one certified by the AIME (American Institute of Mining, Metallurgical, and Petroleum Engineers) for nuclear applications. Similarly, it is one of two companies, out of fifteen, whose steel is certified by the American Builders of Ships and that therefore do not have to seek certification for each individual job.

Chaparral has a reputation for quality at the low-cost end of its product line as well. A customer's study comparing scrap rates of Chaparral steel to that of the only other company from which the customer purchased, revealed a difference ranging from four to twenty-five times as low for common carbon bar and three to five times for the much more expensive alloys.

NOTES

1. G. Foward interviewed by A. M. Kantrow, 'Wide-Open Management at Chapparal Steel,' *Harvard Business Review*, May–June 1986, pp. 96–102. Organization theorists would see Chaparral's culture as an appropriate response to such an environment. Scholars theorize that learning will not happen without

a certain amount of stress and that complex, uncertain environments require decentralized, laterally linked organizations. See: C. M. Fiol and M. A. Lyles, 'Organizational Learning,' *Academy of Management Review* 10 (1985): 803–813; and R. Duncan and A. Weiss, 'Organizational Learning: Implications for Organizational Design,' *Research in Organizational Behavior* 1 (1979): 75–123.

2. Senge argues persuasively that successful leaders are systems thinkers, able to see 'interrelationships, not things, and processes, not snapshots.' See: P. Senge, 'The Leader's New Work: Building Learning Organizations,' *Sloan Management Review*, Fall 1990, pp. 7–23. Other theorists similarly note how interrelated are strategy, structure, and culture in creating learning environments. See: Fiol and Lyles (1985).

3. I assume that learning occurs if 'through its processing of information, the range of [an organization's] potential behaviors is changed.' See: G. Huber, 'Organizational Learning: The Contributing Processes and the Literatures,' *Organizational Science* 2 (1991): 89. That is, beyond contributing to an accumulation of formal knowledge bases, learning creates 'capacities . . . for intelligent action.' See: G. Morgan and R. Ramirez, 'Action Learning: A Holographic Metaphor for Guiding Social Change,' *Human Relations* 37 (1983): 21.

   A growing literature on the topic emphasizes that organizational learning is more than an aggregation of individual learning. See, for instance: B. Hedberg, 'How Organizations Learn and Unlearn,' in *Handbook of Organizational Design*, eds. P. Nystrom and W. Starbuck (New York: Oxford University Press, 1981), pp. 3–27. While the four critical activities proposed here have not been previously combined into a framework, each has been identified as characteristic of a learning organization. On problem identification and solving, see: E. Hutchins, 'Organizing Work by Adaptation,' *Organization Science* 2 (1991): 14–39.

   On integration of internal information, see: Duncan and Weiss (1979). On experimentation, see: R. Bohn, 'Learning by Experimentation in Manufacturing,' (Cambridge, Massachusetts: Harvard Business School, Working Paper No. 88–001, 1988). On acquisition and use of external information, see: Huber (1991), pp. 88–115.

4. Chaparral managers have verified the accuracy of the descriptions of activities and events offered here, but they are not responsible for the characterization of learning laboratories in general or for the way I have analyzed their organizational culture.

5. Other researchers also imply the utility of stretch goals as stimuli for learning. Such goals may be thought of as 'performance gaps' deliberately induced to motivate knowledge generation. See: Duncan and Weiss (1979). Itami suggests that 'overextensions' and 'dynamic imbalances' created to challenge the organization characterize the most successful Japanese manufacturing companies. See: H. Itami and T. Roehl, *Mobilizing Invisible Assets* (Cambridge, Massachusetts: Harvard University Press, 1987). Moreover, the goal for this particular project fits Senge's prescription of a blend of extrinsic and intrinsic visions, in that both outside competition and improvement over prior performances are invoked: Senge (1990).

6. Morgan and Ramirez (1983) suggest that a 'holographic' organization (which epitomizes a learning organization for them) is designed so that 'the nature of "one's job" at any one time is defined by *problems facing the whole*' (emphasis in original, p. 4). Similarly, from his study of knowledge creation in some of Japan's top firms, Nonaka concludes that 'every single member of the organization should be able to suggest problems . . . and . . . solutions.' See: I.

Nonaka, 'Managing Innovation as an Organizational Knowledge Creation Process' (Rome: Technology Strategies in the Nineties Conference Paper, 21 May 1992), p. 44.

7. Quoted by B. Dumaine, 'Chaparral Steel: Unleash Workers and Cut Costs,' *Fortune*, 18 May 1992, p. 88.

8. Argyris and Schon point out that 'espoused theory' does not always influence behavior; 'theory in practice' does. See: C. Argyris and D. Schon, *Organizational Learning* (Reading, Massachusetts: Addison-Wesley, 1978). See also: S. Kerr, 'On the Folly of Rewarding A, While Hoping for B,' *Academy of Management Journal*, December 1975, pp. 769–783.

9. Von Glinow argues that the most effective organizational reward system to attract and retain highly skilled people is an 'integrated culture' that combines a concern for people with very strong performance expectations. Chaparral's system appears to fit her description. See: M. A. Von Glinow, 'Reward Strategies for Attracting, Evaluating, and Retaining Professionals,' *Human Resource Management* 24 (1985): 191–206.

10. In a macro-analysis of sixteen studies using forty-two different data samples that estimated the effect of profit sharing on productivity, the authors conclude that 'these studies taken together provide the strongest evidence that profit sharing and productivity are positively related.' See: M. L. Weitzman and D. L. Kruse, 'Profit Sharing and Productivity,' in *Paying for Productivity* (Washington, DC: The Brookings Institution, 1990), p. 139.

11. This advantage was confirmed in a study by: K. Clark and T. Fujimoto, 'Overlapping Problem Solving in Product Development,' in *Managing International Manufacturing*, ed. K. Ferdows (North Holland: Elsevier Science Publishers, 1989).

Huber (1991) suggests a reason for the advantage: 'When information is widely distributed in an organization, so that more and more varied sources for it exist, retrieval efforts are more likely to succeed and individuals and units are more likely to be able to learn. Therefore information distribution leads *to more broadly based* organizational learning' (pp. 100–101). Fiol and Lyles (1985) similarly cite research showing that learning is enhanced by decentralized structures that diffuse decision influence.

12. Nonaka (1992), after describing very similar policies at Kao Corporation, observes: 'Asymmetrical distribution of information destroys the equality of relationships and leads to unilateral command instead of mutual interaction' (p. 48).

13. For an understanding of the impact on communication patterns of physical proximity and centrally located common facilities, see: T. Allen, *Managing the Flow of Technology* (Cambridge, Massachusetts: The MIT Press, 1977), ch. 8.

14. Interview by A. M. Kantrow (1986). A remarkably similar philosophy was observed in four Japanese companies, where 'employees are trained from the first day on the job that "R&D is everybody's business."' See: M. Basadur, 'Managing Creativity: A Japanese Model,' *The Executive* 6 (1992): 29–42. Itami (1987) similarly proposes '"excessive" experimentation in production' since 'experimentation and learning do not take place only in the lab' (p. 95).

15. Descriptions of Japanese best practices reveal similar strong emphasis on both on-the-job training and formal education. See, for example: J. Sullivan and I. Nonaka, 'The Application of Organizational Learning Theory to Japanese and American Management,' *Journal of International Business Studies* 17 (1986): 127–147.

16. For an interesting contrast in stimulating learning, see the carefully con-

structed routines in the 'learning bureaucracy': P. Adler, 'The "Learning Bureaucracy": New United Motor Manufacturing, Inc.,' in *Research in Organizational Behavior*, eds. B. M. Staw and L. L. Cummings (Greenwich, Connecticut: JAI Press, forthcoming).

17. Clearly a tradeoff exists between stability in the workforce and the diversity needed to stimulate innovation. March proposes that 'a modest level of turnover, by introducing less socialized people, increases exploration and thereby improves aggregate knowledge.' See: J. March, 'Exploration and Exploitation in Organizational Learning,' *Organization Science* 2 (1991): 79.

    However, others point to the 'insistence on selection of company members at an early point in life and avoidance of the introduction of new people at higher management levels' as an important influence on an information-sharing culture: I. Nonaka and J. Johansson, 'Japanese Management: What about the "Hard" Skills?' *Academy of Management Review* 10 (1985): 184. Simon observes that turnover can become a 'barrier to innovation' because of the increased cost of socialization: H. Simon, 'Bounded Rationality and Organizational Learning,' *Organization Science* 2 (1991): 125–134. Chaparral's management takes pride in its low turnover rate.

18. Interestingly, Hanover Insurance CEO William O'Brien made a similar reference to Maslow's hierarchy: 'Our traditional hierarchial organizations are designed to provide for the first three levels [of the hierarchy] but not the fourth and fifth: . . . Our organizations do not offer people sufficient opportunities for growth.' Quoted in Senge (1990): 20.

19. Such experience and knowledge sharing even at managerial levels is noted as a characteristic of Japanese organizations, which are 'able to cover for an absent individual quite easily, because other individuals have a relatively greater understanding of the requisite information': Nonaka and Johansson (1985): 185. See also the discussion of designing organizations with redundant skills: Morgan and Ramirez (1983): 5.

20. Again the parallel with Japanese practice, at least as described in literature, is striking. Nonaka and Johansson describe how Japanese firms consult with outside experts, not as troubleshooters, but as educators on the general topic. It is up to the company's own personnel to translate that newly acquired intelligence into application. See: Nonaka and Johansson (1985).

21. Kantrow (1986): 101.

22. I have argued that core capabilities almost inevitably have a flip side, core rigidities, that hamper nontraditional projects and can hobble an organization in moving to new competencies. See: D. Leonard-Barton, 'Core Capabilities and Core Rigidities in New Product Development,' *Strategic Management Journal* 13 (1992): 111–126.

23. Huber (1991) discusses this limitation. See also: J. Kimberly, 'Issues in the Creation of Organizations: Initiation, Innovation, and Institutionalization,' *Academy of Management Journal* 22 (1979): 437–457.

24. This includes Japanese transplants such as New United Motor Manufacturing, Inc., whose employees are mostly rehires from the same United Auto Workers workforce that had one of the industry's worst labor records. See: R. Rehder, 'The Japanese Transplant: A New Management Model for Detroit,' *Business Horizons*, January–February 1988, pp. 52–61.

25. See the profiles of these two men in: O. Port, 'Dueling Pioneers,' *Business Week*, 25 October 1991, p. 17.

26. Nonaka and Johansson (1985). In fact, some management practices now being imported into the United States were advocated by younger US con-

temporaries of Deming such as Chris Argyris, whose early books were translated into Japanese within a year of their publication in the United States. See: C. Argyris, *Personality and Organization* (New York: Harper Brothers, 1957) and *Integrating the Individual* (New York: John Wiley & Sons, 1964).

27. See, for example, R. Rehder and H. Finston, 'How is Detroit Responding to Japanese and Swedish Organization and Management Systems?' *Industrial Management* 33 (1991): 6–8, 17–21; R. T. Pascale, *Managing on the Edge* (New York: Simon & Schuster, 1990), ch. 9; and G. Shibata, D. Tse, I. Vertinsky, and D. Wehrung, 'Do Norms of Decision-Making Styles, Organizational Design, and Management Affect Performance of Japanese Firms? An Exploratory Study of Medium and Large Firms,' *Managerial and Decision Economics* 12 (1991): 135–146.

28. See, for example, M. Beer, *Organization Change and Development* (Santa Monica, California: Goodyear Publishing Company, 1980), ch. 3.

Chapter 12

Creating knowledge in practice

Ikujiro Nonaka and Hiro Takeuchi

This chapter uses the Matsushita Electric Industrial Co., Ltd., to illustrate the theoretical framework of organizational knowledge creation. Although a variety of references have been used to illustrate each component of the theoretical framework, this chapter will illustrate the entire process of knowledge creation within a single Japanese company. The Matsushita case is divided into two parts. The first part explains the development by Matsushita of a bread-making appliance, known as 'Home Bakery', and its subsequent effect throughout the company. In the second part, we analyse the continuous process of knowledge creation at the corporate level of Matsushita.

Matsushita's Home Bakery is the first fully automatic bread-making machine for home use, introduced to the Japanese market in 1987. It transforms raw ingredients into freshly baked bread, doing everying from kneading and fermenting the dough to actually baking bread of a quality that compares favorably with what a professional baker would produce. All that is required is the mixing of flour, butter, salt, water, and yeast. For even further convenience, a premeasured bread-mix package can be used to save the trouble of measuring out the required ingredients. The machine is remarkable in that it embodies the skills of a master baker in a device that can be operated easily by people with no knowledge of bread making. It captures the skills of a baker in such a way that the critical dough-kneading process, which previously depended on the baker's tacit knowledge, can be reproduced consistently using electromechanical technology.

The Home Bakery's development story supports our theory in two ways. First, it illustrates the four modes of knowledge conversion – socialization, externalization, combination, and internalization. It is especially suited to show how tacit knowledge is mobilized in the pursuit of creative innovation. Second, it illustrates enabling conditions as well as the five phases of knowledge creation – sharing tacit knowledge, creating concepts, justification, building archetypes, and cross-leveling of knowledge. We will discover that knowledge creation is not a linear process, but rather a cyclical and iterative process. As evidence of this, the development of Home Bakery required knowledge creation to move along the five phases a total of three times or cycles.

The second half of the case shows how the knowledge created through the development of Home Bakery was elaborated within Matsushita, resulting in a broader spiral of knowledge creation. The developments that took place in the Cooking Applicances Division eventually triggered changes in other parts of the company and strongly affected corporate strategy. The case also highlights the importance of an organization's ability (1) to identify the type of knowledge required by the changing competitive environment, and (2) to enhance the enabling conditions continuously. With knowledge being perishable, organizations cannot become complacent with today's knowledge, as different types of knowledge will be required as the competitive environment changes. And as we have already seen, it is this ability to create new knowledge continuously that becomes the source of competitiveness in the knowledge society.

CORPORATE BACKGROUND

We start the case by describing the corporate background leading to the development of Home Bakery. As the Japanese household appliances market matured in the 1970s, Matsushita's operational profitability diminished in the face of strong price competition. By 1977, 95.4% of Japanese households already owned color television sets, 94.5% owned vacuum cleaners, 98.4% owned refrigerators, 98.5% owned washing machines, and 94.3% owned irons. In addition, rivals from newly industrialized countries had been improving their position as low-cost competitors.

A three-year corporate plan called 'ACTION 61' was announced in May 1983. ACTION was an acronym that stood for 'Action, Cost reduction, Topical products, Initiative in marketing, Organizational reactivation, and New management strength.' The number 61 stood for the sixty-first year of Emperor Hirohito's era, or 1986. The objectives of this plan were twofold: (1) to improve Matsushita's competitiveness in its core businesses through careful attention to cost and marketing, and (2) to assemble the resources necessary to enter new markets historically dominated by competitors such as IBM, Hitachi, NEC, and Fujitsu. These two objectives were expressed in a slogan that came to be known as 'Beyond Household Appliances.' Naoki Wakabayashi, then chief of the Strategy Planning Section, recalls the sentiment in those days:

Looking at market share, we were losing share in TV sets and in radios.

The whole market was for replacements and not growing. That's why we needed to move into the industrial market. We felt that we might not be able to survive without moving into a new world . . . Of course, the household appliances were our core business and we were not going to retreat from them. . . . [We wanted to move] beyond but not out of household appliances. (Yanagida, 1986, p. 31)

Creative chaos was brought into the Household Appliances Group in 1983 as the company shifted its strategic focus from household appliances to high-tech and industrial products. This strategic shift led to the restructuring of the core business and also led to the integration of three divisions into the Cooking Appliances Division, as we shall see below. This integration brought further *chaos* and *requisite variety* into the newly formed division and put pressure on the Household Appliances Group to develop innovative products. Improving competitiveness and assuring survival were the name of the game.

Integration of the three problem children

In May 1984, three divisions were integrated into the Cooking Appliances Division as part of ACTION 61. The intent was twofold: to improve organizational efficiency by eliminating the duplication of resources and to restore the growth track by combining the technology and know-how of the three divisions. The three divisions were the Rice-Cooker Division, which made microcomputer-controlled rice cookers; the Heating Appliances Division, which made hot plates, oven-toasters, and coffee makers using induction heater technology; and the Rotation Division, which made motorized products such as food processors.

All of these products faced market maturity (see Figure 12.1). The market for rice cookers was no longer growing, with the only growth coming from microcomputer-controlled rice cookers replacing conventional types. The oven-toaster market was not growing as well, while the demand was shrinking for food processors because consumers felt the setup and cleaning after use were inconvenient.

The benefits of the integration were not initially apparent (see Figure 12.2). In the two years immediately following the integration, the new division's profitability improved from 7.2% in 1984 to 9.0% as a result of eliminating excess capacity. However, the division still suffered declining sales, from 62.7 billion yen in 1984 to 60.4 billion yen in 1986. Consequently, people in the division as well as in other parts of the company started to question the benefits of the integration. Ikuji Masumura, the Strategy Planning Section chief, said:

It was apparent that sales had been slowing after the integration. Many discussions took place on the benefits of integration on sales. We thought it was not enough to combine existing businesses, reduce fixed costs, and

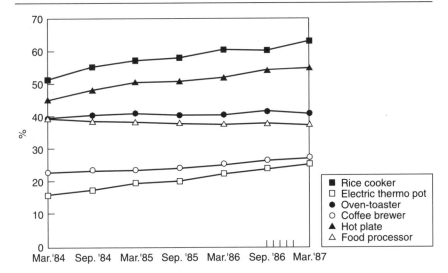

Figure 12.1 Market penetration rates of the main products
Source: Matsushita Electric Industrial Co., Ltd.

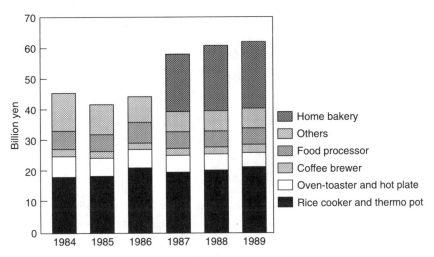

Figure 12.2 Sales of the Cooking Appliances Division
Source: Matsushita Electric Industrial Co., Ltd.

survive. There was a sentiment that something new had to be started, utilizing the characteristics of the three divisions.[1]

Enabling conditions at Matsushita

The company's strategic shift and the integration of the three divisions introduced a sense of crisis into the Cooking Appliances Division. The resulting *creative chaos* inspired individual *intention* and commitment throughout the division. These employees, who had pride in the traditional core business, felt that unless they could develop a home-run product, a completely new product based on a unique technology that combined the knowledge of the three divisions, their ability to improve competitiveness would be questioned.

The integration also brought in *requisite variety*. The three divisions contained a total of 1,400 employees coming from completely different divisional cultures. It was apparent that they had different backgrounds and different ways of doing business. It almost seemed as though they spoke different languages.

Following the introduction of *creative chaos*, communications had to be improved in order to foster the *redundancy* of information. The fact that the three divisions had totally different cultures, ways of doing things, and even languages made it very difficult for communication to flow with any ease. To deal with this problem, the new division sent 13 middle managers from various sections to a three-day retreat to discuss the division's present situation and future direction, which was an attempt to mobilize and share their tacit knowledge. To diffuse explicit knowledge within the division, the personnel department published a newspaper called 'Hot-Line' for factory workers. Keimei Sano, the Cooking Appliances Division chief, commented on the importance of communication as follows:

Speaking a common language and having discussions can assemble the power of the group. This is a vital point, even though it takes time to develop a common language.[2]

The final enabling condition was the development of organizational *intention*, which was to guide a group of diverse individuals toward one goal, one direction. To find clues and suggestions about what that direction might be for the division, a planning team was sent to the United States in 1984 to observe trends in the daily lives of Americans. What they observed there were 'more working women, increasingly simplified home cooking, and poorer diets,' according to Masumura. Recognizing that the same trends were evident in Japan, the team came to the conclusion that cooking appliances should make meals simpler to prepare but at the same time make them tasty and rich in nutrition. As a result, the division came up with an overall concept that came to be known as 'Easy & Rich'. The team believed that an appliance that could produce delicious and nutritious food easily would respond to the needs of working women and gourmet aficionados.

THE FIRST KNOWLEDGE-CREATION SPIRAL AROUND THE DEVELOPMENT OF HOME BAKERY

It was not long after the return of the planning team to Japan that a rough design for an automatic home bakery machine was proposed by Hoshiden Electronics Co., Ltd.[3] From this development, Matsushita's team immediately saw that 'Easy & Rich' could be associated with an automatic bread-making machine. The idea of a fully automatic bread-making machine also embodied many qualities that were appropriate to the division's new objectives. It was completely new, and it involved multiple technologies, such as computer-controlled heating systems from rice cookers, motors from food processors, and heating devices from hot plates.

The idea of an automatic bakery was not entirely new to Matsushita. Some development work had been done at Kyushu Matsushita, its subsidiary, in 1977, but it was suspended in 1980 because of technological difficulties and the prediction of a small anticipated demand. The former Heating Appliances Division also developed and marketed an electric oven in 1973 to ferment and bake bread, but attempts to develop an oven that kneaded dough had failed. This experience was instrumental in Matsushita's decision to reject Hoshiden's proposal for joint product development. Nevertheless, Matsushita was still attracted to the idea of an automated bread maker and elected to develop its own machine in-house.

Given this background, we are now ready to look in greater depth into the specifics of the product development process for Home Bakery. We will observe three cycles of the knowledge-creation process. Each cycle starts with the sharing of experiences among the team members. From these shared experiences, concepts and/or archetypes are created. These concepts and/or archetypes are justified against the organizational *intention*. The next cycle starts either to improve upon the outcome or to overcome the shortcomings of the previous cycle.

The first cycle started with the sharing of experiences by the members of the pilot team. They then externalized the product concept into specific product features and assembled a prototype. However, the original prototype could not produce bread tasty enough to be justified against the concept of 'Rich'. As a result, the process went into the second cycle.

The second cycle started with a software developer, Ikuko Tanaka, sharing experience with a master baker to learn how to knead bread dough properly. To put this difficult know-how into a machine, Tanaka created the mental image of a 'twisting stretch' motion to explain kneading. The skill of kneading was then materialized into specific mechanics such as the movement of the propeller, which kneaded dough, and the design of the special ribs. Because the new prototype succeeded in producing tasty bread, the development moved into the third cycle with the new challenge of meeting cost requirements.

The third cycle began with sharing of tacit knowledge among members of the commercialization team. New members from the manufacturing and marketing sections were added to the team. An innovative way to control fermentation, known as 'Chumen' in Japanese, was developed by the team. This innovation, which added yeast during the kneading process, produced even better bread at lower cost. The resulting bread was justified against cost and quality requirements set when the product concept was originally developed. The perfected Home Bakery machine differentiated itself from competing brands that eventually entered the market and became a hit product. The success of Home Bakery led to the cross-leveling of knowledge at the corporate level.

The first cycle of the Home Bakery spiral

Keimei Sano, who headed the Cooking Appliances Division, initiated the development work on Home Bakery in April 1984. He formed a pilot team, bringing together employees from the Household Appliances Laboratory, an R&D lab for four divisions including the Cooking Appliances Division, with a mechanical designer and a software developer, both of whom were familiar with bread making. This ad hoc team conducted several discussions to develop the product concept that would realize 'Easy & Rich', Masao Torikoshi, who was with the Household Appliances Laboratory, served as the leader. He developed the following product specifications himself in order to avoid any compromises:

1 The machine must knead, ferment, and bake bread automatically once the ingredients are put into the machine.
2 It should not need a special mix of ingredients.
3 A built-in timer must allow the user to prepare the ingredients at night and have bread ready to serve in the morning.
4 Bread making must not be affected by room temperature.
5 The bread should have a good shape.
6 It should taste better than a mass-produced and mass-marketed one.
7 The retail price should be between 30,000 yen and 40,000 yen.

Since these specifications were defined in terms of ideals rather than technological feasibility, many hurdles still had to be cleared.

In January 1985 the project was formally approved by the company, and an official team was formed jointly between the Lab. and the Cooking Appliances Division. But the 11-member team was drawn from several sections, with Torikoshi serving as the project leader. One

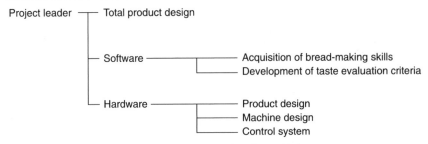

Figure 12.3 Product development tasks for Home Bakery
Source: Matsushita Electric Industrial Co., Ltd.

member came from product planning, three from machines, two from control systems, and three from software development. They came into the project from completely different cultures, having been assembled into one division as the result of the integration that had occurred the previous year.

Because the machine itself was new to the company, everything had to be developed in-house. Several activities – such as developing the taste-measurement system and recipes for the automatic bakery, learning bread-kneading and baking skills, and developing the body of the machine, machinery, and control system – were conducted simulta-neoously (see Figure 12.3).

The first prototype produced something that could hardly be described as bread, since it had an overcooked crust but was raw inside. Several problems had to be resolved. The very shape of the dough case presented the initial problem. Because English bread was square, the case had to be square. However, kneading would be much easier if the case were round. The difference in electric cycles presented another problem. The eastern and western parts of Japan had different electric cycles, which affected the motor's rotation and therefore required an adjustment in the control system. The team also discovered that tem-perature had a significant effect on the fermenting and baking process. The ideal temperature for fermentation was 27 to 28 degrees centigrade, yet the variation in summer temperatures in the different regions of Japan ranged between 5 and 35 degrees centigrade. At too high a tem-perature, the bread overfermented and became sour. At temperatures too low, the bread did not ferment enough and the dough did not rise. In addition, different brands and kinds of flour and yeast further compli-cated the control system. The system had to be robust enough to produce tasty bread under any circumstances.

In the first cycle of knowledge creation, we can observe the five enabling conditions at work. First, the pilot team was given full *autonomy*. Second, *requisite variety* existed because each member of the pilot

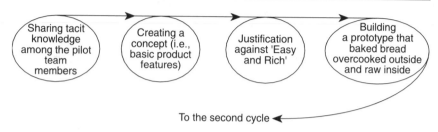

Figure 12.4 First cycle of the Home Bakery spiral

team came into the project with a unique knowledge base. Third, there was *redundancy* of information because members with diverse knowledge bases had basically the same job description. Fourth, *creative chaos* was introduced after the three divisions were integrated. Finally, the concept of 'Easy & Rich' was the organizational *intention* that served to coordinate and direct the activities of the Cooking Appliances Division employees.

On the pilot team, many discussions took place about what exactly Home Bakery should be. The overall divisional concept of 'Easy & Rich' served as a guideline for discussion (*sharing tacit knowledge*). It was general enough to accommodate ideas that reflected each member's tacit knowledge. At the same time, the concept was specific enough to clarify the critical requirements of all product development in the Cooking Appliances Division, namely ease of use and the realization of genuine quality.

In realizing ease of use, the tacit knowledge of each team member and the wants of consumers were *externalized* into product features that specified that 'the machine must knead, ferment, and bake bread automatically once the ingredients set' and 'a built-in timer must allow the user to prepare the ingredients at night and have bread ready to serve in the morning.' A concrete product *concept* was *created* after sharing tacit knowledge. This product concept was then *justified* against the organizational intention. In this case, the specific product features were justified against 'Easy & Rich' and accepted. Once the concept was justified, an *archetype* was *built* by combining explicit knowledge. In other words, a prototype of Home Bakery was built by *combining* existing technology. However, this prototype, which over-cooked the crust while leaving the dough raw inside, was *not justified* against the original product concept. As a result, the knowledge-creation process moved back to the beginning of the second cycle (see Figure 12.4).

The second cycle of the Home Bakery spiral

The second cycle began with a software developer, Ikuko Tanaka, sharing the tacit knowledge of a master baker in order to learn his kneading skill. A master baker learns the art of kneading, a critical step in bread making, following years of experience. However, such expertise is difficult to articulate in words. To capture this tacit knowledge, which usually takes a lot of imitation and practice to master, Tanaka proposed a creative solution. Why not train with the head baker at Osaka International Hotel, which had a reputation for making the best bread in Osaka, to study the kneading techniques? Tanaka learned her kneading skills through observation, imitation, and practice. She recalled:

At first, everything was a surprise. After repeated failures, I began to ask where the master and I differed. I don't think one can understand or learn this skill without actually doing it. His bread and mine [came out] quite different even though we used the same materials. I asked why our products were so different and tried to reflect the difference in our skill of kneading.[4]

Even at this stage, neither the head baker nor Tanaka was able to articulate knowledge in any systematic fashion. Because their tacit knowledge never became explicit, others within Matsushita were left puzzled. Consequently, engineers were also brought to the hotel and allowed to knead and bake bread to improve their understanding of the process. Sano, the division chief, noted, 'If the craftsmen cannot explain their skills, then the engineers should become craftsmen.'[5]

Not being an engineer, Tanaka could not devise mechanical specifications. However, she was able to transfer her knowledge to the engineers by using the phrase 'twisting stretch' to provide a rough image of kneading, and by suggesting the strength and speed of the propeller to be used in kneading. She would simply say, 'Make the propeller move stronger', or 'Move it faster'. Then the engineers would adjust the machine specifications. Such a trial-and-error process continued for several months.

Her request for a 'twisting stretch' movement was interpreted by the engineers and resulted in the addition inside the case of special ribs that held back the dough when the propeller turned so that the dough could be stretched. After a year of trial and error and working closely with other engineers, the team came up with product specifications that successfully reproduced the head baker's stretching technique and the quality of bread Tanaka had learned to make at the hotel. The team then materialized this concept, putting it together into a manual, and embodied it in the product.

In November 1985, the team succeeded in developing a machine that could make tasty bread. As illustrated in Figure 12.5, the product had a kneading mechanism with a motor, a dough case, and a yeast case that held the yeast until exactly the right moment. A microcomputer controlled the heater and yeast case by way of a timer and temperature sensor.

The prototype was now ready for trial. Members of the project team as well as the heads of the cooking appliances sales department, the technology department, and the division all took the prototype home for trial. Their spouses and children made bread with the prototype and provided feedback. Their comments proved that the goal of producing homemade, quality bread was finally achieved.

In the second cycle, the team had to resolve the problem of getting the machine to knead dough correctly. (See Figure 12.6.) To solve the kneading problem, Ikuko Tanaka apprenticed herself with the head baker of the Osaka International Hotel. There she learned the skill through *socialization*, observing and imitating the head baker, rather than through reading memos or manuals. She then translated the kneading skill into explicit knowledge. The knowledge was *externalized* by *creating the concept* of 'twisting stretch'. In addition, she *externalized* this knowledge by expressing the movements required for the kneading propeller, using phrases like 'more slowly' or 'more strongly'. For those who had never touched dough before, understanding the kneading skill was so difficult that engineers had to *share experiences* by spending hours at the baker to experience the touch of the dough. Tacit knowledge was *externalized* by lining special ribs inside the dough case. *Combination* took place when the 'twisting stretch' concept and the technological knowledge of the engineers came together to produce a prototype of Home Bakery. Once the prototype was *justified* against the concept of 'Rich', the development moved into the third cycle.

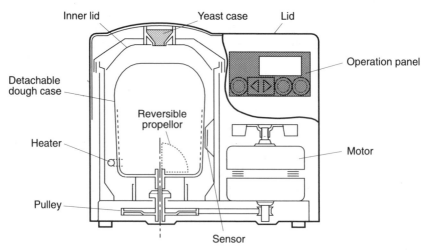

Figure 12.5 Schematic of Home Bakery
Source: Matsushita Electric Industrial Co., Ltd.

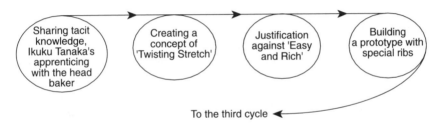

Figure 12.6 Second cycle of the Home Bakery spiral

The third cycle of the home bakery spiral

Seeing the success of the new prototype, Sano moved the project from technological development to the commercialization stage, and transferred the project from the lab to the division. The design staff was expanded, and members from the marketing and manufacturing departments were added at this time. The project team had to deal with industrial design, quality stabilization, and cost reduction as the main issues at this stage.

Although the project leader switched from Torikoshi to Yuzuru Arao, head of the division's planning department, Torikoshi continued to attend major meetings so that his tacit knowledge could be utilized. The other ten original members also remained on the team. Even though the tacit knowledge of bread making had been captured in the prototype, the tacit knowledge of the original members was still needed. In the commercialization stage, several changes were expected in order to meet the cost requirement. The original members' tacit knowledge of bread making was considered to be indispensable in finding a way to make these changes without harming the quality of bread.

The biggest challenge in the commercialization stage was to reduce the overall cost so that the retail price would become less than 40,000 yen. The major cost concern was over the cooler, which kept the yeast-laden dough from overfermenting in high temperatures. Chief Engineer Tsuneo Shibata recalls, 'We were behind schedule and did not have a machine that could make tasty bread within the cost requirement. Everybody was very nervous.'[6] A major advance came when someone on the team discovered that it was possible to mix the other ingredients and then add the yeast at a later stage in the process, a process known as 'Chumen' in Japanese. It was the way people had made bread in the past, when means to control the temperature were not available. Matsushita obtained a patent on this technology, which subsequently proved to be an important factor in enabling the company to maintain its technological edge over rival companies that entered the market later.

The process of bread making using an automatic machine is shown in

Figure 12.7. In total, the development process involved the baking of more than 5,000 loaves of bread using 1.5 tons of flour, 66 kilograms of butter, and 100 kilograms of sugar.

The only problem with the new process was that it required design changes – such as developing a new yeast case controlled by a timer, as well as taking out the coolant – that would postpone market introduction by at least four months. Home Bakery had been enthusiastically welcomed at a distributors meeting in February 1986, and its market introduction in November 1986 was much anticipated. It was also rumored that competitors were trying to develop automatic bread-making machines of their own. In a hard choice between quality and market-introduction timing, an important factor in the competitive Japanese market, Sano's commitment to 'Easy & Rich' won out, and the changes were made.

Matsushita's Home Bakery was introduced to the market in February 1987 at 36,000 yen and sold a record-setting 536,000 units in its first year. It hit the top of the list of Mother's Day gifts. Its success was so extraordinary and rare in the mature cooking appliances market that *Fortune* magazine featured the machine in its October 26, 1987, issue. Six months after market introduction in Japan, Matsushita began exporting Home Bakery to the United States, West Germany, and Hong Kong. Shipments were later expanded to Sweden, Thailand, Australia, and New Zealand. Though prices were set much higher than in the domestic market, Home

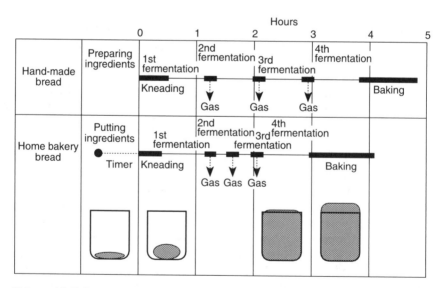

Figure 12.7 Comparison of bread-making processes by hand vs. Home Bakery
Source: Matsushita Electric Industrial Co., Ltd.

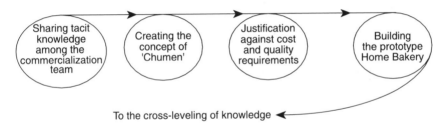

Figure 12.8 Third cycle of the Home Bakery spiral

Bakery has been selling well worldwide beyond the expectations of the manufacturing plan. In the United States, according to Matsushita, the entire market for an automatic bread-maker expanded to as much as one million units, as new competitors entered the market.

Justification played a critical role in the third cycle. (See Figure 12.8.) During the commercialization stage, the team faced the problem of having to reduce the cost of the machine significantly while maintaining the initial quality requirement. The team dealt with this problem by coming up with an innovative solution that did away with a costly yeast cooler. The solution was to put in yeast at a later stage of the dough-kneading process, instead of mixing it with the other ingredients at the very beginning. This improved quality and lowered cost at the same time. This method, referred to as 'Chumen', was the result of the *socialization* and *externalization* of the team members' tacit knowledge.

However, a change in the design required the postponement of market introduction, which was a major dilemma, since market-introduction timing is considered crucial for a product's success in the Japanese market. Sano's commitment to the *organizational intention* of 'Easy & Rich' allowed him to *justify* the decision to incorporate the design change despite the delay in market introduction.

The three cycles of the five-phase process are presented in Figure 12.9. As shown, the first cycle passes through four of the five phases of knowledge creation, then repeats the cycle two more times before moving into the cross-leveling phase, which we shall discuss in the next section. This figure clearly shows how knowledge is created through an iterative and spiral process, not through a one-time linear process.

Cross-leveling of knowledge within the division

The success of Home Bakery is especially remarkable in light of the fact that Matsushita's previous image was as a price-based competitor for relatively standard products in mature markets. Its corporate culture had become conservative and status quo-oriented. Thus the emergence

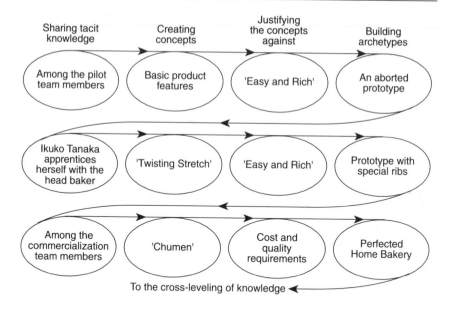

Figure 12.9 Three cycles of the Home Bakery spiral

of a 'new' product and a 'new' process was a sharp break with past tradition. This case provides insight into how established organizational procedures can be revitalized to support the generation of creative approaches that foster innovation.

The experience of developing Home Bakery dissolved the rigid boundaries within the organization through the initiation of interdepartmental project teams, which provided a forum for debate covering a wide cross-section of organizational activities. Home Bakery also brought the users' voices close to the engineers, which seemed like a breath of fresh air to the Cooking Appliances Division. Having previously dealt with mature products, the process brought a sense of enlightenment to the engineers. Comments like the following were heard. 'It was shocking that I laughed with joy'; 'I almost shouted, "unbelievable"! Thank you for developing this.'

The success of Home Bakery changed the engineers' attitudes toward new projects. Their experience brought confidence and a desire among Matsushita employees to develop another innovative product. Prior to Home Bakery, engineers developed products to compete within the company. After its introduction, the focus shifted to creating products with genuine quality that met real consumer needs. In addition, engineers started to investigate the desires of consumers when developing concepts. Sano said, 'By asking what dreams people have in their daily lives and how they realize them, we can get to the next breakthrough.'[7]

Inspired by the Home Bakery's success, products intended to enhance the 'quality of life' of consumers began to follow. One such product was an automatic coffee brewer that came equipped with an integrated coffee mill, the first in Japan, introduced in the autumn of 1987. It ground beans and brewed coffee automatically, so that users could enjoy fresh, delicious coffee, like that served at coffee shops or restaurants, at home. The mill-integrated coffee brewer was extremely successful, and this category now accounts for half of Matsushita's unit sales of coffee makers in Japan.

Another product that followed in Home Bakery's footsteps was the 'Induction Heating (IH) Rice Cooker', which cooked rice in a manner similar to the traditional *kamado* (Japanese steam oven) with an automatic electronic system. Introduced in 1988, this new rice cooker has an induction heating system that achieved higher temperatures and allowed for more accurate contol. Though priced at 59,000 yen (about $480), which was nearly twice the price of a conventional electric rice cooker, it sold well and now accounts for more than 40% of rice cooker sales within Matsushita. Thanks to the IH rice cooker, Matsushita rice cooker sales increased overall by 50% and its market share rose by 7% since the market introduction in 1988.

The new knowledge created by developing Home Bakery spilled over beyond the product development team. It showed that an innovative product could be developed through cooperation rather than through internal competition. It also showed that consumers would respond positively to products that fulfilled 'Easy & Rich'. Furthermore, it demonstrated the value of asking people what kinds of dreams they had in their daily lives and of *creating* a product *concept* that met those needs.

The success story of Home Bakery spread throughout Matsushita by word of mouth and in-house publications. As mentioned above, the newly created knowledge was transferred among division members beyond the development team, which we refer to as *cross-leveling of knowledge*. It radically changed employee perspectives about the potential of home appliances and inspired other people within the organization to develop other innovative products similar to Home Bakery. The fully automatic coffee maker with an integrated mill and a new generation of rice cookers followed the example of Home Bakery, but all these products were based on the same concept of 'Easy & Rich' (organizational *intention*) (see Figure 12.10).

Cross-leveling of knowledge between divisions

The development of Home Bakery inspired Akio Tanii, the CEO, to adopt 'Human Electronics' as the umbrella or grand concept for Mat-

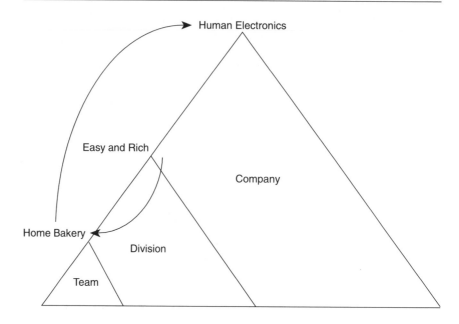

Figure 12.10 Cross-leveling of knowledge within Matsushita

sushita at large in January 1986. Under 'Human Electronics', Matsushita was going to develop more 'human' products utilizing high technology (electronics). A 'human' product, to Tanii, was a product that could free and elevate the human spirit through ease of use. Electronics would enhance the satisfaction and happiness of consumers by providing 'genuine' quality. Matsushita's managing director, Hiroyuki Mizuno, said, 'Household appliances is the very place where electronics technology will have a big bang at last' (Shiozawa, 1989, p. 196).

Home Bakery provided a good fit with 'Human Electronics' since it (1) allowed people to have fresh-from-the-oven bread every morning at home, freeing and elevating the human spirit through ease of use and genuine quality, and (2) was realized as a result of the application of microcomputers, sensors, and other electronics. Home Bakery stimulated a new spiral of knowledge creation that had far-reaching effects on organizational procedures. The new tacit knowledge gained can be expressed as follows: have engineers develop a product by interfacing directly with consumers and by pursuing genuine quality without any constraint. This knowledge was informally conveyed to other Matsushita employees, who used it to develop new products with equivalent quality standards for TV sets, kitchen appliances, audiovisual equipment, and others (see Figure 12.11).

One example of a new product that embodied 'Human Electronics' was 'Gaoh' (named 'The One' in the United States), a series of large-screen TV sets introduced in October 1990. Gaoh owed its success to the pursuit of genuine quality and consumers' wishes for TV sets. As Toshihaya Yamanashi, director and TV department chief, said, 'Gaoh was developed after a re-examination of the function and design of existing TV sets from every aspect' (Kohno, 1992, p. 79).

Matsushita started the development of Gaoh in 1987, just when the large-screen TV market was taking off and competitors were racing to introduce new products. With the knowledge gained from Home Bakery, namely that the pursuit of genuine quality should take precedence no matter what technological difficulties came up, Matsushita's development team tried to surmount all the shortcomings of existing large-screen TVs. Ultimately, the Gaoh development team came to the conclusion that producing a television that offered genuine quality would make consumers happy. In other words, if consumers can have genuine quality in terms of sharp image, high-fidelity sound, beautiful design

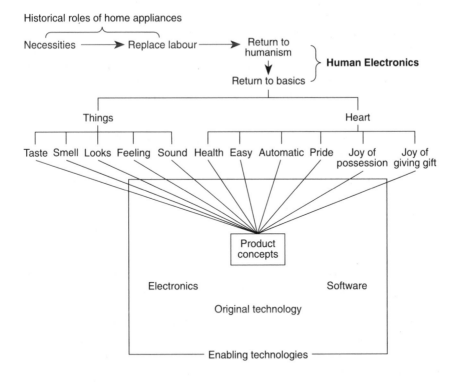

Figure 12.11 The impact of Human Electronics and 'Things and Heart' on product conception
Source: Matsushita Electric Industrial Co., Ltd.

(including hidden speakers), and easy usage, their spirits would be elevated; TV sets, in fact, could be 'tender to humans'.

Development of a new TV set usually takes six months and few technological changes are undertaken. However, it took the TV division at Matsushita two years to release Gaoh, which contained a number of major technological breakthroughs. As one development team member recalled:

Technological development was tough and required changes up until four or five months before market introduction. We were under enormous pressure. . . . We had a sense of crisis . . . that the TV division may not survive.[8]

Gaoh sold more than one million units within 14 months of its introduction, which was equivalent to more than 10% of all domestic TV-set sales in Japan. With sales of 16 billion yen a month on average, Gaoh was ranked third among the 'Top 20 Hit Products of 1991' (measured in terms of sales volume by Mitsubishi Research Insitute), following the Honda Civic Ferio and the Sony camcorder. It was remarkable that a mature household appliance like TV was ranked in the top 20.

To summarize, the success of Home Bakery validated the idea behind 'Easy & Rich' that genuine quality and ease of use will create successful products. To *cross-level* this *knowledge* beyond the divisional boundaries, Matsushita developed an umbrella concept called 'Human Electronics', which inspired such products as Gaoh (see Figure 12.10).

THE SECOND KNOWLEDGE-CREATION SPIRAL AT THE CORPORATE LEVEL

In the previous section we presented a detailed description of the first spiral of knowledge creation. It started with Tanaka's apprenticeship, continued onward to the success of Home Bakery, and ended with the diffusion of knowledge beyond the original development team and the Cooking Appliances Division, resulting in other successful products such as Gaoh.

In this section we will analyse Matsushita's efforts to create knowledge continuously at the corporate level. The output of knowledge creation in the first spiral took the form of a product such as Home Bakery or Gaoh. But products are not the only output of knowledge creation. New knowledge can also be created with respect to ways of doing business, operating a division, developing new products, or managing people. In the second cycle, we focus our attention on the 'soft' side of knowledge creation, as opposed to the 'hard' side, which focused on product development. The 'soft' side deals with less tangible outcomes – such as management systems, operational mechanisms, or

human resource management programs – which are equally as important in creating innovation within a company and, in turn, gaining
sustainable competitive advantage in the marketplace.

The second spiral takes us through a search for the 'ideal' of what
Matsushita should be in the twenty-first century and a discussion of
what Matsushita people should be like under that umbrella concept.
This process is termed the first cycle of knowledge creation at the
corporate level. Having decided what kind of a company Matsushita
should be and what kind of individuals Matsushita employees should
be, the next cycle of the knowledge-creation process takes us through the
development of managerial and operational systems that can accommodate the 'new' ideal.

The first cycle of the corporate spiral

Matsushita began the process of establishing its corporate vision for the
twenty-first century in 1989. Top managers questioned where the company was heading and what kind of company they would like it to be.
While the whole nation was caught up in the economic bubble euphoria,
Matsushita's top management was quite skeptical about the company's
position. Thus they decided to evaluate the company critically (Hirata,
1993).

Realizing that the young people of today would be the leaders of the
company in the future, Matsushita asked 200 employees in their 20s and
30s to formulate the company's corporate vision for the twenty-first
century. Originally, the task for developing the corporate vision was
entrusted to the Human 21 Committee, composed of upper-middle
managers with heavy responsibilities. Since original and stimulating
ideas rarely emerged from these managers, Matsushita decided to
form another group composed of younger employees, most of whom
were between 25 and 32 years old. Called the Human 200-People Committee, it started out with 200 'stars' selected from a large pool of
applicants.

The Human 200-People Committee was organized in each of the 12
companies in the Matsushita Group. Approximately 20 teams were
formed, and the members, who would be the company's leading forces
in the twenty-first century, discussed their visions for the coming century and wrote reports on their discussions. The Human 21 Committee
then played the ombudsman's role by examining the reports and deciding if the company should adopt their suggestions.

Meetings were held every other weekend in either Tokyo or Osaka.
One of the questions that the group tried to answer was: 'What type of a
group should Matsushita employees form?' The concept of 'a group of
voluntary individuals' emerged from their discussions. The younger

employees felt that people's value systems would change in the future. More specifically, people in the twenty-first century would pursue not only material affluence but also spiritual contentment. In such a society, each member of the corporation should be what Matsushita called 'voluntary individuals', who embraced values such as volunteerism, ambition, creativity, and mental productivity. Each employee of Matsushita should thoroughly rethink work and management, and try to be not only a good businessperson but also a good citizen, family member, and individual. Such efforts will lead to 'a group of voluntary individuals'. This idea was the fruit of the project members' reflections on how the corporation could be truly spontaneous, ambitious, and creative.

The idea of 'a group of voluntary individuals' became the basis for the Human 21 Committee to develop a 'possibility-searching company' as Matsushita's corporate vision. In such a company, a group of voluntary individuals with rich and diversified individual knowledge bases would share similar ideals and values. In short, Matsushita envisioned itself as becoming a knowledge-creating company. But because the idea of becoming a knowledge-creating company was radical and new, it was not surprising that some senior managers of the company were reluctant to accept this vision. However, the enthusiasm of the younger employees eventually won over top management.

In April 1990, Matsushita officially announced to the outside world its corporate vision of becoming 'a possibility-searching company'. Under this vision, Matsushita set forth the following four objectives in the areas of business, technology, people, and globalization:

1 'Human innovation business': business that creates new life-styles based on creativity, comfort, and joy in addition to efficiency and convenience.
2 'Humanware technology': technology based on human studies such as artifical intelligence, fuzzy logic, and neuro-computers as well as on chip systems and networking technology, all necessary for the 'human innovation' business.
3 'Active heterogeneous group': a corporate culture based on individuality and diversity.
4 'Multilocal and global networking management': a corporate structure that enables both localization and global synergy.

Notice that the first two objectives are derived directly from the umbrella concept of 'Human Electronics', with a heavy emphasis on customers and high technology. The third objective corresponds to one of our enabling conditions, *requisite variety*. Matsushita knew that knowledge creation would not be possible without the diversity of individual experiences. The fourth objective points out the importance of transcending the dichotomy between localization and globalization.

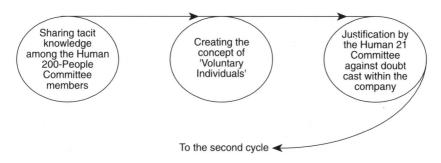

Figure 12.12 First cycle of the corporate spiral

The first cycle of knowledge creation at the corporate level started out with 200 people *sharing their experiences* and carrying on a dialogue in the Human 200-People Committee. The dialogue was centered on what society would be in the future and what that would mean for Matsushita. The *concept* of 'voluntary individuals' emerged as a result, which was *justified* by the Human 21 Committee. The five-phase model is not fully represented, but the first cycle of the knowledge-creation process takes us through three of the phases (see Figure 12.12).

We can also observe the five enabling conditions at work here. Through the Human 21 program, top management cast its doubt on the status quo and developed a new ideal or organizational *intention* regarding what Matsushito should be like. This redefinition brought about a chain reaction, heightening the anxiety among employees (*fluctuation/chaos*), which in turn induced young employee's commitment to the Human 200-People Committee. The committee was composed of 200 people from various divisions and group companies (*requisite variety*). This diversity was vital when the committee was trying to deal with an uncertain future, since uncertainty (of the environment) is often reduced or absorbed by uncertainty itself (i.e. uncertainty of membership). The fact that 200 people shared their tacit knowledge resulted in *redundancy* of information, which provided a common knowledge base for all the members. This committee of 200 young employees was given full *autonomy* by the Human 21 Committee to come up with innovation.

In addition, we can clearly observe two of the four modes of knowledge conversion in the first cycle of the knowledge-creation process. *Socialization* took place among the Human 200-People Committee members as they shared their experiences. *Externalization* took place when their discussion of what type of individuals Matsushita would need in the future was articulated explicitly as 'voluntary individuals'.

The second cycle of the corporate spiral

In the second cycle, the concept of 'voluntary individuals', which was created in the first cycle, was operationalized. The objectives of 'voluntary individuals' were to have Matsushita employees become voluntary, ambitious, creative, and mentally productive, and also become not only good businesspersons but good citizens, family members, and individuals. One of the operational means of achieving these objectives was the reduction of working hours. By eliminating or reducing time spent on routine jobs (e.g. information processing), employees would be able to be more mentally productive, ambitious, and creative. By increasing private time, their personal lives as citizens or family members would be enriched.

Matsushita discovered that inefficiencies at work were blocking the creativity of its employees and taking away their personal time. People in the staff organization were suffering from low productivity, while productivity of line activities had reached a plateau, which led to routinized overtime work. Matsushita's average yearly working hours in 1990 were 2,131 hours for staff people and 1,903 hours for line people, for an average of 2,036 hours for the company.

To solve this problem, Matsushita set a goal in 1991 to reduce its annual working hours to 1,800 hours under the program called MIT'93 (Mind and Management Innovation Toward 1993). Osamu Tanaka, general manager of the MIT'93 Promotion Office, emphasized that the purpose of the program was to enhance employee creativity rather than to simply reduce working hours or costs:

We do not need MIT if we only want to reduce working hours. We can just tell employees that the company will not pay for any overtime work. Lay-offs might be another alternative during a recession like this. But we must remember the purpose of MIT. It is not a simple reduction in working hours. We have wanted to improve the productivity of our staff organization through this project. . . . The company wants to give time back to individuals for their creativity. How can anyone be creative if he works until twelve midnight everyday? People's sense of value is rapidly changing. You cannot make original products just by looking at plans at the office every night.[9]

To enhance creativity, Matsushita felt that innovation had to take place both in people's mindset and in the management system, hence the name of the program. The 1,800-hour project was considered a symbol of Matsushita's innovation with respect to management and operation systems.

The MIT'93 Promotion Office asked every division of Matsushita to develop new managerial and operational systems that would enable annual working hours to be reduced to 1,800 hours. Three committees were established – in labor-management relations, personnel, and general accounting – in order to coordinate that effort. But the actual development of new managerial and operational systems to reduce working hours was left up to self-organizing teams within each division. No specific details on how to go about reducing working hours were provided. The only guidelines that the MIT'93 Promotion Office provided were: (1) to analyze existing working hours and business processes; (2) to uncover causes of inefficiencies; and (3) to make people actually experience a 150-hours-a-month schedule (equivalent to 1,800 hours a year).

The analysis of existing working hours and business processes in the staff organizations led to the following findings:

- 45% of working hours in the R&D sections were spent on non-developmental work, which consisted of follow-up work necessitated by additional design changes that took place after product designs were handed over to the production division.
- 40% of working hours in the materials management sections were spent on follow-up work caused by changes in product designs or production plans.
- 20% of working hours in R&D were spent on internal meetings, contacts with visitors, and interviews unassociated with development work.
- Less than 20% of the sales staff's working hours were spent talking with customers.

These findings revealed ample opportunities to improve current operating systems. Team members in the R&D sections and materials management sections discovered that the inefficiencies were largely due to the shortcomings of the Japanese-style product development process. Matsushita's product development was conducted using the rugby style, in which several functional areas – such as engineering, manufacturing, planning, and marketing – worked together in a multi-functional team, exchanging information and sharing tacit knowledge through dialogue held in meetings or camps. This system had some advantages, such as allowing coordination to take place more easily, enabling development to be completed in a shorter period of time, and ensuring that the resulting new products met customer needs. But it also led to the disadvantage of having the original designs and specifications changed constantly. The rugby-style development had the tendency of overreliance on the socialization mode, which led to inefficiencies as the number of people involved in the project increased and the number of suggestions for change multiplied.

Having employees actually experience a 150-hours-a-month schedule, for example, helped those involved in product development realize the pitfalls of rugby-style product development. They had first-hand experience of what can and cannot be done within a shorter working schedule. Their bodily experience convinced them that a lot of design changes cannot be accommodated and certain unnecessary work had to be eliminated. This experience led to the tacit knowledge of what it meant to work 1,800 hours a year.

This experience also resulted in the development of an innovative product development process called 'concurrent engineering', which could set all the specifications at an early stage of development and consequently reduce design changes at later stages. The experience of working 150 hours a month led people to realize that they could not have as many face-to-face meetings as before, and that communication using computer networks had to be more fully employed. By relying on concurrent engineering, specifications of product features were documented in detail at the early stage of product development through the use of electronic media, such as CAD/CAM. Front-loading explicit information helps product engineering (upstream) 'to do it right the first time' and affords process engineering (downstream) earlier exposure to product design specifications, which reduces problem-solving lead time. CAD/CAM assures more accuracy in communicating information and reduces the length of the communication chain.

In the second cycle of the corporate spiral, a new operational system was created to give employees more time so that they could become creative (see Figure 12.13). For this purpose, Matsushita established a self-organizing team in every division and group company. The knowledge-creation process started when members of each team *shared tacit knowledge* on what types of work employees at Matsushita should do and should not do to utilize their creativity fully. The teams also analysed existing work patterns and uncovered causes of inefficiencies. For instance, they felt that R&D people should be spending most of their time on actual research and development, and not on follow-up work for additional design changes. The *concept* of 'Mind and Management Innovation Toward 1993' was *created* to enhance creativity and reduce working hours. This concept was *justified* against the objective of reducing annual working hours to 1,800, allowing it to be developed into an operational system (*archetype*) that combined elements of concurrent engineering into existing operational systems. The objective has been achieved, and Matsushita dissolved the MIT'93 Promotion Office in March 1994.

In this cycle, we can also observe the five enabling conditions at work. Matsushita's challenging goal to reduce annual working hours to 1,800 brought *fluctuation/chaos* into the organization. A sense of crisis took hold, inducing people's commitment to search for the causes of ineffi-

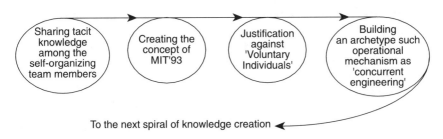

Figure 12.13 Second cycle of the corporate spiral

ciencies. Matsushita's organizational *intention* to produce 'voluntary individuals' reoriented people's commitment to one direction. Teams, consisting of people with different backgrounds, were set up in all the divisions and group companies, and given full *autonomy* to develop ideas for improvement. *Redundancy* of information prevailed within these teams in the form of common knowledge held about the rugby style of product development process, for example. This redundancy helped members of the teams by providing a common language with which to share their tacit knowledge. *Requisite variety* was enhanced by involving people whose working environments differed from division to division.

Among the four modes of knowledge conversion, *internalization* played an important role. Being forced to experience shorter working hours (150 hours a month) experimentally, people actually felt (*internalized*) how short such a curtailed schedule was and how much work had to be eliminated. They engaged in 'learning by doing'. In addition, team members exchanged their own tacit understandings of what it meant to limit their working hours to 150 (*socialization*), and came up with a new development system called concurrent engineering (*externalization*). This mechanism was combined with existing operational systems and other explicit knowledge to form a new operational system (*combination*).

ENHANCING ENABLING CONDITIONS FOR KNOWLEDGE CREATION

Thus far, we have seen two spirals of the knowledge-creation process within Matsushita. The first was around Home Bakery, a product, and the second around MIT'93, an operating system. But in both spirals, enabling conditions played a key role in stimulating and promoting the knowledge-creation process. Matsushita's case illustrates that for knowledge creation to continue, enabling conditions should be enhanced or upgraded continuously as well. Next, we shall briefly describe the company's ongoing efforts to continuously upgrade the enabling conditions.

Matsushita recently enhanced one of the enabling conditions, *redundancy* of information, by improving its communication infrastructure. Matsushita installed a new communication infrastructure called Market-Oriented Total Management System (MTM) in 1991. By connecting R&D organizations, factories, and retail stores on line, Matsushita was able to eliminate excess inventory and avoid out-of-stock situations for popular items. But its greatest impact, from a knowledge-creation perspective, resides in the free flow and sharing of information among different functional groups. Under this system, the sales and the manufacturing departments shared the same explicit knowledge (i.e. sales information at retail stores). This common knowledge, which represents *redundancy* of information, helped the sales and manufacturing groups exchange their mental models and gut feelings about the future. In this sense, MTM has facilitated the coordination of production plans between the two departments and, as a result, improved overall efficiency.

MTM allowed product development teams to obtain instant feedback on how well a particular product or model sold at retail. This detailed market information, as opposed to warehouse shipment data, was *internalized* by the development people, bringing variety into their knowledge base (*requisite variety*). Development people could develop a variety of 'what if' solutions more precisely in anticipation of customer reactions. In this sense, MTM paved the way for joint knowledge creation between customers and development teams. Vice president Shoji Sakuma stressed the importance of retail-based information as follows:

If I told my staff members, 'Go to the front lines because they are very important,' they would all rush to the front line of the manufacturing sector. But if you really care about consumers, you would soon know there is another important front line, the store fronts of retailers, where you could have contact with consumers. Matsushita, however, has tended to isolate itself from consumers, clinging to the manufacturing sector.[10]

Another effort on the part of Matsushita to enhance *autonomy*, one of the enabling conditions, can be seen in the change it initiated in 1993 to terminate its business group system, which was a layer created above the divisional layer to coordinate interdivisional activities. The predecessor of this business group system was the sector system, introduced in 1984, to coordinate activities such as joint product development or joint marketing across the divisions. But after nine years, Matsushita realized that the extra umbrella layer (business group system) was inhibiting the divisions' *autonomy* and commitment to innovation. Elimination of the group layer led the divisions to take more initiative in coordinating activities across the divisions through a more flexible and ad hoc system, such as an interdivisional project team.

Matsushita also enhanced *intention* and *fluctuation/chaos* by setting extremely challenging goals. On January 10, 1994, Matsushita announced 'The Revival Plan', which stipulated that by fiscal 1996 profitability would be increased to 5% return on sales (ordinary income-to-sales ratio) from 1.4% in 1993. In order to achieve this profitability level, Matsushita identified the necessity to shift its strategic domain to multimedia, an emerging industry in which the company could capitalize on its capabilities in hardware equipment (e.g. audiovisual, television), computers and communication equipment, and software (e.g. entertainment). At the same time, the company decided to increase the productivity of its staff organization by 30%. This challenging goal introduced *creative chaos* throughout the company, which forced its employees to relinquish the status quo and seek brand new solutions. 'The Revival Plan' also upgraded organizational *intention*, which had the effect of reorienting the employees toward one ambitious goal.

SUMMARY AND IMPLICATIONS

We used the Matsushita case to illustrate the actual process by which organizational knowledge is created within a company. Several implications can be drawn from the case on how a successful organizational knowledge-creation process can be implemented. The case points out the importance of: (1) leveraging the tacit knowledge base of an individual and making use of *socialization* to transfer it throughout the organization; (2) amplifying knowledge creation across different levels of the organization, i.e. *cross-leveling*; (3) enhancing the enabling conditions; and (4) continuing to create new knowledge constantly. Each implication is elaborated below.

First, Home Bakery's development process emphasizes the importance of tapping into an individual's tacit knowledge, which in this case was represented by the head baker's kneading skill. By its very nature, tacit knowledge is hard to formalize and communicate. But this skill was critical in making the machine knead the dough correctly. The Home Bakery example also shows the importance of *socialization* as a means to share tacit knowledge between individuals. Ikuko Tanaka apprenticed herself to the head baker and learned the skill by observation and imitation. Engineers had to experience the actual bread-making process to learn that skill.

Second, the success of Home Bakery led to the creation of 'Human Electronics' and a series of successful products that embodied that concept. In order to make knowledge creation truly dynamic, knowledge created at one level needs to be amplified across different levels of the organization. Only by *cross-leveling* can companies obtain the true benefits of organizational knowledge creation. In Matsushita's case, we saw how the knowledge created in developing Home Bakery spiraled itself to create new knowledge at the corporate level. Umbrella concepts such as 'Easy & Rich' and 'Human Electronics' played a significant role in connecting one knowledge creation to another.

Third, Matsushita's knowledge-creation process highlights the importance of enhancing organizational enabling conditions, which promote the four modes of knowledge conversion as well as the five-phase process. We saw how Matsushita tried to (1) increase *redundancy* and *requisite variety* by providing the R&D people with up-to-date sales information; (2) bring *autonomy* back to the divisions by restructuring organizations; and (3) instill *intention* and *creative chaos* into the organization by setting challenging goals, represented by the shift to multimedia or the improvement of productivity by 30%.

Fourth, the case illustrates that organizational knowledge creation is a never-ending process that requires continuous innovation. Because the competitive environment and customer preferences change constantly, existing knowledge becomes obsolete quickly. We saw how the rugby style of product development, which had provided a source of competitive advantage for Japanese companies in the past, was already becoming obsolete as their competitors in the West began utilizing the same style and as the recession rekindled the search for eliminating inefficiencies. The continuous upgrading of organizational *intention* or values is important, since new knowledge must be constantly *justified* against the latest *intention*.

NOTES

1. Interviewed on April 1, 1988.
2. Interviewed on April 1, 1988.
3. Hoshiden Electronics Co., Ltd., is a manufacturer of electronic parts and devices, and not affiliated with Matsushita.
4. Interviewed on July 19, 1988.
5. Interviewed on April 1, 1988.
6. Interviewed on April 1, 1988.
7. Interviewed on April 1, 1988.
8. Interviewed on December 2, 1993.
9. Interviewed on December 2, 1993.
10. Interviewed on July 2, 1991.

Chapter 13

Leveraging competencies across business

Michael Goold, Andrew Campbell and Marcus Alexander

EDITORS' PREFACE TO THIS CHAPTER

The following case studies of Canon, Cooper Industries and 3M are taken from Corporate-Level Strategy.[1] *In the book, the authors use a framework and vocabulary which may not be familiar to some readers.[2] Goold, Campbell and Alexander describe corporate-level strategy as the quest for* parenting advantage, *meaning that the businesses in the corporate portfolio perform better than they would as independent businesses, or as part of another corporate portfolio. To gain parenting advantage, a corporate parent must have* value creation insights *which enable it to recognize and focus on specific opportunities to improve performance in its businesses. The parent must also have* distinctive parenting characteristics *or capabilities which enable it to exploit opportunities for performance improvement in its businesses. Finally, the parent must focues on* heartland businesses, *meaning that the businesses in the portfolio are ones which will gain benefits from the parent's value creation insights and from its distinctive parenting characteristics. The parenting advantage statement for each company summarizes how its value creation insights, distinctive parenting characteristics and heartland businesses create parenting advantage in each firm.*

CANON

Shared resources and core competences

Canon was originally founded in 1933 as 'Precision Optical Research Laboratory', developing camera products for the domestic Japanese market. By the early 1990s, it had become a significant world player in a wide array of products from photocopiers and laser copiers, facsimile transceivers and bubblejet printers, to cameras and videos, X-ray equipment, calculators, and even computers.

Canon's matrix structure is a series of product division 'spokes' emerging from a central corporate 'hub', and bound together by strong global functions in R&D, production, and marketing. The product division spokes (such as 'Peripherals' or 'Camera Operations') provide the major thrust into the markets, but the functions and shared resources at the center enable full and frequent communication between all parties interested in a decision. This allows for global coordination of product group strategies, but also for local coordination of sales and channel strategies within national marketing organizations. Yasutaka Obayashi, Head of Corporate Strategy, believes that the weighting within the matrix is both clear and appropriate: 'Although, as with any matrix structure, there are some confusions and ambiguities, it works well. The key to this is a clear sense of priorities. The product group is the primary axis in the matrix and the functional and geographical axes are secondary.' For a decision to be reached, many individuals may need to be convinced, but, according to executives such as the general manager of the Copying Machines Product Group, this does not cause intolerable delay: 'The process is not a step-by-step, level-by-level review, as might be typical of a Western company. Rather, the people concerned meet together and decide simultaneously. This speeds up the decision process and makes it less cumbersome.'

There are around 1,000 administrative staff and over 1,000 R&D staff at Canon's headquarters. These staff are not so much an overlay on the Canon matrix, as a central resource from which, and into which, much learning flows. For example, most of the product groups share overlapping technologies that come together in the research rather than development phase, and central technologists are able to stimulate new combinations and generate new ideas. In this way, Canon maintains considerable corporate resource outside the business units,. The hub-and-spoke image suggests clearly the notion that all product groups radiate out of the company's resources; these product groups are conduits for corporate resources to generate value in specific markets. In the *Canon Fact Book* of 1991–92, an interesting display shows how basic product groups (at the center of the circle) fan out into product families and in turn into specific end products (see Figure 13.1). A note under the diagram reads: 'The composition of Canon's complete product lineup as shown here is the result of constant efforts to maximize the potential of the company's resources.' At Canon the resources are essentially owned by the company as a whole, but are on loan to the individual units.

Despite the emphasis on corporate resource and shared corporate identity, Canon is by no means a unitary, functionally organized company. Its product groups have significant autonomy, and it is to them that the various functions in marketing or R&D are accountable. How, then, does the company maintain access to the skills and capabilities that are distributed across its units?

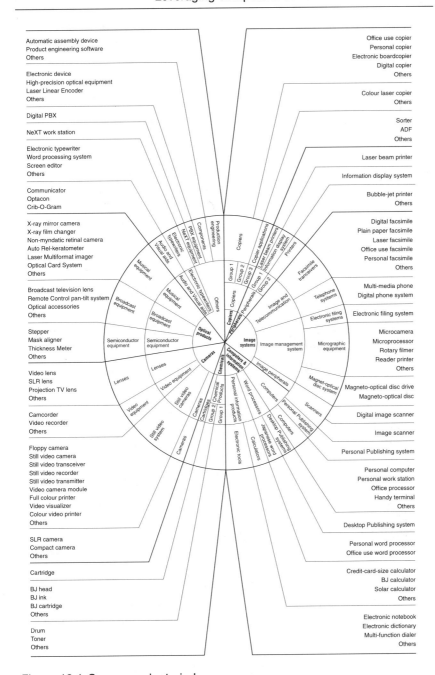

Figure 13.1 Canon product circle
Source: *Canon Fact Book, 1991/1992*. The composition of Canon's complete product lineup as shown here is the result of constant efforts to maximize the potential of the company's resources.

One crucial mechanism is the formation of short-term taskforces. These taskforces, which bring together employees from across the organization, have the authority, through their membership and the blessing of the most senior management, to act rather than merely recommend. They are not exempted from management review or veto, but they do have the same status in decision taking and action as more structurally fixed organizational forms. A classsic example of Canon's approach was the large cross-company taskforce brought together to develop the AE-1 camera. This group combined skills and know-how from around the company to create the world's first electronically controlled totally automatic single lens reflex (SLR) camera with a built-in microprocessor unit. Following its introduction in 1976, the AE-1 achieved enormous success as a world trend-leader. Furthermore, the speed and success of the development process encouraged other break-through projects within Canon. One of these was focused on a new type of personal photocopier.[3] As in the case of the AE-1, the organizational unit for the development of the personal copier was the taskforce.[4]

This group, known as 'Taskforce X', was given high visibility. It was formally inaugurated on September 1, 1980, by Ryuzaburo Kaku, President of Canon. As with other Canon taskforces, its members were appointed by the company president, giving further organizational weight to this temporary entity. Taskforce X was very different from the lightweight teams that many companies establish to create linkages across units. It had around 200 members, divided between two prime development groups and six staff groups. Members were selected from many departments, including the reprographic products development center; the production engineering research center; the corporate technical planning and operation center; the corporate patents and legal center; the reprographic products planning and administration center; and the copier sales planning department. This membership reveals something of the importance and role of centralized groups at Canon. For example, much of the specialist know-how and expertise of the production engineering research center had been gained from work on the mass production of cameras. This enabled K. Naito, Director of the Center, to redesign the copier production line using principles developed in camera manufacture. Furthermore, production engineering staff were involved from the earliest stages of the project, helping to shape product design with mass production in mind.

Canon's central staff provide another important mechanism for facilitating linkages. First, their briefings to senior executives help to enhance the understanding of cross-business or cross-functional issues, and to improve the flow of information. Second, the mere existence of so many staff positions provides an opportunity for many managers to spend some time in these roles. This can be an important part of 'socialization' into Canon as a whole and provides a perspective from outside any given product group. Third, in a way that parallels the large negotiating staffs on international treaties, their existence enables a great deal of groundwork to be put in place. This smooths the way to multipartite decisions and lessens the danger of significant gaps developing between different parts of the company.

The center also plays an important role in gathering and disseminating information that can aid linkages. Data on the performance and cost structures of all the overseas manufacturing and sales subsidiaries are prepared in Tokyo and circulated to all locations. This 'can stimulate questions which result in improvements', as one manager commented. Senior executives from the different dimensions of the matrix meet regularly face to face. At the top of the company, under the chairman and president, is an 8-man corporate team of senior managing directors. These are joined by the heads of the product divisions, the heads of the sales organizations for Japan, Europe, and the United States, and the heads of the main staff and functional departments to form a 22-man corporate executive committee that meets weekly and has final decision-making authority. This regular contact greatly reduces the risk of fragmentation or the development of unnoticed gulfs.

The culture of Canon, as of many Japanese organizations, is also well suited to a matrix structure with significant central resources.[5] On the one hand, the matrix reduces inappropriate deference to hierarchical authority by deemphasizing a single chain of command. This can help to flush out problems or disagreements that might otherwise be submerged. On the other hand, given a strong disposition toward consensus decision making, the matrix is unlikely to break down due to insoluble conflicts. Having flushed out the difficulties, there is a will to find solutions that are acceptable to all.

Another important mechanism to enhance linkages is the centrally driven career management process. This process not only moves individual managers through different functions and product groups, but recognizes and rewards the ability and inclination of individuals to network effectively. There is a strong central personnel department, with 25 staff who keep records on all employees, and are influential in promotion and training decisions for all senior staff. The systematic appraisal process includes written exams. The most senior personnel managers are themselves likely to have enjoyed a broad range of positions, perhaps starting in sales in one product group, then moving into a financial role in another group, then taking up an international position, before moving into the personnel function. The ability to create such career paths for many managers depends both on the parent's attitude to staff development and on the loyalty and long service of employees.

Finally, Canon's unifying culture creates an important backdrop in the search for linkages and their effective realization. Although there is lively competition between different product groups, there is a strong sense that all employees are primarily members of Canon as a whole. This sense of shared identity is based on a wide range of factors. The decision to grow organically rather than through major acquisitions has limited the risk of importing rival cultures. The movement of staff across units, the large number of centrally held resources, the formation of cross-company taskforces, and the clear corporate vision statement all support the sense of one enterprise.

The success of Japanese corporations such as Canon, which have substantial shared corporate resources available to their businesses, together with the tantalizing and mysterious accounts of building and leveraging tacit know-how and core competences, have led several Western companies to feel that they should explore this way of managing.[6] In many cases, however, companies have come to the conclusion either that they have no 'core competences' or that the shared resources approach is of marginal relevance to their particular portfolio. In what business contexts, then, is the approach liable to be appropriate? Although it is important to distinguish between expertise in a particular technology and 'core competences',[7] it is easy to see that in technologically rich and fast-moving areas, this approach is more likely to be relevant than in mature, low technology areas. Similarly, if opportunities exist for new combinations of skills and resources previously held in separate business domains, the approach is more likely to tease out these new combinations than one that is organized around tightly defined business units and business-specific ways of working. The role of the center is to encourage flexibility in product and business definition, and to avoid self-standing, complete divisions getting locked into ways of working that only optimize performance for a brief time span.

This fits with the notion that core competences can be applied to a number of different markets and that they remain the concern of the company as a whole. By maintaining a large center through which information and individual business managers regularly pass, the organization can benefit from local experiments and consolidate experience. It can also develop patterns of behavior that cross the organizational boundaries of the time. This fosters core competences that can be deployed in new settings and newly defined businesses.

Corporate strategy

A parenting advantage statement for Canon is provided as Table 13.1. Its *value creation insights* are all intimately related to its approach to linkages. First, shared resources in core technologies allow all Canon's businesses to benefit from relevant expertise that they could not afford individually. Second, complex linkages are achieved through the use of

Table 13.1 Canon parenting advantage statement

Value creation insights	Individual businesses have resourcing difficulties in pursuing a range of technologies in depth and can benefit from shared resource within the parent.
	Businesses find it difficult to create linkages and cross-fertilization between different areas of technology, between technologists and market needs, and between different markets; and there is a role for a parent in facilitating these linkages.
	An inspiring corporate vision can help businesses to stretch for growth beyond the confines of each business.
Distinctive parenting characteristics	Ability to manage cross-fertilization: • Across different technologies. • Between technical and market specialists. • Across different markets. A high level of corporate commitment to technology and learning. Company vision that energizes staff toward growth and stretch without prompting inappropriate risks.
Heartland businesses	Businesses in which overall performance depends heavily on product performance and new product development, which in turn are driven by superior understanding and linking of three core technology areas: precision mechanics, fine optics, and micro-electronics; where technology advantage is embodied in certain key components; where international presence and ability to manage multiple channels to market provide a major advantage; selling business machines, cameras, and specialist optical products.

large central staffs, the matrix structure, career development paths, and taskforces. Third, employees form an identification with Canon that goes beyond their current business unit and is based on shared access to the company's resources. But Canon's insights are not only supported by parenting characteristics concerned with sharing and linkages. Other *distinctive parenting characteristics* are also important.

Canon's commitment to technology development is spelled out in one of the company's corporate objectives, which states: 'We will create the best and most unique products based on leading edge technologies. We have a responsibility to create the best products possible. To achieve this goal, we will concentrate our efforts in the areas of R&D, product planning and marketing, adopting an enterprising attitude.' This involves both funding R&D and placing it in a central position within the company. Canon's total R&D expenditure averaged nearly 11% of sales in the second half of the 1980s and totaled $2.8 billion over the 5-year period from 1986 to 1990. Canon was granted a total of 3,363 patents in the United States between 1987 and 1990, which placed it in the top three achievers for each year, with Hitachi and Toshiba as its consistent fellows, well ahead of some much larger technology firms.

Commitment to R&D is not just demonstrated in the level of funding, but also in the parent's willingness to invest for long-term payoffs. As the 1992 annual report puts it: 'In R&D, Canon will concentrate on developing products that will sell in the long term rather than making instant bestsellers.' R&D has also had a distinctive status and role within Canon. As a Japanese business school professor, who had worked for many years at Canon, summed it up: R&D drives Canon's strategic thinking and is central to Canon's behavior and management style. As an example, the medium-range management plan of each product division is drawn up by the development center of the product group. This 3-year product and development plan is then presented for discussion to the international meeting for product strategy held every autumn. Canon's R&D staff therefore believe that their work is essential to the growth of Canon.'[8] This level of R&D commitment is clearly important in realizing benefit from the first value creation insight.

The third insight concerns the danger of psychological constraints imposed by rigid business definitions. These constraints are partly reduced by the linkage mechanisms and somewhat fluid organizational structure of the company. But Canon has also been unusually successful in creating companywide visions that challenge employees to stretch well beyond their current businesses.

Canon has been guided by three company visions that have opened up new thinking and aspirations by concentrating on some form of strategic intent for the enterprise as a whole. Growth and stretch have been heavily emphasized in these visions. In 1976, Canon launched the first 'Premier Company' plan. At that point, Canon was suffering badly from its overhasty entry into pocket calculators, and the devastating effects of the 1973 oil crisis. As Chairman Kaku later described it, 'Canon was like a ship that constantly changes course and goes nowhere.' Against this difficult backdrop, Kaku, then a junior director, was the driving force in launching a plan to make Canon 'The world's leading company.' The plan covered a 6-year period aiming to make Canon a premier company within Japan during the first 3 years, and a premier company internationally during the second 3 years. The plan included high-level goals such as: 'to time perfectly the release of new products which offer performance and quality unequaled anywhere in the world'; 'to manufacture goods with the highest quality, at the lowest prices, and in the shortest time'; 'to strengthen sales companies to achieve utterly efficient sales.' The plan was not specific about how these objectives were to be attained but stressed issues such as the importance of innovation in technology, the need to develop human resources to the maximum, and Canon's social responsibilities. However, immediate practical steps were also taken, such as reorganizing the company into product groups, increasing automation in factories and offices, and supporting the corporate image. Furthermore, the grandiose high-level objectives were applied to specific projects, stimulating a level of aspiration that challenged basic assumptions. Middle-level managers were pressured into creative and unconventional ideas as the only possible way of meeting such aspirations. The development of the AE-1 camera or the personal copier were based on almost preposterous price targets. These acted as a ceiling under which the desired product functionality had to be delivered.

The extraordinary level of stretch in the 1976 vision was repeated in the second 'Premier Company Plan' in 1982, and in the 'Vision that Starts a New Canon' in 1988, which exhorts the 'building of an ideal firm.' These plans are strongly influenced by top management, but can involve a broad spectrum of Canon's employees. Their value lies not in the goals themselves, such as the apparently unreachable 'trillion yen' sales goal proposed in 1976, but in the efforts that the vision and goals inspire. This inspiration is not simply generated by a document of intent. Senior management in general, and chairman Kaku in particular, regard the development and constant reemphasizing of the vision as their crucial role in the company. The company plan is not, therefore, seen as merely the output of senior management brainstorming, but as the driving force and energizer of the company as a whole.

Canon's *heartland* criteria emphasize the role of three core technologies. These technologies have been linked together to create innovative products for many different markets. Indeed, the ability to cross-fertilize ideas and know-how between these areas has been cited as a prime example of 'core competences'.[9] The competences are relevant to cameras, special optical products, and a variety of business machines, not just because all these areas use the three technologies, but also because they depend heavily on product performance and new product development. If this was not so, the relative value of the technological competences would be diminished. Within its heartland businesses, Canon also aims to produce the key components that embody technological advantage. By controlling these components, Canon is not reliant on the speed and capabilities of outside suppliers. It can also sell the key components to others, controlling the flow of technology, reducing reliance on single end product applications, and locking out would-be competitors through its own global dominance.[10]

But for a business to be included in the heartland, it is not enough simply to share benefits from a given core competence. To avoid the risk of value destruction, a parent must also understand the critical success factors of its businesses. Canon has proved itself particularly adept at achieving this requirement by acquiring a feel for new businesses. Its large center has helped it address the learning needs of the parent.[11] Its emphasis on organic growth rather than acquisition has also given it time to practise parenting new areas in comparatively low-risk contexts. Finally, it has so far focused on businesses that have elements of commonality beyond the importance of the three core technologies. For example, the value of international presence and the use of multiple sales channels are common to most Canon businesses. The parent is familiar and comfortable with the sorts of decisions that are important in such contexts. In contrast, a business that involved large-scale projects sold to government entities would be unfamiliar territory for Canon, even if it involved use of the three core technologies.

The nature and rate of Canon's growth is an impressive testimony to the quality of its parenting. It has grown organically rather than by acquisition and has successfully entered markets where it faced entrenched and dominant competitors. Its challenge to Xerox in photo-copying was as audacious as its earlier challenge to Leika in cameras. But, to the extent that its parenting advantage has depended on techno-logical competences and new product development, it may face new challenges as technologies mature in its major businesses. In the past, it has shown an unusual ability to bring new businesses successfully into its heartland. If it is able to continue this process in the future, for example with its current investments in computer businesses,[12] its parenting advantage will not play out for many years.

COOPER INDUSTRIES

Cooper Industries is a $6 billion company, headquartered in Houston, Texas. Until the 1960s, it was primarily a manufacturer of engines and compressors for natural gas pipelines. Since then, the company has diversified substantially, and now has businesses in hand tools, power tools, electrical products, electrical power equipment, and automotive parts, as well as in a variety of petroleum and industrial equipment sectors. A common factor in all these businesses is that manufacturing is an important part of the overall cost structure, and a key to competitive success.

Manufacturing function

Bob Cizik, the chairman and chief executive officer of Cooper, is personally committed to the importance of manufacturing for Cooper. He, and the other members of the parenting team, all have long experience of manufacturing businesses, and they believe that a focus on improving manufacturing is a key source of Cooper added value. Cizik has written about this in a company publication entitled 'Manufacturing: Give Me an M', which deals with Cooper's so-called Big M manufacturing philosophy. The essence of the philosophy is that all functions in Cooper need to work together to recognize the importance of manufacturing. Manufacturing issues are high on the agenda in discussions between representatives of the parent company and the businesses, and feature prominently in planning and budgeting reviews.

The parent's influence on manufacturing is reinforced by the role of the corporate Manufacturing Services department. The department has a staff of 15 people, most of whom are divisional manufacturing people on 3- to 4-year tours of duty. 'It is better,' says Cizik, 'to have people with a bit of grease under their fingernails.' For many years, it was led by Joseph Coppola, a senior vice president with 14 years' service at Cooper, and a lifetime of experience in manufacturing positions.[13] The department is organized around different subfunctional specialisms, such as automation engineering, materials management, and environmental technology.

The department is involved in screening all Cooper acquisitions and is always brought in to advise on postacquisition improvement opportunities. It has a major role in vetting capital investment proposals from the ongoing businesses and will help them to develop their proposals if requested to do so. It is also available to advise any Cooper business on manufacturing issues. In addition, the department organizes a number of Cooper-wide 'councils', which meet two or three times a year and bring together functional staff from different businesses around specific topics such as logistics management. The department also organizes a 2-year graduate training scheme in manufacturing management. The department therefore combines a functional influence role with a central service role.

Cooper's Manufacturing Services department can add value because the different Cooper businesses nearly all face similar manufacturing issues. 'You would be amazed at the similarities in the processes in our division,' explained Coppola. 'Machining, fabrication, assembly, work measurement, materials management, quality assurance, and so on are all similar.' This means that Cizik and the parenting team can develop a good sense of the issues and tradeoffs that the businesses face in their manufacturing operations, and that the Manufacturing Services department can become experts in these processes. Experience gained in one business carries over and is relevant to other businesses, and the department can draw on benchmarks and best practice established in one business in advising others. This raises standards and develops skills throughout the company. Cooper typically finds that new acquisitions fall far short of the company's expectations for manufacturing productivity, and major savings can be made by working with the Manufacturing Services department. Productivity at Champion Spark Plug, for example, increased by 30% during the 3 years after its acquisition by Cooper.

The Manufacturing Services department recognizes, however, that its skills do not cover all types and forms of manufacturing. 'We can contribute less on the sort of sophisticated forging they do in the Cameron business,' stated Coppola. 'And if we went into something like a speciality chemical, I doubt whether we could contribute much at all.'

The way in which the Manufacturing Services department exercises its influence is also noteworthy. Except with new acquisitions, the department only works with Cooper businesses if it is invited to do so. Businesses are free to establish their own specialist departments or to use the services of an external consultant, if they so choose. However, in the words of one division head: 'It would be very difficult to have all that expertise within the division, and outside suppliers would be very expensive and probably not as close to the state of the art as the Manufacturing Services people.' It is seen as crucially important for the department to regard the businesses as 'clients', who must be persuaded of the views of the department. 'We give out no edicts,' was Coppola's claim. Furthermore members of the department are trained to treat the personal relationships in client businesses with care, and to aim to win the respect and support of the businesses for the department. To achieve this end, the department always tries to involve divisional staff closely with projects on which it works, and to structure the projects to show early successes. A quick identification of a measurable cost reduction opportunity gains credibility for the department, and improves the chances of major, longer-term proposals being accepted. Although the department draws on its experience with other divisions in making best practice suggestions, it is careful to avoid 'gossip' about problems or personalities elsewhere. Establishing a confidential relationship with each business, in which openness about issues is possible, is the goal. To encourage divisions to seek the help of the department, Cooper makes no charge for its services, a policy that applies to all of Cooper's central departments.

Cizik believes that an internal department working in this way can create much more value than outside consultants and advisers. 'It helps us to demonstrate our commitment to manufacturing. Our people know Cooper plants, products, and people better than outsiders, and can spread the Cooper way of doing things. And, with our own staff, we can control the interpersonal interfaces better and make sure that we are developing the skills in our people throughout the company.'

The attention and priority given to manufacturing in Cooper reflects the key success factors in its businesses. The Big M concept and Cooper's understanding and support for manufacturing investments distinguish the company from many other parents that have neither the commitment to, nor the feel for, what is necessary to succeed in manufacturing businesses. Furthermore, the Manufacturing Services department creates value because it has a unique depth of expertise, based on its extensive experience with Cooper's particular types of businesses, and ways of working that develop positive relationships with the businesses. The fact that businesses do not have to pay for the services of the department obviously means that they are seen as good value. But the primary purpose of the 'no charges' policy is to overcome any initial resistance to calling on the department for advice; our clear impression is that Cooper businesses that have experience of working with the department would continue to use it, even if it made 'commercial' charges for its work.

Corporate strategy

Table 13.2 is a parenting advantage statement for Cooper Industries. Cooper's basic *value creation insight* has been to perceive that many US businesses in the manufacturing sector have failed to make the most of their opportunities. Often, their parent companies have become disenchanted with manufacturing, seeing it as an unattractive or unglamorous activity in which to engage. As a result, these businesses have not been aggressively managed. They have suffered from underinvestment, have given up the initiative to strong labor unions, have allowed unnecessary costs to be taken on, and have lost focus on those products and markets where their profit opportunities were best. A typical example was Champion Spark Plug, acquired by Cooper in 1989.

Champion was the leading US manufacturer of spark plugs and wipers, with a strong domestic market share in these products, and a brand name that was recognized throughout the world. However, the company had been reinvesting only 2% of sales revenues in its businesses since the mid-1970s, and the main thrust of Champion's strategy during the 1980s was to deemphasize its core products, and to diversify into new products that could carry the Champion brand name. These included oil additives, hand cleaners, automotive tools, and even a chain of car washes in Mexico. Most of these new businesses proved unprofitable, and in 1988 Champion incurred an operating loss of $6.4 million in its US operations. Cooper believes that a corporate parent that is committed to manufacturing can help businesses such as Champion to realize their true potential, by focusing them back on their core businesses and helping them to identify ways of improving their productivity and profitability in those businesses. Thus Champion is now

Table 13.2 Cooper Industries parenting advantage statement

Value creation insights	Companies that see manufacturing as unattractive lose focus on their profit opportunities, give up the initiative to strong unions, and fail to control their costs. This gives opportunities for a parent committed to manufacturing, particularly if it has specialist expertise in manufacturing technology and other relevant areas. Many independent businesses serving similar markets can derive synergy benefits in manufacturing and distribution, if brought under common parental ownership.
Distinctive parenting characteristics	Commitment to manufacturing: • Strong, specialist corporate staffs in manufacturing and other related areas. 'Cooperization' process: • Structuring into semiautonomous divisions that report directly to the corporate center, with no intermediate layers. • Reviewing top management appointments in the businesses, and bringing in managers from elsewhere in Cooper as needed. • '80/20' focus on most profitable opportunites. • Imposing Cooper policies and practices, and clarifying what issues will be handled by the center and by the business. • 'Clustering' businesses with linkage potential into the same division.
Heartland businesses	Manufacturing businesses, drawing on selected, fairly mature technologies, with leading positions and brand recognition in their markets; focusing mainly on the US market; where consumer marketing is not key to success; and preferably where individual customers do not have high bargaining power and capital intensity is not high.

concentrating on spark plugs, wipers, and aircraft ignitions. With the help of the Manufacturing Services department, it has also consolidated five North American production facilities down to two, and has introduced major process changes and investments and eliminated restrictive practices at the remaining plants. The business is now much more profitable.

Cooper's second value creation insight concerns the synergies available from bringing together different businesses that serve similar markets into divisional 'clusters'. The clusters allow Cooper to overcome the competition and mutual distrust that prevent independent businesses from achieving the sort of benefits that are possible. Cooper now has clusters in hand tools, oil field equipment, and lighting products, as well as automotive parts.

Cooper's value creation insights are supported by *distinctive parenting characteristics* that stress the importance of manufacturing, and the role of the Manufacturing Services department and other corporate staff departments, such as industrial relations, management development, finance, and planning. Other distinctive parenting characteristics are drawn together in the concept of 'Cooperization', an approach to parenting that is applied to all Cooper businesses, but especially to new acquisitions. The ingredients of Cooperization include:

- Fitting the business into the Cooper organization structure and, in particular, cutting out unnecessary layers of overhead and reporting. The Cooper structure stresses 'semiautonomous' divisions (for example, the Lighting division, the Hand Tool division, the Oil Tool division) that report direct to the corporate center. There are some 20 divisions, which each report to one of three executive vice presidents. The EVPs have very small, one- or two-person staffs and do not act as a consolidation or review level in the corporate structure. Rather they act as representatives of Bob Cizik and the corporate center for the divisions in their areas. The structure therefore has a minimum of layers and often allows substantial cost reductions for new acquisitions. Champion's corporate, international, and regional head offices, for example, were all closed by Cooper. The divisions are largely free to propose their own strategies, subject to corporate functional policies, as described later in this section. If necessary, Cooper also tightens up on redundant working capital, SG&A costs and other areas of overhead.

- Appointing new managers from elsewhere in Cooper to senior positions in the business, as needed. Typically, the general manager and financial controller in newly acquired businesses come from other Cooper businesses and, in some cases, a much larger number of new appointments are made: in Champion, for example, 19 out of the top 20 positions were filled by new Cooper people after the acquisition. Cooper's human resource planning tracks the top 800 people in the company, with the expectation that cross-divisional moves will be common and beneficial. In 1991, no fewer than 45 senior managers moved into new divisions.

- Insisting that all businesses focus on their most profitable products, markets, and customers. Cooper believes strongly in the 80:20 rule, especially for companies that have strayed into peripheral diversifications. A firm steer from the parent is sometimes needed to move business managers away from peripheral products to which they have become unduly committed.

- Imposing Cooper's policies and approaches on industrial relations, management development and succession planning, environmental issues, benefit plans, accounting, planning and budgeting, and real estate. In areas such as real estate and industrial relations, corporate functions take over responsibility from the divisions, and believe that they can achieve economies of scale and specialization not open to individual divisions. With accounting, planning, budgeting, and benefit plans, it is more a matter of following the Cooper way of doing things. 'When we make an acquisition,' says Alan Reidel, vice chairman of the board, 'we tend to impose the Cooper culture and processes. To begin with, we were less confident in doing this, but during the last few years we have gained increasing confidence that this is right for the sort of businesses we acquire.' Support for this view comes from most of the division heads. One, from a recent acquisition, observed that during the first year of Cooper's ownership he felt that he was being 'mothered' and became restive. But now that the disciplines have been established, he accepts that they work well. 'It is more supportive than restrictive.'
- Bringing in the Manufacturing Services department to identify manufacturing improvements and investments that should be made. Often, this involves factory relocation and the introduction of new working practices.
- Lastly, designing the divisional structure to facilitate resource sharing between businesses clustered into the same division. For example, with the acquisition of Moog Automotive in 1992, a new automotive parts cluster has been created, with a view to sharing and rationalizing distribution and sales between Cooper's 'under-car' chassis part businesses. The structure is intended to locate businesses with significant potential for sharing within the same division, and to avoid the need for strong linkages between divisions.

Cooperization is possible due to the similarities between Cooper's businesses, and the opportunities this gives for common approaches between them. Indeed, sharing best practice between businesses is a pervasive philosophy in Cooper. As one division head claimed: 'To me, the strength that comes out of corporate is that if they see something that works in one division, then they get it into the others too.' Thus, although Cooper's portfolio has evolved over the past 25 years to include a variety of different businesses, they all conform to the *heartland criteria*. Most essentially, all of Cooper's businesses have manufacturing as an important part of their cost structure, and a significant basis for competitive advantage. 'The business of Cooper Industries is value-added manufacturing. We come from a long line of people who forge, cast, draw, drill, bore, grind, heat treat, and fabricate things out of metal. Now we use other materials and processes as well. But it all comes down to manufacturing. We know a lot about that.'[14] Continuous process manufacturing or simple assembly businesses do not build on Cooper's particular competences, but businesses where cell-based manufacturing is the key to success are particularly suitable.

In addition to the manufacturing theme, Cooper concentrates on businesses in relatively mature technology areas, where high levels of R&D spending and rapid product obsolescence are not found. Cooper is less comfortable judging the risks in more rapidly changing, technically unstable businesses. Ideally, businesses should, however, have some distinctive products or technologies to give them a competitive edge. Cooper prefers businesses that have leading market share positions and enjoy brand recognition in their markets. It is also familiar with the types of issues that arise where products are handled through extensive channels of distribution, involving wholesalers, dealers and for consumer goods, retailers. Most of Cooper's businesses are primarily focused on US production for US markets. Cooper avoids businesses that require high consumer marketing expenditures or that are dominated by a few large customers. It also avoids high capital intensity businesses and businesses that face intractable labor relations problems or large environmental or product liability risks. Businesses should also be large enough to support the Cooper overhead.

Nearly all of Cooper's many acquisitions during the past 25 years conform, to a greater or lesser extent, to these specifications. Companies such as Crescent, Lufkin, Nicholson, and Triangle in the Hand Tool division, Crouse Hinds, McGraw Eddison, and RTE in Electrical Products, Cameron and Gardner-Denver in oil field equipment, and Champion and Moog in automotive parts, all fall within the heartland. Equally, Cooper Airmotive, an aircraft engine overhaul and service business, the Industrial Machinery division of Gardner-Denver, the specialty forged products business of Cameron, and other smaller businesses have been divested because they did not fit the heartland criteria.

Bob Cizik, Cooper's CEO, expresses the importance of the heartland criteria as follows: 'Because our businesses are all reasonably closely related in terms of depending on basic manufacturing processes and using similar sorts of distribution channels, we can get a pretty good understanding of the issues they each face quite quickly.' 'You don't have to know the details of how a turbine is made as against a file, but the language is the same. There are tremendous similarities in the sorts of strategic issues that come up in the different businesses in our group.' 'Flags pop in your mind when certain ratios are getting out of line. I know what sort of ratios we need to make money, given the cost structures in our sort of businesses. These sort of understandings get developed over time due to constant experience with our businesses.' It is in the heartland businesses that Cooper's manufacturing-based corporate strategy adds the most value.

Cooper's record through the 1980s is one of significant success in the majority of its businesses. Its Cooperization approach has yielded real performance improvements in many businesses and has allowed profits before tax to rise from $240 million in 1982 to $625 million in 1993, on sales up from $2,390 million to $6,274 million. Earnings per share have risen during the same period from $1.38 to $2.75.

These impressive results would have been even better without the negative impact of the oil and gas sector, which has remained depressed for the bulk of the past decade, and which is likely to cause 1994 earnings to fall. Cooper's long-term commitment to this sector has prevented the quality of its corporate strategy from being fully reflected in its bottom-line results since the early 1980s. Oil and gas equipment is one of Cooper's original businesses and provided excellent profits, particularly during the late 1970s oil boom. But Cooper's willingness to continue to support and invest in it during bad times and good has proved expensive. During the late 1980s and early 1990s, Electrical Power Equipment has also faced a depressed market.

Cooper also paid full prices for its major late 1980s acquisitions, such as Champion, Cameron, and RTE, with the result that, by 1992 it was carrying $2.8 billion of intangible assets, primarily goodwill, in its balance sheet. This has depressed return on assets and means that Cooperization needs to yield high levels of performance improvement in these businesses to justify the acquisitions. Progress has already been made, but Cooper will be looking for substantial advances when the markets in which these businesses compete improve.

Cooper's success has come, therefore, not from corporate development activities that have positioned it in profitable sectors or allowed it to make cheap acquisitions, but from performance improvement in the businesses in its portfolio. Its parenting influence, based on its manufacturing commitment and skills and its Cooperizations process, creates unusual value. Some commentators point to Cooper's diversity as the source of its strength. We believe, in contrast, that it is its focus on the kinds of businesses and the sorts of parenting opportunities that it knows best that accounts for its success.

3M

For many years, 3M has been one of the most admired companies in the United States. It has an enviable record for innovation and new business creation, and it has a portfolio diversity that most rivals have found difficult to manage. The company's \$14 billion of sales are derived from some 40 product divisions. The product divisions range from businesses selling abrasives to the automotive industry to businesses selling dental products to the pharmaceutical industry. One division makes roofing tile granules, another makes Post-it notes for use in office work. But there is a common factor within this diversity. Nearly every product made by 3M has been developed by its technical staff in its divisional laboratories. On average, 3M's laboratories produce many more successful new products than its rivals. Much of this success is due to the parenting influence of 3M's central technical function.

Technical function

Each division in 3M has its own laboratory for developing new products, and the duty of the divisional technical director is to develop products that secure the business's future. It is the technical function, not the marketing function, that is the main source of new product ideas. The management of laboratories, the prime task of the divisional technical director, is therefore a vital activity in 3M. In total, there are some 150 laboratories working on some 1,500 new product development programs. Divisional technical directors report to divisional chief executives. But they also have dotted-line relationships with sector technical directors and the central technical function. The sector technical director has overall responsibility for the technical development of the sector and works closely with the central technical function. Good relationships between technical people at the center, the sector level, and the divisions are essential to the smooth working of the 3M system.

In this description of 3M's technical function, we will focus on two areas of influence – improving the quality of laboratory management and ensuring that technology is shared throughout 3M. The quality of laboratory management is maintained and improved in a number of ways. First, the central technical function helps to develop and select technical directors. The final selection decision is made by the division chief executive, but the candidates will all be internal technical people, identified by the technical function and imbued with 3M's approach to laboratory management. One unusual aspect of 3M's approach is the close working relationship between marketing and technical staff. Technical staff frequently visit customers and go on calls with marketing staff. As a result, 3M technical people are usually skilled in marketing and new product development as well as technical research. It is the central technical function's responsibility to make sure that these qualities are being developed in the technical staff and that there are sufficient potential candidates for new technical posts.

The second way that the quality of laboratory management is developed is through an audit process. The central technical function manages a peer audit process, in which technical directors from other laboratories visit a laboratory and write a report on their findings. The main focus is on operational procedures such as how patents are handled or how the new product introduction system is working. The importance attached to these audits helps to reinforce the natural desire of technical directors to get a clean bill of health from their peers. Both the audits themselves, and the work that goes into deciding what the audit standards should be, help to accelerate the continuous learning process at 3M. In addition, learning flows both ways, from those doing the audit to those being studied and vice versa.

The third way of raising the quality of laboratory management is through the policies, procedures, and cultural norms that have grown up and become institutionalized in 3M. The managers in the central technical function are the keepers of these '3M ways of doing things', and they have the task of deciding whether to enforce a particular policy or norm. They recognize the need for continuous improvement and experimentation, and hence, they keep a healthy balance between rigid policies and management chaos. One policy or norm is the 15% rule. This 40-year-old norm permits technical people to spend 15% of their time pursuing their own ideas. It is a management policy that 3M has cherished as part of its technical culture. Not all technical people choose to use the opportunity to follow their own projects. But some do, and the fact that the opportunity is available encourages individuals to take more responsibility for innovation. Another part of the '3M way' is the new product introduction system. This consists of a centrally written four-page guideline, stating that all laboratories should have an organized system for product introduction. The guideline was developed in 1967 and has been revised a number of times since then. As a divisional technical director explained: 'I don't feel constrained by the guideline. It is not an instruction. I am free to develop my own system if I believe it will be more effective. But it is a standard against which to measure yourself and it is used in the audit process.'

The fourth way of raising the quality of laboratory management is through the Technical Forum. All technical staff in 3M are members of the Forum, and the Forum has its own central staff. It is like a professional association within 3M. There are regular meetings to discuss the 'hottest technical areas' and the 'hottest management issues'. Attendance is voluntary, ensuring that managers only attend if they consider the sessions useful.

Another important role of the central technical staff is to ensure that technology is shared between 3M's 150 laboratories. This commitment to share is backed by a strong 3M policy that technology belongs to the company not the division. 'We have many different ways of encouraging people to talk to one another' explained Tom Wollner, Staff Vice President, Corporate Research Laboratories. 'We don't have any organized plan for networking. But we encourage it to happen as much as we can.' The campus environment of 3M Center in St. Paul, Minnesota, is important. 'We have definitely created something unusual here. It is not easy to repeat.' In fact, 3M has found it hard to recreate the same closeness of working relationships in Japan and in Europe, and even in the new technology center in Austin, Texas. But networking is not the only way of encouraging sharing. 3M has an extensive library system recording all the new product development programs both past and present. Technology fairs are held annually in which each laboratory displays its wares, and marketing and production people are invited to browse the stalls. These systems encourage information flow and make it easy for technical directors to access work going on in other laboratories.

In other companies, many of the features of 3M's technical function – technical forums, peer audits, networking, and strong cultures – lead to bureaucracy and time wasting. In 3M, these processes are highly positive and fit well within a corporate strategy that stresses decentralization, new product development, and a performance orientation, and which concentrates on businesses in which these characteristics pay off best. Thus, 3M's technical function plays an important role within its overall corporate strategy.

Corporate strategy

Table 13.3 is a parenting advantage statement for 3M. The company's *value creation insights* have been built up over its 90-year history. They have their roots in the early days, when 3M had to find a way of succeeding against stronger, established competitors. The key to success in 3M's businesses has been to insist on superior products, based on technically unique qualities that can be defended against competitors. To achieve this, 3M's parenting emphasizes the role of the technical function in promoting creativity and innovation. This is about the quality of the technical function in each division; it is about the way the technical functions in different divisions coordinate and network together; and it is about the way central technical units nurture common technologies and provide support in specialist areas to help divisions bring products to market quickly. It is also about an approach to sales and marketing that creates a close link between the customer and the rest of the business. This approach was originated by William McKnight in 3M's earliest history. Describing events in 1913, 3M's *Our Story So Far*[15] explains McKnight's early influence: 'McKnight trained his salesmen to do what he had learned could be done, get into work areas, find what kind of abrasive materials were best suited for customer needs, demonstrate

Table 13.3 3M parenting advantage statement

Value creation insights	Innovative new products and whole new businesses can be developed by effective parenting of the technical function, within a structure of small decentralized divisions that encourage close relationships between sales and technical people and share common technologies.
Distinctive parenting characteristics	Decentralized management philosophy: • The division is the building block. • Financial performance is the main measure of success; but divisions cannot cut back on investment in research. • Close relationships between sales and technical staff. Technology and innovation-led culture; • Commitment to innovation. • Commitment to the innovator. • Status of the technical function. Long tenure, cooperative, consensus-seeking cadre of senior managers: • Few outsiders. • Supportive culture. • Trust relationships.
Heartland businesses	Businesses developed from 3M's core coating technology, particularly those that sell products to the automotive industry and the office products industry, have clear technical leadership, and can earn the return on sales needed to support a high research expenditure.

3M's products and report problems precisely to the factory with samples of poor quality sandpaper.' The link between sales, marketing, production, and technical staffs is still as close as it was in these early days, and 3M managers believe that it is central to their ability to innovate and get new products accepted by customers. The closeness of the relationship between the technical staffs and salespeople is a particularly unusual feature of the 3M approach.

In implementing 3M's insights, several *distinctive parenting characteristics* justify special mention. First, 3M is a highly decentralized company, but care is taken to decentralize to units that are large enough to be self-standing and, therefore, capable of funding their own research. Equally, 3M attempts to prevent divisions from getting so large that individual innovations no longer have any impact. 'Over the years, we've discovered that when a division reaches a certain size, it has a tendency to spend too much of its time on established products and markets, and a lesser amount on new products and businesses.' The size of divisions varies according to the size of the market being addressed. But most divisions have at least $100 million in sales. Divisions are measured against profit targets, with return on investment and return on sales as vital performance ratios. Divisions are expected to earn enough to fund their own growth and are encouraged to grow as fast as resources allow.

Decentralization is prized. McKnight is often quoted as having said, 'The mistakes . . . [of individuals] . . . are not as serious in the long run as the mistakes management will make if it is dictatorial.' However, divisions operate within a web of functional guidance and are closely monitored by line management to ensure that the decentralized divisions are managed in the 3M way. For example, spending on research is closely monitored and attempts to increase profits by cutting back on research investment would be quickly picked up.

The second distinctive characteristic is the careful nurturing of 3M's technology and innovation-led culture. 3M is a company that talks more about innovation and innovators than almost any other company and is used worldwide as an exemplar of innovation. 3M's commitment to innovation is symbolized by its long-standing public target of having 25% of sales from new products launched in the past 5 years, which has recently been upgraded to 30% of sales from new products launched in the past 4 years. Another public target is its commitment to spend around 7% of sales on research. 3M is also unusual in its commitment to and support for the individual innovator and has many ways of recognizing exceptional technical efforts. Its Golden Step awards (for US employees) and Pathfinder awards (for international employees) are given to individuals and teams who achieve important product developments. Individuals with unusual technical records are elected to the 'Carlton Society', named after one of 3M's most prominent technical leaders. 3M believes in the individual as the driver and champion of new ideas.

Supporting 3M's commitement to innovaton and to the innovators are two other distinctive features of the parenting approach – the status of the technical function and the technical background of many of 3M's senior managers. The technical function in 3M is 'first among equals'. Managers are at pains to point out that success depends on good technology, good production, and good marketing. But, within this triad, the technical people feel special. 'The great weight of the long-term commercial responsibility falls on the technical director in the 3M system. My role is to make sure we have the technologies that will enable us to have a long-term business position,' explained one divisional technical director. The status of the technical function encourages an unusually commercial attitude, which has been carefully fostered from the earliest days and ensures the close working relationships of the three functions. Technical directors are continually trying to get a customer's perspective on development projects. They encourage technicians to visit customers, spend time with marketing people, and work with production.

This highly cooperative, technically-led culture is supported by a third distinctive characteristic: the long tenure, consensus-seeking cadre of senior managers. Many of 3M's top managers have worked together for 20 years or more, and they have developed networks and relationships that make for unusually close and supportive working relationships. This both helps to maintain the 3M way of doing things and encourages the exchange of technical information and ideas that is so essential to success.

The final distinctive parenting characteristic, which we have already discussed, is the way 3M parents the technical function.

3M's *heartland businesses* draw off a common set of related technologies: More than 80% of 3M's 60,000-item product portfolio is linked to the technologies that have developed from the need to understand how to coat substrates with materials. 'Over 80% of our business is involved in precision coating and probably more than 90% works with polymers.' Within this technological heartland, the ideal 3M business fits a particular mold. It is based on technology that is patentable or sufficiently protectable so that 3M can gain reasonable returns for its technical investments. The product area is a niche, differentiated from a mass-market positioning. The product area is small enough that 3M can gain a number one or number two position and large enough to make its investment in technology worthwhile. 'Obviously we are not in heavy machinery or any low profit business environments. If the average profit is only 5%, we would steer away from the business.' Internally, managers look for a return on sales of 25% in new product or business areas. Returns at this level are only possible in markets where the product can achieve a clear technical advantage.

Another feature of an ideal 3M business is a focus on the early stage of a technology life cycle. 'When we get into mature product areas, we don't seem to do so well,' explained one manager. More recently, however, 3M has attempted to extend its heartland to these maturer areas. 'Since the mid-1970s there are fewer opportunities for us, so we can no longer afford to reduce emphasis on a business that has become more competitive. We now have to be prepared to fight competitors with our manufacturing skills and learn how to compete in the mature stages of the market.'

A final feature of an ideal 3M business is that a high percentage of its products should be sold to the office products, the automobile, or the metalworking markets. 'We are probably now number one in companies that serve the office market. Our office market division probably understands the customer and distribution channels better than anyone else,' commented one manager. The same depth of sales knowledge exists in the automobile and metalworking industries, where 3M had most of its earliest successes. Businesses have frequently grown out of sales or technical relationships that identified a customer need and developed a solution to it. 'We were selling abrasives to the auto industry. Because of contact with the factory floor, we noticed that they were having problems with paintwork. They would glue newspaper over the parts they did not want to paint. But then they would have problems removing the glue.' From this recognition of customer need and a 2-year research effort, 3M developed masking tape and its product portfolio of pressure-sensitive tapes.

3M's long-term performance has been the envy of many of its competitors. A pretax return on sales averaging over 16% has been combined with a return on equity around 20% and a compound growth rate of 7.5%. But, as 3M has grown, its rate of growth has inevitably slowed. In 1980, the compound growth rate was 13%, but in 1990 the company was more than twice as large as it had been in 1980 and growth in percentage terms became harder. In the future, 3M faces the challenge of learning how to compete effectively in more mature market sectors, where manufacturing costs, volumes, and prices are the keys to success, rather than technology. In the past, growth from new products has made it possible for 3M to deemphasize markets as they matured and the products became commodity items. But in tapes, and more recently in computer diskettes, 3M has decided to stand and fight. It is an alien strategic battle, one that does not play to 3M's historic parenting strengths. It will be interesting to see whether 3M will succeed in these businesses.

NOTES

1. Goold, Michael, Campbell, Andrew, and Alexander, Marcus, *Corporate-Level Strategy*, John Wiley & Sons, Inc., New York, 1994.
2. For a more complete explanation of the parenting advantage framework, see 'Corporate Strategy: The Quest for Parenting Advantage' in Part II.
3. See Teruo Yamanouchi, 'Breakthrough: The Development of the Canon Personal Copier,' *Long Range Planning*, vol. 22, no. 5, pp. 11–21, 1989.
4. Yamanouchi, 'Breakthrough'.
5. Nigel Campbell, Michael Goold, and Kimio Kase, *The Role of the Centre in Managing Large Diversified Companies in Japan*, Ashridge Strategic Management Centre Working Paper, September, 1990.
6. See, for example, Walter Kiechel, 'Corporate Strategy for the 1990s,' *Fortune*, February 29, 1988, p. 20. See also Hiroyuki Itami, *Mobilizing Invisible Assets*, Cambridge, MA: Harvard University Press, 1987.
7. Core competences involve an ability to combine technologies in ways that are not easy for others to replicate. It is the ability to transfer and cross-fertilize

particular technologies in developing products that best exemplifies technological core competence.

8. Yamanouchi, 'Breakthrough'.
9. See C. K. Prahalad and Gary Hamel, 'The Core Competence of the
   Corporation.' *Harvard Business Review*, May–June 1990.
10. Applying this logic, Canon had reputedly achieved an 84% share of the
    world market for desktop laser printer 'engines' by 1990, although these
    were incorporated in many products and brands other than its own.
11. See Goold, Campbell and Alexander, *Corporate-Level Strategy*, chapter 10 for a
    fuller discussion of Canon's approach to learning.
12. For a discussion of Canon's past heartland extensions and current moves, see
    Goold, Campbell and Alexander, *Corporate-Level Strategy*, chapter 10.
13. Coppola left Cooper in 1993 to become chairman and chief executive of
    Giddings and Lewis Inc. He was replaced by Nishan Teshoian.
14. 'Cooper Industries Management Philosophy: The Nature of Cooper's Busi-
    nesses' (company publication, p. 3).
15. *Our Story So Far*, St. Paul, Minnesota: 3M, 1977.

Appendix 1: Sources of readings by chapter

PART I UNDERSTANDING COMPETENCIES

Looking Inside for Competitive Advantage, Jay B. Barney
Academy of Management Executive, vol. 9, no. 4, 1995, pp. 49–61.

Understanding Organizations as Learning Systems, Edwin C. Nevis, Anthony J. DiBella and Janet M. Gould
Sloan Management Review, Winter 1995, pp. 73–85.

Managing Core Competency for Corporate Renewal: Towards a Managerial Theory of Core Competencies, Yves Doz
INSEAD Working Paper 94/23/SM (Rev. 17/05/94)

PART II COMPETENCIES AND CORPORATE STRATEGY

Unexplored Assets for Diversification, Gordon R. Conrad
Harvard Business Review, Sept.–Oct. 1963, pp. 67–73.

Related Diversification, Core Competences and Corporate Performance, Constantinos C. Markides and Peter J. Williamson
Strategic Management Journal, vol. 15, 1994, pp. 149–165.

Targeting a Company's Real Core Competencies, Amy Snyder and H. William Ebeling, Jr.
Journal of Business Strategy, vol. 13, no. 6, Nov.–Dec. 1992, pp. 26–32.

Corporate Strategy: The Quest for Parenting Advantage, Andrew Campbell, Michael Goold and Marcus Alexander
Harvard Business Review, March–April 1995, pp. 120–132.

PART III MANAGING CORE COMPETENCIES ACROSS BUSINESS UNITS

Building Core Skills, Andrew Campbell and Michael Goold
Working Paper, January 1992, Ashridge Strategic Management Centre

Knowledge Creator vs. Knowledge Broker: Corporate Roles in Technology Development in Diversified Firms, Anil K. Gupta and Ilkka Eerola
Working Paper, Revised July 1991

Intra-Firm Transfer of Best Practices, Gabriel Szulanski,
American Productivity & Quality Center, October 1994.

The Factory as a Learning Laboratory, Dorothy Leonard-Barton
Sloan Management Review, Fall 1992.

Creating Knowledge in Practice, Ikujiro Nonaka and Hiro Takeuchi
The Knowledge-Creating Company, Oxford University Press, New York, 1995. Chapter 4, pp. 95–123.

Leveraging Competencies Across Businesses, Michael Goold, Andrew Campbell and Marcus Alexander
Corporate-Level Strategy, John Wiley & Sons, Inc., New York, 1994. Extracts: pp. 168–176; 191–205 (and relevant notes).

Index

ACTION 61 267, 268
activity-based benchmarking 129–30
adaptive learning 31
alien-territory businesses 150–1
alliances 257–8
American Airlines 15, 38
AMP 231
Andersen Consulting 63
Apple Computers 68–9; Macintosh
   25–6
apprenticeships 248–9
archetype 274, 290
assets: accumulation 104–8;
   amortization 97, 98; creation 97, 98;
   fission 97–8, 107–8; improvement
   97, 98; processes 100–2; see also
   channel assets
AT&T 16, 17, 38, 67, 196
AT&T Paradyne 231
autonomy 273, 287, 291, 292, 294

ballast businesses 149–50
BCP 61–2
benchmarking 38, 229; external 61
best practice: exchanges 62; imposition
   of 174; transfer milestones 214–18;
   transfer profile 213; typical transfer
   218–21; see also Intra-Firm Transfer
   of Best Practices Project
British Aerospace 59, 65
British Petroleum 231
'brokering across' 201–2
'brokering in' 200–1
BTR 145–7
Burmah Castrol 231–2
business process reengineers 123

CAD/CAM 290
Canon 31, 68, 70, 98, 106–8; corporate
   strategy 300–04; shared resources
   and core competences 295–300
career paths 253–5
Caterpillar 18–19, 22, 194–5, 196;
   selectivity 197
central developments 173
central resources 154
centralization 195–6; responsiveness to
   SBU needs 108–9
Champion International Corporation
   142–3; 307–8
channel assets 108; indicators 111
chaos 268, 287, 290, 293, 294
Chaparral Steel 261; see also learning
   laboratories
Chevron Corporation 232
Coca-Cola, Inc. 23–5
cola wars 23–5
combination 274, 276, 291
commercial imperatives 175, 177–8;
   creation of 184
company profile 90–2
competence development 58–61, 71
competence diffusion 56–7, 61–5, 67,
   71
competence integration 65–6, 71
competence leverage 57–8, 66–9
competence renewal 58, 69–71
competency transfer 63, 104, 119
competitive advantage sources 14
competitive challenge 59
complementary resources 22
continuous education 45
continuous experimentation 250–2
Cooper Industries 142–3; corporate

strategy 307–12; manufacturing
    function 304–7
coordinating solutions 173–4
coordination of divisions and markets
    204
core skills 163–5, 181–2, 183–4;
    identification 165–70; managing
    172–5; research sample and methods
    183; role of centre 170–5; role of key
    components 175–81
corporate creativity 67
corporate hierarchy 189
corporate HQ roles 199–200
corporate strategy 96, 98
corrective learning 31
costs and benefits 60–1
creating a company way 174
creating value 154
critical mass 195
critical success factors 137–8, 152
cross-leveling of knowledge 293, 294;
    between divisions 281–4; within a
    division 279–81
cultural constraints 175, 177
customer assets 108; indicators 110-11
customer needs 87–8

decentralization 163–4, 189, 194–5, 199;
    contract 154
decision making 89
decisions' importance 19–20
Deluxe Check Printers 132
demerger decisions 135–6
Digital Equipment Corporation 45, 46
dissemination mode 39–40
distribution 89–90
diversification 83; broader approach
    85–90; fallacies and failures 84;
    talent and experience 90–3; see also
    related diversification
diversified firms' challenges 194
divestment decisions 136–7
documentation mode 39
double-loop learning 31, 40

'Easy & Rich' 271, 272, 274, 279, 281,
    284, 294
economies of scale 195
economies of scope 105–6
EDF 38–45, 49
edge-of-heartland businesses 148–9
EDS 232

education 248–9
effectiveness learning 66–7
efficiency learning 66–7
egalitarianism 243
Electricité de France 30, 33
employee and asset distribution
    129–30
environmental opportunities 15
environmental scanning 42
exaggerated relatedness 105
executive learning 88
experimentation mind-set 44
external imagination 67
external scientific community 203–4
externalized knowledge 274, 276, 287,
    291

facilitating factors 36, 42–7
Fiat 30, 33, 39–45, 47
five forces model 13, 16
flicking the switch 215
format uniformity 62
franchises 88
future commitments 60

General Electric 15, 19–20, 45, 127–8
generative learning 31
group-moves 84
group-think 84
growth/share matrix 134, 135

heartland businesses 147–8, 318–19
heartland criteria 303–4, 310–12
hiring practices 253–5
Honda 59, 103–4, 127
Huber's learning process model 32–3
Human 21 Committee 285, 286, 287
Human 200-People Committee 285–6,
    287
'Human Electronics' 281–4, 293–4
Hunter Fan Company 16

IBM 15, 26, 19, 42, 68
ICI 135–6, 196
independent problem-solving 241–3
information redundancy 274, 287, 291,
    292, 294
input assets 108
INSEAD study see Intra-Firm Transfer
    of Best Practices Project
integrating knowledge: external 255–7;
    internal 245–8

intelligence gathering 88
inter-disciplinary focus 195–6
internal attributes *see* resources and
   capabilities
internal flexibility 67, 68
internalized knowledge 291, 292
internationalization: product 178–81
Intra-Firm Transfer of Best Practices
   Project 208–9; best practice and firm
   performance 209–11; difficulties
   221–2; findings 213–21; intuition
   test 211–13; managing the transfer
   224–8; mechanisms 222–4;
   participants' feedback 231–3
involved leadership 46

justification 274, 276, 279, 290, 294

K-Mart 17–18, 22
Kaiser Permanente 232
key activities identification 129
key components 175–81; *see also* 3M
key skill components 169
'knowledge broker' 199, 200–3
'knowledge creator' 199–200; key
   factors 203–4
knowledge source 38
knowledge-creation: enabling
   conditions 273–4; *see also*
   Matsushita's Home Bakery
Komatsu 19

learning by doing 60
learning capability improvement
   49–51
learning focus 40
learning laboratories (Chaparral Steel)
   236–7, 258–61; challenging the
   status quo 250–5; definition 237;
   knowledge 245–9; near net-shape
   project 239–40; networking 255–8;
   organic system view 237–8; owning
   and solving the problem 240–5
learning organizations 30–4, 230–1; *see
   also* facilitating factors; learning
   laboratories; learning orientations;
   learning systems
learning orientations 36, 38–42;
   support for 48–9
learning process model 32–3
learning systems: enhancement 47–51;
   model themes 34–6; *see also* learning

organizations; model of
   organizations
leverage *see* organization
leveraging capabilities 199
leveraging competencies see Canon,
   Cooper Industries, 3M (case studies)

Macintosh *see* Apple Computers
Malcolm Baldridge Quality Award 20,
   40
management by objectives 43
management concensus 129–30
management of competencies 53–4,
   71–3; development 58–61; diffusion
   56–7, 61–5; integration 65–6; issues
   and dilemmas 54–8; leverage 57–8,
   66–9; renewal 58, 69–71
management tools 71–3
managing tensions 175, 178–81
market knowledge assets 109
market relatedness 108–12
Marriott Corporation 201, 206–7
Matsushita's Home Bakery knowledge
   creation 266–7; at corporate level
   284–91; for development 271–9;
   enabling conditions 291–3;
   implications 293–4
Matsushita Electric Industrial Co. Ltd
   266, corporate background 267–8;
   corporate vision and objectives 286
McDonald 61–2
measurement 43
mental maps 153
milestones 214–16; activities between
   216–18
Mind and Management Innovation
   Toward 1993 (MIT'93) 288–91
mindsets 60
mismanagement by the centre 164
mobilization 68
model of organizations 36–8;
   facilitating factors 42–7; learning
   orientations 38–2
Motorola 30, 31, 33–5, 38–47, 59;
   development milestones 61
multiple advocates of learning 46

near net-shape project *see* learning
   laboratories
NEC 17 negotiating 88
networks 62; resources for 257–8;
   stimulation 173

new business arenas 196
niche competitors 163
not invented here syndrome 212–13, 228, 229
Nucor Steel 14, 15

openness 44, 257
opportunities 67
organization: external sharing 131–2; internal leverage 130–1
organizational behaviour 152
organizational intention 271, 279, 281, 291, 293, 294
organizational knowledge creation 266–7; 293–4
organizational learning inventory 50–1
organizations: balance of power 60; culture 15, 34–5; generic processes 35–6; historical development 18–19; as learning systems 34; styles of learning 35

parent characteristics 141–3
parent organization 135, 153–4
parenting advantage 134–7; assessing fit 137–44; changing characteristics 152–3; fit assessment at BTR 145–7; improving fit 147–52; reviewing the organization 153–4; statement 300–1
parenting: characteristics 300–2, 309–10; 316–18; framework 135; opportunities 138–41; structures, systems and processes 154
PepsiCo, Inc. 23–5
performance analysis 143–4
performance competencies 70
performance gap 42–3
performance rewards 243-5
personnel 195
Philips 68, 169, 181–2, 192
political backing 203
Porter's model see five forces model
predictors of difficulty 221–2
prices 87
process assets 109; indicators 111–12
product concept 274, 276, 281, 290
product customization 111–12
product ideas 87
product–process focus 38–9
Profit Impact of Market Strategies (PIMS) methodology 143–4
programme management tools 65–6

project management tools 65–6

quality deployment 59
quality improvement 59

R&D integration 194
ramp-up 215–16
Rank Xerox 22–3, 59, 192; INSEAD study 232–3
reasons for success 70
related diversification 96–8, 118–19; dynamic view 104–12; hypotheses, data and methodology of study 112–16; measuring relatedness 98–104; study results 116–18
requisite variety 268, 273, 286, 287, 291, 292, 294
resources and capabilities 14, 26–7; competitive implications 23–5; competitive position 25–6; imitability 18–21; organization 22–23; rareness 17–18; value 15–17
respect 243
response to market needs 194
risk 252–3
risk avoidance 70
riskier projects 196

selectivity 197–8
shared knowledge 248
single business firm 192–4
single-loop learning 31, 40
skill component analysis 166–8, 170
skill development: focus 41–2; process 170–1
skill level 112
skill transfer process 171–2
skill tree 167, 170
skills 86–90, 154; management of 164–5, 169–70; scarcity 164; understanding 166–9; see also core skills
slicing knife example 124–5
socialization 276, 279, 287, 291, 293
socially complex resources 20–1
Sony 15, 21
sources of difficulty 221–2, 224–6, 230, 233–4
staff departments 154
strategic assets 99–100; catalysts in the 'production function' 102–4

strategic assets: classes of 108–10;
    exploiting 119
strategic managers' responsibilities 15
success and failure analysis 143
superior know-how 169
SWOT analysis 13–14
systems perspective 47

'T-shaped engineers' 65
tacit knowledge 274, 276, 279, 290, 293
talents 85–6
targeting real competencies 123–4;
    activity perspective 124–9; four
    imperatives 129–32; redefinition 132
team learning 41–2
team processes 65
technical service 89
technological discontinuities 203
technological skills 15
technology development 188–92;
    corporate office 204–6; diversified
    firms' dilemma 192–6; 'knowledge
    broker' role 200–3, 206–7;
    'knowledge creator' role 203–4;
    selectivity 196–200

technology transfer 202–3
tensions: creation of 184–5; see also
    managing tensions
The Mailbox, Inc. 20
3M 30, 44, 68, 86, 92–3; corporate
    strategy 315–19; key skill
    components 174–5; skill area 165;
    technical function 313–15
thumbs up 215
total quality management 38, 59
transfer seed 215

Unilever 45, 165, 175, 182
unions 87

validating judgments 143–4
value creation insight: 300–1; 307–9,
    315–16
value-chain focus 40–1
value-trap businesses 151–2

WalMart 14–15, 17–18, 22, 31, 38, 44, 46
'what if' scenario development 129–30
Whitbread Restaurants 166–8, 169